Reworking Culture

Reworking Culture

Relatedness, Rites, and Resources in Garo Hills, North East India

ERIK DE MAAKER

OXFORD
UNIVERSITY PRESS

OXFORD
UNIVERSITY PRESS

Oxford University Press is a department of the University of Oxford.
It furthers the University's objective of excellence in research, scholarship,
and education by publishing worldwide. Oxford is a registered trade mark of
Oxford University Press in the UK and in certain other countries

Published in India by
Oxford University Press
22 Workspace, 2nd Floor, 1/22 Asaf Ali Road, New Delhi 110 002, India

© Oxford University Press 2022

The moral rights of the author have been asserted

First Edition published in 2022

All rights reserved. No part of this publication may be reproduced, stored in
a retrieval system, or transmitted, in any form or by any means, without the
prior permission in writing of Oxford University Press, or as expressly permitted
by law, by licence or under terms agreed with the appropriate reprographics
rights organization. Enquiries concerning reproduction outside the scope of the
above should be sent to the Rights Department, Oxford University Press, at the
address above

You must not circulate this work in any other form
and you must impose this same condition on any acquirer

ISBN-13 (print edition): 978-8-19-483169-3

ISBN-10 (print edition): 8-19-483169-5

ISBN-13 (eBook): 978-8-19-511127-5

ISBN-10 (eBook): 8-19-511127-0

ISBN-13 (OSO): 978-8-19-511126-8

ISBN-10 (OSO): 8-19-511126-2

DOI: 10.1093/ oso/ 9788194831693.001.0001

Typeset in Minion Pro 10/13
by Newgen KnowledgeWorks, Chennai

Printed in India by Rakmo Press Pvt. Ltd

for Jiji
and those who have taken her place

Contents

List of Figures	ix
Maps	xiii
Glossary of Terms	xv
Transliteration, Pronunciation, and Quotation	xix
Preface and Acknowledgements	xxi

1 Customizing Culture?	1
1.1 Locating Garo Culture	1
1.2 Creating Community	5
1.3 Continuing Conversations	13
1.4 Structure of the Book	21
2 Frames, Labels, Locations	25
2.1 Spatial Divides	25
2.2 Garo Conversions	29
2.3 Becoming Citizens	37
2.4 Constituting 'Tribe'	45
2.5 Ethnic Politics, Militancy, and the Demand for Statehood	51
3 Housing Matters	58
3.1 Jiji's Plight	58
3.2 Modelling Relatedness	63
3.3 Living with Houses	68
3.4 The Birth of a House	74
3.5 Bracing for Social Pressure?	80
3.6 Houses of Relatedness	83
4 *Niam*, Houses, and Land	86
4.1 'It would be good if he died!'	86
4.2 Practising *Niam*	90
4.3 Living with the Spirits	94
4.4 Occupying the Land	100
4.5 Landed Responsibilities and Religious Stature	108
4.6 Negotiating the Growth of the Crops	113

5 Engaging the Dead	128
5.1 The Religiosity of Funerals	128
5.2 Souls and Their Wanderings	130
5.3 Anticipating Death	134
5.4 Death's Demands	136
5.5 Engaging Gifts	139
5.6 Acknowledging the Source	146
5.7 Vouching to Slaughter a Cow	155
5.8 Putrefaction and Presence	162
5.9 Separating, Distancing, and Reconnecting	169
6 Claiming Relationships, Spaces, and Resources	173
6.1 Replacing Baka	173
6.2 Constituting Mutuality	182
6.3 Showing Commitment, Acknowledging Debt	191
6.4 Rural Workers, Rural Entrepreneurs	199
6.5 Accessing Swidden	203
6.6 From Rotating Swiddens to Permanent Occupation	210
6.7 Living on the Land	216
7 Customizing Traditions	221
7.1 The State as a Resource	221
7.2 Reinterpreting Status, Wealth, and Prestige	231
7.3 Polarities and Convergences	239
8 The Modernity of Garo *Niam*	245
8.1 Cherishing Tradition	245
8.2 How *Niam* Facilitates Social Change	247
8.3 Reworking *Niam*	248
Notes	251
References	277
Index	293

List of Figures

0.1	Garo Hills covers the western one-third of the Indian state of Meghalaya.	xiii
0.2	Map of South and South East Asia, showing Garo Hills.	xiv
1.1	'Meet a Garo Couple'.	7
1.2	'Modern Garo Couple'	8
1.3	Jiji M. Sangma with the author.	15
1.4	A framed picture of my father reading to my children when they were toddlers, which is kept in the household of one of Jiji's children.	20
2.1	Bathing and washing in the open: spring water is guided through an iron pipe from a nearby source to a communal bathing and dish-washing spot.	27
2.2	In villages like Sadolpara, people are in many ways less prosperous than those living in town, but to a good degree master of their own time, and value taking a break whenever they feel like.	28
2.3	Drinking rice beer after the burning of the new fields, the day before A'galmaka. Rice beer drinking brings people together to relax and enjoy with their relatives and neighbours.	34
3.1	The floor plan of the house in which Jiji lived.	60
3.2	Early morning in Sadolpara: Jiji (second from right) chatting with three of her daughters, her sister, two sons-in-law, and a cousin before they all leave for their fields for the day.	61
3.3	Jiji's *kram* (below) and *natik* (above) drums are the seats of spirits, according to the traditional Garo community religion.	62
3.4	Jiji and Baka belonged to a House that had been created by Aki and Ginjing.	70
3.5	The gazebo (*kachari*) at the centre of the ward in which Jiji lived.	73
3.6	Chicken intestines are interpreted as omens on various occasions.	77
3.7	Tami and Gushen, about a month after they had been married. By then, it was more or less public knowledge that they had agreed to the marriage, but they were still shy to acknowledge that, and careful to keep a certain distance apart.	79
4.1	Oldap diagnosing spirit-induced illness with the use of a *pongsi*. Mentioning the name of the spirit responsible, made the bow tremble.	98

LIST OF FIGURES

4.2 Gatjeng sacrificed a chicken to the spirit Risi, as part of a healing ritual (*amua*) intended to bring about the release of his nephew Gotjen. 99

4.3 The *kusi* boulder of Sadolpara, standing in between two supporting boulders. A third supporting boulder has fallen over, and is lying in front. 103

4.4 The *kusi* boulder at Ringre in Tura, with plaques inscribed in both Garo and English. 104

4.5 Map showing the boundaries of the land belonging to Sadolpara, finalized on 15 June 1926 by the administrators of what was then Garo Hills district. 105

4.6 On the morning of A'galmaka, a family has ritually cleansed their new field of *marang*, and is now preparing to have rice beer and food. 116

4.7 Neighbours drinking rice beer together with Jiji's daughter Waljak (second from left) on the rear veranda of her house at A'galmaka. Plying one another with rice beer is an enjoyable way to strengthen social bonds. 117

5.1 The vessel in which Sisi used to store the rice she cooked. It was broken at her funeral to disconnect her from the house she had lived in. 138

5.2 At Jiji's funeral, Songarek women fanned the corpse with cocks' tail feathers and Christian women did so with white paper flags. Heirloom jewellery and coins were displayed on her chest, and guests had placed the unginned cotton wool that they had bought for her near her head. 140

5.3 After Genna's funeral, young men and women stayed up all night playing cards in the gazebo near the house in which she had lived. 141

5.4 Men driving a small bull ahead of their relatives, as the group from Sadolpara walks together on their way to attend a funeral. A boy playing a *kram* drum is walking between them and the rest of the party. 143

5.5 At Sisi's funeral, one of her uncles uses an heirloom sword to hack at the posts of the entrance door of her house. 144

5.6 Large stacks of gongs, representing great wealth, kept in the storeroom of the house of a village head in Madhupur (Bangladesh). 148

5.7 A valuable gong being presented as *ma'gual* by widower Dising (second from right) at the funeral of his wife Sisi. 150

5.8 The morning after Sisi's cremation, Nenchi and Nokmi collect pieces of bone from among the ashes of the funeral pyre. 164

5.9 Oldap discovered the imprint of a tiger's paw among the ashes of Sisi's funeral pyre. 164

5.10 Jiji posing with the effigy of her daughter Waljak, who had died in her fifties.	166
5.11 An effigy after one or two years: the face has disappeared, and most of the clothes in which it was initially dressed have fallen off.	167
5.12 The size of a cluster of *kimbrong*s near a house gives an indication of its inhabitants' capacity to offer cattle for their own dead, as well as for the dead of other Houses.	168
6.1 Jiji's cherished picture of herself and Baka dancing at Wangala, which was most probably taken in the 1990s.	174
6.2 The Facebook post dedicated to the cremation of Jiji, displayed on Rakkan Sangma's Timeline.	181
6.3 A man from Sadolpara mining coal on village land. The coal-bearing layer is close to the surface, and mined using a pickaxe.	202
6.4 Jiji returning home after a day in the fields, carrying a heavy load of cotton on her back and a bundle of tapioca stems in her hands.	208
6.5 An orchard of areca nut trees. The undergrowth is cleared regularly so that it does not disturb the trees' growth.	212
7.1 Dising was highly respected as a figure of authority due to his extensive knowledge of *niam*.	222
7.2 Meltrona Marak ('Tuna') giving a speech at Sadolpara during the award ceremony that concluded an Independence Day football tournament.	225
7.3 A Tura marriage, celebrated in style.	239

Maps

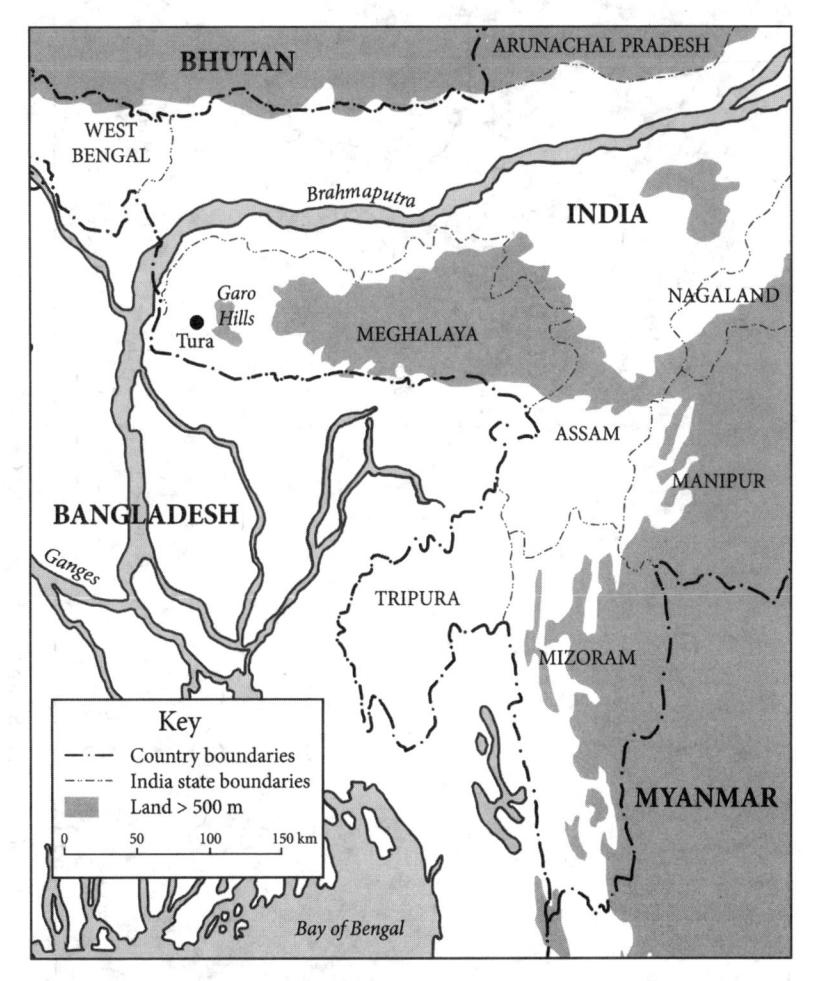

Map 0.1 Garo Hills covers the western one-third of the Indian state of Meghalaya.

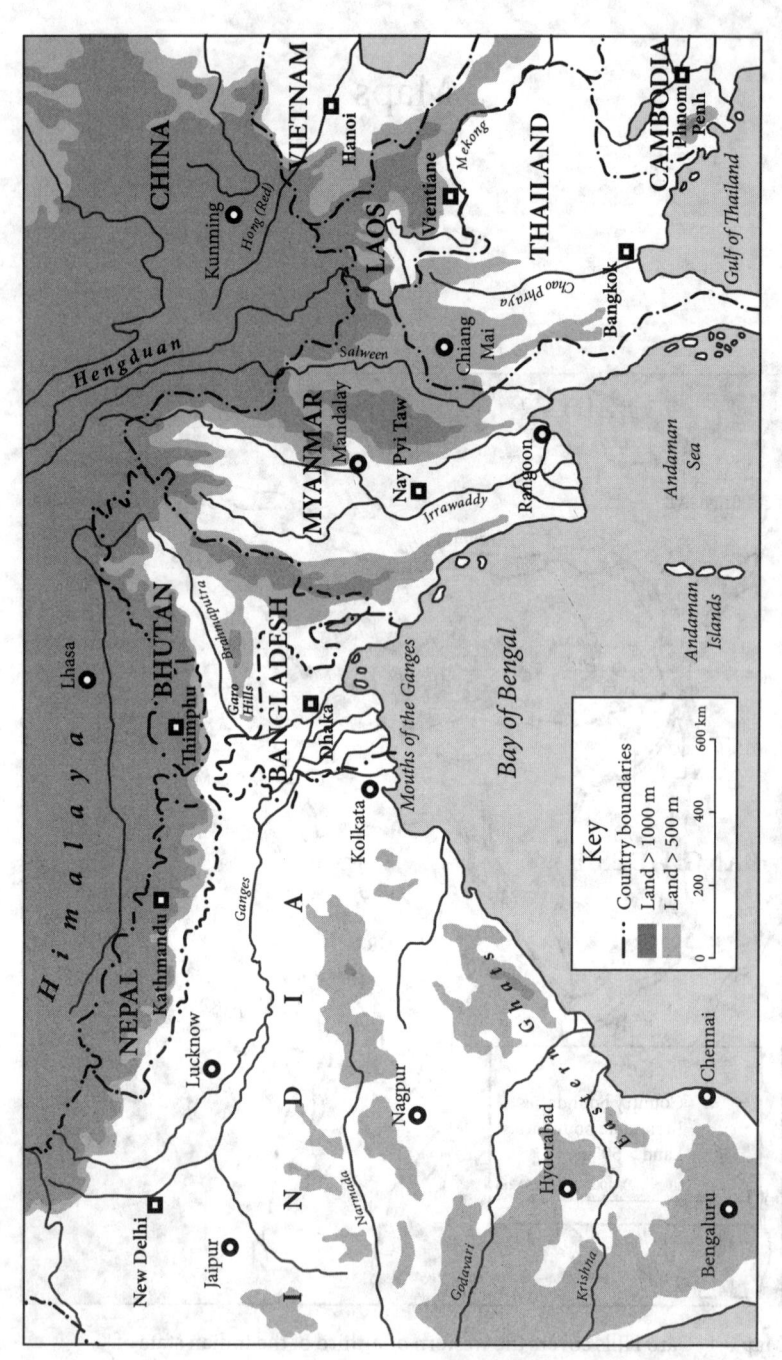

Map 0.2 Map of South and South East Asia, showing Garo Hills.

Glossary of Terms

A'galmaka Festival of the annual agricultural cycle, celebrated by followers of the traditional Garo community religion. It begins on the morning following the burning of the new swidden fields. *A'a*: earth; *gal'mak*: black ashes; hence 'blackened earth'.

a'kim Customary marriage alliance, which obliges the matrilineal kin groups or matrilineages of both partners to replace the respective spouse upon death.

a'king Land that belongs to the matrilineal group of a particular village, including fields, forest, and streams as well as the plots on which houses have been built. Several matrilineal groups within a village can own *a'king* land. In addition, all the land that belongs to a village is referred to as the *a'king* of that village.

chra A person's male matrilineal relatives (uncles, nephews, brothers, sons, and grandsons in the matrilineal line).

dama Large wooden drum, which is played for Wangala dancing

du'sia The ritual initiation of a marriage in accordance with the traditional Garo community religion.

community religion In this book, 'community religion', or 'traditional Garo community religion' refers to the practices, ideas, and myths that make up the religious epistemology that was dominant prior to the widespread conversion of Garos to Christianity. I use the term 'community religion' rather than 'religion' or 'Garo religion' in order to avoid implying that these practices and ideas have been codified in a way comparable to established religions that are organized hierarchically, base their teachings on sacred texts, and employ professional religious specialists.

GHADC Garo Hills Autonomous District Council, the elected body that governs the five Garo Hills districts. The GHADC operates under the Sixth Schedule of the Indian Constitution, and Garo customary law is supposed to guide the way it governs. The area under its jurisdiction is excepted from many of the 'generic' laws that apply in most of India's federal states and territories.

'head' of a House A House belongs to the matrilineal group of the wife, but her husband is its 'head' (*skutong*).

House/house I use House, written with a capital 'H', to refer to a unit of property, rights, and belonging that is created when a couple marries. A House and all of its assets belong to the matrilineal group of the wife. When I refer to a house as a building, I use a lower case 'h'. The Garo term *nok* denotes both meanings.

jhum Generic term, used throughout North-East India, to refer to swiddening or the practice of shifting cultivation. In Garo, the word *jhum* is not used; people refer to a field cultivated in this way as an *a'ba* (first year of cultivation) or an *a'breng* (second year of cultivation).

kachari A gazebo with a raised floor and a roof, but no walls, built on the beaten earth in between the houses of a village ward, and maintained collectively by its residents. A *kachari* provides a sheltered place where residents as well as visitors can sit, rest, or sleep.

kram A large conical wooden drum that is associated with the spirit Risi in the context of the traditional Garo community religion. The keepers (or 'tamers') of a *kram* drum maintain a dedicated relationship with Risi, which establishes their House as senior within their matrilineal group.

kusi A boulder that is a seat of the spirit Guira, according to the traditional Garo community religion. The boulder represents an exclusive claim to the land that surrounds it on behalf of those who 'planted' it, or their descendants.

ma'gual A gift offered by the House of a recently deceased person to Houses of women who classify as 'mothers'. *Ma'gual* should ideally be given in the form of heirloom objects such as brass gongs, jewellery, or swords, but these are often substituted by larger or smaller amounts of money.

marang 'Pollution', associated with violence, blood, and death. *Marang* is dangerous and potentially lethal, hence its management is a prime concern in any Garo cultural context, but most crucial in relation to birth and death.

mande, mandi 'People'. *Mande* is used self-referentially in rural West Garo Hills by followers of the traditional Garo community religion (Songsareks), distinguishing themselves from Christians, who they call *ruri*. In parts of Garo Hills where Christianity prevails, the term *mande* is used to refer to Garo people in general.

matrilineal group A group of people who are related through the female line (*ba'saa*: 'born of the same'), while also encompassing in-married men. Garo emphasize relatedness between mothers, daughters, grandmothers, and granddaughters. Sons are much more closely tied to their mother's than to their father's relatives.

militant groups Politically motivated groups that engage in violence to challenge the legitimacy of the Indian state. Various 'underground' militant groups have emerged in succession in Garo Hills since the 1990s.

niam *Niam* refers to cultural principles, the situational interpretation of which is negotiated as a consensus reached among people who are recognized as figures of authority. *Niam* refers to ideas, norms, values, and practices that are believed to have been passed down from preceding generations and are in that sense traditional.

nokma An owner of *a'king* land or an otherwise wealthy person. *Nokma* is often used as the short form for *a'king nokma*, or village head.

ruri 'Outsider'. In rural West Garo Hills, *ruri* include Christian Garo who have adopted customs 'from outside'. In parts of Garo Hills where Christianity prevails, *ruri* refers to people who are not Garo.

Songsarek Follower of the traditional Garo community religion.

Toma 'Kin trial'. A meeting held in order to make decisions regarding important issues, typically involving people who belong to distinct matrilineal groups or matrilineages. May also be referred to as a *bichel*, if the meeting includes the interrogation of persons accused of misconduct or involved in conflict.

Ukam A pledge exchanged between the House of a recently deceased person and another House. *Ukam* should ideally be an inexpensive gong, but often a small amount of money is given instead. A House that accepts *ukam* agrees to slaughter a cow in honour of the person who has died. Subsequently, when a death occurs in the House that took the *ukam*, the gift can be returned to the House that initially gave it, obliging that House to slaughter a cow for the latter deceased person.

Wangala The most extensive of the celebrations of the annual agricultural cycle, Wangala encompasses the offering of the last of the first fruits to the spirits, and calling for an omen for the next agricultural year. Since the mid-1970s, Wangala has also been celebrated with an annual state-sponsored dance competition that brings together Christian and Songsarek Garo from across Garo Hills.

Transliteration, Pronunciation, and Quotation

This book is based on research that was done in an area in which people speak Am'beng Garo. To many of the speakers of 'standard' Garo, which is A'we, Am'beng is a rustic dialect. One of the ways in which Am'beng Garo differs from A'we is that in Am'beng the vowel 'o' tends to become an 'u'. For example, the word for chicken in A'we is *do'o*, whereas in Am'beng it is pronounced *du'u*. At the instigation of some of my Am'beng-speaking field assistants, I have transliterated spoken Garo in a way that reflects the sound of the Am'beng spoken, rather than A'we-fying it.

Spoken Garo features the glottal stop: a sudden break in the vowel, after which the rest of a word is pronounced. The glottal stop acts as a kind of consonant, and is crucial to pronunciation. In this book, it is indicated by an apostrophe, as in the word *du'u*. For someone who is not a native speaker of Garo, the correct identification and insertion of the glottal stop can be quite challenging, as I know from first-hand experience.

Garo words and sentences are written in italics in this book, with the exception of proper nouns. I have pluralized Garo words, by adding a non-italicized '-s' to the transliteration. When quoting spoken Garo, I first give the English translation in the text, followed by the original Garo phrases in round brackets. I have kept the translations as close to the original spoken language as possible, and where necessary inserted clarifications into the quotations, marked by square brackets. Where quotations have been shortened, I have marked omissions with ellipses.

Whenever the source of a quotation is known, it is referenced in an endnote. Many of the dialogues quoted took place during events that I attended, and often recorded, while doing fieldwork. These conversations were transcribed from video or audio, and translated with the help of both field assistants and research interlocutors, as detailed in section 1.4. In addition, I also quote things people said that I did not record electronically, but translated from Garo and noted down while doing fieldwork.

Preface and Acknowledgements

In rural Garo Hills, within the time of little more than a generation, radical social, economic, and religious transformations have taken place. This book focuses largely on a part of Garo Hills where some of these transformations have, at least to some degree, been resisted. My choice of focus has not been motivated by a wish to engage in 'salvage ethnography', to document and preserve relics of cultural practices perceived to be destined for extinction in the face of greater forces such as globalization. Not that I see no merit in documenting culture per se, but from a sociological perspective, it strikes me as far more urgent to explore why people continue to be committed to practices that are considered obsolete elsewhere in the same region. As I finalize this manuscript, in 2021, the world is still reeling under the Covid-19 pandemic. In South Asia, the virus has already taken the lives of tens of thousands of people, and continues to pose a formidable threat. In addition to the direct hazards it poses in terms of health, the measures taken to curb the spread of the virus are having grave economic consequences for the poor, and not least among them, for many inhabitants of rural Garo Hills. The pandemic creates hardship, which people can only overcome by falling back on their resources. In rural Garo Hills, these resources include extensive networks of relatives, the land on which people live, as well as the access they have to funding and goods made available through local administrative and political structures.

Garo Hills, the western extension of the hill and mountain range that separates India from Bangladesh, is part of North-East India. North-East India came into existence as a region in the aftermath of the hasty partition of British India, which created international boundaries that severely restricted land-based connections with the rest of India. Particularly in the first few decades following independence, these borders rendered the area distant from the perspective of the Indian 'mainland'. North-East India became notorious for political conflict. Multiple secessionist movements resisted the incorporation of 'their' ethno-territories into the Indian state, which responded in turn with militarization and violent counter-insurgency measures (Baruah 2009). These conflicts were brutal, but primarily concentrated in the central and eastern parts of North-East India. Garo Hills remained a somewhat tranquil backwater for the first four decades following independence, especially in its rural areas. This changed from the mid-1990s, when ethnic militancy emerged in Garo Hills to become a significant political factor for at least two decades. From the early 2000s, the Indian government began to allocate very substantial sums of money for development measures in the North-Eastern region, formalized as the 'Look East Policy' (Baruah 2005b: 222–226). For places like Garo Hills, where people living in the rural areas were typically quite poor (in a monetary sense), the novel funding was substantial, and as it began to pour in through a wide variety of schemes and programmes, it accelerated the processes of transformation that have been central to my research.

This book is built upon an engagement with Garo Hills that has extended over two decades. It began with the two years that I lived in Garo Hills to conduct my PhD research, from July 1999 until August 2001. Living in a Garo village, without many of the comforts of 'modern' life, I learned a lot about living in a face-to-face context, where people shared much with one another, but were at the same time careful to hide what should not become public. Life in rural Garo Hills could be very hard, with people dying from illness at any age, or as a result of fatal accidents such as snake bite. There were times when some families had only two meals a day, and what they ate was mostly white rice with some tiny dried fish and hot chillies for flavour. Jackfruit can make a good curry, but it also proved to be a last recourse for families that had run out of rice. On other occasions (or, more specifically, in other seasons), food was available in abundance and conspicuous consumption almost mandatory. I was also sometimes overwhelmed by what I experienced as the hostility of the environment, which revealed itself differently depending on the season. I encountered periods of intense heat, of endless rains and soaring humidity, months of slushy mud, leeches, snakes, and mosquitoes, as well as a few brief weeks when the nights were biting cold. In dealing with these conditions, people relied on skills and knowledge that had been carried over from previous generations, which equipped them to live in and with their environment. As I stumbled along my own steep learning curve, I recognized that these kinds of skills and knowledges cannot be taught formally but must be gained through lived experience, if they are to become part of one's habitus.

My connection to South Asia in general, and Garo Hills in particular, was aroused by the region's apparently insatiable preoccupation with defining cultural difference in terms such as caste, religion, or 'tribe', which led me to question how social and cultural forces can at once create ground for conflict, while also holding people together in compelling and meaningful ways. My own positionality is manifest in several ways in this book. I have always been fascinated by people who do not feel the need to subscribe to (Western) consumerism but shape their lives in accordance with ideals, practices, and material conditions that are valued in their local context. Our assessment of the world around us tends to be filtered through stereotypes, which often present themselves with such veracity that we forget to question them. Garo are frequently portrayed as a 'timeless' indigenous people who seem to be inherently connected to their territory. Rejecting such ahistorical if not naïve renderings, I have explored how Garo who I have encountered personally both sustain culturally anchored ideas and practices and (re)interpret them as they adapt to changing economic and political contexts.

One of the aspects of life in West Garo Hills that I have often found difficult to deal with, especially initially, is the gradual marginalization of practices and ideas associated with the traditional Garo community religion. The vast majority of Garo are Christians these days, and I use the term 'community religion' to refer to the practices, ideas, and myths that make up the religious epistemology that was dominant prior to the widespread conversion of Garo to Christianity. I have felt particularly uncomfortable on occasions when some—particularly non-Garo—Christian missionaries have expressed disdain for the community religion. This was all the more disturbing for me, knowing that the Christian missionary effort has its roots in European, North American, and Australian organizations. It has made me want to distance myself from the European middle-class context in which I grew up, which was shaped by Christianity—even if religion played a rather marginal role in my family. Over the years, I have gradually been able to gain more appreciation of the nuances and intricacies of religious belonging in Garo Hills, which has allowed me to become less judgmental than I was initially. People the world over are part of complex social networks, which they can sometimes choose to a certain degree, but which are usually at least partially, and often inescapably, ascribed by others. I will never forget an ardent young Garo Christian who asked me about my faith one day in Tura. When I told him that I had left the church before I even reached adolescence and did not consider myself bound to any specific religion, he replied: 'You can say that you are not a Christian, but to me you remain an ethnic Christian.' His answer perfectly summarized the South Asian principle of the *jat* ('birth group'). One is born into a particular *jat* and that means taking on its ethnic and religious characteristics, at least in the eyes of others. Whether one likes it or not. Religious belonging can involve some degree of choice, but equally, and often more importantly, it is ascribed.

In rural West Garo Hills, people speak the Am'beng dialect of Garo. To gain an introduction to the language, I took classes with several young high school teachers in Tura, and I continue to be very grateful to Lorinda Marak and Meringpole Sangma for their unending patience. Yet, although they did manage to teach me some of the basics, I learned most of my Garo in the conversations I had with the people who I met in the course of my fieldwork. My language skills gradually improved, but I never reached the level required to understand and dissect the dense and highly poetic Garo that people speak when they address their relatives formally. To analyse such conversations, I have always relied on linguistic support. In Sengjrang Sangma, Henysing Sangma, Nixon Dango, and Zhandi Marak, I have found aides who have made crucial contributions to my research at different times and in different capacities. In addition, my research would never have been so fruitful without the help of Finuza Bruseby-Panto, Rubi Gogoi, Suzoy Hazarika, Daniel Ingty, John Momin, Skylance Momin, Daboo Thulsyan, Rakkan Sangma, and the late Rafael Marak.

During the initial two-year fieldwork period, my partner Nandini Bedi made a major contribution to the research. We lived together for much of that time, and she did the sound recording for most of the video footage that was at the core of my research. As a documentary filmmaker, she produced numerous short features for the Sri Lankan-based television channel Young Asia Television during our stay. She also made the documentary film *Notes on Man Capture*. This documentary, which has been well received, explores how Garo engage with the widespread practice of 'capturing' bridegrooms (discussed in section 3.4) (Bedi 2007b; 2009). A couple of years later, in 2003, she returned to the village in which we had lived during the initial fieldwork period and made the documentary *Ambi Jiji's Retirement* for India's Public Service Broadcasting Trust (Bedi 2007a). This latter documentary engages with the ongoing transformations that are redefining upland agriculture and highlights farmers' increasing dependence on cash crops and monetary income.

Anthropology, as a discipline, has allowed me to probe the processes by which people locate and define themselves in a cultural sense. I received my undergraduate training at the University of Amsterdam and went on to do my PhD at Leiden University. While my PhD research[1] focused explicitly on the enactment and negotiation of relatedness in the context of Garo funerals, subsequent projects looked at land relations[2] and place making.[3] I am very grateful to the Dutch Research Council (NWO), the Indian Council of Social Science Research (ICSSR), Leiden University's profile area Asian Modernities and Traditions (AMT), and the International Centre for Integrated Mountain Development (ICIMOD) for their generous support of the research projects that I have conducted in Garo Hills.

As a student, I benefitted from the guidance I received from scholars based both in the Netherlands, in India, and in the United States. At the University of Amsterdam, the late Hein Streefkerk introduced me to the sociology of South Asia and always emphasized the importance of scrutinizing societal models for their (hidden) class biases. At Leiden University, Steef Meyknecht, who is also unfortunately no longer among us, taught me the value of 'being there' (at the right moment and well prepared) when using video in ethnographic research. His colleague Dirk Nijland inspired me to conduct event-oriented ethnography and was persistently optimistic and supportive of my endeavours, even at times when I myself began to falter. The late Danielle Geirnaert granted me the rare privilege of conducting fieldwork together in Sumba (Indonesia), where we researched the relevance for people's everyday lives of maintaining relationships with ancestors. This experience made me recognize the centrality of funerals in many societies and the continuing significance that the dead can have for the living. And, during the initial phases of the research that this book is based on, when I was working on my PhD, I benefitted tremendously from the profound sociological knowledge concerning relatedness, religion, and ritual of Jarich Oosten, who also sadly passed away much too soon. True to the Leiden tradition of ethnography, Jarich consistently emphasized the importance of fieldwork and the invaluable insights from research interlocutors that no other method can deliver so well. While working on this book, I reread many of the notes I had taken during our long conversations and discovered that they continue to serve as a source of inspiration.

Willem van Schendel of Amsterdam University has long insisted on the need to conduct research on the impact and imposition of state borders, particularly in Asia (Baud and Van Schendel 1997). His critical reassessment of assumed demarcations of culture areas and groups have proven valuable in defining the questions that I have been exploring, which also translated in important suggestions in the early phases of writing this book. Over the last ten years, we have also been working together as members of the team that organizes the international 'Asian Borderlands' conferences, supported by the International Institute of Asian Studies (IIAS), Leiden, which are held biennially and offer a forum for scholarship that transcends the boundaries of traditional approaches to studying countries and regions.

I am also immensely grateful to the late Robbins Burling, who conducted ethnographic research in Garo Hills in the 1950s as an anthropologist and linguist. Burling's seminal writings on the Garo, most notably his monograph *Rengsanggri*, have been, and continue to be, very influential. With its emphasis on attending if not participating in events, ethnographic research can often lack historical depth, and the conversations which I had with Robbins Burling, notably at the time that I conducted PhD research and in the years immediately after, proved very valuable in addressing this potential lacuna. At the North-Eastern Hill University in Shillong, Meghalaya, I was greatly inspired by the work of Tanka Subba, who advised me on my research in its early stages. I am also very grateful for the sustained support, both intellectual as well as practical, which I received from historian Milton Sangma. Numerous colonial sources are available concerning the history of North-East India, particularly the uplands, and many continue to be considered authoritative. Milton Sangma was among the first from the region to initiate the production of histories that offer perspectives not focused by a colonial lens.

Many more people have contributed to this book, and I apologize to anyone I have not mentioned here. I want to thank the two anonymous reviewers from OUP, who gave me valuable suggestions that have improved the manuscript. Pip Hare undertook a very thoughtful editing of the text, resulting in significant improvements in terms of both language and style. I am hugely indebted to my colleagues at Leiden University, both at the Institute of Cultural Anthropology and Development Sociology (especially the Asia Research Culster) and at the Leiden Institute of Area Studies, who have been a source of inspiration, as well as flexible and accommodating when I have needed to withdraw in order to write. Thank you to Annemarie Samuels, Bart Barendregt, Ratna Saptari, Patricia Spyer, Nira Wickramasinghe, Sanjukta Sunderason, Tim van den Meerendonk, Andrea Ragragio, Cristina Grasseni, and Peter Pels. In Guwahati, the North Eastern Social Research Centre (NESRC) has always been very welcoming, and I cherish the many weeks that I was able to write there. I am particularly grateful to Melvil Pereira, Walter Fernandez, Meenal Tula, and the late Alphonsus D'Souza. Caroline Marak and Fameline Marak of the North-Eastern Hill University's Tura campus have also been very supportive of my endeavours. Henysing Sangma and Rehannah Marak have provided me with a home away from home in Tura. I am indebted to many scholars of Asia who have over the years all in one way or the other contributed to the completion of this book project. This includes Arzuman Ara, Ellen Bal, Sanjib Baruah, Sanjay Barbora, Meenaxi Barkataki-Ruscheweyh, Anjuman Begum, Timour Claquin-Chambugong, Sanjay Hazarika, Ute Hüsken, Vibha Joshi, Beppe Karlsson, Margareth Lynghdoh, Rajini Palriwala, Surajit Sarkar, Dan Smyer Yü, Mélanie Vandenhelsken, Philippe Ramirez, Eric Venbrux, and Jelle Wouters. Joek, Sara, and Suzanne have been important friends who have kept me focused over the years. I want to thank my parents for their enduring trust and consistent support, and the same goes for my siblings and brothers-in-law: thank you Jan, Henriet, Hugo, Iris, Piet-Hein and Param. Lastly, I want to thank Amar, Kiran, and Nandini for their patience with me, and for the many ways in which they continue to enrich my life. Nandini has been my first reader, and the connection we share to Garo Hills continues to inspire.

Parts of this book that specifically focus on funerals have drawn on my PhD, 'Negotiating Life: Garo Death Rituals and the Transformation of Society', which I defended in 2006 (de Maaker 2006a). Some other parts are concerned with themes that I have addressed in journal articles and book chapters published more recently. I have written about cultural fissure and continuity in: 'Have the Mitdes Gone Silent? Conversion, Rhetoric, and the Continuing Importance of the Lower Deities in Northeast India' (2013a) as well as in: 'Performing the Garo Nation? Garo Wangala Dancing between Faith and Folklore' (2013b). Offering gifts at Garo funerals is the focus of 'Assessing Gifts, Mothers and Marriages' (2012), which was published in Garo as 'Nokdangko Man·rikani: Gamrangko Sualani, Ma.gipa Ong.rikani aro Bia Ka.anirang' (2019). I have discussed material representations of the dead in: 'Ambiguous Mortal Remains, Substitute Bodies, and other Materializations of the Dead among the Garo of Northeast India' (2015). Lastly, I have written about land and land relations in 'On the Nature of Indigenous Land: Ownership, Access and Farming in upland Northeast India' (2018) as well as in 'Who Owns the Hills? Ownership, Inequality and Communal Sharing in the Borderlands of India' (2021a).

Most of this book is based on ethnographic fieldwork conducted in rural West Garo Hills. People there have actively contributed to my research, keen for their stories to be told, and, at times, their claims to be stated. Since this book is about their stories and their lives, it would have been odd to anonymize them all. Echoing an argument advanced many decades ago by Adrian Gerbrands, a Leiden scholar who did groundbreaking work on material culture, people who anthropologists work with in the field are all too often deprived of their individuality in anthropological writings (Gerbrands 1967). Therefore, where appropriate, I have used real names. Where it did not seem right to do so, for fear of harming people's interests, I have changed the names of people and places. By and large, these decisions have been mine and I hope I have taken the right ones. Any mistakes or misrepresentations are obviously mine.

1
Customizing Culture?

1.1 Locating Garo Culture

'It's good that these buildings are being made', said the young man who had accompanied me to the hilltop. It was 2014, and we were looking at a couple of quite large and solid concrete frames, each about six metres by twelve metres, commissioned by the local Department of Tourism. Once completed, the buildings were to accommodate visitors, who would then be able to experience, in relative comfort, the tranquil atmosphere of a Garo village. The buildings' design was intended to emulate the raised houses, made of entirely natural materials—wood, bamboo, and thatch—that had been all but ubiquitous in the region until recently. Yet the floors, pillars, and roof of the new structures were concrete, which was by no means a traditional building material. The concrete was to be later masked by split and flattened bamboo. While a bamboo weave would line the walls, the concrete of the roof was to be covered by a thin layer of thatch. My young companion looked with appreciation at the concrete, admiring its strength and durability. He knew it would be able to withstand the damp climate and the omnipresent termites. Climbing up from their underground nests, termites consume and hollow out any wood or bamboo that is in contact with the earth, except perhaps some of the local hardwoods that have become very rare and hence expensive. The cottages were located in a densely forested area, with no houses in the immediate vicinity. I talked about the project with people who lived in a neighbouring village ward. None of them expressed any misgivings about the project. They assured me it was 'good' that the cottages were being built; they welcomed them as a sign of 'development'. The construction workers had been outsiders. Locally, no one knew how to work with concrete, alien as it was to traditional building techniques. So far, the project had not resulted in any cash flowing to the villagers, but 'development', as a blanket term, carried the promise of an overall increase in living standards. People expected that it would bring more and better opportunities to earn cash, or at least bring in more people from outside, creating what would presumably be opportunities for enjoyable and perhaps profitable social interaction.

At the time of our conversation, the cottages had been under construction for more than two years, but were yet to be completed. People living close by told me that neither the person in charge of the building work (they believed it was someone from Tura town) nor any construction workers had been seen for a long time. No one knew why the work had been halted, but they supposed that the money required for its continuation had somehow run out. I wondered about the viability of the project. For years, there had been sporadic exchanges of violence between ethnic insurgents and counterterrorism units in the wider region within which the village was located, making West Garo Hills a rather unlikely destination for rural tourism. Recently, the ethnic insurgency had waned. In its wake, however, rural gangs had emerged, and West Garo Hills regularly continued to make headlines with abductions of traders for ransom. It was, in short, an unlikely place for tourists to want to stay for any extended period of time.

The cottages were being built at a location of great natural beauty. While the hilltop itself was bare, one side had an enormous banyan tree that branched out some ten to fifteen metres above the perimeter. During the day, the tree provided shade, with sunlight filtering through its foliage creating a picturesque atmosphere. Villagers referred to the hilltop as the 'old village' (*songgitcham*), which is a generic term used throughout Garo Hills to refer to abandoned former settlement sites. A man with whom I visited the site in 2017 told me that there had once been an entire village ward on the hilltop, but that it had been abandoned 'more than ten generations ago' when its residents had 'fallen ill in large numbers' and 'many had died' of unknown illnesses. This had revealed that the location had 'bad earth'—an explanation for misfortune that I encountered on numerous occasions, and a common reason for shifting a house to a new location. None of the villagers were unaware of the unsuitability of the particular hilltop as a place to live, but that was not the sort of information that they would want to convey to anyone from outside. They knew, I guess, that even if their knowledge about the place ever reached the staff in charge at the tourism department, it probably wouldn't be taken into consideration. Garo from town, educated and Christian, would be inclined to dismiss such knowledge as unfounded superstition.

The cottages were meant to facilitate 'ethnic tourism'. For several years, the Garo village where they were being built, Sadolpara (also spelled Sadolbra), had attracted interest among local tour guides. It is not unlikely that this interest emerged—at least partly—due my enthusiastic accounts of life in Sadolpara, which at least for some towns people brought the place and its people into the limelight. Despite the somewhat unpredictable situation in terms of security, several guides had brought travellers over, both Indians and foreigners. A regional newspaper had referred to the village as a 'famous destination for foreign and domestic tourists' and praised how its residents had 'preserved' 'age old A'chik [Garo] traditional beliefs, customs and practices' (*Meghalaya Times* 2012). It had also become loosely included within what the *Lonely Planet Northeast India* refers to as 'the tribal circuit' (Bindloss 2009: 24). A young resident of Tura town, who sometimes worked as a tour guide, told me that he occasionally took tourists there who wanted to 'experience real Garo culture'. The village is home to a substantial number of people who follow the traditional Garo religion and whose livelihoods depend to a good degree on shifting cultivation (generally referred to as *jhum* in North-East India). The former, in particular, is becoming increasingly rare. The traditional Garo religion has lost most of its earlier centrality, with ever fewer people practising it. This is due to the religious conversion of Garo to Christianity, a process that started more than 150 years ago. In Sadolpara and other villages nearby, support for the traditional Garo community religion has remained strong, although numbers of followers are falling even there (section 2.2).

The Garo are an ethnic community. Rather than assuming that such communities are characterized by cultural homogeneity, in this book I explore how cultural coherence can be understood as 'an internal feature of local social relations and local social practices' (Stasch 2009). Like Stasch, who studied the mortuary rites of the Korowai (West Irian), I focus specifically on social relationships that are maintained by people within their community, while acknowledging that these relationships are influenced and shaped by people's relationships with the state, as well as with non-Garo. Based on my prolonged ethnographic engagement, this book challenges prevailing perspectives on culture in 'indigenous' upland North-East India. Often portrayed as egalitarian, in harmony with nature, and deeply traditional, upland societies also tend to be regarded as outdated and doomed to die out. Contesting one-dimensional and ahistorical notions such as these, this book focuses on the vibrancy and efficacy of practices deemed traditional among the Garo. I argue that while people perceive the traditional or customary as carried over from the past, it is always subject to ongoing processes of reinterpretation and revision.

North-East India is among the culturally and linguistically most diverse regions in South Asia, and this is particularly true of its uplands. Administrative boundaries and the majority of ethnographic studies suggest that the uplands are divided into more or less exclusive 'tribal' domains, such as the Khasi, the Jaintia, and the Garo Hills in Meghalaya. In reality, most of these domains are home to various ethnicities, membership of which is much more fluid and open than often presumed.

Academic approaches to 'writing culture' (Clifford and Marcus 1986) have, over the last three decades, moved away from a former tendency in anthropology to assume an isomorphism between people, territory, and language (Gupta and Ferguson 1997). In order to break this down and do justice to the situational and contextual contingency of cultural normativities, the latter have since been located in 'flows', 'scapes' (Appadurai 1996: 33), and 'styles' (Ferguson 1999: 86). Foregrounding fluidity and processuality, this book does not present an account of an isolated, static society in North-East India's uplands, as many ethnographies of the region have done, but instead takes steps to unravel the interrelatedness of economic, social, and religious change. It shows how swidden cultivators are also becoming sedentary farmers and wage workers, as their relationship to the environment changes. And as religious ontologies diversify, land, which used to be primarily held collectively by larger kin groups, is increasingly being privatized. Changes such as these are radical and unsettling, challenging earlier cultural normativities.

Modernization theory typically associates development with the diminishing relevance of traditions. I show how traditional normativity can instead be invoked to facilitate and legitimize the revision of economic and political relationships. The diversification of the religious landscape, new measures of wealth and prestige, and increased involvement with the modern Indian state prompt the adaptation, reformulation, and thus 'reworking' of cultural ideas and practices. As long as the latter continue to be perceived as traditional, and thus rooted in the past, they can serve as legitimation for decisions that shape the relationships and commitments that define people's lives.

This book is not a village study, but it is based on fieldwork that has been localized to a large extent. It foregrounds the local, focusing on a rural area in which land continues to constitute the most important resource that people have access to. My research centred on how people negotiate their positions within social networks, particularly in the context of dramatic events such as funerals, and it proved best to study this by connecting to a relatively small group of people. I conducted most of the research for this book in and around the village of Sadolpara. Many of the issues at stake there, such as the growing influence of state and markets on people's lives, also pertain throughout the larger contiguous uplands of South and South East Asia, across states such as

India, Myanmar, Bhutan, Thailand, China and Vietnam (Van Schendel 2002; Scott 2009).[1]

In Garo Hills, as anywhere else, what happens 'locally' is dependent on processes that encompass higher levels of scale as well. Reconnecting to the opening vignette of this chapter, the question arises: With reference to which ideas, and with what practical consequences, do the tourist cottages being built in Sadolpara link villagers to government staff, to townspeople, and (eventually) even to foreign tourists? How do such relationships channel money, mobilize political authority, and confirm or challenge assumptions about cultural hierarchies? This book addresses questions such as these, focusing on the agency of local actors within the normative realms in which they locate themselves.

1.2 Creating Community

It is common for Garo and non-Garo alike to view the community religion as paradigmatic of traditional culture. The project proposal that paved the way for the construction of the tourist cottages described above, written by a high-ranking officer of Meghalaya,[2] called for Sadolpara to be classified as a 'heritage village' in order to facilitate 'preservation of the true traditions and culture of the Sengsarik [Songsarek] Garos.'[3] ('Songsarek' is the term commonly used to designate a follower of the traditional Garo religion.) The proposal described the village as '[t]he most genuine pearl of uncorrupted ethnic Garo culture, that needs to be preserved at all costs'. It detailed the merits of the site, emphasizing its natural beauty and cherished inhabitants. 'Nestled in the lap of nature, it has a picture-perfect setting of a gurgling rivulet gushing nearby, luxuriant foliage, . . . and on raised mounds the most beautiful settlements primitive simple minds could conjure and construct.' The 'primitive simple minds' appear to be people from the past, rather than contemporaries, as the proposal continues: 'To a curious passer by, someone seems to have turned the clock back. It feels like being transported back in time to a fossilized past of leisure and plenitude, forlorn traditions and customs, self-sufficiency and contentment.' The village, presented as an anachronous remnant of a 'fossilized past', is a haven of 'uncorrupted ethnic Garo culture' where 'the true traditions and culture of the Sengsarik Garos' are maintained.

Heralding Songsareks as the guardians of 'real' or 'original' Garo traditions is by no means uncommon. It is, for instance, also a key theme in *The Pristine*

6 REWORKING CULTURE

Culture and Society of the Garos of Meghalaya (2002), a book published by the Directorate of Information and Public Relations of the government of Meghalaya. The glossy work includes many photographs, most of which feature Songsarek villagers, who can be recognized as such by their turbans and earrings. In the captions, these followers of the traditional community religion are simply referred to as 'Garo'. This contrasts with images of a couple identified as 'modern Garo'. Here, the woman is dressed in a Punjabi-style *salwar kameez* while the man is wearing a polo shirt and pleated trousers, which makes it clear to anyone familiar with the region that they are Christians. The distinction between the 'ordinary' Garo and the 'modern couple' is also one of class and education. In addition to the differences in attire, visible details reveal lifestyle and literacy: the 'modern' man is wearing a wristwatch and has a pen in his shirt pocket (Figure 1.2). In striking contrast, the Garo man in Figure 1.1 appears to be bare-chested, while both he and the woman are wearing earrings (*nariki* and *nabal*) and a necklace (*rikgitok*) that are strongly associated with the traditional community religion. Essentially reducing Garo culture to practices associated with the traditional Garo religion, and glossing over the disparities that exist among Garo, the chief minister of Meghalaya stated in his foreword to the book: 'Garo tribals enact their lives more or less as they have for centuries.... The purity of their culture is evident in the fact that the Garos are a truly classless and casteless society'.

Regarding the traditional community religion as the epitome of what is 'real', 'genuine', and 'pure' Garo culture meets the expectations of an 'ethnographic state', as India has been labelled by Dirks (2001: 44). In their attempts to control India, British colonizers conducted extensive ethnographic surveys from the late 19th century onwards, charting and ranking the characteristics of what they perceived to be discrete groups, often distinguished on the basis of religion. Today, from a policy perspective, upland societies continue to be predominantly perceived as culturally homogeneous, geographically contained, and isolated. Processes of modernization and differentiation, as a consequence, are likely to be seen as deviations from a static cultural core. Such distorted, ahistorical portrayals serve the interests of 'indigenous' political activists and local state actors alike. Indigenous activists' political demands are often made with reference to bounded ethno-territories, which are also the basis of many of the Indian state's policies (Baruah 2009: 11; Middleton 2013: 257). The ethnographic accounts that are at the core of this book focus on the vibrancy and adaptability of local cultural configurations, and question what cultural homogeneity and cohesion mean in relation to the Garo.

Figure 1.1 'Meet a Garo Couple'.
(Directorate of Information and Public Relations 2002, 26).

In any social context, 'community' becomes manifest in the relationships that people create and maintain. I focus primarily on how people position themselves within the resulting networks, with reference to what ideas and which conventions. Thus, I approach community foremost as an emic category, a 'category of practice' as it is understood and defined by the people it applies to (Brubaker 2012: 2). At the same time, community is also shaped by the interpretations of others, by what Brubaker refers to as a 'category of analysis'. Inevitably, there is 'heavy traffic between the two', since both categories

Figure 1.2 'Modern Garo Couple'.
(Directorate of Information and Public Relations 2002, 27).

inform each other to some degree. By foregrounding practice and enactment, I am able to explore the ambiguities, situationality, and conflicting interests that shape people's experiences of community.

Challenging earlier primordialist and essentialist approaches, the relationship between community, culture, and tradition has been hotly debated in the social sciences. Anderson has famously argued that because the ethnic or national groups in which people locate themselves are typically far too large for all members to know each other personally, a sense of belonging typically hinges on how people 'imagine' such groups (Anderson 1983: 6). This makes the dissemination of such imaginations politically significant. Also exploring the factors that underlie effective claim-making, Hobsbawn and Ranger have shown that traditions tend to be most highly valued if they are considered relevant and important in the present, irrespective of whether they are historically accurate or have been 'invented' (Hobsbawm and Ranger 1983: 1). Both works were preceded by Barth (1969) who, in his approach to ethnicity, argued that the identification and emphasizing of differences between groups, which he called 'boundary maintenance', was more relevant than the 'cultural stuff' that might at first sight seem to define an ethnic community (Barth 1969: 15). Combined, these three contributions have been instrumental to the emergence of a research agenda focusing on how community, culture, and tradition inform ethnic identities (Eriksen 2001: 44).

Such a focus on identities, produced in dialogue and interaction with ethnic 'others', emphasizes conscious agency and reflexivity within political contexts. But it cannot explain why some cultural ideas and practices are more meaningful to people than others, nor how they relate to personal experiences and emotions (Eriksen 2001: 60). What renders certain cultural practices significant or normative? How are they anchored in values and why do they matter? Introducing what he called the 'inventiveness of tradition', Sahlins (1999: 408) argued that cultural practices have the capacity to generate, validate, and thus substantiate symbolic and moral frameworks. In other words, cultural practices are conveyors of meaning, rather than constituting somewhat arbitrarily 'invented traditions'. As Otto and Pedersen have pointed out, however, Sahlins' 'inventive traditions' seem to be imbued with an inherent significance, which locates agency with the cultural traditions themselves (Otto and Pedersen 2005: 21). Rather than assuming such a priori 'cultural agency' (Li 2006: 126), the ethnography presented in this book adopts a more relational or transactionalist point of view in exploring how the efficacy of tradition derives from its sustained enactment: from its being repeatedly expressed, (re-)interpreted, and performed in dedicated cultural contexts.

In this book, ritual practices such as funerals provide the starting point for an ethnographic analysis of experiences of relatedness and community. Funerals provide a particularly opportune context for studying the articulation and interpretation of ideas about life and death. Dealing with the dead—caring for them as well as taking their guidance—is an important concern in cultural contexts worldwide, and extensive investments in mortuary rituals are by no means unusual (Bloch and Parry 1982; Huntington and Metcalf 1991). The responsibilities that people load upon the dead, and the ways in which the dead make demands on the living, have been the subject of much debate. Typically, scholars have either focused on mortuary practices as social events, or on the fate of the deceased. Contemporary anthropological studies of death and mortuary practices continue to draw on the seminal work of Hertz (1960 [1907]). In his analysis of the funerals of the Ngaju of Kalimantan, which included double burials, Hertz paid particular attention to temporality. Mortuary practices included a first burial but were not concluded until a second burial had taken place, years later. Focusing on the decay of the corpse and the various stages of its 'processing', he approached dying as a process of extended disintegration and transformation. As the dead body putrefies, is buried, cremated, or otherwise substituted, the soul of the deceased also becomes repositioned. Likewise, Hertz argued, the state of the mortal remains affects the condition of the mourners. The correlations or interdependencies that Hertz identified highlight a tension between the agency of the mourners in guiding the dead and the capacity of the dead to direct the living. This friction renders funerals a prime context for the redefinition of social as well as cosmological relationships (Hertz 1960 [1907]: 86).

The emotional impact of death is culturally specific. There are situations in which it does not cause great emotional upheaval, as Nancy Scheper-Huges (1992) has argued is the case for infant mortality in the slums of Brazil, for example. The nature of the loss perceived, the presences the dead assume, and the degree to which they affect relations maintained among the living define their emotional impact (Huntington and Metcalf 1991). In a Garo context, death triggers strong emotions, but the number of people emotionally affected varies—to a large extent in accordance with the age and social significance of the deceased. The death of an infant typically 'moves' fewer people than the death of a senior person. Likewise, a death that occurs in a family that is economically and politically powerful has more of an impact than one that occurs in a family that is poor. Garo funerals call for acknowledgement of the dead, both in terms of the social person they used to be, and as the deceased they have become. At the same time, funerals encompass the reorganization of claims and responsibilities that pertained to the deceased. This requires people to clarify how they relate to each other, which makes such occasions a prime ground for the articulation and redefinition of social networks, and for reworking the cultural conventions these are rooted in.

Mortuary rituals can shed light on societal contexts characterized by religious diversity and political inequality. In a recent monograph on the Sora of highland Odisha (India), Vitebsky (2017) shows that Sora Hindu and Christian converts have challenged their community's former dialogic engagement with the dead. Hinduism and Christianity, as 'new' ontologies to the Sora, have disencouraged a continued agential presence of the dead among the living. Closer to the Garo, writing about the Mizo of North-East India, Pachuau links transformations in death-related practices that have taken place since the imposition of colonial rule to changes in Mizo settlement patterns. Mizo were migratory in precolonial times, but despite having long since become sedentary, especially in urban contexts, they continue to lack a hereditary connection to place. In precolonial days, Mizo did not inter the dead but took their bones with them when they migrated. Nowadays, burial serves to create—upon death—a permanent linkage to place and consequently also to the other people living there (Pachuau 2014: 215–222). The dead demand the expression of relationships that can define social groups as well as the places these groups connect to.

For Garo, the authority that underlies cultural practices such as funerals rests with *niam*. *Niam* (related to the Sanskrit *niyama*) is an overarching term for the orally transmitted principles that uphold ideas, norms, values, and practices that are believed to have been passed down from preceding generations and are in that sense traditional. *Niam* centres on principles, the interpretation of which varies according to the situation at hand. *Niam* refers to a normativity that constitutes a conceived order, yet takes shape in dialogue with everyday interaction. *Niam* defines one's relationships to other people as well as to the environment more generally. *Niam* also stipulates what counts as false conduct: ways in which people should not behave because that would be disloyal towards other persons, or disrespectful towards animals, spirits, or plants. At funerals, *niam* connects social obligations to religious commitments. Because the interpretation of *niam* is situationally specific, and thus always partially dependent on the people involved in a given situation, it can never be translated into hard-and-fast rules or laws that are simply to be enacted. For Garo, it is *niam* that, perhaps even more then language, sets them apart from 'neighbouring' communities such as the Hajong, Koch, Rabha, Bengali, or Khasi, all of whom have their own versions of *niam*.

At the village level, *niam* is imparted orally: it is talked about and discussed, with the most weight attributed to the voices of kin seniors, primarily men. Garo *niam* can encompass anyone who agrees to submit to it. I have come across Assamese, Nepali, and Hajong who (through marriage) have ended up living in Garo villages, and they follow Garo *niam*, at least in certain respects. This quality of Garo *niam* explains how Garo can at once mix with and stay separate from surrounding communities. In my experience, notably people belonging to ethnicities that are distinct yet 'near', such as Hajong, Koch or Rabha can to a good degree become part of the Garo community as long as they subject themselves to Garo *niam*. Conversely, anyone who does not follow Garo *niam* effectively excludes themselves from that group. The importance attributed to compliance with *niam* has probably been instrumental to ethnic permeability. Upland communities such as the Garo have, at least historically, been relatively open to allowing outsiders in.[4] Such openness has also been documented by Ramirez in what he called 'ethnic conversion' between Karbi, Tiwa, and Khasi in the Meghalaya–Assam borderland (Ramirez 2013: 279).

Although there are obviously common denominators, interpretations of Garo *niam* differ from context to context as well as from place to place. There are differences between rural and peri-urban contexts, and also between religious orientations. As mentioned above, following *niam* means 'obeying' (*mania*) it, and what is obeyed is at once social (the larger kin group, kin seniors) and superhuman (the spirits of the traditional community religion or the Christian God). Those who 'obey' the Songsarek spirits follow the *niam* of the *mande*, which is said to have existed since time immemorial, the 'time of grandfather and grandmother' (*atchu-ambini somoi*) and is therefore referred to as 'real' custom (*niam chongmot*). At the time of my fieldwork in Sadolpara, *mande* was consistently used to refer to Songsareks, and *ruri* ('modernists' or 'outsiders') to Christians, marking Christianity as something comparatively new. In settings where Christianity is considered quintessentially Garo, the term *mande* refers to Garo people in general and *ruri* to 'outsiders', non-Garo, such as Bengali or Assamese.

What Garo call *niam* is akin to what Astuti and Bloch (2013: 109) refer to as 'deference', that which people 'follow', since they are expected to. Taking this perspective, 'observance' provides a more apt translation of the term *niam* than the much more common 'customary law'. Obeying *niam* is comparable to the 'carrying' of *zan* by the Akha of northern Thailand described by Tooker (1992). Akha are an upland community who—at least historically—depended on shifting cultivation for their livelihood, with a form of social organization that is similar to that of the Garo in certain respects. *Zan* encompasses 'religious practices, technological practices and rules for action'. Rather than a set of ideologies or beliefs, it comprises a 'way of life', a 'way of doing things' that needs to be practised or 'carried' (Tooker 1992: 803). Tooker showed that Akha distinguished between different kinds of *zan*, depending on whether families followed the Akha community religion or were Christians. She argued that what mattered in relation to 'carrying' *zan* was that people followed the principles and guidelines that it encompassed. Belief or faith were less relevant; the emphasis was on how *zan* was practised. Although distinctions between the various types of *zan* have gradually become more marked, they have not come in the way of a sense of shared Akha-ness. Shared Akha-ness is becoming ever more important, especially as Akha make efforts to maintain connections that transcend the national borders of Thailand, Laos, and China, which they live divided across (Tooker 2004; Morton, Wang, and Li 2016). A comparable dynamic seems to operate among the Garo. Although Songsarek and Christian Garo interpret *niam* differently, as do Garo Christians of different denominations (such as Baptists, Catholics, and Seventh Day Adventists), these distinctions are frequently and easily played down to emphasize a shared sense of Garoness.

Niam also corresponds with a Durkheimian notion of morality, which encompasses the kinds of values that 'compel and constrain human action, manifest in their being simultaneously obligatory and desirable' (Laidlaw 2013: 173). Morality, in this sense, refers to what are presumed to be collective understandings of what is desirable, what brings prestige, what is detested, and what is taboo. Garo culture does not constitute a singular body of ideas, values, and practices, but it does converge on the moral commitments that are central to Garo *niam*. *Niam* becomes manifest in commitments to relatives and friends that define one as a social being. Focusing on interpretations of *niam*, this book explores what people experience as Garo culture.

1.3 Continuing Conversations

This book is based on ethnographic fieldwork conducted primarily in rural West Garo Hills between 1999 and 2019, comprising about thirty months in total. Following an initial intensive fieldwork period of approximately two years, I have returned every one or two years, but at times there have been longer gaps in between (de Maaker 2014).[5] This prolonged period of ethnographic engagement enables a diachronic perspective, revealing how changes take place over time. Yet, some observations are not necessarily time bound. Although valid at the time of writing, these are clearly open to future change and should not be interpreted as representing an eternal 'ethnographic present'.

In West Garo Hills, people live dispersed across numerous village wards (*gittims*), which are clustered together as village territories (*a'kings*). Towns are small, few, and far apart, and most have government buildings, shops, schools, and the houses of the people these services employ. The towns offer important facilities, but the vast majority of the population live in the rural areas. Sadolpara is one of the larger village territories of West Garo Hills. It encompasses more than ten village wards and (by 2016) at least 1,700 inhabitants,[6] spread out across a territory that I estimate at 20–25 square kilometres. I ended up in Sadolpara, initially, rather coincidentally. When I first came to Garo Hills I could not speak Garo and was travelling together with a friend. We had set out on a walking tour in West Garo Hills, without much of a plan. At the end of a long day, Sadolpara was the last village we came to. One of the people we met there was Jiji. She lived in a traditional Garo house (*nok mande*). Like many of the village wards in its vicinity, the majority of people living in Jiji's ward, Chenggalgre, practised the traditional Garo community religion. Jiji invited us inside, offered tea, and then rice beer. She was an elderly widow and shared a household with her youngest daughter and her two children. Jiji was thin and looked frail, but she liked to crack jokes that made everyone roll over with laughter. For her, I was a 'white skin' (*bigil gipok*), but I don't think she had much of an idea where I came from. Jiji was quick to formalize our relationship, announcing she would call me her son. That meant that I not only gained an adoptive mother, but also brothers, sisters, uncles, aunts, cousins, and so on. Garo generally frame social relationships in kin terms, and by making me her adopted son, she incorporated me into that framework. I could not help but feel a bit awkward about this, and rather than calling her 'mother', I came to call her 'grandmother' (*ambi*), which is a respectful term that is also used to address senior women more generally. Jiji nonetheless persisted in calling me her 'child' (*pisa*), and every now and then she would command me as a (Garo) mother might her son. Over the years that followed, until her death in 2015, she never ceased to claim the authority over me that my filial position warranted (Figure 1.3).

Sadolpara seemed a good place to conduct fieldwork from, and I moved there a couple of weeks after the initial visit. I was soon joined by Nandini (my partner) and then by Sengjrang, my first field assistant (when he took a job as a teacher a couple of months later, I received essential linguistic support from Henysing and Nixon). Jiji, or a member of her close kin, told us that we could construct a house next to hers. She held title to the land on which the village ward was located, which her relatives said entitled her to make such an offer. We also consulted the village head (*nokma*) of Sadolpara, Motchang Chambugong Marak, who gave his consent but cautioned us that we should not 'depend on the village for our rice'. When we

Figure 1.3 Jiji M. Sangma with the author.
Photograph: Henysing A. Sangma, 2014.

reassured him that we would buy our rice from the market, he agreed to our stay. We requested various people to construct a house for us, but initially no one wanted to do so. Thatching grass and wood were scarce at the time, so it would take a lot of effort to obtain them. Long negotiations followed, and in the end a group of men offered to build a house that would last for at least a year, for the price of INR 5,000. They did a really good job and the house ultimately outlasted our two-year stay.

Moving into the house transformed my relationship with Jiji and her relatives. Jiji never once asked me for anything and left it to me to figure out how to deal with the disparity in wealth between us. From the very first day, Jiji's youngest daughter, who lived with her, provided us with drinking water and firewood. This was heavy work; drinking water had to be collected from a spring at the bottom of the steep hill on top of which we lived. We asked one of Jiji's granddaughters, who lived next door, if she would be willing to help us in the mornings and evenings in the house. She readily agreed and so did her parents. Every day, she cooked us lentils and a vegetable dish and washed the dishes afterwards. We paid her some money and took care of her meals.

Villagers were determinedly self-sufficient and never asked to be given anything, even though they could see that money provided us with access to a seemingly unlimited supply of tea, sugar, milk, rice, lentils, vegetables, and the like. I knew from previous fieldwork experiences that structural inequality in terms of food could create an extremely uneasy situation. In an attempt to pre-emptively address this, I asked Jiji and her daughter to cook our rice. This meant that we bought rice (at least 10 kg at a time) or gave money for rice to be bought. In return, we received a number of shares of cooked rice twice a day. The amount of rice that came into Jiji's household this way covered our needs as well as those of Jiji and her daughter, compensating them for the cooking. In addition, it allowed them to share out rice to relatives and neighbours. The granddaughter of Jiji who helped us with the daily chores took some food from us for her own family as well. In addition, there were less regular food exchanges with other people living in the same area of the village. People would offer us eggs, or a bowl of curry, gestures we would invariably reciprocate. All this contributed to our being tied into a web of exchange relationships that extended well beyond food.

Our household helpers never stayed for longer than a couple of months. When Jiji's granddaughter decided not to work for us anymore, her elder sister volunteered to replace her. The elder sister was succeeded by the daughter of another neighbour, and then again others. That these commitments were short-lived was not unusual. Every now and then, village youth in search of adventure and an education would leave for one of the towns in Garo Hills, such as Tura. There, they would combine working as a domestic helper with attending school. Very few of those youths stayed away for more than a couple of months. The most common reason for leaving their posts was 'feeling ashamed' (*kracha'a*): they felt humiliated when they had to obey someone who was not a parent, grandparent, uncle, or aunt. Even though Jiji saw me as a son, we were not truly kin, and it seemed inevitable that soon after they agreed to work with us, our household helpers began to feel uncomfortable about doing our daily chores.

I intended to research funerals, since going by the ethnographic insights that I had obtained thus far, these seemed to bring many things together. Initially, I felt rather daunted by the prospect and unsure about how I would be able to attend such events. Jiji helped to allay those fears. Being associated with her, a well-known and senior figure, opened many doors for me—sometimes literally—that otherwise might have remained closed. My presence at funerals was no doubt unusual, but as long as I focused on what happened relatively openly and did not invade anyone's private space, people did not really seem bothered by my presence. Garo funerals are, to a good degree, public events, which anyone is welcome to attend. Jiji did not consider my interests extraordinary at all. Death itself is 'bad' (*namja*), but that does not prevent funerals from including enjoyable elements. Funerals provide people with an occasion to catch up with friends and relatives and the provision of abundant food (and, among Songsareks, rice beer) by the deceased person's close relatives is obligatory.

Robbins Burling, in his seminal Garo ethnography *Rengsanggri: Family and Kinship in a Garo Village* (1997 [1963]), only mentions funerals briefly. Despite never having attended a Garo funeral himself, he offers a perceptive if rather a short analysis. Burling asked people to describe funerals but found that they were often hesitant to talk about the practices involved or the ideas associated with death. In an essay titled 'Garo Beliefs in the Afterlife', Burling writes how he asked people about creation and the nature of the human soul. One typical response was to throw such a question back at him: '"I don't know", they would say, "what do you think?"' (Burling 1988: 31). I have tried to overcome these difficulties by observing what people did in certain contexts, and then trying to engage them in conversations about the events they had been part of, often aided by video recordings I had made, in an attempt to understand what had motivated their actions.

I was particularly interested in the obligations faced by kin towards widows or widowers to 'replace' a deceased person, and the connection between these obligations and the gifts that are offered at funerals. Given the complex and sensitive interactions involved, and my limited proficiency in Garo, video recordings were crucial towards detailed analysis. I had received training in audiovisual methodology at Leiden University and was experienced at creating research video recordings (Nijland 1994; de Maaker 2000, 2006b). When people speak, the tone and volume of their voice matters. Communication is not just verbal but also embodied. It includes facial expressions, gestures, the distance people maintain between one another, and how these develop over time. Video recordings show material objects, spaces, buildings, time of day and season, and much more. In more conventional interviews, researchers are almost inevitably obliged to formulate 'What if ... . ?' questions, calling upon respondents to speculate upon their own and others' behaviour. Social science data, consequently, often consists of what people say they have done, or will do, rather than on what they actually do. Interlocutors may describe or reflect on an expected or 'ideal' course of action, but in prestige-oriented cultural contexts, such as Garo funerals, the ideal is seldom met in everyday life. In other words, if the ideal is barely achievable—even if only due to economic limitations—it can be socially acceptable for people to perform within their means as long as they seem to be striving for the ideal. Research that proceeds from 'enactment', from what people actually do, can reveal, contextualize, and situate such discrepancies between ideals and actual practices.

The research video recordings were designed to spur discussions with interlocutors at a later date. Working with video involved several steps. In order to obtain good images and clear sound, two people made the recordings: I myself operated the camera, while Sengjrang or Nandini took care of the sound. I then compiled a description of the shots. Next, one of the field assistants transcribed the spoken Garo, to create a word-by-word translation from Garo into English. This gave a very general impression of the content of the dialogues but not more than that. The field assistants typically understood the words spoken, but coming from 'town' were often less sure what they meant in the respective context. Much of the research centred on watching footage together with different people, including those present in the recordings, discussing their perspectives on what had happened. The video recordings certainly proved to be conversation starters, reminding people of what they had experienced and sparking discussions and retrospective reflections on the events recorded. Frequently, we viewed the same video recordings with different interlocutors on different occasions, which resulted in complementary or even conflicting interpretations. These sometimes meticulous analyses provided insights into how people traced relationships to one another, while also producing detailed and annotated translations of spoken Garo into English. The case studies that resulted from this work are the building blocks of this book. Most of them continued to evolve over time, as subsequent phases of fieldwork expanded upon earlier interpretations. Combined, the video footage, translations, and interpretations provide a densely rich resource. Yet the fine detail of the data has also had its drawbacks: at times I have felt I was virtually 'drowning' in it. That is a problem that Adrian Gerbrands, the doyen of Leiden Visual Anthropology (he referred to it as 'ethnocommunication') had already noted in relation to his early experiments with film elicitation in ethnographic research (Gerbrands 1971).

However, the enormous amount of data did provide me with many openings to pick up on old conversations on my visits to Sadolpara for the next two decades. I have been able to refer back to past discussions and build on them to address new questions. Even more significantly, my earlier presence and the experiences that we shared in the past have created a level of trust that has stood the test of time. Sadly, many people who were already old when I started my research have since died, and unfortunately this is also true of quite a few people who were much younger. At the same time, a whole new generation has emerged, as many of those who were teenagers at the time of my initial stay are now young parents.

This book contains many accounts of events that I have been a part of, or been told about, during my research. Other passages are based on cumulative observations and interactions and draw less on first-person accounts. I have attempted to remain close to the perceptions of my interlocutors and address the world as they experience it as much as possible. As time has passed, I have found that some events that had been difficult to handle at the time they occurred later lost their edge (de Maaker 2020). When Nagal died, following a snake bite, her widower was overcome by grief. About six years later I met him again, and asked whether I could use some of the images I had recorded at her funeral in a publication. He immediately agreed and commented: 'It doesn't matter, it's from the past.'

The new generation welcomed me into their homes as their elders before them had done. On one visit, someone showed me a framed picture of my father reading to my two infant sons who had been born some years before. I had brought the photograph along during an earlier visit and she had managed to acquire it and kept it along with other family pictures. The photos, some of which were stained with rice beer or mouldy at the edges, were kept in a plastic bag. They did not have a camera of their own, so the bag contained pictures given by me, Nandini, or other people who had visited them over the years. While I looked at the picture of my father and his grandsons, I realized that while the villagers had become part of my life as I worked with the images I had collected during fieldwork, in some ways I had become part of theirs too (Figure 1.4).

In Sadolpara, over the past two decades much has changed, but perhaps even more has remained the same. During my initial two-year stay, there was no electricity from the grid. On cloudless nights, the stars shone with a clarity that I had never seen in Europe. People would chat for long hours, sitting in the dim light of a kerosene wick or a smouldering wood fire. When, in December 2011, electricity lines reached the village, the nights lit up with the bright light bulbs that have become a common sight ever since. A few people who could afford to bought televisions, dethroning the one or two that had previously provided nightly amusement for the entire village, powered by solar-charged truck batteries. A couple of years later, cellular phone masts emerged, and when prepaid services became affordable, mobile phones were

Figure 1.4 A framed picture of my father reading to my children when they were toddlers, which is kept in the household of one of Jiji's children.
Photograph: Erik de Maaker, 2008.

in the hands of quite a few people. Most of rural West Garo Hills had never really had landline telephone connections, so the sudden availability of mobiles brought a radical change. People were quick to appreciate the advantages of connectivity, and these days even those with a very moderate cash income own a phone. With the exception of mobile phones, however, standards of living have remained remarkably unaltered in the past twenty years, and, so far, rural West Garo Hills has seen little of the dramatic economic growth that is transforming India as whole.

Nonetheless, people in rural West Garo Hills are now increasingly cultivating cash crops and using the money gained to buy food, clothes, and consumer goods. Many new schools have opened, some of which demand monthly tuition fees that currently range from INR 150 to 300 per month. This may be a nominal amount for people who are salaried, but it can be a substantial burden for families who have to earn each and every rupee by either selling their produce or their labour. On the flip side, the returns on many of the crops people sell in the market have hardly kept pace with inflation. For some crops, wholesale prices have fluctuated significantly over the years. In the year 2000, a basket of ginger could fetch up to INR 450. By 2012 this had fallen to INR 150–200, which then increased to INR 700 or even more in 2019. Prices paid for the villagers' agricultural produce slumped drastically during the infamous demonetization of November/December 2016, when wholesale traders reputedly haggled down the amounts they offered by claiming to have 'no cash' to hand. Irrespective of the economic strains people face, Sadolpara currently has more inhabitants than ever before. Locally, people gauge the size of a village ward by the number of households (or 'Houses', see section 3.3), rather than by counting inhabitants. Reliable figures to confirm the increase in population are not available, but in 2018 I was told that, as a village domain (including the villages Sadolpara and Mangdugre) Sadolpara had 272 households. With 59 more households than the 213 that were counted in the census of 2011, this suggests an increase of about 27 per cent. Since household sizes are declining (couples are having less children), this does not mean that the population has also grown by 27 per cent, but there is no doubt that it is on the increase. There has been some outmigration, but many of the people who have tried to make a living 'outside', for instance in Tura, have eventually returned and seem to prefer to make do with what they can earn using the resources the village offers.

1.4 Structure of the Book

This book sets itself apart from the majority of existing ethnographic literature on North-East India's upland societies in three ways. First, it forces a rethinking of the all too often taken-for-granted assumption that upland societies are characterized by cultural homogeneity and strong internal cohesion. The book explores the creation and continual transformation of the multiple relationships through which people are connected to one another. These relationships are embedded in normative frameworks that are demanding, yet leave room for ambiguity and negotiation. Garo 'society' and 'Garoness' emerge in reference to shared norms, values, and the fulfilment of mutual obligations. Far from being immutable, these need to be constantly expressed, (re-)interpreted, and enacted. Second, the book shows how traditions, referred to as *niam*, are continuously revised and reworked in response to new economic and political opportunities and a changing ontological landscape. Yet, it is the perception of *niam* as having been carried over from the past that imbues it with the ability to induce and legitimize social change. Third, this book takes customary practices as a vantage point from which to consider the importance of ideas, beliefs, and notions of relatedness. It demonstrates that religious ideas and beliefs do not exist on their own, but are intricately linked to, and produced by, the enactment of customs and rituals. In certain respects, 'practices' even take precedence over ideas and are likely to shape the latter.

I contextualize the people that this book is about in chapter 2 ('Frames, Labels, Locations'). How are Garo located socially and what has been their trajectory of becoming? In Garo Hills, a rather sharp distinction divides people who earn their livelihood as cultivators and those who live in town and have salaried jobs. Sources of income and land relationships create contrasting realms that overlap to a certain extent. But instead of the urban simply encapsulating and transforming the rural, the latter also has an asset of its own—it constitutes the source of the very traditions that define Garo ethnicity, including in urban contexts. The urban, as the seat of the state bureaucracy, oversees rural land management arrangements. A certain degree of village level administrative autonomy is upheld, but defining the rural areas as exclusively Garo also translates into a kind of ethnic incarceration. For instance, land management laws in Garo Hills benefit Garo, but such laws do not apply to Garo who live outside Garo Hills. There is a significant disparity in terms of access to state resources between urban middle-class Garo and rural dwellers. Structures of governance are urban-centric, and rural areas do not have much political leverage at a state level.

'Being Garo' finds expression first and foremost in terms of relatedness that are at the core of chapter 3 ('Housing Matters'). What relational categories are relevant to Garo, and how are they experienced across distinct social domains? Proceeding from ethnographic narrative, I discuss how roles and responsibilities are shaped, in part, to fit real-life needs. Garo express relatedness with reference to matrilineal descent and affinity. Marriages that can be continued across generations provide shape to hierarchically structured residential groups. Belonging to such groups brings access to resources, the most important of which is land. While the relationships within these groups might appear immutable, over time they can be adapted and reinterpreted in accordance with changing political and economic strengths and weaknesses. Among practitioners of the traditional Garo community religion, political and economic responsibilities are linked to religious responsibilities. Kin groups shape people's relationships to one another, but at the same time these groups are shaped by the actions of individuals.

Chapter 4 ('*Niam*, Houses and Land') focuses on connections to place as experienced in rural West Garo Hills. How do people interpret their environment and negotiate their existence within it? The traditional Garo community religion provides strategies and (ritual) techniques for living among omnipresent spirits. Religio-political structures that developed before the colonial era have been assimilated and transformed by the modern state. In Sadolpara, people encounter various sources of authority, ranging from the spirits of the traditional Garo community religion, to the Christian God, to the Indian state. Focusing on Songsareks, I discuss how land relations are historicized, reflected, and articulated in religious responsibilities as well as in hierarchical relationships within the matrilineal group. Proceeding from an examination of the relationships maintained by practitioners of the traditional community religion with the forest and its spirits, and the practices undertaken to secure fruitful growth of the swidden crops, I discuss how the concomitant rituals and celebrations are taking on new forms and attaining new significances in a variety of contemporary contexts.

The relationships within which people locate themselves are not a given but need to be enacted in order to be recognized. Chapter 5 ('Engaging the Dead') explores how and why funerals in rural West Garo Hills are significant occasions for the assertion of matrilineal and affinal relationships. Funerals allow people to guide a deceased person to the afterworld, while simultaneously facilitating their reconnection and reintegration among the living. As they assess their obligations towards the dead, people are led to consider the extent to which they identify with the larger groups that they are part of, and the kinds of loyalties they face as a result. Funerals involve a wide range of ritually significant gifts, most of which are embedded in some sort of reciprocal relationship. For some gifts, reciprocation may take place more or less immediately, for others, it may be drawn out over subsequent funerals involving distinct matrilineal groups. Funerals also connect people to place, not only with the interment of bodies or (following cremation) pieces of bone but also in the various locations and objects that the dead are made to associate with.

Chapter 6 ('Claiming Relationships, Spaces, and Resources') focuses on how obligations, rights, and claims towards other people, as well as to essential resources, become manifest. Here, the replacement of deceased spouses is a major concern. Achieving replacement is a complex and often difficult process that risks triggering conflicting interests between individual persons and the larger groups of relatives to which they belong. Replacement is of particular importance where claims to land are implicated. Such claims, which have only partially been absorbed into the interpretation of customary arrangements of ownership and tenure accepted by the state, depend on the continuation of marital bonds across generations: this is what in the context on rural West Garo Hills makes spouse replacement crucial. While these customary arrangements enable communal access to land, they also include mechanisms that are facilitating the demise of communal land tenure. The increasing integration of rural West Garo Hills into a monetary, market-oriented economy, fuelled by a growing need for cash among a steadily rising rural population, encourages the gradual privatization of land.[7] Not everyone benefits equally from these developments, and economic inequality is increasing. Nonetheless, people also make significant efforts to continue to practise shifting cultivation, which requires collaboration—even across religious divides.

How do relatedness and custom gain new significances with the transformation of the resources that people depend on for their livelihood? Chapter 7 ('Customizing Traditions') explores this question from various angles. The state has long been an established presence in Garo Hills but has only relatively recently become a source of funding for a wide range of development-related activities. The relationships that people in rural West Garo Hills maintain with civil servants and politicians are deeply personalized and hierarchical. This does not render other notions of social hierarchy obsolete, but sees them reinterpreted and transposed to adapt to the new status quo. The obligation to replace deceased spouses remains, not least because it is essential for the passing on of inheritances. The consolidation of privatized wealth, however, is transforming the nature of ownership and sharing, resulting in a gradual easing of the mutual dependencies that have historically defined relationships between households.

Chapter 8 ('The Modernity of Garo *Niam*') revisits the main questions addressed in this book. In rural West Garo Hills, *niam* (custom) continues to be upheld, valued as a source of guiding principles in negotiations that ultimately define land use and organize other socio-economic aspects of life. As long as *niam* is perceived as traditional, deep-rooted, and authoritative, it can continue to underpin the relationships that people trace among one another, which influence how they share, or sometimes compete for, the resources they depend on in everyday life.

2
Frames, Labels, Locations

2.1 Spatial Divides

Tura town, together with adjacent smaller towns and villages, comprises a substantial peri-urban area. With a population of more than 75,000 people, Tura is home to at least 10 per cent of the population of the combined Garo Hills districts, and it is by far the largest town in Garo Hills.[1] Many houses are located on plots with big gardens that are used for the cultivation of cash crops. Tura has many trees, and it is probably one of the greenest towns in South Asia. Especially towards its outskirts, urban and rural blend into each other. The oldest part of Tura, the town centre, is located at the foot of the Nokrek mountain. On a clear day, the mountain offers spectacular views of the plains of Assam and Bangladesh. Tura has the best educational institutions and hospitals in Garo Hills and is its political, administrative, and commercial centre. It is currently the 'headquarters' of West Garo Hills district, but before the division of Garo Hills into its current five districts, it used to be the district capital of the entire Garo Hills region.[2]

Tura is home to the majority of the college-educated, wealthy, and politically influential Garo. It is the town that Garo who have left to work in Delhi, Bangalore, Shillong, or elsewhere eventually return to. Although dominated by Garo politically, Tura has always had substantial numbers of non-Garo minorities who identify themselves either in terms of their regional or linguistic background. This includes minorities who have historically always been located in the Garo Hills, such as Koch, Hajong, and Rabha, as well as groups who typically trace their origins from much further away, such as Bengalis, Assamese, Marwaris, Biharis, and Punjabis. Tura was founded in the late 19th century as a small colonial administrative centre, which was initially primarily home to Bengalis and Europeans (Majumdar 1980: 163). Many of the other migrant groups have also been present for a long time, and often came to Tura to make use of opportunities created by the incorporation of Garo Hills into the British colonial state. After Indian independence, the importance of the town grew, and by the 1980s Tura had become a 'centre for the educated Garo elite' (Majumdar 1980: 164). In recent decades, Tura has

Reworking Culture. Erik de Maaker, Oxford University Press. © Oxford University Press 2022.
DOI: 10.1093/oso/9788194831093.003.0002

attracted migrants from rural Garo Hills, as well as increasingly large numbers of migrants—often unskilled workers—from elsewhere in India and reputedly also from Bangladesh. Some of the other towns of the Garo Hills region also have ethnically mixed populations, as do the densely populated plain areas at the northern and western borders of Garo Hills, where Bengali Muslims comprise the majority, whereas people in the mostly sparsely populated hilly 'interior' are predominantly Garo. Nonetheless, throughout the hills, road works, construction labour, mining, and many other physical or menial jobs tend to be done primarily by non-Garo.[3] Garo Hills stretches across an area of about 200 by 100 kilometres as the crow flies. According to the most recent census, it was home to 1.1 million inhabitants (of whom approximately 900,000 were Garo) in 2011, but it can be safely assumed that these numbers have increased since.[4]

Even though towns like Tura can feel fairly rural at times, the contrast between urban and village life is often stark. Like Sadolpara's residents, most Garo villagers primarily depend on agriculture for their livelihood. Shifting cultivation involves clearing forest, sowing, weeding, and harvesting. This work is physically demanding and typically has to be done in the hot sun. What is more, the heavy rain that falls during the growth season produces a very high humidity. Harvesting fruit trees means climbing them, which can be really dangerous. Level patches of land such as river valleys are used for growing wet (paddy) rice, but even this work is typically un-mechanized and involves a lot of arduous labour in often hot and muddy conditions: making dykes, planting, and harvesting are often all done by hand. Everyday domestic life also involves a great deal of physical labour. Rice is husked by pounding, with a heavy six-foot-long pole used as a pestle. Most people have to collect water for home use from a well or spring. Carrying vessels or buckets of water is strenuous, particularly as houses tend to be constructed on higher ground, with water sources located somewhere below. Men sometimes carry water, but the task is more usually done by women and children. Often, water sources also serve as a collective bathing place. Men and women bathe in public, arranging their sarongs in such a way that all critical body parts remain covered (Figure 2.1). Most households have a latrine, but this is a relatively recent development. At the time of my first fieldwork period, latrines were very rare, and people took recourse to the forest instead.[5] By contrast, even in small towns most people have a bathroom, water may come from a tap, and those with a cash income buy their food from shops or markets.

In villages, people live exposed to the elements. In the dry season (October to March) the environment may seem pleasant, but it is much less so during

Figure 2.1 Bathing and washing in the open: spring water is guided through an iron pipe from a nearby source to a communal bathing and dish-washing spot.
Photograph: Erik de Maaker, 2003.

the rainy season (April to September). Garo Hills has a high annual rainfall, and it can rain for days at a time, particularly from May to July.[6] The incessant rains, combined with unrelenting heat, produce a very high humidity. The earth, which is hard as rock in the dry season, is transformed into a soft, slippery, but also fertile clay. The rains also herald other dangers. They bring out large numbers of leeches that try to attach themselves to both people and animals, inflicting large bleeding wounds. Biting flies and mosquitoes become omnipresent; some of the latter are infected with parasites that can cause lethal cerebral malaria. The rains and the heat also draw out snakes, scorpions, tarantulas, poisonous millipedes, and many other kinds of dangerous insects and animals. Villagers who grow up with these discomforts as part of everyday life have the knowledge, skills, and resignation required to live with them. People who have grown up in town often do not. This holds for Garo, but even more so for non-Garo who have been posted to the region by a government body or NGO. Such people perceive Garo villages as uncomfortable and dangerous, at least during the rainy season. In addition, villages—and villagers—are considered dirty. This commonly held view is not only stated with the mud, the leeches, or the lack of 'urban standard' sanitation in mind.

It is also a judgement passed upon the way of life of those who live in the rural areas. In many villages, pigs run freely, which means that their dung can be encountered anywhere. Given the many discomforts and dangers, many townspeople are reluctant to visit, let alone stay in a village, at least during the wet season. The urban–rural disparity is also one of wealth: while government officers earn relatively high salaries and can afford large solid houses and big cars, such luxuries are beyond the reach of villagers. In villages like Sadolpara, people are unlikely to go hungry, but in comparison to townspeople they are clearly poor (Figure 2.2). This can create uneasy relations, and a sense of social distance that is sometimes difficult to overcome.

Many villagers, as a consequence, do not feel very comfortable in town, and that is particularly true for Tura. When I started my fieldwork in 1999, many of Sadolpara's residents had never been to Tura. This was particularly the case for women. Some of the more enterprising men used to go there occasionally to meet civil servants or politicians to 'get things done'. Even now, most people only make the trip rarely—perhaps once or twice a year—or even less often. More than the physical distance (it takes about two hours

Figure 2.2 In villages like Sadolpara, people are in many ways less prosperous than those living in town, but to a good degree master of their own time, and value taking a break whenever they feel like.
Photograph: Erik de Maaker, 2003.

by bus), or even the cost of travel, it is the rather heavily monetized environment that deters them from visiting Tura. Compared to salaried employees, villagers literally have very little cash to hand, and being in town brings this home in an unpleasant manner. It is simply not easy for villagers to obtain cash. People either have to sell their produce or work as daily wage labourers. Remarks made by Jiji and some of her children after visits to Tura indicated that this sense of discomfort can border on humiliation: they were made to feel poor, which was not how they felt in their everyday lives. Townspeople sometimes visit villages, and villagers occasionally go to town, but the disparities in (cash) wealth outlined above serve to render the 'peri-urban' and the 'rural' quite separate societal realms.

Within Garo villages there are also disparities of wealth and income, but these are nowhere near as pronounced as the class distinctions that are manifest within towns. The middle-class Garo who live in Tura, some of whom are very affluent, typically work at one or another of the many government bodies, educational institutions, or NGOs located there. In their homes, as in middle-class households elsewhere in South Asia, cooking, cleaning, and gardening is often done by live-in domestic helpers, often 'poor' Garo villagers or village youth who combine working as a domestic with attending a good quality school. Townspeople who are less well off tend to live lives that are in a practical and social sense not too far removed from village life, except that they primarily depend on a cash income for their livelihood. Despite these differences of class and environment, in towns and villages alike, most people continue to see being loyal to one's kin and extending mutual support to relatives as essential and admirable virtues. Homelessness or genuine destitution are rare—perhaps because it is almost impossible to deny food or shelter to needy relatives.

2.2 Garo Conversions

There are Hindu temples, mosques, and at least one Sikh gurdwara in Tura, but with the exception of an almost negligible number of Hindu Garo, they are only attended by the town's non-Garo minorities. The identification of the vast majority of Garo with Christianity is so well established that, along with Nagas and Mizos, Garo are often regarded as one of the 'fully' Christian communities of North-East India (Marak 1999: 186). The majority of Garo perceive the traditional community religion primarily as something from the past, which prevents it from constituting a challenge to the hegemony of Christianity. Christianity, which has now been practised in Garo Hills for more than 150 years, has become firmly entangled with Garo cultural practices and has become a tradition in its own right (M.S. Sangma 1984; de Maaker 2013a). Garo Christianity is divided across several denominations and interdenominational friction is not unknown. Approximately half of Garo Christians belong to the Garo Baptist Church (A'chik Dalgipa Baptist Krima – ADBK). Most of the others are Roman Catholics. In a relatively recent development, charismatic Protestant Christian churches have also gained popularity, attracting people who have defected from the mainstream Baptist and Catholic constituencies (de Maaker 2013a). Christianity is also well established in the rural areas, with the exception of a few pockets in both the West Garo Hills and East Garo Hills districts, where the traditional community religion continues to be practised.

'Outsiders' to the community religion, such as Garo Christians, or non-Garo, tend to refer to the followers of the community religion as Songsareks. The term *songsar* may relate to the Sanskrit *saà-sâra* (from *saà-sù*): 'to be in the world', as opposed to being a 'world renouncer'. Adopting this interpretation, the term may have been coined by Bengali or Assamese, with whom Garo have a long history of interaction. The traditional Garo community religion perceives the world as a place populated by a great diversity of visible and invisible entities. It emphasizes that the world in which people find themselves is 'animated', if not alive.[7] In this sense, it is a 'relational epistemology' (Bird-David 1999: S67), one which proceeds from the premise that people are in some sort of a symbiotic relationship with non-human entities. This kind of ontology implies that 'persons are constituted by the shifting interactions of continuously negotiable relational acts' with a multiplicity of entities, the majority of which are non-human (Harvey 2019: 80). The traditional Garo community religion centres on the idea that 'different phenomena have a similar human-like interiority even while their outward physical forms differ', as Vitebsky (Vitebsky 2017: 8) wrote in relation to the community religion of the Sora of Odisha. A key aspect of the traditional Garo community religion is the continuous (re-)negotiation of relationships with omnipresent spirits (*mitde*), hence its practitioners generally refer to themselves as 'the ones who obey the spirits' (*mitde manigipa*). Elsewhere I have referred to these *mitdes* as 'deities', but that term suggest a degree of institutionalization as in polytheistic religions like Hinduism, which renders it less appropriate to the Garo belief system. I refer to Garo animism as a 'community religion' since it is not an institutionalized 'religion' in the conventional sense of the word. The ideas, knowledge, and practices that the traditional Garo community religion encompasses have not been codified in religious texts, nor are there any professional officiants who claim religious authority (Lambek 2016: 12). A person who conducts a sacrifice is a *kamal*, a term which is often translated as 'priest', but many people have such skills, and the role is not a professional qualification. I do not, however, completely reject the term religion with my choice of 'community religion' since there has been a certain degree of systematization in terms of practices and ideas, notably in contrast to Garo Christianity.

The Garo were introduced to Christianity in the late 19th century, soon after the Garo Hills region was incorporated into the colonial state. In *A Garo Jungle Book* (1919), a publication intended to garner support for the activities of Baptist missionaries in the 'Garo field', Reverend William Carey recounts how the first Garo who converted to Christianity developed an aversion to the community religion, resulting in what became—at least from his missionary perspective—a major cultural fracture. Affordable reprints of *A Garo Jungle Book* continue to be sold in bookshops in Tura and are available in college libraries, allowing it to serve as an early account of modern Garo history. According to missionary history, Garo converts themselves were the first to spread the gospel and then invited foreign missionaries to Garo Hills. By contrast, colonial sources indicate that it was the colonial government that invited American and English missionaries to introduce education among the Garo (Bhattacharjee 1973: 519). The colonial government maintained a policy of religious non-interference in the parts of British India that were dominated by Hindus and Muslims but not in regions like Garo Hills, where the population were perceived to be animist or simply lacking religion, since the colonial administration only acknowledged recognized world religions (Nongbri 2014: 86). After the establishment of the Garo Baptist Church in 1868, missionaries worked in partnership with the colonial government, organizing both formal education as well as healthcare (Chaube 1973: 56; Downs 1983: 274; Marak 1998: 171).[8] The missionaries transcribed the dialect (A'we[9]) spoken by the people with whom they first came into contact into the Latin script, and this transliteration continues to be used today. The A'we dialect was adopted as the standard variant of the Garo language to be taught in missionary as well as government schools, which has given it the status of 'cultured' (or educated) Garo (Majumdar 1966: 24; Sangma 1983; Allen et al. 1993 [1909]: 505). The adoption of the Latin alphabet for the transliteration of Garo (rather than the Bengali script, as had previously been undertaken) has been conducive to the emergence of a Garo ethnic identity that is markedly distinct from those of Hindu and Muslim communities of the surrounding plains, all of whom use Indic scripts like Bengali or Assamese (Bhattacharjee 1973: 520).[10] The same holds for some other upland communities in the North-East, such as Khasi and Mizo, that have also adopted the Latin script under comparable circumstances. Government schools emerged from the 1940s, but to this day Baptists and the more recently established Catholics continue to have a reputation for providing good quality education, and maintain a substantial number of schools in Garo Hills. The foreign missionaries gradually left after independence, and for decades church leaders have now been people from within the Garo community. In addition, there are a good number of South Indian Catholic priests in Garo Hills, many of whom work as teachers in Catholic schools.

The predominance of Christianity among Garo is nonetheless a relatively recent phenomenon. Missionizing started during the last decades of the 19th century, but, according to census data, by the 1920s less than one per cent of Garo had converted to Christianity. Their numbers only started to significantly increase in the second half of the 20th century. In 1961, about one-third of Garo had converted, and by 1971 more than half had done so (Bose 1985: xix).[11] Initially, Christianity remained largely confined to Tura and the other small towns. According to anthropologist and linguist Robbins Burling, who conducted extensive ethnographic fieldwork in Garo Hills in the 1950s, Songsareks still vastly outnumbered Christians at that time (Burling 1997 [1963]). In the second half of the 20th century, the gradual expansion of primary education into rural areas, and of basic biomedicine, was accompanied by a rapid increase in religious conversions to Christianity.

The current strong association of Garo ethnicity with Christianity has created a sense of commonality with other Christian hill communities in the North-Eastern region, fortified by frequent mutual visits of reverends, priests, and youth groups (Marak 1999: 186). Christianity also enables ongoing linkages with global denominational networks that are keen to support counterparts seen to be followers of a minority religion within India. Roman Catholics are part of a global church organization, while Garo Baptists maintain strong connections with influential Baptist groups in the United States, such as the Billy Graham Evangelical Association. One explanation for Christianity's advancement among the North-Eastern hill communities is that it has 'proved to be a religion that gives dignity, self-respect and preservation of one's culture' (Marak 1999: 187). Several scholars have suggested that had Songsarek practices been Hinduized, and Garo become Hindus, they would have ended up being categorized as Dalits. Christianity was spread by Western missionaries, and (like Islam) did not—at least in theory—require assimilation into a caste-based system of discrimination, but instead propagated that every human being is equal before God (Raj and Dempsey 2002: 67). Islam would probably have been less compatible with Garo society, since its egalitarian ethos might have been unable to accommodate the existing prestige- and status-oriented political structures (Bose 1985: xviii). Adopting Islam would have also made pork consumption problematic, and pork is a very popular kind of meat. More significantly, like Hinduism, Islam was followed among communities in the surrounding plains, with whom relations were often fraught.

There can be little doubt that the introduction of formal education provided the single most important drive for people to adopt Christianity (Burling 1997 [1963]: 28). Garo school teachers always were and continue to be Christians, irrespective of whether they work in (secular) government or Christian schools (Marak 1998: 174). Garo (primary) schoolbooks therefore, unsurprisingly, include references to Christian prayer, and to the Christian God (Skichengani Ki'tap I 1995 [1920]).[12] More significantly, the kinds of knowledge, skills, and attitudes that schooling imparts are integrated within a 'modern' ontology that renders the beliefs and practices that are central to the community religion old-fashioned, superstitious, if not simply obsolete (Van Der Veer 1996; Keane 2007). Consequently, if Songsareks attend school, the attitudes and knowledge that they acquire there encourages them to distance themselves from the body of thought associated with the traditional community religion, and the commitments that it calls for. Given the supposed incompatibility of these distinct epistemologies, attending school encourages and endorses baptism.

The traditional Garo community religion involves numerous collective rituals and celebrations that require the participation of large numbers of people. As long as the number of Christian converts in a certain village remains low, Songsarek religious practices are not particularly affected. But once the number of converts crosses a certain threshold, and especially if a village head (*nokma*) converts, it becomes very difficult for the remaining practitioners of the community religion to sustain their religious commitments. People who convert to Christianity are expected to renounce worship of the Songsarek spirits. They should cease to participate in the sacrificial rituals that are conducted in relation to the growth of swidden crops, the construction of houses, and—most significantly—to cure illnesses. When the rituals for the Songsarek spirits can no longer effectively be performed because insufficient participants are available to conduct them, reorientation to worship what Christian Garo claim is a superior religious authority—the

Christian God, or Jesus—becomes all the more attractive. Christians and Songsareks do not participate in one another's rituals, with the exception of funerals. Perhaps this is because funerals provide a prime ground for evaluating and publicly expressing commitments towards the dead, as well as to relatives and friends.

The Baptist missionaries who established the Garo Baptist church were teetotallers, and from the outset they banned the brewing and drinking of rice beer. This prohibition is also strictly followed by other Protestants across much of India's North-East. Rice beer is an important element of most of the Songsarek celebrations, where it is offered to the spirits as a libation.[13] The spirits are provided with a small offering, and people drink most of the rice beer themselves (Figure 2.3). Among the upland communities, the acceptance or refusal of rice beer continues to be seen as a decisive indicator of one's religious commitments (Longkumer 2016: 445). Christians usually explained their avoidance of rice beer to me in civilizational terms. They said that brewing rice beer is 'wasteful' since it implies 'spilling' rice that people require as food. In addition, getting drunk, and the loss of self-control that

Figure 2.3 Drinking rice beer after the burning of the new fields, the day before A'galmaka. Rice beer drinking brings people together to relax and enjoy with their relatives and neighbours.
Photograph: Erik de Maaker, 2000.

induces, may result in sexually explicit jokes, loud arguments, and sometimes even scuffles and fights, all of which fit in with stereotypical images of Songsarek villagers as boorish and uncouth. Adopting a more pragmatic stance, several Catholic priests have told me that 'drinking (rice beer) in moderation' can be acceptable, as long as it is mentioned as a sin (*pap*) at the time of confession. Nevertheless, in rural areas where both Christians and Songsareks reside, drinking or refraining from rice beer continues to serve as an important indicator of whether one is loyal to the community religion or not.

While some Garo Baptists completely shun alcohol, most do not abstain from industrially produced alcoholic beverages. Meghalaya is a so-called 'wet' state, and beer and distillates can easily be obtained from an abundance of government-licensed stores. The distillates sold, such as rum, whisky, and gin, are marked by the acronym 'IMFL', which is short for 'Indian made foreign liquor'. This foreignness refers to their having being introduced from abroad, during the colonial period, but their production has long since been taken over by Indian manufacturers (hence 'Indian made'). In Sadolpara and the surrounding area, people refer to IMFL as 'red wine' (*chu gitchak*), whereas rice beer is simply called *chu* (in the Garo language, English categories such as beer and wine are thus more or less interchangeable). In comparison to a vessel of rice beer, 'red wine' is expensive, too costly for most villagers to afford. They like to drink it, especially the distillates with a high alcohol content, but these are seldom available in quantities large enough to facilitate long hours of socializing. Politicians, high-ranking government officers, and police commanders often brought at least a few bottles of liquor when they visited Sadolpara during my time there, and such gestures were always very well received.

Most of the followers of the traditional Garo community religion with whom I have become acquainted over the years have told me that they have, on various occasions, contemplated converting to Christianity. The conflation of Christianity with the modernity of literacy, science, and—in Garo Hills, the state—imbues it with a sense of prestige, if not epistemic authority. This authority is associated with the Bible, which, by virtue of being a written text, is inaccessible to the illiterate. When I was staying in Sadolpara, the Catholic priest who regularly came there in order to conduct mass and baptize 'heathens' used to emphasize the Bible's authority by claiming that it had been 'written by God himself'. He was well aware that Songsareks had no holy texts or professional priests, and—as they themselves would often remark—were often unsure about the intentions and requirements of their spirits. Further exacerbating the uncertainties that he knew Songsareks struggled with, he repeatedly warned that heathens would suffer unbearably after death. One of my neighbours once told me that she was considering getting baptized because she was afraid she would otherwise 'burn (in hell)' (*kamgen*). As she spoke, sitting in our kitchen, she kept her arms close to her body, shaking them as if in despair, but then laughed to indicate that the priest's threats had not truly scared her.

According to missionary writings, Garo followers of the community religion were 'victims of dirt, ignorance and superstition' (Carey 1919: 256), who lived in 'demon-haunted' (Pianazzi 1934: 44) hills. For some people, the missionaries' take on the traditional community religion, and their stance towards Garo traditions as a whole, has resulted in a loss of cultural pride. During one of my visits to the region, a senior government officer, who conflated the community religion with Garo 'culture', told me that Christianity had made Garos 'feel shy about Garo culture'. 'We feel deprived of our own culture. We have been diverted, we have not been allowed to grow within our own culture. Our own culture should not have been rejected. Our Gods should not have been called demons.' Remarks such as these echo a sense of loss and regret, as noted by scholars such as Oppitz (2008: 9). Many Garo are second- or third-generation converts, and the rejection of the community religion that is expected of Christians often creates an uneasy ambivalence among urban and educated Garo when they identify their cultural past with the traditional community religion. But this sense of loss or even alienation has never (yet) sparked the kind of revivalist religious movements among Garo that have emerged among the Khasi, the Naga, or the Apatani[14] (Longkumer 2010; Thomas 2016).

When Garo, converts and Songsareks alike, talk about conversion from the traditional community religion to Christianity, they describe it as a watershed event. It results in the 'cleansing' (*rongtala*) of the soul of the convert, rendering that person 'new' (*gital*). This language echoes the missionary notion of spiritual rebirth. The 'radical discontinuity' that this implies requires the convert to cast aside 'all older codes of conduct', as Robbins (2004: 244) has noted regarding the process of religious conversion among the Urapmin of Melanesia. It seems inevitable that shifting orientation towards a more globalized Christian realm of ideas and practices results in 'sociocultural transformations, transcultural engagements and even language, which permanently transcend local structures of action and conviction' (Joshi 2012: 8). Nonetheless, globalized Christian ideas and practices are interpreted locally, inevitably engaging and becoming entangled with existing local epistemologies and practices. In the Garo context, this is probably most explicitly revealed in approaches towards disease and illness, which relate to both Christian divinity, 'modern science', and the spirits of the traditional community religion.

Despite the rhetoric of non-Garo missionaries, the distinction between Christianity and the community religion has never been strictly upheld in practice. Garo herbal medicine (*sam A'chik*) is very popular among Garo irrespective of their religious orientation, but it is based upon sources of knowledge that are conceptually very close to those concerning Songsarek spirits (de Maaker 2013a). Moreover, on several occasions I have heard Christian Garo conclude that an illness had been caused by a spirit and could only be countered by making sacrifices of the kind prescribed by the traditional community religion (de Maaker 2013a).

By the turn of the 21st century, more than 80 per cent of Garo had adopted Christianity and that percentage slowly but steadily continues to rise. The 2001 census records that there were still more than 20,000 followers of the community religion in Garo Hills at the time it was conducted.[15] My own observations over the last couple of years suggest that the number has decreased since then. In Sadolpara, in 2019, I estimated that about a quarter of the residents were Songsarek (sixty-seven of the village's 272 Houses), which was considerably less then at the time of my doctoral fieldwork (1999–2001), when approximately half the Houses followed the traditional Garo community religion. The expansion of primary education has raised literacy levels in the rural areas, and in the words of Reverend Krickwin Marak, 'No educated Garo want[s] to remain a Songsarek' (Marak 1998: 174). At the same time, it is remarkable that to this day a substantial number of people continue to resist the pressure to convert. This goes against the assumption generally held by Christian Garo that the community religion is obsolete: a remnant of the past that is a hindrance to prosperity. People who have resisted pressure to convert live mostly in clusters of villages in either West or East Garo Hills district. The persistence of the community religion provokes the question of what it offers to the people who continue to follow it, and how they manage to sustain it within an overall context in which it is perceived as marginal and outdated.

2.3 Becoming Citizens

In the 18th century, the British colonial state in South Asia gained a secure hold of Bengal. After the battle of Palashi (Plassey) in 1757, in southern

Bengal, the British gradually expanded their territory northwards. Goalpara, the plains area to the west and north of Garo Hills, was conquered in 1765. The Mymensingh region (now in Bangladesh), which lies beyond the southern border of Garo Hills, became part of the colonial state from 1787 onwards. These expansions aimed towards a conquest of the Brahmaputra valley, an area that included large tracts of land suitable for the cultivation of tea, which would soon prove to be extremely profitable (Gait 1963). With the plains to the south, west, and north occupied by the colonial state, Garo Hills had become a frontier region by the early 19th century (Eliot 1799; Barooah 1970).

Most historical sources that relate to Garo Hills derive from colonial era administrators and travellers. Their writings initially served to facilitate and further the expansion and consolidation of colonial rule. Yet for upland communities that did not maintain a script in those times, the absence of other written sources has led these colonial era texts to be drawn upon as appreciated historical records. This is certainly true of Playfair's *The Garos*, which was published in 1909 as part of a government effort to document the various upland peoples. Affordable reprints of the book continue to circulate in Garo Hills, which has gained an iconic status (1909; Marak 2012 for a recent assessment of this work).

The earliest accounts relating to Garo Hills derive from British travellers and explorers such as Eliot (1799) and Francis Hamilton (1940 [cf. 1807–1814]), who surveyed the fringes of the hills at a time when they had yet to be conquered. Their texts refer to people called 'Garrow', later spelled 'Garo'; a term that Bengali used to refer to the people living in and close to the area now known as Garo Hills (Majumdar 1977: 77; Martin 1990 [1838]: 91). In precolonial times, it seems likely that the inhabitants of these hills located themselves primarily within smaller linguistic and cultural units. Only later, due to the categorization induced and imposed by the colonial state, did 'Garo' emerge as a common identification.[16] In the Garo language, the self-referential term used is *a'chik* (hill dweller) or *mande* (person), but 'Garo' has also come to be used self-referentially, especially in English, which is why I have chosen to use it in this book as well.

The accounts of early British travellers and explorers suggest that in the precolonial period, Garo villages in the 'interior' of the hills were largely autonomous. Political relations between these villages included protracted feuds that at times seem to have involved violent conflict and headhunting (Majumdar 1977: 40). In order to trade with people from the plains, Garo living in the hills were dependent on markets[17] in the foothills that were controlled by feudal landlords (*zamindars*) from the nearby plains. The latter imposed high taxes on Garo, a source of friction that sporadically triggered 'raids' by the uplanders upon the plains throughout the 18th and 19th centuries (Barman 1994; Mackenzie 1995 [1884]: 250; Misra 2011).[18] In the words of the colonial chroniclers, Garo were 'bloodthirsty savages', a 'source of terror' who were 'eager to capture the skulls' of innocent Bengali peasants (M'cosh 1975 [1837]; Mackenzie 1995 [1884]: 164). Whereas there can be little doubt that Garo practised headhunting (the memories of that are still alive, with people remembering the places where severed heads used to be kept), the number of their victims seems to have been negligible in comparison to the violence inflicted upon local populations by the frequent punitive expeditions of the British in the first half of the 19th century (Sangma 1986: 217–224). In 1866, when Stoddard told him he was to become a missionary among the Garos, the then Lieutenant-Governor of Bengal Sir William Grey reportedly remarked: 'They are a bloodthirsty set of savages, and deserve extermination. Government is now considering that question' (Carey 1919: 107). The colonial government had vested interests in the fertile plains surrounding the Garo Hills and therefore perceived the uncontrollable inhabitants of the uplands as a menace.

Initially, the colonial government did not attempt to occupy the Garo Hills. As it did in the Himalayan foothills (*terai*), endemic malaria posed a serious threat. M'cosh noted: 'Above all jungly countries in India, that of the Garrows is perhaps, the most fatal for a European to visit.... three-fourths who have done so, have fallen victims to its baneful climate' (M'cosh 1975 [1837]: 165). Moreover, the hills had little to offer in terms of revenue. Moffat Mills wrote: 'There is nothing to be gained by occupying the country; the revenue that could be derived from it would not cover one-sixth of the cost of maintaining the Police force; the expense of Government would be considerable, and the loss of life in all probability appalling' (Mills 1853 [1984]: 45). Nevertheless, colonial records state that the British eventually did conquer Garo Hills in order to safeguard the people of the surrounding plains from the violence regularly inflicted on them by the hill-dwelling Garo (Kar 1970; Bhattacharjee 1978). Perhaps it was no coincidence that the conquest took place at a time when the colonial economy was developing a growing need for high-quality hardwood; significantly, substantial parts of Garo Hills were covered by extensive teak forests (Saikia 2011: 74–75). In 1866, the Lieutenant-Governor of Bengal decided 'to put an end to the independence of the savages inhabiting this nook in the midst of British territory' (Allen 1980 [1906]: 21). The financial arguments formulated previously remained nonetheless pertinent and contributed to the decision to develop an administrative structure that largely allowed the Garo to settle their own affairs.

Upon its incorporation into the colonial state, Garo Hills was given an exclusionary status. This status was similar to that of frontier areas elsewhere in Assam that were located beyond the 'Inner Line'.[19] The Inner Line constituted an internal boundary, which separated the plains (including the tea estates) from the surrounding hills areas. It was complemented by an 'Outer Line', which marked the border between the territory claimed by the British and that of neighbouring states. Large areas of land located beyond the Inner Line were thus considered part of British territory, but de facto not administered. The Inner Line was 'supposed to demarcate "the Hills" from "the plains", the nomadic from the sedentary, the jungle from the arable' (Kar 2009: 52). The Line was created in order to restrict the movement of people between the plains and the hills (Sangma 1981: 39). British subjects were not permitted to cross it without a licence; more specifically, the Line was meant to stop tea planters from acquiring lands beyond it. However, since Garo Hills was surrounded by territory controlled by the British, there the restriction of movement was never effectively enforced (Sangma 1988: 415).

In 1822, before the Garo Hills were actually occupied, they were given a distinctive administrative status that was based upon the notion that its inhabitants comprised 'races of people entirely distinct from the ordinary population'[20] (Mackenzie 1995 [1884]: 250). This administrative status was intended to 'free' the Garo from the obligation to pay taxes to the landlords of the plains, as well as to allow for a system of administration of justice exclusively for the Garo that was deemed appropriate to their 'peculiar custom and prejudices' (Barooah 1970: 62). In 1869, Garo Hills became a separate district (administered as a Frontier Tract from 1884), in 1910 it was designated a Scheduled District, then a Backward Tract (1919) and then a Partially Excluded Area (1935) (Das 1990: 10–11). These successive exclusionary demarcations all served to exempt the area from many of the laws that applied elsewhere in British India (Galanter 1984: 147) and ensured that Garo *niam*, albeit in a codified form, could continue to play a central role in people's day-to-day affairs.

The creation of Garo Hills district following the defeat of the last of the independent Garo villages in 1873 (Sangma 1981: 36) resulted in the political and legal encapsulation of the Garo 'village republics' (cf. Naga village republics (Wouters 2018: 55)). Until then, the authority of village heads had been based in local politics, which allowed for contestation between contenders to power. A village head who failed to perform in accordance with expectations could be replaced by someone else (Burling 1997 [1963]: 230). Once the colonial state had gained supremacy, however, the position of village heads gradually came to depend on the district authorities as well. In addition, the colonial state created an intermediary layer of administration and taxation. Garo Hills District was divided into eight *mouzas* ('revenue districts'), for each of which a *mouzadar* became responsible for tax collection. A *mouza* was again divided into *elekas* ('judicial units'), for each of which the district administration appointed a *loskor* ('village magistrate') and several *sordars* ('police constable') (Kar 1970: 204). All these officials were locally influential men, often—but not necessarily—village heads, who came to enact colonial rule, while at the same time representing the rural population.[21]

As a 'downward extension' of colonial rule, the village heads and other men enlisted by the colonial government became crucial to the enactment of indirect rule in a similar way to how 'tribal leaders' were essential to the administration in colonial Southern Africa, as Comaroff and Comaroff have shown (Comaroff and Comaroff 2018: 1). As such, they were 'an indispensable armature of colonial governance' (Comaroff and Comaroff 2018: 8). But where colonial rulers depended on local 'power holders', such as Garo village heads, to implement their policies, the villages—in their economic, religious, and political manifestations—constituted realities that the district authorities were obliged to live with. Local power holders in Garo Hills, confronted with the power of the colonial state, were sometimes able to resist and fight back. One example of this is the revolt that was led in the early 20th century by village head Sonaram Sangma when the colonial state made claims to large tracts of his village's land (Sangma 2002; Sinha 2003), intending to repurpose it as forest reserve for commercial forestry (Karlsson 2011: 142). The protest, supported by hundreds of people, resulted in a lawsuit, Sonaram's conviction, and significant publicity. Instances such as these—admittedly rare—most probably helped village heads to retain their authority in the eyes of the people who depended on them.

After independence, Garo Hills became one of the Autonomous Districts of Assam, governed by the Sixth Schedule of the Indian Constitution. The Sixth Schedule was established to enable the creation of dedicated regimes of governance for the 'tribal districts and tracts' of (erstwhile) Assam (Kumar 1996: 18–19). This led to the formation in 1952 of the Garo Hills Autonomous District Council (GHADC), an elected body granted limited legislative, executive, and judicial powers, primarily in relation to land, water, forest, and the appointment and succession of village heads (Kumar 1996: 19; Sangma 1998: 131). Most of the area under the jurisdiction of the GHADC consists of communally owned village land (94.25 per cent). Much of the remaining 5.75 per cent is a densely populated plains belt along the Brahmaputra river, where Muslims comprise the majority (Das 1990: 12).

When language politics in the state of Assam, of which Garo Hills was then a part, led to Assamese becoming the state's dominant language in the early 1960s, political leaders from various hill districts resisted the decision, and jointly founded the All Party Hill Leaders Conference (APHLC) (Kumar 1996: 39). Under the leadership of Capt. Williamson A. Sangma (a Garo), the APHLC demanded a separate state for Assam's hill areas. This resulted in the creation of the state of Meghalaya in 1972. Meghalaya included Garo Hills as well as the Khasi and Jaintia Hills. In addition to the state administration, the governance structures already created under the Sixth Schedule continued to function. These were the Garo Hills Autonomous District Council, the Khasi Hills Autonomous District Council, and the Jaintia Hills Autonomous District Council (Das 1990: 10–11; Sangma 1998).

From the inception of the state onwards, the relationship between the GHADC and the state administration of Meghalaya has not necessarily been easy. It is often unclear, in a legal and administrative sense, how the two levels of governance are related or are supposed to cooperate, which creates scope for confusion and conflict (Kumar 1996: 20). Although the District Council is autonomous according to the Indian Constitution, any laws it passes 'require the assent of the governor, failing which they will not have the sanctity of law' (Nongbri 2014: 16). In addition, the Sixth Schedule includes a clause (12A), which states that in case of incompatibilities between laws formulated by the District Council and the State of Meghalaya, the latter shall prevail Nongbri (2014, 16). One occasion when this clause was utilized was when the so-called 'timber ban' was imposed in Meghalaya following a Supreme Court order in 1995–6. The implementation of this order completely bypassed 'the jurisdiction of the Autonomous District Councils in Sixth Schedule Areas' (Barik and Darlong, 2008: 19–20, quoted in (Nongbri 2014: 17)). In addition, in Garo Hills, many of the functions formerly fulfilled by the GHADC have—at least partially—been taken over by the state of Meghalaya. One factor that contributed to this was that the GHADC had always had very limited means of taxation, and thus of acquiring funding, which rendered it weak as a policymaking body. Moreover, a significant proportion of the GHADC's funding is channelled through the state government, which has further intensified this relationship of dependency (Nongbri 2014: 18).

In addition, the efficacy of the GHADC has been hampered by overtly personalized governance. Prominent historian Milton Sangma published a critical assessment of the District Council in 1998. Evaluating the performance of the GHADC since its inception, he wrote:

> Human weakness like greed for money and chair also mellowed down the enthusiasm and enchantment with which it was started. The funds allotted for running the Council have been diverted to meet their own selfish ends without going to the actual fields for which it was sanctioned. The power struggle for chairs and wooing the members and the electorates ate away the developmental funds. The Secretariat is overstaffed and the corruptions among Executive Members [the 'board' of the GHADC] and the M.D.C.s [Members of the District Council, the elected representatives] have been percolated to the officers. (Sangma 1998: 136)

In other words, political and executive powers appear to have been channelled along relations of patronage, which is congruous with the person-centric political traditions of the region.

The GHADC has continued to use the structures of governance that were developed during the colonial era, when Garo Hills was administered as an autonomous district. At that time, a distinction was made between the relatively densely populated plains areas along the western and northern side of the district, and the 'interior' hilly areas, which had a comparatively low population density. The plains were surveyed in the 1930s, resulting in the registration of lands there in the names of individual landowners. Such individual land titles were—and continue to be—referred to as *patta*. In the 'interior' areas, land was registered with villages as collective property, albeit in the names of village heads (*nokmas*). People living on those collective holdings did not have to pay taxes on land, but were obliged to pay an annual fixed 'house tax' for each household to the District Council. Otherwise, villages continued to be largely self-governing. Minor disputes relating to marriages, inheritances, or land were to be settled by villagers among themselves. If they could not be resolved, cases could be referred to the court of the GHADC. Serious violence, such as murder, went beyond the powers of villagers and the District Council, and would always be dealt with by the courts of the state of Meghalaya. This tiered judiciary system still applies today, underlining the importance of the GHADC for people who are under its jurisdiction.

The constitution of the GHADC exempts Garo living in the 'interior' hills from laws relating to land, marriage, and inheritance (among others) that apply elsewhere in India (Kusum and Bakshi 1982: 30). The GHADC has produced extensive detailed laws and regulations of its own, but many of them are not followed. The council lacks the personnel to impose them, while villagers would probably perceive any attempts to do so as an infringement upon their hereditary rights to land, embedded in their interpretations of Garo *niam*. Yet Garo *niam* is also what guides the District Council regarding relationships between people and land, as well as among one another (Marak 2000 [1986]; Garo Hills Autonomous District Council 2007). Since the District Council is mandated to strive to enact *niam*, and its courts are to settle disputes in accordance with Garo *niam*, demands have been made for *niam* to be codified in writing, as customary law has been elsewhere in the colonized world. Many such attempts have been made, the most important of which by Alan Playfair (1909), Gulio Costa (1954), Jangsan Sangma (1973), Chattopadhyay and M.S. Sangma (1989), and Julius Marak (Marak 2000 [1986]).[22] However carefully compiled, these codifications have never been able to fully account for the situational and relational character of *niam* as it is enacted on a day-to-day basis. Codification almost inevitably results in ideal-typical descriptions, which focus on rules and categories, but cannot take into account the agency of people, of the dead, and of material objects as playing out in specific situations. Nonetheless, District Council judges in Meghalaya tend to base their conclusions on the above-mentioned published texts, rather than listening to interpretations of custom by members of the communities concerned (Karlsson 2011: 268). Attributing so much authority to texts, which in many ways can never provide more than partial insights, is part and parcel of an attempt to approach custom from a kind of neutral or objective ground. In my understanding, however, custom can never be enacted without taking interpersonal relationships into consideration. Robbins Burling provides an extensive account of a dispute over land which illustrates this. The dispute dragged on over several generations, and its outcome was ultimately influenced by the political status of the actors involved (Burling 1997 [1963]: 269–271). The interpretation and enactment of Garo *niam* is always embedded within social relationships, which in turn are subject to the larger social field in which they are located.

As a lasting heritage of British colonial rule, in 1947, upon Indian and Pakistani independence, an international border emerged along the southern edge of Garo Hills. This border created a division between India and East Pakistan (which after 1971 became Bangladesh). The border separated Garo who lived in the hills from those living in the adjacent plains of Mymensingh. It was virtually indiscernible for the first couple of decades after independence. With measures to curtail the smuggling of arms and the movement of Bangladeshi citizens into India, the border has gradually 'hardened' since the 1990s (Van Schendel 2005: 296). Along almost the entire border that India shares with Bangladesh, including the 443 km in Meghalaya, fences have been erected, many of them high barriers topped with razor wire, which are notably on the Indian side intensively patrolled by border guards. Every year, dozens of people are killed while attempting to cross the border illegally, marking it as one of the most violent borders in Asia (Van Schendel 2005).

The hardening of the border has made life for people who used to cross it regularly much more difficult, depriving them of opportunities to trade their produce at nearby markets on the other side of the border. Sadolpara is less than 40 kilometres from the border as the crow flies, but that was well beyond villagers' radius of interaction with relatives and markets at the time I stayed there, and to my surprise no one there ever seemed to feel that the border had an impact on their lives. Elderly people did have memories of Indian air force planes flying sorties at the time of the Bangladesh war. I was also told of Garo refugees from East Pakistan/Bangladesh who had due to the war, and violent conflicts that happened both before and after, resettled in Garo Hills. But rather than the border presenting itself as a physical reality, its creation and subsequent hardening resulted in the residents of Sadolpara becoming citizens of India.

2.4 Constituting 'Tribe'

Within India, the Garo are classified as a tribal community. The term 'tribe' was first used in colonial era accounts that set out to describe and categorize the people of British India. The colonial administration interpreted terminology used by the (high-)caste Hindus who were their primary Indian interlocutors (Bates 1995: 13; Bayly 1999: 109). These Hindus referred to the inhabitants of the forests and hills as *atavika* (forest dwellers), *girijan*, or *pahari* (hill people), terms with the implicit connotation—from a higher-caste normative perspective—that such people were less 'cultured' than those settled on the plains. Combined with evolutionist 18th and 19th century European interpretations of race, which presumed a teleological progression from the 'primitive' to (European) 'modernity', people of the uplands and the hills were thus relegated to the lower end of the social spectrum (Pels 2000: 83). In addition, these were communities deemed to have been marginal or external to the dominions of precolonial states.[23]

After independence, in an attempt to mitigate and redress the grave social inequalities that characterized Indian society, compensatory discrimination became a key policy instrument. A commission instituted by the central government, in consultation with the state governments, created lists for each state enumerating 'schedules' of 'tribal' groups that qualified for preferential treatment (hence 'Scheduled Tribes').[24] Decisions regarding which communities were included in these schedules were based on 'habitat and geographic isolation, but even more on the basis of social, religious, linguistic, and cultural distinctiveness' (Galanter 1984: 150). While no 'uniform test for the distinguishing the Scheduled Tribes' could be formulated, 'tribal origin, primitive way of life, remote habitation, and general backwardness in all respects' came to serve as 'common elements' (Galanter 1984: 152). This 1950s definition, although revised since, continues to resonate in the present. The National Tribal Policy, which was drafted in 2006 by the central government's Ministry of Tribal Affairs, states that tribal communities '... are known to dwell in compact areas, follow a community way of living, in harmony with nature, and have a uniqueness of culture, distinctive customs, traditions and beliefs which are simple, direct and non-acquisitive by nature' (2007: 2). While the language here moves away from earlier derogatory references to tribal communities as 'primitive' or 'backward', it nonetheless maintains that such groups are simple, live in 'harmony' with nature, and are thus implicitly excluded from 'modernity'. This demonstrates how, in a South Asian context, it remains all but impossible to sever 'tribe' from its evolutionist connotations (Srivastava 2008: 30; Rycroft and Dasgupta 2011: 6).

Political parties such as the Indian National Congress have been very supportive of preferential discrimination policies, which has contributed significantly towards the sustenance and gradual extension of the schemes initiated. Other national parties, such as the Bharatiya Janata Party, while less supportive of the principle of preferential treatment, have not been able to revoke it. Preferential discrimination has come to encompass valuable economic, political, and educational benefits. These are highly desirable and quite a few 'non-tribal' communities have made attempts to become classified as Scheduled Tribes (Middleton 2013: 13). In many contexts the practical benefits of being categorized as a tribe are seen to outweigh the negative image that its evolutionist connotations might bring (Karlsson 2003: 406; Xaxa 2008: 39; Middleton 2011: 525).

In the Garo language, a widely used term for 'a community' is *jat* (cf. Hindi *jāti*). As elsewhere in South Asia, the term is used to refer to groups that one acquires membership to by birth. By definition, then, *jat* can refer to both castes and tribes. *Jat* serves both self- and other-identification, albeit primarily in multi-ethnic contexts. Locally, among Garo, 'tribe' is used as a term of self-identification for people who are familiar with English, and it is not necessarily seen to have negative connotations. A couple of years ago, in an academic workshop on social change in North-East India, some of the scholars present expressed doubts regarding the sociological relevance of the term 'tribe'. A Garo scholar, in reaction to the critical remarks made, raised her voice to declare: 'Even so, I am a tribal!', implying that her own experiences were at odds with what may have come across as academic attempts to dispute the validity of the label (Béteille 1998: 189; Bal and Van Schendel 2002: 126; Karlsson 2003; Mcduie-Ra 2019: 70-72). 'Tribe' has evidently become a 'category of practice' (Brubaker 2012: 2–5), which is relevant in its function to define Garo as a specific category within a multi-ethnic state.

Garo are the second most populous Scheduled Tribe (ST) in Meghalaya. According to the 2011 Census of India, 86.1 per cent of Meghalaya's population of 2.5 million are members of one of the state's STs. Of these, the Khasi/Jaintia[25] comprise the majority (49.5 per cent), with Garo as the second largest group (30.9 per cent). The remaining 5.7 per cent of the STs belong to a variety of numerically small groups such as Hajong, Rabha, and Koch. A minority of Meghalaya's population (13.9 per cent) are 'non-tribals', which makes Meghalaya one of the few 'tribal majority' states of India. These non-tribals include Assamese, Bengali, Punjabi, Marwari, Bihari, Nepali and others who are perceived as (the descendants of) migrants to the state (Haokip 2014: 305). In Meghalaya, people who belong to an ST are exempted from income tax. Moreover, according to the 1971 Meghalaya Land Transfer Act, only those who belong to an ST community can buy land and/or houses.[26] Hence, anyone who does not belong to an ST community and needs real estate for a project is obliged to collaborate with an ST partner. Furthermore, 85 per cent of the government jobs in Meghalaya must be taken by someone from an ST community.[27] Given the virtual absence of commercial enterprise, and with trade dominated by Marwari, Bengali, and Assamese, the government is a very important employer for STs. Government jobs are relatively well paid, secure, and therefore highly desirable. In addition, the majority of 'seats' in all the important elected bodies of the state of Meghalaya (such as its parliament, the State Legislative Assembly) are reserved for the ST communities.[28] Preferential discrimination also secures access to government schools and colleges for students from the STs, allowing them to gain admission with lower grades than those required by candidates who have to compete in what is called 'the open category' for non-reserved seats.

At a national level in India, Hindu perceptions of social order are the norm. Social hierarchies are expressed, to a good degree, with reference to what people eat, and with whom they do so. Different kinds of food are not only associated with different regions (North Indians prefer bread, South Indians rice, for example), but also with hierarchies of 'purity'. Meat is the most controversial in this regard, and many Hindus abstain from it altogether, associating vegetarianism with 'purity' (Fuller 1988: 33). 'Purity' here is linked to social/religious status, suggesting that claiming a greater degree of purity can reflect a higher social status (Dumont 1981: 47). Consequently, abstaining from meat can be a way for a community to try to claim a higher status, in an attempt to move up the social scale (Srinivas 2003: 32). According to the dominant Hindu perspective, different kinds of meat are imbued with different connotations: while many Hindus consider the consumption of fish, chicken, or goat acceptable, pork, and above all, beef, are much more controversial. Although there have always been Hindus who eat beef, the recent rise of Hindu nationalism is making this increasingly unacceptable, and a growing number of states have prohibited the slaughter of cows and bulls (Staples 2019: 1126).[29] While eating beef is generally presumed to be marginal among Hindus, the opposite is true for Muslims. Many Hindus seem to assume that only low-caste Hindus (Dalits) eat beef, and from a 'casteist' perspective, taking beef consumption as in indicator, Muslims then analogously end up at the bottom of the social hierarchy. The same applies for Christians, who typically also eat beef. Alternatively, the acceptance or rejection of (certain kinds) meat is often taken as an indicator for religious belonging, and a measure of the cultural distance existing between distinct religious locations.

Among the upland communities of North-East India, meat is popular, with pork and beef as favourites. Garo, Khasi, and Naga, to name a few, try to have fish or meat at least once a day. And whenever there is something to celebrate or commemorate, such as a marriage or a funeral, it is compulsory for the hosts to provide meat, preferably several kinds, prepared in different ways. Serving a meal that has meat is also important at political rallies, especially those held in rural areas. Cooking and offering meat on such occasions is a way of inviting and including people who appreciate it; at the same time, it excludes those who abstain from it. For several years, a Hajong family lived in Sadolpara. The Hajong were Hindus, and from a majoritarian Hindu perspective their standing was equal to that of Dalits. They earned a living by herding the villagers' cattle. When the practitioners of the traditional Garo community religion celebrated their largest annual festival Wangala, the family could not join the festivities, even though the events were in principle open to all. Central to the Wangala celebrations is the slaughter of numerous bulls, and the consumption of their meat over days of feasting. The Hajong did not eat beef. It was so repulsive to them that they did not even want to be in the vicinity when a bull was slaughtered and its meat cooked. This effectively excluded them from the Wangala celebrations.

The consumption of dog meat is even more controversial than the consumption of beef. Eating dog meat is fairly common among people who live in the uplands of North-East India, as well as across large parts of South East and East Asia, and Garo are no exception. In Sadolpara, dog meat was not a regular part of the diet, and I never saw it offered for sale. On rare occasions, however, men, typically youth, did eat dogs. This would usually be a dog known to be vicious ('biting everyone'), or a dog that somehow had no owner. I was also once told of some boisterous young men who had cooked and eaten a stray puppy. And, a stray dog that we had adopted during our stay in the village but had to leave behind in the care of others, was reportedly eaten by Garo who had come to the village for construction work. Many middle-class Garo in Tura keep dogs as pets, or as watch dogs, and would not dream of eating them. But I have heard it said that even Tura youth occasionally consume dog meat. Doing so is typically considered rather 'rough', and people tended to giggle when they talked about it, but at the same time it certainly did not seem to be something to be ashamed about (see also: Marak 2014: 113).

Muslims consider dogs impure creatures, and even though Hindu scriptures entertain no such premise the same goes for a good many Hindus, which makes the idea of eating dog meat abhorrent to them. One day during my two-year stay in Garo Hills, I was sitting on a bench near the entry gate of a camp of the Border Security Force in Tura. My partner, who was an Indian citizen at that time, had been allowed inside to visit a branch of the State Bank of India located inside the camp. As a foreigner, I could not enter the camp, so I waited outside. The guard posted at the gate was a young man, probably in his mid-twenties. His impressive dark moustache, in a style very popular in the Indian armed forces, gave his face a truly martial expression. The sentry was in a chatty mood and told me that he was from Bihar. When I asked him how he felt about being stationed in Garo Hills he told me frankly: 'People here are very bad. They eat cats and dogs!' I had never heard of any Garo eating cat meat, but later on I learned that it does indeed sometimes happen. As described above, his claim about the consumption of dog meat was not entirely unfounded, but what struck me was his conclusion: because 'people here' 'eat dog' they were 'very bad'. This illustrates that Garo Hills is not exempt from the Indian tendency to take food taboos and eating habits as a basis for moralizing and imposing and justifying perceived cultural hierarchies.

It is important to note that imposed cultural hierarchies are not always unequivocally accepted, but may be disputed and challenged, resulting in diverging interpretations. For example, on more than one occasion middle-class Garo told me that the Bengali Muslim migrant labourers who do much of the menial labour on building sites and for road construction are 'like vermin'. This was evidenced, one such speaker argued, by the fact that they only needed to be paid a pittance to work ten hours a day. Not only did they work without complaint, they hardly needed food at all and did not require more in terms of accommodation than a tarpaulin stretched above their heads. In other words, the exploitative working conditions endured by the Bengali labourers were used to justify their subordinate social position. In the eyes of the Garo who expressed such sentiments, these Muslims were less than human, echoing the stratified perspective on society described above despite shifting the hierarchical order asserted.

People in Sadolpara also expressed negative views on Muslim Bengali, who they encountered among others as traders who bought their produce at the weekly market. The villagers felt, not entirely without justification, that the traders often tried to trick them into selling their crops for prices that were far below the market value. Presented with a large basket filled with the best quality ginger, such a trader would offer just a small amount of money, which the Garo producer would refuse—until the market was about to close, and he or she had no choice but to accept the offer or haul the ginger back home. Garo referred to these trading techniques as 'Bengali cunningness' (*Bangal chalak*), ascribing difference in terms of ethnicity rather than religion. At the market, the Garo felt dependent on the Bengali. Clearly aware of their more powerful position, the traders knew that ultimately the Garo villagers had no choice but to sell, so they did their utmost to pay the lowest possible price. The rather fierce arguments that resulted created bad feelings, at least among the Garo. Hence, while people are free to interpret social hierarchies according to their own perspectives, ultimately political, economic, and social inequalities are what define the relationships that matter in their everyday lives.

Social hierarchy and ethnic and religious diversity thus play out in various ways in Garo Hills. While a hierarchical and derogatory 'Hindu perspective' on 'tribals', which dominates at the national level, is expressed by non-Garo who are temporarily or permanently located in the region (the Bihari guard), middle-class 'town' Garo do not necessarily feel that it applies to them. While Muslims also tend to locate themselves higher in terms of cultural hierarchy than Garo 'tribals', that does not win them much traction in everyday interactions. In predominantly Garo contexts, Bengali Muslims are often despised and exploited as cheap and semi-skilled workers. As traders, they are suspected of cheating villagers at the market. Interpretations of social hierarchy in Garo Hills thus vary according to the situated perspective of the person interpreting; the experiences they have had, and the significance they attribute to categorizations like ethnicity, religion, and class.

2.5 Ethnic Politics, Militancy, and the Demand for Statehood

The framing of the Garo as a 'tribe', as a discrete cultural and political community, is predicated on the assumption that they share a common Garo language and culture, coupled to residence in a more or less contiguous territory. This notion of community is (obviously) not a given, but has been shaped in the context of state formation, grafted on political and economic patterns that have their origins in precolonial times. As a result of this process, a variety of cultural and linguistic groups, predecessors of the current Garo, became redefined as a shared ethnicity. The five Garo Hills districts of western Meghalaya have come to constitute the Garo heartland, and serve as a geographic and cultural reference for a Garo political community that extends to Goalpara (Assam) and Mymensingh (Bangladesh), as well as to a diaspora in cities as far apart as Dhaka, Delhi, Guwahati, and Shillong.

Garo ethnicity is largely defined by the cultural practices of the Am'beng (or A'beng), who comprise approximately 50 per cent of all Garo, according to some estimates. As mentioned in section 1.1, an important point of reference for 'Garoness' is the traditional community religion, for which the annual Wangala celebrations are a key event (section 4.6). In the state of Meghalaya, Wangala, which was originally primarily celebrated among Am'beng and A'we, has become an annual state-wide holiday. It is also officially celebrated as a large-scale state-sponsored festival held each year at dedicated grounds in Asanangre (some 20 kilometres from Tura). While the celebration has been adopted as an expression of a shared Garo culture that is expected to bring together people of all generations, from both the rural and urban areas, historically it had little relevance for the people of East Garo Hills (de Maaker 2013b). Like many such cultural festivals held across North-East India, Wangala presents a rather formulaic consolidated representation of 'culture' and plays a crucial role in both defining and expressing politicized ethnicity (Kikon 2005; Barkataki-Ruscheweyh 2018).

In a political sense, performances of ethnicity can serve to advance claims to land, laws, and resources (such as government jobs). The massive protest led by Sonaram Sangma at the turn of the 20th century is now often taken as the inception of a Garo political consciousness (Sinha 2003: 206; Karlsson 2011: 302). Remembrance of the protest continues to be invoked, perhaps all the more passionately because it was held in a Garo-dominated area that is currently part of the state of Assam. Garo nationalist groups such as the Garo Student Union (GSU) commemorate Sonaram Sangma every year at Bakrapul (near Damra, Assam), where he died on 27 August 1916 and where a statue of him has been erected (Sangma 1985: 333; Karlsson 2011: 136). The commemoration serves to reiterate the long-standing demand for the Garo-dominated areas of Assam to be incorporated into the state of Meghalaya. The ultimate political aim of such groups is the creation of a separate Garo state, which would continue to be part of the Indian union. In the run-up to the 2014 elections for the Lok Sabha (the lower house of the Indian parliament), even the mainstream National People's Party (NPP), which went on to win the Garo Hills constituency, acknowledged the demand for a separate Garo state. At an election meeting in the town of Jingjal, veteran politician Purno Sangma announced, as reported in the *Times of India*, 'I seek your vote for Garoland.' According to a journalist who attended the rally, his statement was met by 'thunderous applause' (*The Times of India* 2014). The demand for a separate Garoland state is but one of many calls for 'new states' that have been put forward by a variety of political movements in India. Their hopes of actually realizing their goal are boosted each time the central government grants a new state. In the year 2000, the states of Uttarakhand, Jharkhand, and Chhattisgarh came into being, and more recently, in 2014, the state of Telangana was inaugurated.

As elsewhere in South Asia, the unemployment and under-employment of educated youth is a growing problem among Garo, and contributes to a further widening of the already substantial disparities of class that characterize urban life (Jeffrey 2010). Ever more schools and colleges are opening in Garo Hills, and the number of graduates continues to increase. Garo graduates seek jobs in teaching or in the government administration, but these are scarce and not easy to obtain. Earning a college degree does not guarantee future employment, particularly as people often complain, if one lacks the 'right' contacts within the bureaucracy.

The demand for a separate Garo state is rooted in the conviction that if it were realized, Garo politicians would have more control over the resources provided by the Indian state than they have under the current administrative arrangement, in which Garo share the state of Meghalaya with Khasis/ Jaintias. The control desired relates primarily to the allocation of money and the recruitment of employees for government jobs. Young, educated Garo complain that a disproportionate number of these jobs are posted in and around Shillong, the state capital of Meghalaya, which is located in the neighbouring Khasi Hills. Like other hill states in the North-East, Meghalaya only generates very limited revenue from within the state, and according to some sources at least 60 per cent of the state budget depends on funding that derives from the Indian central government (D. Gupta 2012). Since the early 2000s, North-East India as a whole has received abundant funding from the central government, intended to promote the integration of the region with the rest of India, not least in the light of repeated Chinese claims to large parts of the region. The funding was supposed to improve infrastructure and raise the general standard of living (Nongbri 2014: 8). It enabled the appointment of additional state government employees, as well as financing a wide range of schemes to develop infrastructure (roads, electricity, drinking water), and to improve people's livelihoods (such as subsidized rubber saplings, funding for the construction of fish ponds). In addition, citizens of the region qualified for national schemes to support the rural poor, such as materials or grants to improve housing (corrugated iron roofing sheets, houses for widows and widowers), direct income subsidies (distribution of subsidized rice and kerosene, pension schemes for poor widows and widowers), as well as the provision of subsidized work (the Mahatma Gandhi National Rural Employment Guarantee Act (MGNREGA), which aims to provide 100 days of paid labour to every household in rural areas). Acquiring, directing, and controlling the flow of these benefits, which involves numerous diverse government departments and schemes, is closely tied to the distribution of political power in the state of Meghalaya. Again and again, people have told me that due to relationships of patronage if not corruption, much of the funding allocated to the state as a whole ends up with the Khasi elite. While it is impossible for me to ascertain the extent to which such allegations are based on truth, many Garo, particularly large sections of the middle class, are convinced that a separate Garo state would bring a larger share of the resources provided by the central Indian government to Garo Hills.

The NPP's adoption of the 'separate state' demand, mentioned above, is a relatively recent development. Political parties such as the Garo National Council, and student unions such as the GSU, have been putting forward the demand for a separate Garo state for decades, and continue to garner support for it. Since the 1990s, this call has also been taken up by militant groups. From the time of independence onwards, North-East India has seen many movements that have violently challenged the legitimacy of the Indian state.[30] Various Garo militant groups have emerged in succession since the 1990s. All of them have claimed that their objective is to defend Garo rights to land and to keep out 'encroaching' non-tribal migrant settlers. One of the groups that was particularly explicit about such demands was the A'chik National Volunteers Council (ANVC), a relatively large and well-organized militant group that was active from the late 1990s until the end of the first decade of the 2000s. In 2006, the ANVC published a 'Memorandum on the demand for the creation of separate Garoland' (2006), in which the authors state: 'We have been divided into Garos of Garo Hills and Khasi Hills within the Meghalaya State itself; the Garos of Assam and Meghalaya in the national level; the Garos of India and Bangladesh in the international level, even though we possess a geographically compact area.' (ANVC p.7., cited in C.R. Marak 2005: 102). The memorandum included a detailed map of a proposed new Garoland state, which encompassed territory currently located in the states of Meghalaya and Assam. The ANVC was cautious not to claim Garo-inhabited areas located across the Indo-Bangladesh border, presumably in order to avoid a clash with the Bangladeshi government. The militant group was at least partly dependent on camps located in Bangladesh.

Frequent attempts were made by the Indian government to broker peace with the militants, often with the active involvement of local church leaders, offering attractive rehabilitation packages in exchange for surrender. Such packages generally included the promise of immunity from prosecution for former conduct as a militant, free housing, and a monthly allowance. In 2009, the ANVC agreed to engage in negotiations with the Indian government and gave up its armed struggle. But soon afterwards some of its members regrouped and formed new movements. Failing to regain its former unity, this time the movement splintered, and until recently Garo Hills had approximately sixteen active militant groups, which varied considerably in terms of size and activities.[31] While all these groups at least ostensibly strove for the creation of a separate Garo state, I rarely read more than brief statements of their intentions in the press, and I have never heard of any group having published their demands in detail. Over the years, Garo militant groups have earned themselves a reputation for ambushing police convoys and even taking on police stations. This has triggered counter-insurgency measures involving the Meghalaya State Police and the Central Reserve Police Force,[32] resulting in frequent violent encounters between security forces and militants, as well as in civilian casualties. For decades, militant activity and counterterrorism operations have been a persistent feature of life in large parts of Garo Hills. The conflict reached a new height in February 2018, when Nationalist Congress Party candidate Jonathone Sangma was ambushed with an improvised explosive device (IED) and then shot dead by members of the Garo National Liberation Army (GNLA) (The Shillong Times 2018b). Jonathone had been campaigning in the run-up to the elections for the Meghalaya Legislative Assembly. Soon after, perhaps in retaliation, 'Garo Hills Police and Meghalaya's Special Force-10 commandos' killed the leader of the GNLA (Loiwal 2018). This created a leadership crisis within the group, which had an impact on other militant groups as well, and eventually brought militant activity in the Garo Hills to a standstill.

The militant groups derived much of their income from the 'taxation' of trucks that transported coal from the coalfields in East Garo Hills to the plains of Assam and Bangladesh.[33] In addition, they acquired funds by means of extortion and at times abduction of non-Garo traders, mostly Bengali, but also Assamese, Bihari, and Marwari. Affluent Garo were also sometimes the victims of extortion and/or abduction. Since the wealth of the latter was seen to result from their (privileged) access to flows of income from the state, the militants' infliction of violence upon such Garo suggests that they felt entitled to demand a share of that wealth (de Maaker 2021a). Some high-ranking state security officers even told me that the monopolizing of state resources by sections of the Garo elite was one of the main reasons that militancy had emerged in the region in the first place, even though the groups' rhetoric argued otherwise.

During the time I was living in rural West Garo Hills, militants often came to Sadolpara. However, they never tried to meet me, and I always stayed away from them. Villagers referred to the militants as 'men from the jungle' (*mande burung*). On one occasion, I was later told, five men had demanded to stay overnight in someone's house. They were unknown to any of the villagers but demanded that rice and lentils be cooked for them. Between them, they carried one automatic weapon, presumably an AK-47. Rather than inciting political talk, they ordered the villagers to tie up their pigs, saying it was unhygienic to let them wander around freely. They threatened to come back and beat up the villagers it they did not obey. People told me that these 'men from the jungle' were fighting the 'soldiers' (*siphei*), but nobody seemed to know which organization they belonged to, nor did the villagers express much interest in the militants' political agenda.

In the early 2000s, it was not uncommon for middle-class Garo from Tura to express at least some degree of sympathy towards the militants and their cause. As one person remarked to me, their presence 'helped' to keep the non-Garos 'in their place'. Once the ANVC had started peace negotiations, and the subsequent militant groups had begun to emerge, support became less widespread. Much more frequently than before, Garo middle class came to be among the targets of extortion. And after 2010, when the number of militant groups mushroomed, even giving in to the demands of one group offered no safeguard from demands made by others. Popular support had never seemed very high, but by then it appeared to have all but evaporated. The press started to report instances of militants being lynched by people who simply did not want to give in to their demands (*The Assam Tribune* 2015; *Newmai News* 2016).

One important reason why militant groups in the North-Eastern region have been able to flourish is its geography: large areas of densely rugged, forested hills and long international borders. Many groups have maintained camps in Myanmar, Bhutan, or Bangladesh (*The Assam Tribune* 2013), which functioned and to some degree continue to function as safe havens. The governments of these countries have often shown little interest in dismantling these camps, while Indian forces were and are unable to operate outside their national territory. Since the 1990s, Garo Hills has also gained strategic significance for some of the North-Eastern region's largest militant groups, such as the National Socialist Council of Nagalim-Isak Muivah (NSCM-IM), which used it as a conduit for the smuggling of arms from Bangladesh into India. Some press reports have even claimed that the NSCM-IM was instrumental to the emergence of militant groups in Garo Hills in the first place (Choudhury 2011).

Throughout Garo Hills, the main language of communication is Garo. Non-Garo are typically able to communicate in several languages, and also speak Garo. In this respect, Garo Hills is very different from other parts of North-East India such as Arunachal Pradesh, where Hindi is the lingua franca, or Nagaland, where Nagamese (a derivative of Assamese) serves as the common language. In Garo Hills, the widespread use of the Garo language reduces the need for Garo to become proficient in Assamese, Bengali, or English—or, for that matter, Hindi. While this puts the Garo language less at risk of extinction than some other indigenous languages, their limited knowledge of Hindi, for instance, can be a disadvantage for Garo college students who want to continue their studies outside the North-East. This often leads them to choose universities in South India such as Hyderabad or Bengaluru where Hindi does not play such a significant role as in Delhi or other cities located in the 'cow belt'. Likewise, the dominance of the Garo language within Garo Hills can discourage some Garo from moving out and seeking job opportunities elsewhere in India.

The predominance of the Garo language in Garo Hills testifies to the significant capacity of Garo to take in what comes in from 'outside' and assimilate it into a Garo 'world'. Garo, at least in Garo Hills, are a close-knit community, notwithstanding the increasing disparities of class and religious differences. Garo themselves are well aware of this, whether they appreciate it or not. One woman who had a non-Garo boyfriend told me why she was hoping to settle with him somewhere outside Garo Hills: 'You'll never understand; I can never be myself here.' I had asked her why she wanted to leave the place where all her close relatives were. Yet most Garo view close-knit networks of kin as a source of security and support, as will become evident in the chapters that follow.

3
Housing Matters

3.1 Jiji's Plight

When Jiji died, on 16 November 2015, she was one of the oldest residents of Sadolpara and widely respected as a senior kinsperson. Jiji had had multiple talents. She was an accomplished midwife. Committed as she was to the traditional Garo community religion, she was able to perform many of the sacrifices that serve to cure illnesses. She also had a comprehensive knowledge of the traditional funeral chants. As a person, Jiji combined generosity with modesty. She was respected by old and young, men and women alike. Jiji herself did not know her age, but soon after I was introduced to the family, one of her daughters told me she was 'more than a hundred years old'.[1] To me, this was more than unlikely: she was simply too energetic. Saying that she was 'more than a hundred years' of age was, as I understand it, simply a way of saying that she was 'very old'. Going by the age of her eldest child, and taking into account that most women of her generation bore their first child in their late teens, I assume that Jiji was in her late fifties when we first met. As time passed, she became increasingly weak and frail. When she died, some fifteen years later, she was probably in her mid- or late seventies.

Jiji was a widow; her husband had passed away in the early 1990s. Throughout her life she had worked the swidden, and she continued to do so as long as she had the stamina. Hill farming is very demanding physically: the slopes are steep, and during the long monsoon season, days are characterized by extremely high temperatures and humidity. When old age eventually caught up with her, Jiji decided to give up farming. From then on, she spent most of her time with one of her daughters, who lived with her family in a village ward about 2 kilometres from Jiji's house. About two years later, even this twenty-minute walk had become too demanding, and Jiji's daily life was more or less lived out within the bounds of her house. Jiji lost her teeth, one by one—dental care was (and still is) unavailable to poor inhabitants of rural West Garo Hills. No longer able to chew, she lost her appetite and became frail as a bird. Nevertheless, her youngest daughter, who lived next door to her, continued to bring freshly cooked food twice a day. And despite having

Reworking Culture. Erik de Maaker, Oxford University Press. © Oxford University Press 2022.
DOI: 10.1093/oso/9788194831693.003.0003

become withdrawn, Jiji never gave up rice beer. Drinking parties energized her and saw her briefly regain her younger self as she once again cracked outrageous jokes that provoked fits of laughter all round.

Jiji lived in a large house that had been built in accordance with the stipulations of the traditional community religion. A house of this design and materials is known as a *nok mandi* (Figure 3.1). *Nok* means 'house', and *mandi* or *mande*, as mentioned in section 1.2, is used by Garo self-referentially. In rural West Garo Hills, it more specifically denotes practitioners of the traditional Garo community religion (as opposed to Christians). Jiji's house was big: approximately 5 metres wide and 25 metres long. It was built upon the incline of a low hill; at the rear it rested on posts that were nearly two metres tall, facing down the slope. The main entrance, on one of the short sides, overlooked the very wide and fairly level top of the hill. The house had originally been built entirely from materials from the forest, as a *nok mandi* should be. The posts and joists were hardwood, but the floor, walls, and large parts of the roof were made of bamboo. Between the bamboo poles, flattened bamboo was woven to form strong wall panels. All the joints were fastened with thin strips of bamboo, tightly knotted. No metal nails are required for this kind of construction. The roof was initially covered with a thick layer of thatching grass. Jiji's children took care of the essential yearly maintenance work, but keeping the roof in decent shape proved challenging. As well as having to be patched up annually, a thatched roof must be entirely renewed every four to five years. Thatching grass became difficult to obtain from the early 2000s onwards, as more and more land was taken up by orchards. Because of this, one year Jiji's sons, sons-in-law, and grandson-in-law covered the old decaying thatch on the roof with corrugated iron sheets that had been provided by the local Block Development Office as part of a scheme to provide low-cost housing. Ideally, a *nok mandi* should be entirely rebuilt every ten to fifteen years, but Jiji's relatives tried to avoid doing so, and over time the house began to look increasingly dilapidated. Here and there, the mesh of the floor became brittle, and more than once it gave way when someone broke through it. None of this seemed to matter much to Jiji.

Jiji had given birth to eight children. Her youngest daughter, a single mother of two, was in her late teens when I first met Jiji. Upon marriage, which took place during our initial two-year stay in Sadolpara, she moved out of her mother's house. Her husband was a Christian. She had decided to get baptized as well, and it was therefore not appropriate for the couple to live in a *nok mandi*. Otherwise, as the youngest daughter, it would have been expected that she and her husband would live with Jiji. Since that was not an

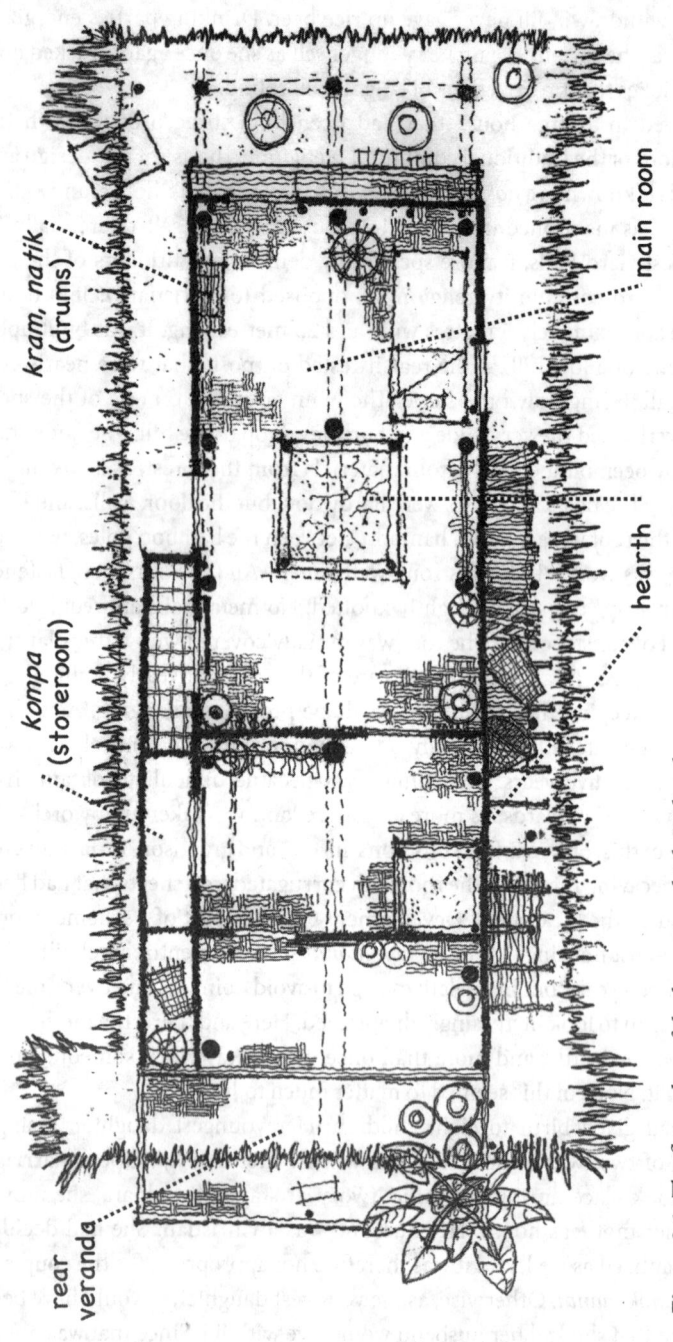

Figure 3.1 The floor plan of the house in which Jiji lived.
Drawing courtesy of Param Bedi, 2001.

option in her case, once married she lived with her husband and children in a house next to that of her mother. Most of Jiji's other daughters, and quite a few of her granddaughters, all of whom were married, lived nearby as well. Together, these ten to fifteen houses comprised a village ward. Most of the women who lived in these houses regarded Jiji as a mother, an aunt, a niece, a grandmother, or a mother-in-law. In other words, there were no women in the village ward who she did not in one way or another consider a close relative. A few of the women's husbands were her consanguine relatives as well, particularly those who had been born in Sadolpara (Figure 3.2).

As Jiji grew older, her diminishing ability to look after herself made me wonder whether it wouldn't be better for her to move in with one of her daughters. Once her youngest daughter had left, she was lonely in the big house. But she had to stay there. She could not 'leave her drums alone', as she explained to me.

In the main room of Jiji's house, there were two drums: a *kram* and a *natik* (Figure 3.3). According to the traditional community religion, each of these is the seat of a spirit. Jiji had to care for her drums, which meant that she had

Figure 3.2 Early morning in Sadolpara: Jiji (second from right) chatting with three of her daughters, her sister, two sons-in-law, and a cousin before they all leave for their fields for the day.

Photograph: Erik de Maaker, 2001.

Figure 3.3 Jiji's *kram* (below) and *natik* (above) drums are the seats of spirits, according to the traditional Garo community religion.
Photograph: Erik de Maaker, 2003.

to provide them with shelter, company, and occasionally rice beer and food. The *kram* drum, the larger of the two, was a seat of the spirit Risi. The *natik* drum housed Risi's daughter, whose name was never mentioned to me, and may not even be known. The *natik* drum was a supplement to the *kram* drum and people seldom referred to it. As with all the other spirits recognized in the traditional community religion, Risi is primarily known as a potential cause of illness: she can 'bite'. Although such biting is invisible to the human eye, it weakens its victim. Someone who is bitten by Risi loses their appetite and suffers from fevers that fluctuate sharply (*sin'na-dinga*, 'hot-cold').[2] For children or elderly people, this ailment can even prove fatal. Risi can bite anyone, whether they keep a *kram* drum or not. But maintaining a *kram* drum creates a privileged relationship with Risi: it provides a means of making contact with her, so she can be approached if she is suspected of inducing illness.

Only very few Houses in Sadolpara maintained a *kram* drum. Someone who keeps a *kram* drum is a 'tamer' (*jilgipa*) of Risi. This taming is taken literally. A *kram* drum is kept in a fixed place inside a house, hanging from a hook. Risi is believed to be able to make the drum swing on the hook. The movement of the drum is restricted by pillars at either side of it, suggesting that it might be dangerous to keep a drum without such constraints. Nowadays, with the sharp decline in the traditional community religion, no new *kram* drums are being made. But when Jiji's was young, powerful men used to sometimes dream that Risi ordered them to made a new seat for her, and accordingly they arranged for a new *kram* drum to be carved out of hardwood. Risi needs to be provided with regular offerings of food on specific occasions, such as when the roof of the house is replaced, or in relation to the annual agricultural cycle. As a rule, the food offered includes meat curry (requiring the slaughter of an animal) as well as rice beer. Moreover, the food and rice beer have to be provided in quantities that are sufficient to feed one's larger kin group as well. For Songsareks, hosting such events, and thereby displaying one's capacity to provide, brings prestige.

Each of the keepers of a *kram* drum holds title to a certain portion of the village land. These land titles bring religious responsibilities: dedicated rituals, linked to shifting cultivation, that can only be conducted by those who maintain such drums. The land titles of the *kram* drum owners are respected within a village, but significantly, minor title holders are not mentioned in the land registers kept by the Garo Hills Autonomous District Council (GHADC), which mainly records the holdings of village heads (Karlsson 2011; de Maaker 2018). These partial registrations are common throughout the region that is under the jurisdiction of the GHADC (Burling 1997 [1963]: 225). Locally, maintaining a *kram* drum therefore serves as a reminder to others that one holds title to land. This is not only in the interest of those directly in charge of such a drum, but also relevant for a fairly large circle of matrilineal relatives and in-laws. Most of Jiji's relatives were Songsareks and therefore continued to acknowledge Risi, as did Jiji herself. That was why Jiji had no choice but to stay in her house and care for her *kram* drum. It was not only for her own good, but also for that of her relatives who recognized the importance of the drum and the land titles it substantiated.

3.2 Modelling Relatedness

Garo trace descent in the female line, and as a rule a child acquires its mother's clan name as a surname. People emphasize relatedness between mothers, daughters, grandmothers, and granddaughters. Sons are much more closely tied to their mother's than to their father's relatives. Foregrounding the female line of descent produces matrilineal groups, which consist of matrilineally related women but also involves in-married men (Burling 1997 [1963]: 22). Garo kinship terminology is complex and elaborate but also open to interpretation. Ties of kinship can, to a good degree, be tailored and reinterpreted to accommodate the relationships that prevail in everyday life.

Men and women who trace descent to a common female predecessor whose name is known are said to originate from a single womb. They belong to a single matrilineal group (*ba'saa* or 'born of the same'[3]). Such a group can vary in size from a few dozen to a few hundred people. In addition to matrilineal groups, people acknowledge even wider categories of descent. All matrilineal groups that are believed to share the same origin constitute a matrilineage (*ma'chong* or 'mother core'). Affiliated matrilineages comprise a clan (*chatchi*), the widest unit of matrilineal relatedness. There are five clans, but the vast majority of Garo belong to either the Sangma or the Marak clan (Burling 1997 [1963]: 22). Garo surnames, in full, indicate each of the three categories of descent: the first middle name denotes the matrilineage, the second middle name the matrilineal group, with the clan name as the surname. To give an example using a fictive man's name, consider 'Sujon Mrong Waknol Marak'. 'Sujon' would be his first name, 'Mrong' the name of his matrilineage, 'Waknol' his matrilineal group, while he belonged to the 'Marak' clan.

Relationships between matrilineal groups are sometimes explained in legend. For example, the Mrong Waknol Marak group is believed to have branched off from the Mrong Gisim Marak group (*gisim* means 'black'). The corresponding legend narrates that a long long time ago, when warfare between villages was common, a member of the Mrong Gisim Marak matrilineal group was held responsible for the death of someone who belonged to another descent group. Men from that latter group took revenge, killing nearly all the Mrong Gisim Marak in that particular village. Just one woman managed to survive: by hiding in a pigpen (*waknol*), where the killers did not find her. Since her survival had depended on the place where she had taken refuge, her descendants became known as the Mrong Waknol Marak.

Close kin relationships are denoted by terms like *ama* (mother), *apa* (father), *abi* (elder sister), *angjong* (younger brother), *mama* (mother's brother), *de* (child), and *su* (grandchild). Each of these terms refers to ties of 'blood' but may be equally well applied to adoptive relationships. Moreover, most kin terms are also used in a classificatory sense: 'mother' applies not only to one's biological mother but to her sisters as well. This is primarily the case when referring to women of the same matrilineal group, but if deemed appropriate it can be extended to the matrilineage, or even to the clan. Likewise, all women and men who consider a certain group of women to be their 'mothers' can consider each other to be siblings. Consequently, people not only have many brothers, sisters, grandmothers, and grandfathers but also many mothers and fathers. With this broad and classificatory tracing of relationships, any one person maintains a seemingly endless number of kin ties.

People evaluate classificatory relationships in terms of proximity. Children of mothers of the same matrilineal group consider themselves to be more closely related than those who only share membership of the same matrilineage or even clan. Likewise, people refer to the woman who actually gave birth to them as their 'real mother' (*ama chongmot*), whereas other mothers are 'mothers by kin' (*ama maharigita*). However, even the term 'real' is open to interpretation and is not necessarily limited to 'blood' relations. Children who have been raised in the same household can express the intimacy of that relationship by stating that as babies they 'have drunk [milk] from the same breast' (*sok apsan ringjok*). This expression is usually used to explain the nearness of 'biological' siblings, but it can also refer to siblings who were adopted (*deregata*) into a household when they were still very young. The latter are also likely to refer to their adoptive mother as their 'real' mother, showing their appreciation of the 'nearness' of the relationship.

The classificatory approach to motherhood (and, likewise, fatherhood) makes it easy for children to be adopted by sisters, nieces, and aunts. It is not uncommon for children to be adopted at an early age, particularly by couples who have no children of their own. For instance, one of Jiji's granddaughters gave birth to twins. Soon after their birth, one of the twins was adopted by one of Jiji's daughters, who was unable to get pregnant but desperately wanted a child. This meant that the girl, who was adopted as a baby when she was just a couple of weeks old, had to be raised on (relatively expensive) powdered baby milk since her adoptive mother could not breastfeed. Custody of the child was transferred from the biological parents to those who raised her. Even though the adoptive mother came to be talked about as the 'real' mother, people also continued to acknowledge the relationship that the girl traced to the mother (and father) to whom she had been born.

With matrilineal descent at the core of Garo conceptualizations of relatedness, it might be expected that one has to be 'born' a Garo in order to qualify as one. In practice, however, Garo kinship terminology is remarkably flexible and encompassing. For example, over the years, I became acquainted with a man who had a Nepali mother and a Garo father.[4] Given that Garo trace kinship along the matriline, and (most) Nepali do so via the patriline, formally, the man could not trace descent within either of the communities. But he grew up in the household of his father, who married a Garo woman after splitting up with his Nepali partner. Consequently, the man with the Nepali mother took on his adoptive mother's (Garo) surname. Having grown up in Sadolpara, he spoke perfect Garo and was fully versed in the cultural codes of everyday life. Sometimes people teased him about his Nepali origins, typically when they were drinking rice beer together, but otherwise it didn't seem to matter that his biological mother had not been a Garo. The assimilation of the descendants of non-Garo men who live with Garo women into kinship structures is even simpler. All children with Garo mothers simply belong to the mother's matrilineage.[5]

Relationships among kin are not only evaluated in terms of proximity or 'nearness' but also of seniority. It matters whether someone is an elder or a younger sibling: a younger sister is an *ano*, an elder sister an *abi*. A younger brother is *angjong*, an elder brother *ada*. Relative age is not only relevant for the children of one mother but extends to those of closely related households of the same matrilineal group. Addressing someone as junior to oneself implies assuming authority over them. Being spoken to as a senior means that respect is bestowed upon one. Siblings who have been raised in the same household trace seniority according to their order of birth. However, people who classify as sisters or brothers but grew up in different households are positioned in accordance with the birth order of their respective mothers. Thus, the children of one's mother's elder sister are always senior to oneself, even if they are younger in actual age. Similarly, all children of the younger sisters of one's mother are junior, although they can be older in terms of age. Among people who belong to a single matrilineal group, such rankings are part of everyday life. But if people belonging to distinct matrilineal groups meet, and certain relationships are unknown, it may require some enquiries back and forth in order to identify a common relative, however distant, so as to clarify how to address one another.

Being able to address each and every other Garo as a relative, either as a cognate or as an affine, is an important marker of community belonging. In everyday life, it is common and polite to use such relational terms of address. Calling someone by their first name is highly unusual. It implies an assumption of authority and is therefore only appropriate towards a child. Even when people talk about others in their absence, the first names of anyone except children are generally avoided. Instead, reference is made to the 'father of so-and-so', 'mother of so-and-so', 'brother-in-law', 'maternal aunt', and so forth. For me, this indirect and roundabout way of referencing was often very confusing since it required knowing who was whose mother, father, or other relative in order to trace the chain. Seeing my puzzled expression as I once again failed to figure out who people were talking about, someone would typically come to my rescue and softly mention the name of the person I was trying to identify.

The habit of framing social relationships in terms of kinship explains why Jiji felt the need to fit me into her relational grid as a son. This made me, like her, a Mangsang Sangma. In terms of inclusion, the nickname that I received soon after was an even greater success. My nickname was acquired after I had made a video recording of a man who attracted ridicule by publicly declaring that he had divorced his wife, only to rejoin her a couple of months later. Because I had recorded his foolhardy statement in order to research the hearing and thus expressed what might have come across as excessive interest in the couple's marital quarrels, people somehow decided to 'wrongly' name me after the ex-husband (who quite quickly became her husband again) whenever they wanted to poke fun at me. The ex-husband was tall for a Garo, and we more or less resembled each other in height. Each time I return to Sadolpara, people enjoy recounting the prank, re-evoking the memories that we share, and reiterating that I am included in their relational network. Joking with names, as well as intentionally using a 'wrong' kin term to address someone, is a favourite pastime. Especially when people spend time together socially, for example, when (Songsareks) have rice beer, intentionally addressing someone incorrectly as, for instance, 'father of so-and-so' is guaranteed to bring salvos of laughter. The 'father of so-and-so' would have had sex with the 'mother of so-and-so', which is why such insinuations provoke such amusement. The victim's role is to reject the way they are being addressed with a loudly exclaimed 'Tsssch!!'. Amidst the ensuing laughter, the insulted party can then counter the jest by 'wrongly' addressing someone else—usually one of the people laughing the loudest. Along the same lines, most people have nicknames[6] that refer to a specific bodily characteristic and are again (mildly) offensive. One rather innocent example is 'fat belly' (*chengbong*). Others are vulgar and reserved for when people are getting drunk. On one such occasion a man's virility was played on by calling him 'seven bamboo pipes [penises]' (*wa'tok sni*). This triggered an explosion of laughter, which the victim took part in as well. Name jokes, especially if told when drinking alcohol, are guaranteed to bring people together.

3.3 Living with Houses

Ideally, according to Garo *niam*, marriages should take place between distinct clans, and indeed the vast majority of marriages bring together a Sangma and a Marak.[7] Since everyone from a single clan is related, even if only distantly, marriages within the clan would be incestuous. Marriages between members of distinct clans are the norm, and, particularly when people in socially significant positions are involved, the rule is followed quite strictly. Such normative marriages create an *a'kim* obligation between the partners' respective kin groups. This means that when either partner passes away, the deceased's relatives are obliged to find a new spouse as a 'replacement' for the one who died. This is referred to as 'to put back' (*datanga*) or 'to give instead' (*on'songa*). The replacement spouse should belong to the same matrilineal group or at least the same matrilineage. Ideally, a deceased woman is replaced by someone who classifies as her sister, cousin, or niece, and a deceased man by someone who classifies as his brother, cousin, or nephew.

The building in which Jiji lived was her 'house' (*nok*), but the same term was also used for the persons, property, rights, and responsibilities associated with it. In this latter sense, the *nok* encompassed Jiji herself, the unmarried daughter with whom she lived (when I first met her), the daughter's two children, as well as valuable heirloom objects, bulls and cows, and a considerable amount of land. To distinguish between these two senses of *nok*, I write 'house' with reference to a building with a lower case 'h', and 'House' as a unit of property, rights, and belonging with a capital 'H'.

The House of Jiji held title to the land upon which her house stood, as well as to large plots located elsewhere within the village domain (*a'king*). This made Jiji 'a *nokma*' (a landowner, person of importance), as some of her close relatives told me, which was why she felt she could offer us a place to make a house without having to acquire prior permission from the village head. Her daughters and their husbands, her granddaughters and their husbands, and her sons and grandsons all supported her in that decision. They all belonged to the matrilineal group of which Jiji was the most senior member. The House also encompassed powerful ceremonial objects (such as the *kram* drum), which enabled—and obliged—Jiji and the other members of her matrilineal group to take on certain religious responsibilities. The House, in short, was significant for Jiji's matrilineal group as a whole. It was therefore in that group's interest that the House should continue to exist after Jiji's death, which could be accomplished by eventually replacing her as well as her deceased husband. If an *a'kim*-inducing marriage has taken place, it is in fact obligatory to provide replacement. 'once established', a House 'should ideally remain forever' (Majumdar 1978: 77).

As an organizational concept, the 'House' in various manifestations is of significance across South East Asia, as has been shown in the work of Waterson (1990), Sparkes and Howell (2003), and Carsten and Hugh-Jones (1995). Waterson noted that throughout the South-East Asian archipelago, 'we find societies in which the word "house" designates not only a physical structure, but (also) the group of kin who are living in it or who claim membership in it' (Waterson 1990: 142). Further afield, the House emerges as a relevant concept in an even wider range of regional contexts (Joyce and Gillespie 2000). For instance, in his ethnographic work among the Kabyle of North Africa, Bourdieu found that the symbolic connotations of the House shaped people's understandings of themselves, as well as their relationships with others (Bourdieu 1977). The House, Lévi-Strauss noted, provides people with a means to combine societal principles that tend to be mutually exclusive, such as descent and residence (Godelier 2018: 173). Marriages need to bring together spouses who are not close kin in order to avoid incestuous relationships. Yet marriages between partners who are not closely related may result in either of the partners becoming disconnected from their descent group. Where Houses represent the descent groups of both spouses, they can reconcile these two contradictory demands, which makes them particularly important in contexts where people depend on shared resources (Lévi-Strauss 1991). Due to *a'kim* replacement, the continuation of a Garo House is perceived as a progression from mothers to daughters. At the same time, in the male line of the House, *a'kim* replacement allows for continuity from uncles to nephews. A man marries into the matrilineal group of his wife, gaining access to the assets of her House and becoming positioned as its 'head' (*skutong*).

A social organization that centres on Houses is never overtly person-centric, because a House is not to be confused with those who belong to it. Houses can own property, claim statuses, and hold responsibilities. But rather than people owning Houses, Houses define people (Godelier 2018: 173). People who belong to a House are not so much its owners, but rather have custody over the wealth, responsibilities, rights, and obligations associated with it. If Houses are central to social organization, they are typically perpetuated over generations to ensure that they do not peter out (Lévi-Strauss 1983: 176).[8] Where property and rights are vested with Houses, people stand to lose access to those assets if their House 'ends', and often conventions exist that enable Houses to be continued from one generation to the next

(Lévi-Strauss 1991). So, if Houses can be continued following the death of one or more partners of the marriage that established or led them, great effort is taken to ensure that they will be.

The House that Jiji belonged to had existed for several generations. Going by the available genealogies, it had most probably come into being early in the 20th century. The House had reportedly been founded when a woman named Aki had married a man called Ginjing (Figure 3.4). Aki was a daughter of the village head. Somehow, her House acquired title to part of the land that belonged to the House of the village head. Logically, Aki belonged to the same matrilineage as the wife of the village head. When Aki died, her daughter Songrit took her place. Songrit married Tujen, who was a close relative of her father. Songrit and Tujen had three children. Many years later, when Songrit died, her niece Dajap married Tujen to replace her. When Tujen died, years after that, his relative Baka married Dajap. When Dajap was in her

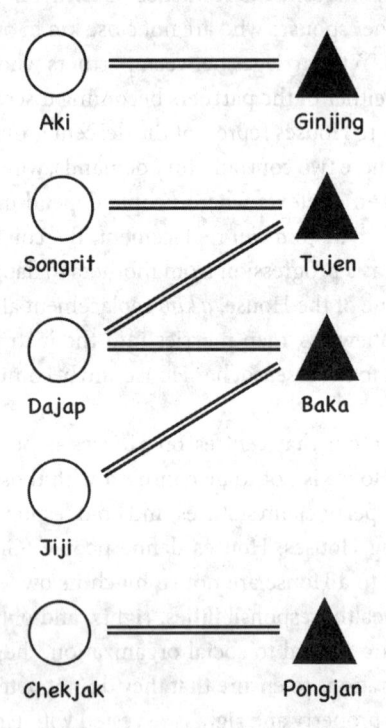

Figure 3.4 Jiji and Baka belonged to a House that had been created by Aki and Ginjing.
Diagram: Erik de Maaker.

thirties or forties, Baka married a second wife, Jiji, who was a cousin of Dajap. (It is not uncommon for Songsarek men to have two wives.) At the time of the marriage, Jiji must have been in her early teens, and the age difference between Jiji and Baka was probably about twenty or thirty years. Jiji and Baka had eight children together. Dajap died before Baka. By the time Baka died, Jiji was probably in her late thirties. His relatives made numerous attempts to provide Jiji with a new husband to 'replace' Baka, as they were obliged to according to Garo *niam*, but ultimately none of the matches worked out, and Jiji lived the rest of her life as a widow. Jiji's House had thus been created with the initial marriage of Aki and Ginjing and was continued after their death as they were replaced by successive others.

A new person who 'enters' a House as a spouse, replacing someone who has died, acquires the kinship designation of their predecessor. A daughter who replaces her deceased mother becomes the 'mother and stepmother' (*ama-ma'de*) of the children of her House, and a 'grandmother' (*ambi*) to its grandchildren. The replacement of a deceased man becomes 'father and stepfather' (*apa-awang*) to the children of his House, and a 'grandfather' (*atchu*) to its grandchildren. The relationships created by replacement are supplementary to those that people acquire by birth. A daughter who replaces her deceased mother thus comes to trace double relationships to her siblings: she becomes their stepmother while continuing to be a sister. A young couple who have taken the place of deceased senior kin may need to be addressed by others from their matrilineal group as 'grandmother' and 'grandfather', even by people who are their seniors in terms of age. Over successive generations (*chasong* or *wa'pak*), as long as a House is continued, kin titles continue to be inherited. This means that everyone, regardless of age, continues to have fathers, mothers, and grandparents.

Waterson, referring to island South East Asia, has drawn attention to relationships maintained among Houses and how these are shaped by economic factors as well as by 'hierarchies of status, prestige and ritual power' (Waterson 1995: 51). In the Garo context, inter-House hierarchies define and structure relationships among people and the resources they depend on. Simultaneously, the capacity of a House to negotiate certain resources (access to land, maintaining religious responsibilities), influences how it is positioned vis-à-vis other Houses. Matrilineal groups have one House that is the most senior (or apical), which all other Houses are thought to originate from. Relationships between this House and more junior ones are modelled on the mother–daughter ties traced between their foundresses. Relationships among Houses depend on ties between women, but Houses are nonetheless talked about with reference to the men who 'head' them, which reflects the dominant status of men in everyday life. The most senior House is that of a grandfather (*atchu*). The House that was the first to branch off from this apical House is the second most important. It is referred to as the House of the 'biggest son-in-law' (*chawari dal'gipa*). The Houses junior to that of the 'biggest' son-in-law are referred to as 'smaller' sons-in-law, grandsons-in-law, great-grandsons-in-law, and so on. Consensus regarding these hierarchical inter-House positionings generally goes unchallenged as far as Houses that are right at the top or bottom of the hierarchy are concerned. But with regard to Houses positioned somewhere in between, the hierarchy is much more open to interpretation, as the following example illustrates.

A number of people told me that the House of a man named Oldap had been the first to branch off from that of the village head, which was regarded as the most senior House in Jiji's village. This made Oldap the village head's 'biggest son-in-law' (*chawari dal'gipa*). In turn, the House of Jiji had been founded by a daughter of the House of Oldap, making Jiji's House that of a grandson-in-law of the village head. Jiji herself disputed this, however. She claimed that her House had branched directly off from that of the village head: hence, her House was not that of a grandson-in-law but of a son-in-law. This branching off had, according to her, happened prior to that of the House of Oldap. Therefore, Jiji maintained, her House should actually be acknowledged as that of the 'biggest son-in-law' of the House of the village head. Other people argued that the House of a man named Dising was that of the 'biggest son-in-law'. Dising had become rich as a dealer of government-supplied rice, offered through the Public Distribution System. He sold this 'fair price' stock at a subsidized rate to his fellow villagers. Dising was considered very knowledgeable with respect to *niam*, and indeed the village head consulted him regularly when faced with disputes to resolve. Nevertheless, yet other people claimed that Dising's House was no more than that of a 'grandson-in-law' of that of the village head. All this suggests that the ways people interpret and adjust the genealogies of Houses is influenced by both their own positionality, and by the reputations and capacities of the Houses involved.

Assets are vested with Houses, as are obligations and responsibilities. For example, people would speak about 'the assets of the House of Jangmi' (*Jangmini nokoni mal*), with Jangmi being the name of the widow who 'headed' a particular House. These assets (referred to collectively as *a'ma*) include the residential house, implements, the granary and its contents such as food stocks and seed grains, cattle, and the crops that are on the fields.

It also includes heirloom objects such as jewellery,[9] gongs,[10] weapons, and drums that are said to have been passed down since time immemorial, as well as any titles to land. The greater a House's assets, the more likely it is that significant efforts will be made to perpetuate it. The obligation to replace deceased spouses and thus provide *a'kim*, theoretically applies to all Houses, but genealogies show that only a few Houses are successfully continued over many generations, while others 'end' sooner or later. Consequently, the most senior Houses, which will typically be vested with the most substantial assets, have the greatest chances of being continued. Their continuation contributes to the memorialization of their dead: as long as a House exists, its deceased former residents are likely to be remembered in (oral) genealogy.

House relationships are also manifested in spatial organization. Sisters' houses are often located close to one another. Upon marriage, men generally leave where they used to live in order to join their wives. This often means moving from one village to another. However, in Sadolpara, quite

Figure 3.5 The gazebo (*kachari*) at the centre of the ward in which Jiji lived. It functioned as a place to meet, chat, and relax, and was maintained by the ward's residents.
Photograph: Erik de Maaker, 2000.

a few marriages took place within the village, which meant that the newly wedded men only had to relocate from their parents' ward to that of their wives (Figure 3.5). One advantage of this matrilocality is that when it comes to negotiating access to land, it is easier for couples to gain access to land held by the matrilineal group of the wife than of the one from which the husband originates (Agarwal 1994: 103). There are no differences between Christians and Songsareks in this regard. Christians do not challenge the principles of matrilineal descent and residence, so their property continues to be inherited in the female line (Sarmah 1977: 51).

Garo interpretations of kinship are at the core of Robbins Burling's seminal ethnography *Rengsanggri: Family and Kinship in a Garo Village*, which was first published in 1963 (1997 [1963]). Based on his extensive ethnographic fieldwork, Burling identified many of the patterns and rules fundamental to Garo kinship. At the time of his research, shifting cultivation was still the dominant mode of cultivation throughout West Garo Hills, while in the rural areas the traditional community religion went by and large unchallenged. When Burling was able to revisit the people he had worked with some forty years later, he discovered that radical changes had occurred. Christianity had become the dominant religion in Rengsanggri, and many people had adopted alternative livelihood strategies to supplement or replace shifting cultivation. Yet he was struck by the 'continuity of the kinship system' and the 'continuity of particular families' (Burling 1997 [1963]: 345). Burling's analysis takes a normative perspective, at times underestimating the wide variation that results when norms are interpreted within specific situations. The transformations that have since *Rengsanggri* taken place with respect to the resources people depend on for their livelihood, and with respect to their religious affinities and political loyalties, have directed my own focus to contestations and divergent interpretations of Garo *niam*.

3.4 The Birth of a House

For months, jokes had been made about Tami needing to get married. Tami was one of Jiji's granddaughters, aged about 16. She was our next-door neighbour. One day in early November, Tami's parents paid a visit to her father's village, 'to meet his kin', as they told me. I noticed that they left dressed in their best clothes and that her mother was carrying an earthenware rice beer vessel. A few days later, Tami's younger brother told me that the purpose of their visit had been to arrange a groom for Tami. Tami was more than embarrassed about the issue and gave only evasive answers accompanied by expressions of shyness. Her parents did not want to talk about it either. Then, one evening, Tami's father explained to me that during their visit to the village where he himself had grown up, one of his relatives had suggested that a young man named Gushen could be an appropriate groom for Tami. Gushen was a Marak, while Tami was a Sangma. Moreover, like her he was a Songsarek and not inclined to get baptized. Tami and her parents were also Songsareks, and if she were to marry a Christian that would most probably result in Tami getting converted, which they were eager to avoid. Also, they would prefer a Songsarek son-in-law because he would be able to help and support them in the performance of religious rituals, most of which require the involvement of several people. On the day of that visit in early November, Tami's parents had contacted Gushen's parents to hear their views on a possible marriage. They were open to the idea, and in accordance with custom they did not inform their son about the enquiry.[11] Many months later, after Tami and Gushen had become a married couple, Tami's mother confided to me over early morning tea: 'Tami had spotted Gushen at the weekly market, and told me that she liked him.' I was aware that the weekly market offered youth a lot of excitement in terms of glances cast and gossip exchanged. But Tami persistently refused to acknowledge having played any part in the selection of her husband. Gushen told me that he had not known about his impending abduction. He had met Tami once before, he said, but they had never spoken to one another.

On a Sunday afternoon about a week after Tami's parents' visit to her father's village, Tami's younger brother gathered four or five of his friends together. Most of the youth, but not all, were close matrilineal kin of Tami. One man originated from Gushen's village but had come to live near Tami's home when he married a relatively distant in-law of hers. That evening they went to Gushen's village. Gushen had been out for the day, herding cattle. When he came back they surrounded him and used gentle force to guide him to Tami's house. It was a somewhat playful act since he was not particularly averse to being abducted. He knew some of the men and probably had a vague idea where he would be taken.

Gushen himself had participated in other men's abductions, so he knew what to expect. Upon arrival in Tami's village, he timidly kept his head down and did not speak to anyone. He was made to sit in the main room of Tami's house. Relatives and neighbours of Tami gathered in the house as well and Tami's brother offered Gushen rice beer. (Later, people commented that Tami should have done so herself.) Gushen hesitated initially, but then he took a few sips. That was taken as a good sign since it indicated that he was not unwilling to respond to Tami and the others gathered there. People subsequently told me that it was also a good sign that during the first hours of his abduction, Gushen had refused to make eye contact and had not spoken to anyone. 'Grooms who are eager don't make good husbands', Jiji remarked. Later that evening, Tami behaved timidly as well, not least when she had to offer him rice beer and cooked food, 'inviting him to accept the marriage', as someone explained. Months later, when he was living with Tami, Gushen told me that he had not truly felt shy at the time, but had acted that way because he knew he was supposed to.

On the evening of the abduction, Oldap, a senior man, conducted *du'sia*—or 'beating the large chicken intestine' (*du'bik doka*). *Du'sia* is a ritual that creates a conditional marriage, which may or may not be accepted by the groom and the bride in the weeks that follow. Tami knelt on the floor of the house, at least three metres from Gushen. While holding up a hen by its legs, Oldap beat Tami's back with the flat palm of his hand and chanted 'This is it! For Tami with Gushen. To stay together like before [according to custom]. To tie them like before [according to custom]. Let's hold hands, firmly hold hands. Let's be together, firm like rattan. Let's stay together, firm, like cane. Unite, hooking onto each other's fingers. This is it!' ('*Iahai. Ta'minamingne Gusennamingne. Da'sini donga gita. Da'sini kaa gita. Jakbingihani-jakkaihani. Su'ka gitani. Rimagonggita. Jakstikiha-konkantiiha. Iahai.*').[12] As he spoke these last words, he hit Gushen on the back. Oldap later explained to me that the chant refers to the respective kin groups of the groom and the bride rather than to the individuals themselves. As he clarified, 'Let's hold hands, firmly hold hands' meant 'Let us get along, as kin groups.'

Oldap then broke the hen's neck with his hand and threw it to the floor. As it struggled, it flapped away from him, but only about a metre. This short distance indicated to those present that the bride was likely to stay with the groom, as I was later told. One of Tami's uncles then pulled out the chicken's large intestine (*du'bik*). The intestine provided a forecast of whether the bride would be willing to live with the groom. The man held the intestine up, so that everyone in the room could examine it. Everybody peered at two finger-like protrusions of about two centimetres in length. They pointed away from each other. Moreover, the intestine was not evenly filled with dung, and that was not a good sign. Someone remarked, 'It's not good', but an old woman reacted dismissively: 'Chicken intestines can lie!' (Figure 3.6).

Oldap then took up a rooster and repeated the ritual. This time, he mentioned Gushen's name first, hitting him on the back and then Tami. The

Figure 3.6 Chicken intestines are interpreted as omens on various occasions. Here, the intestine was being assessed to indicate the future relationship of the author to Jiji's kin. The omen was favourable: the two protrusions were parallel, faced forwards, and the intestine was evenly filled with dung.
Photograph: Erik de Maaker, 2018.

intestine of this rooster predicted the proclivity of the groom and luckily it provided a good omen. Finally, a third chicken was killed, also a rooster. The blood of this 'chicken of honour' (*du'u rasong*) was dripped onto the floor of the main room, at the rear of the fireplace, where it formed a neat puddle. Someone explained to me that had the blood run further, that would have indicated that the couple were likely to face poverty. Fortunately, the intestine of the third chicken also signified a favourable outcome. It indicated that the couple were likely to beget children, that they would be able to produce food in sufficient quantities, and that their family would not be struck by disease. In other words, since they would procreate, be healthy and prosperous, the House that their marriage was about to create would be 'honourable.'[13]

Tami served the cooked legs of the chicken of honour to Gushen. He ate the meat, which again signified that he was inclined to accept the marriage.[14] Some of Tami's uncles then talked to Gushen, speaking in rather formal and ritualized language, and told him about the resources in terms of forest and fields that he would gain access to by living with Tami. The visitors stayed in the house until late and drank lots of rice beer. That night, Gushen was made to sleep in the main room of the house, not too far from Tami. The young men who had abducted him slept in front of the doorways to prevent him from escaping. This 'guiding while sleeping' (*tusidil'a*) is conducive to leading the bride and the groom to each other, I was told. At the same time, it prevents the marriage being consummated before it has been accepted.[15] In the days that followed, Gushen made several attempts to escape from his captors, but he was caught each time. Tami's brother (accompanied by other young men) took him around the village to meet important relatives. After two days, Gushen was finally allowed to return to his parents. Tami's brother told me that he had seemed positively inclined towards the marriage. Gushen had told him that he liked their place because its jungle had 'lots of bamboo'. Tami also seemed positive about the match, even if she refused to admit that to me (Figure 3.7).[16]

Nevertheless, it took five or six more abductions before Gushen finally agreed to stay. Gradually, he became acquainted with more and more people in Tami's village and worked with Tami and her parents on their swidden. About six weeks after his initial abduction and the performance of the *du'sia* ritual, he moved in with Tami and her parents. Even if the couple might not have needed so long to make up their minds, accepting too quickly would have been inappropriate. It could have been interpreted as eagerness to engage in a sexual relationship and made them easy prey for teasing and ridicule. When Gushen finally accepted the marriage and moved in with Tami, he brought his personal belongings with him (clothes, bedding, bush knife (*atti*), and money), but nothing else. Those were his *a'tot*, his personal property. After he left, his parents could no longer benefit from his labour, which meant that they had to arrange for someone else to herd their cows and bulls.

As a couple, Tami and Gushen seemed well matched in many ways. Both had worked from a young age and were all but illiterate. They wanted to

Figure 3.7 Tami and Gushen, about a month after they had been married. By then, it was more or less public knowledge that they had agreed to the marriage, but they were still shy to acknowledge that, and careful to keep a certain distance apart.
Photograph: Erik de Maaker, 2000.

live off the land, close to their parents and other kin. They were prepared to accept a life of arduous labour with relatively meagre (monetary) returns. Despite the predictions discerned in the intestine of the third chicken at the time of their marriage, life did not turn out to be easy for them. Not only did they remain poor, but much to their regret it was many years until Tami became pregnant. She and Gushen took recourse to expensive treatments of various sorts, both local herbal preparations and biomedicine. Then, when their daughter was just two months old, Gushen died of an illness quite suddenly. Work, social life, and domestic chores are heavily gendered, and it would have been very difficult for Tami to live alone for longer than a short interlude. Since Tami's and Gushen's respective kin groups had endorsed the marriage at the time it was conducted, Gushen's relatives were obliged to provide a replacement spouse soon after his death. And although they did not manage to do it immediately, Gushen's matrilineal kin did provide Tami with a replacement spouse about a year later. The young man agreed to live with her, moved into her house, and became an adoptive father to the child that Gushen had fathered.

3.5 Bracing for Social Pressure?

According to Caroline Marak, at least until a couple of generations ago, young women faced much greater pressure to accept the marriages that were arranged for them than men did (C. Marak 1997: 58–59). But even for young men, 'marriage by abduction' is said to have sometimes involved physical coercion. One elderly man told me how in the 1950s, when even in the Tura area the majority of Garo were Songsareks, he had seen a young man being forcefully abducted to the house of his prospective bride. With his hands and feet tied to a large bamboo pole, the man had screamed loudly as he was carried along by several men. On that occasion, the narrator assured me, force had been used, but on other occasions marriage-related abduction included a degree of playful performance. Enothsing quotes a man who was abducted as a groom, who recalled: 'I was no doubt willing to marry the proposed girl with whom I was already familiar but I did not like to submit easily, rather I was thinking of offering very strong resistance and to know how strong the party is' (E.C. Sangma 1984: 56). Although the use of explicit physical force has become rare nowadays, it has certainly not been completely abandoned. Where a proposed marriage partner is not entirely unwilling, being 'led' has become a matter of loosely placing an arm around a man's shoulder, or holding a woman's lower arm. And in either case, the abductee is surrounded by a group of young men who (at least appear to) prevent escape.

Christians do not practice bridegroom capture nor do they conduct marriage by *du'sia*. They renounce *du'sia* because sacrificing the chickens and drinking rice beer invokes the Songsarek spirits. Among Christians, a prospective marriage is negotiated between the relatives of the potential bride and groom, taking the preferences of the two prospective partners into account. Such a negotiated marriage nonetheless creates an *a'kim* bond, with the concomitant obligation to replace deceased spouses. Following a Christian groom's consent to a marriage, he is brought to the house of the bride, where both parties drink tea together to seal the agreement. The bridegroom is not expected to escape, but if a marriage does not work out, either the groom or the bride have the right to end it—at least in the early days. It is likely that the growing prevalence of Christian marriages has also resulted in a tempering of Songsarek practices, creating more leeway for young men and women of the latter religious orientation to accept or reject a marriage that they have been chosen for.

A marriage between a Songsarek and a Christian is not in accordance with *niam*, so one of the spouses will be expected to convert. Songsareks in mixed relationships typically convert to Christianity, but I have also met quite a few former Christians who became Songsareks in order to marry. If a couple have difficulty reaching a consensus on religious affiliation, the pressure to do so can lead to the breakdown of a relationship, as it did for Salson and Dikji. The couple had lived together for many years and had two children. But when Dikji became a Catholic, Salson remained a Songsarek. According to Dikji, Salson had agreed to become a Catholic as well, but he kept putting it off. The Catholic father who visited the village at irregular intervals repeatedly warned Dikji that she was living in sin. Their relationship became unstable. When Dikji borrowed a shawl from another man because she got cold during nighttime New Year's celebrations, Salson became jealous and created a row. The relationship soured, and when a 'kin trial' (*mahari bichel* or *mahari toma*) was held in the presence of relatives from both sides, the religious differences between the partners were cited as a ground for divorce. Similarly, marriages between Christians belonging to distinct denominations are not accepted. If a Baptist and a Catholic, or a Baptist and a Seventh Day Adventist intend to marry, the woman is expected to convert to the denomination of her prospective husband. Christians who fail to comply with this risk being ousted from their Christian community. Once ousted, one is 'in front of the church' (*mondoli a'pal*), as the saying goes.

The marriage of Tami and Gushen was arranged in accordance with Songsarek *niam*, but couples also come together out of liaisons initiated by the partners themselves without necessarily obtaining the prior consent of their respective kin groups. In rural West Garo Hills, I got to know quite a few couples who had not been formally married but lived together under a 'catch and stay with' (*seki donga*) arrangement. Often, but not always, a 'catch and stay with' relationship came about due to a pregnancy. Premarital sex was not really considered particularly reprehensible, at least not for men, but not necessarily for women either. Where it resulted in marriage, thus lacking prior consent of the constitutive kin groups, that did in a way suggest a lack of respect for the authority of senior relatives. Frequently, 'catch and stay with' relationships were between partners who—in order of the degree of incestuousness—both belonged to the same clan (*bakdong*), to the same matrilineage (*ma'dong*), or more rarely even to the same matrilineal group (*ba'saa*). People were reluctant to admit that in Sadolpara such marriages were not uncommon, but that became obvious once I had started recording genealogies. Relationships within a single matrilineal group were talked about with disapproval, and I was told more than once that they did not create *a'kim* obligations. But rather than *a'kim* being inapplicable in such cases, the distinction is that if problems arise in a marriage, the respective matrilineal kin groups are not obliged to intervene and sort them out. In other words, those who choose a 'catch and stay with' marriage are 'on their own' if problems arise, as people told me. *A'kim* replacement is also complicated when one of the spouses is not a Garo. When the woman is a Garo, the House (and its assets) belong to her matrilineal group, and if these assets are substantial, her group will make efforts to continue the House. Since land and Houses are always associated with the matrilineal group of the woman, there is much less incentive for replacement to be achieved when a non-Garo woman has married a Garo man.

According to *niam*, it is wrong to marry a matrilineal relative, since this constitutes a certain degree of incest, depending on the nearness of the relationship traced. People told me that 'in the days before the white men arrived' (precolonial times) 'catch and stay with' marriages had, on occasion, been punished with violence because they brought shame on the matrilineal group. But, these people would continue with some regret, *niam* has become less strict since then, evolving to the current situation in which such marriages have become more or less accepted. More than once, I was told that 'nowadays' young men and women had ceased to respect *niam*. I took this to indicate that people were still aware of 'the rules', but were becoming increasingly tolerant of transgressions. Invariably, expressions of disapproval of such relationships were accompanied by mischievous sniggering since the couples that violated these marriage prohibitions had deliberately resisted the social pressure to comply with them. In my understanding, the sniggering indicated a certain degree of admiration for people who dared to go against *niam* and engage in 'catch and stay with' marriages.

In rural West Garo Hills, marriages are not large-scale celebrations, and the importance attributed to them comes nowhere near that attached to funerals. That is very different among the urban Garo middle class, who celebrate weddings lavishly, with large numbers of guests, expensive ceremonies, and abundant food. Attendance at these events is more or less compulsory for a large circle of relatives and friends. In terms of catering, to win respect by demonstrating one's generosity, meat in particular needs to be provided in plentitude. Dishes typically include pork, beef, chicken, and fish, all offered in large quantities and prepared according to a wide variety of recipes. All the costs are borne by the bride's family, and providing a well-organized marriage is a significant source of prestige. As in the rural areas, a Garo middle-class groom may only take his personal property from his parents' home, and upon marriage he loses access to their House's assets. At a wedding that I recently attended, the groom's mother was crying, saying the marriage of her son meant that 'he was leaving her'. While her emotions were clearly sincerely felt, she did not stand to completely lose her son—he would also continue to be connected to and share in the responsibility for the House of his parents.

3.6 Houses of Relatedness

In the literature on matrilineality, tracing descent in the female line is sometimes conflated with matriarchy, or 'the rule of women'. In the late 1950s, Gabrielle Bertrand published an entertaining travelogue about her stay in Garo Hills with the intriguing title *Secret Lands Where Women Reign*. Her title implies that women play a dominant role in those lands, but her observations in the book do not support that, as she states: 'matriarchy, in the true sense of the word, does not exist among the Garos' (Bertrand 1958: 62). With land primarily being associated with matrilineages, held in the names of women, and inherited in the female line, Garo women might appear better placed than those of South Asia's patrilineal communities. While there is certainly some truth to this, in the sense that women cannot be dispossessed as easily as they often are in patrilineal contexts, when it comes to controlling economic resources, and in political life, Garo women tend to be subordinate to men (Marak 1997: 59).

The marriage of Tami and Gushen created a new House within the group of Houses of which Jiji's House was the most senior. Tami, Tami's mother Waljak, and Waljak's mother Jiji all belonged to the Mangsang matrilineage, and their Houses were each referred to as a 'Mangsang House' (*nok Mangsang*). A House belongs to the matrilineal group of the wife, and is ranked and positioned according to the female line, but in a rather male-centric way people nevertheless regard the husband as the 'head' (*skutong*) of a House. In the absence of a husband, as in Jiji's case, a woman can take on that leading role, but at exclusively male gatherings she has to be represented by one of her sons-in-law. It is the responsibility of the 'head' of a House to ensure that it lives up to its obligations, and that it prospers. A House gains new members through birth, adoption, or when deceased spouses are replaced. Men and women leave the House into which they were born when they marry, die, or—in the case of children—are adopted into another House. As long as a House is supported by the relevant relatives and affines, and the people who belong to it are successfully replaced, it can continue to exist over numerous generations.

Upon marriage, a man 'enters' the matrilineal group of his new wife. In the period between a man's initial abduction and the couple's decision to accept or reject the marriage, the bride's relatives refer to him as a 'new person' (*mande gital*). The same term is used for a newborn baby. The bride's relatives refer to the joining of the groom as 'entering through birth to stay' (*dongnapa atchia*). From the perspective of his own relatives, a groom is 'thrown alive, like a stone, to enter [the kin group of the bride]' (*tangnapa rongua*). Once the groom has settled in with the bride, his status changes. From then on he is part of her matrilineal group as an affine (*gachi*), and often has to act on its behalf. At the same time, he continues to relate to his own kin as a male matrilineal relative, a *chra*.[17] As such he is a custodian of the Houses of his mothers, sisters, grandmothers, and other female matrilineal relatives. As a *chra* he does not have access to the assets of their Houses, but is nonetheless held responsible for them as well as for the well-being of the people who belong to them. In other words, the 'head' of a House, if a man, is expected to obtain the consent of his wife's *chra*s when making major decisions. If the 'head' is a woman, she must consult her own *chra*s in such situations.

As the backbone of social structure, Houses thus assign responsibility, influence, and authority to men—not only within the matrilineal group a man has married into, but also in relation to the one he was born into. Women only have a say regarding their own kin group, but even there they are frequently overpowered by their brothers and uncles. And yet, even though Garo men are endowed with so much authority, Garo women are not expected to be submissive or shy. Particularly among Songsareks, women can be strikingly vocal and outspoken, often even openly and explicitly poking fun at men. While no individual woman has control over the assets of a House, neither does any single man. All important decisions in relation to a House's assets, responsibilities and people, are to be made by its constitutive matrilineal groups, which are represented by men as the main spokespersons. When conflicts need to be settled between kin, notably senior women make themselves heard as well.

Garo use an idiom of kinship to create a self-contained realm, which centres on Garo *niam*. This idiom describes and connotes the relationships of everyday life, including 'inverted' relationships of mockery and ridicule.

Rather than being inflexibly prescriptive, the relational terms used create a referential framework that can be interpreted in order to organize and validate relationships according to the situation at hand. According to *niam*, marriages and the Houses they create should be sustained across generations. Achieving this requires committed efforts from matrilineal relatives as well as in-laws. Interpreting *niam* is a process that brings mutual expectations to light as they are articulated, whereby the relationships involved may be confirmed, challenged, or redefined.

4
Niam, Houses, and Land

4.1 'It would be good if he died!'

One afternoon, Sadolpara was unusually empty. Walking through Ajigre, one of the more centrally located village wards, I met Satnak. Satnak was a cheerful woman in her early fifties and a close relative of Jiji. I asked her whether she knew what was going on, and she told me that 'everyone had gone to Mangdugre'—a constituent part of Sadolpara, just a couple of kilometres away. Sensing that something significant was about to happen, Nandini and I walked to the place known as the 'market', a dusty open space adjacent to the main road. It had rows of market booths made of wood and bamboo, which stood empty except when they were used on market days. Sadolpara's market is held every Saturday, hence the location is known as 'Saturday-market' (*Sonibar-bazar*). The market area was never entirely deserted, however; it also had a couple of houses and shops in which people lived. In one of these, near the roadside, we encountered some men. 'There is going to be a trial (*toma*) tonight', we were told. They explained that two men living in Mangdugre, Nagon and Gansing, had had a bad fight.

Nagon had killed a cow that belonged to Gansing, whereupon Gansing had threatened to set Nagon's house of on fire. Gansing's cow had eaten areca nut saplings that had been planted by Nagon. As Nagon chased the cow away, he lunged at it with his bush knife and killed it. When Gansing found the dead cow, which had apparently been quite a large one, he was furious. He cut up the cow and brought the meat home. Nirot, Nagon's daughter, lived close to Gansing. Nagon began telling people that Nirot had overheard Gansing saying he was so angry, he was going to block the door of Nagon's house, trapping its inhabitants inside, and set the house on fire. By now, the conflict had got seriously out of hand, and Gansing requested the village head to hold a public trial, to sort it out.

Nagon was an old, often grumpy, and rather penurious-looking man. Gansing, by contrast, was in his mid-thirties, strong and cheerful, and as far as I could make out he was relatively well placed in the local relational network. That night, the kin trial was an emotive affair. It was pitch dark and not easy for me to see who was speaking. The only light came from a small campfire, around which people were sitting and standing. That evening, I had great difficulty understanding what was being said. Not only did people speak very quickly, they also screamed, shouted, and hurled insults. Luckily, the village head gave us permission to record the kin trial on video. Even though the images were quite dark, the recorded sound allowed me, in the weeks that followed, to get a detailed translation of what was said and—even more importantly—to ask some of the people who had been involved for clarification.

The kin trial was attended by many people, all adults. The majority of attendees were men, but there were also quite a few women present. Nagon and Gansing belonged by birth to the same matrilineage, and everyone who showed up was related to both—either as consanguineal or affinal kin. Nonetheless, the attendees were divided into two 'camps': depending on who they considered their closest kin, some people had come for Nagon, others for Gansing. Yet other people joined these 'camps' according to their relationships to the wives of Nagon or Gansing, who belonged to distinct matrilineages. When Nagon's close kin gathered in the early evening at his house, as they were expected to do in order to support him, he offered them rice with chicken curry. He said he could not offer them beef because he did not own any cows or bulls. His relatives took this as an insult. After all, they had come to support him. It transpired that on the morning preceding the kin trial, Nagon had hurriedly sold all his cows and bulls, ten or eleven in total, to a man from a neighbouring village for about INR 10,000. Rumours began circulating that he had sold the animals in order to avoid having to slaughter one for a meal for his relatives. Gansing served his relatives the beef from the cow that had been killed by Nagon the day before. Once everyone had had their respective dinners, they all gathered in a large circle in the wide open space in front of Nagon's house. In accordance with convention, the kin trial was presided over by the village head. At his side were some senior men who were respected for their extensive knowledge of *niam*.

First, the village head called Nagon forward. Nagon squatted before him—a customary sign of respect. The village head delivered the formulaic lines that open any such event. Addressing Nagon, speaking loudly, he said: 'Whether I am right or wrong, all of you listen to me.... Here standing around you are your wife, your children, your sons and daughters, aren't they? ... Standing around you are your mother-in-law, your niece, your uncle, your grandfather, your brother-in-law and your maternal uncle.' (*'Ong'akuba ong'jakuba gimik knarimbune. Aro nang'jik nang'dirang, nang'ni dipanti dimichikrang dongama dongja? . . . Ia warekkimkim donga nang'ni niu donga, nang'ni sari donga, nang'ni pajong donga, nang'ni atchu donga, nang'ni gumi donga, nang'ni chra donga.*')[1] Then, switching tone rather abruptly, he asked: 'Why are you sitting here, in front of us?' ('*Na'a ia mandi pabileku na'a maini gimin asongonga?*') Nagon explained that he had heard from his daughter that Gansing had threatened to burn his house down, with all its inhabitants inside. The village head then called for Gansing, who also squatted before him. But when asked by the village head about the allegation, Gansing flatly denied having made any such threat. Next, Nagon's daughter Nirot was called forward, as she was the one said to have overheard Gansing's statement and told her father about it. Nirot squatted next to Nagon and Gansing. The village head asked her whether she had indeed heard Gansing make the threat reported by her father. To everyone's great surprise, Nirot answered that Gansing had never said such a thing. She even denied having met her father at the place and time he had recounted. As I began to comprehend her denial, I wondered whether she had really never reported overhearing the threat, or whether she perhaps now felt intimidated by her angry relatives and had decided to retract what she had told her father earlier. Or was her father, maybe rather unwisely, trying to put Gansing in a bad light by accusing him of something he had never said? Gansing admitted that when he had learned that Nagon had stabbed his cow, he had grabbed Nagon by the neck and pushed him to the ground.

After Nagon's daughter Nirot failed to support her father's allegation against Gansing, the crowd grew more and more hostile towards Nagon. The village head was quick to announce his verdict. He ruled that Nagon was to pay a fine of INR 200 for lying about Gansing's intentions, while Gansing was fined INR 60 for beating up Nagon. The death of the cow, which had—as I understood it—initially sparked the conflict, was not mentioned in the verdict. Someone later explained to me that Gansing had taken a risk by letting his cows and bulls roam around freely. It was early March, and although the new swiddens had been burned, they had not yet been sown. According to *niam*, cows and bulls may be left to roam freely at that time, which is a rule that originates from a time when shifting cultivation was the dominant form of agriculture (Majumdar 1978: 135; Burling 1997 [1963]: 44). But over the last couple of decades, growing permanent orchard crops has become increasingly common. Orchard trees are planted together with swidden crops, and when swidden cultivation ceases, after one or two years, the trees remain. Since people have the right to chase away animals that try to eat the crops growing on their fields, that right could reasonably be extended to Nagon's defence of his saplings, even though that did not give him the right to kill someone else's cow.

On the night of the kin trial, once the village head had given his verdict, the atmosphere became increasingly tense. Rather suddenly, or at least so it seemed to me, one of Nagon's close kin came forward. With a loud scream, he used his fists to hit Nagon a couple of times on his shoulder and back. He followed up with some hard kicks. Then another of Nagon's relative came forward and also gave him a beating. Nagon did not even attempt to ward off the blows. Wincing with pain, he fell to the ground and covered his head with his hands. The village head stood up from where he had been sitting to preside over the kin trial—not to call for calm but to deliver Nagon a few blows and kicks himself. While the men continued to beat Nagon, a woman shouted: 'Though I was born, I was born alone, he says!' (*'Angadi aksan atchiuba atchia ini inaha biadi!*') One of Nagon's brothers added: 'He doesn't have any brothers (any more)!' (*'Angjongba dongja, adaba dongja bina!*') And the village head stated: 'Let Nagon die, his life has no value!' (*'Siongkan Nagon, Nagonni siani gimin gamchatja!*') A woman screamed at Nagon: 'You simply lied to people, making them gather. Are you not ashamed, are you a dog?' (*'Mandiku bu'ari jinongitna. Kratcha'jama, achak jatma?*')

It was clear that Nagon had brought shame upon his relatives. Not only had he falsely accused Gansing of planning to burn down his house—that is, presuming that Nirot told the truth at the kin trial—even more seriously, he had failed to provide his relatives the obligatory beef curry. In some rituals of the community religion, chicken may be considered an acceptable substitute for beef, but serving it on an occasion like this had evidently been experienced by his relatives as a slap in the face. One person shouted: 'Can you get people [your relatives] for nothing, by just roasting, smoking an (empty) stick over a fire?' (*'Indin mandiku wal'u ripui gol'u angi man'ama?*') To drive the point home, someone else added: 'Cook rice, slaughter a cow!!' (*'Mi song'buda, ma'su den'buda!!*')

While Nagon was being hit and kicked again and again, and further abuse and accusations were hurled at him, someone remarked that his matrilineal group would need to pay the fine that the village head had imposed on Nagon, since the relatives of Nagon and Gansing who belonged to the same matrilineage would need to 'unite' again. A very senior man, who had kept quiet for most of the evening, came forward with the branch of a tree and a small piece of rock. Hitting the rock against the branch he recited: 'This concludes it! Defilement of the land. Defilement of the water source. Go up high above, go up into the sky. This concludes it!' (*'Iahai! A'song marangko, chiga te'pattangkune. Chujitetnawa, chuduetnawa. Iahai!'*) With this customary invocation, the kin trial was formally closed, but the atmosphere remained loaded. Jiji snatched my flashlight from me without asking and stalked off into the night. Later, when we met her again at home, she was still bristling with anger and could not stop blaming Nagon for being 'shameless.' Significantly, she belonged to the same matrilineage as Nagon (and Gansing).

In the days that followed, many people overtly expressed their satisfaction that Nagon had been given a thorough beating. The day after the kin trial, Nagon had gone to hospital in town where he had received a couple of stitches. He had been humiliated but was otherwise more or less fine. Any subsequent conversations about the kin trial surmised that Nagon had failed to respect his close relatives, which had brought shame upon the whole matrilineal group. He had defiled its honour, and he had done so conspicuously by selling his cows and bulls in the morning preceding the kin trial so that he would be unable to offer beef curry to his relatives. Nagon's defiance of custom resulted in his being disowned by his matrilineage, and worse still, by his closer relatives within his matrilineal group. As recorded in the video that Nandini and I had made that night, some of his relatives had shouted in anger: 'We don't care if Nagon dies, we will just dump him!' 'It would be good if he died!' 'It is good if he really dies!' 'If Nagon dies, his younger brother won't complain about that, and his mother won't complain either!' ('*Nagonni sianadi gamchatja chingadi, dapketketari galinawa.*' '*Sisrangun namare.*' '*Sisrangohana nama.*' '*Nagon siudi sa jonggipaba dongjawa badi, ma'gipaba badi dongjauba.*')

It was not uncommon for public kin trials to give way to violence. Each and every time I saw this happen, it was the accused's kin that meted out violence towards the accused—in order to salvage the honour of the matrilineal group and the matrilineage. Kin trials such as the one described above take place under the aegis of *niam*, a core principle of which is loyalty and respect for the senior Houses, the matrilineal group, and the matrilineage. *Niam* serves to distinguish between good and bad, between what behaviour is considered appropriate and what is antisocial. Calling on relatives for help, yet keeping one's wealth to oneself, as Nagon was seen to have done, is a transgression worthy of punishment.

4.2 Practising *Niam*

'That's not *niam*!' is a common way of denouncing something someone has said or done. Any conflict of opinion, or more general judgement of right and wrong, can lead people to invoke the authority of *niam* (see section 1.2 for an introduction to the concept). Senior men, especially those affiliated with important Houses, know *niam* best—or at least, that is the general assumption. They are also the ones who are able to orate 'the sayings' (*kattarang*). This is a kind of literary speech, replete with metaphors and stylized expressions, which is used on important occasions, such as when matrilineal groups meet to discuss the replacement of deceased kin. Men tend to draw more attention to their expertise on *niam* than women do, but a figure like Jiji was also well respected for her knowledge of *niam*. *Niam* can also be invoked to reprimand children or youth, and—by inverting it—in teasing and mockery.

Niam is built around certain principles, the relative relevance and interpretation of which varies from case to case. In the dispute between Nagon and Gansing, it was most probably contrary to *niam* that Gansing had allowed his cow to eat Nagon's saplings and also that Nagon subsequently killed Gansing's cow, but at the ensuing kin trial, neither event was attributed much importance. What took precedence was the manner in which Nagon had insulted his matrilineal group by failing to serve them beef. This was considered all the more disrespectful since it was known that he could have slaughtered an animal had he not sold his cows and bulls on the morning of the kin trial. It was Nagon's calculated avoidance of the obligation to serve beef that brought shame onto his matrilineal group. The principles of avoiding shame (*kracha'a*) and striving to gain honour (*rasong*) for oneself and for one's House, and even more importantly for one's matrilineal group, are prime motivations for conduct. The degree to which people bow to pressure from their kin, or attempt to evade it, varies from person to person and the situation they find themselves in.

How 'honour' is defined and what is considered 'shameful' also depends on consensus within one's wider social group. It is shameful not to meet one's obligations, but what exactly these are, and at what point failing to meet them constitutes an offence, depends on the context. For Nagon, the need to provide beef to his kin proved—retrospectively—to have been non-negotiable. Nagon was an old man with a somewhat forlorn appearance. Presuming that he had not wanted to be beaten up, had he assumed that serving chicken would suffice? Or had Nagon even attempted to avoid the trial by selling off his cattle, in the hope that his kin would not want to gather if they knew he would be unable to offer them any 'real' meat? Had he misjudged his position, expecting more sympathy and not realizing that sentiments could turn against him? Once the relatives who were displeased with how Nagon had treated them had set the tone, it was imperative—according to *niam*—that his matrilineal group remained united. And irrespective of the outcome of the kin trial, it was also crucial that the relatives of both parties did not remain divided, but instead 'united' to conclude 'in agreement' (*melia*). At the kin trial of Nagon and Gansing this convergence was reached, in part, with Nagon's public scolding and beating by his own relatives. By taking his punishment in their own hands (as is customary), they absolved their own group from the shame that it might have incurred from Nagon's behaviour. This was a necessary prerequisite to the resolution of the conflict at the level of the two constitutive groups.

'Providing', primarily in terms of food, and particularly meat, is an important way of gaining 'good honour' (*rasong nama*). When one's relatives visit, they should be given food, and not offering any can be understood as an insult to the visitors. On the other hand, if one visits relatives and they begin to cook food (and slaughter an animal), it becomes more or less obligatory to stay and eat. Once someone has started to prepare food, leaving without eating would be considered at the very least impolite, if not unacceptably rude. For the practitioners of the traditional Garo community religion, the need to provide animals extends to the spirits. Specific spirits demand the blood of particular animals, ranging from chicken or duck to goat or bull (see the next section). Bulls are expensive, but—at least among Songsareks—their meat is the most highly valued, and providing one bestows the greatest respect upon the spirits and upon one's guests. The need to regularly fulfil these demands has the potential to reduce even the most prosperous House to poverty. In an attempt to excuse providing a less valuable animal, or even none at all, without causing offence, people often emphasize their regret that they are 'unable to give'. Whether that is actually true, or rather a calculated statement, typically remains unclear.

The more one manages to provide, the greater the prestige earned. In this sense *niam* is at the core of the kind of 'big man' (and, among the Garo, to a lesser degree 'big woman') concept that has led the hill societies of North-East India and adjacent parts of South East Asia to be characterized as 'redistributive, competitive feasting systems' (Scott 2009: 22). According to Scott, these systems reflect social relationships that are fundamentally egalitarian, yet flexible enough to allow for differentiation. This differentiation becomes apparent in terms of unequal access to assets, which reflects people's relative positionings among their kin. Yet these positionings are not fixed, but always open to (at least some degree of) renegotiation as individuals achieve merit and prestige in everyday life.

Christian and Songsarek *niam* differ, but are not necessarily incompatible. The kin trial of Nagon and Gansing brought together Songsareks, Baptists, Catholics, and Seventh Day Adventists. All appeared unified in their assessment of the case, and nobody criticized Nagon's relatives' violent reaction to his failure to provide beef. When it comes to recognition of divine powers, however, perspectives inevitably diverge. This becomes evident in relation to the conduct of marriages, funerals, and on any other occasion that involves reference to the spirits of the community religion. The rise of Christianity has reduced the authority attributed to the Songsarek spirits across Garo Hills, with the side effect that the interpretation of *niam* by practitioners of the traditional community religion can now be much more flexible than in the pre-Christian past. Songsareks frequently lament that people are no longer able to comply with *niam* the way preceding generations used to, and that people have become less strict in their interpretations of *niam*.

Niam guides people in their interactions with other people, as well as with animals, plants, spirits, and the dead. Violating *niam* can result in punishment from one's own kin, as in the kin trial of Nagon and Gansing. More frequently, at least according to Songsareks, transgressions are punished by wild animals or by the spirits. Christians are confronted with the wrath of their own God. In everyday life, *niam* continues to be informed and validated by ideas and experiences that are not necessarily limited to a single religious domain. In Sadolpara and the surrounding area, Christians and Songsareks live side by side. Most Christians continue to acknowledge the spirits of the community religion in one way or another, while Songsareks may perceive Jesus as a spirit as well (de Maaker 2013a).

Religious conversion is, to some extent, an individual choice, and can create painful divisions within families. This can lead to friction, as it did when a Catholic Father attributed the very serious mental problems of a teenage girl to her—in his eyes—'heathen' parents. She had taken the decision to convert, although her parents remained Songsareks, and he had baptized her. The girl's mental health struggles became publicly known when, on several occasions, she chased people with a bush knife. Villagers told me that she had gone 'mad' (*pagilla*). One evening, when the Father had come from the nearby town of Dadenggre to read mass, he stopped by to visit her parents' house. In order to cure the girl of the demons that he believed were haunting her and therefore responsible for her illness, he sprinkled the rafters inside her house with holy water. As I watched him do that, I came to better understand what he had meant when he had told me previously that 'one has to understand the beliefs of the heathens in order to truly strike them down'.

Songsareks believe that the rafters of a house are a dwelling place of spirits, who are not to be disturbed. Sprinkling holy water, which is associated with what Songsareks conceive of as the spirit Jesus, was clearly intended to intimidate if not chase away those spirits. The experience was very distressing for the girl's parents. Songsareks, for whom spirits are omnipresent, strive to keep the spirits of their house content at all times so that they won't trouble its inhabitants. The sprinkling of holy water on the rafters created a conflictual situation. For the girl's Songsarek parents, it established Jesus in the house. Since Jesus would be angered by people drinking rice beer, they would no longer be able to do so inside their house. Instead, from then on, they brewed rice beer in their kitchen (a separate small house) and drank it in the house of one of their close matrilineal kin. Drinking rice beer is at the core of all Songsarek rituals, and it is mandatory according to Songsarek *niam*. The spirits are always invited to participate: anyone having rice beer first pours some of it onto the floor as a libation for the spirits. The Father's actions failed to cure the girl. Her parents eventually entrusted her to a 'herbal healer', who took her for treatment to his house, which was located more than a day's travel from Sadolpara. She never returned. A couple of years later, I was told that she had died while at the healer's home. Her parents eventually abandoned the house in which the rafters had been sprinkled with holy water. They built another one, in which they could once again hold Songsarek rituals and serve rice beer.

4.3 Living with the Spirits

Songsareks seldom volunteer to explain their ideas about the spirits. If asked, they maintain that whatever they know is patchy and clouded by uncertainty. What people know about the spirits derives from their own experience, and experiences passed on to them from preceding generations. These experiences indicate that the spirits are omnipresent and innumerable. Most rituals include chants that make references to mythology and cite the names of some of the spirits. Interpreting illnesses or events inevitably leads people to discuss the presences and doings of the spirits. I have never met any Songsarek who had gained their religious knowledge from writings nor do I know any texts that they would consider to be authoritative on the subject. Hence, when a person reputed to be knowledgeable about the spirits dies, that almost inherently implies a loss of valuable expertise. Songsareks are painfully aware of this, and time and again I was told that much of what the preceding generations had known about the spirits had been lost forever.

The spirits of the traditional Garo community religion are invisible in everyday life, but sometimes they show themselves in people's dreams. Someone once told me she had dreamt she saw Dakkara, the spirit of creation, as a man with a long white beard. Risi, the spirit of the *kram* drums that are kept and cared for by important Houses, such as Jiji's House, can show herself as a woman. Jiji told me how, in her dreams, she had encountered spirits who were tall, muscular people. Covered with body hair from head to toe, they lived deep in the jungle, far away from the places where people make their houses. The land that they occupy is referred to as 'strong earth' (*a'a raka*), which at least some people believed should never be cultivated for that reason. Quite a few people had encountered such spirits in their dreams. One of Jiji's sons once told me that, in a dream: 'They tried to tie me up, to beat me to death.' Some spirits may occasionally manifest themselves as animals. These may be fierce, such as a tiger, an electric eel, or a monster lizard, or benign, perhaps a goat or a peacock. Spirits can also be associated with plants, for example, the spirit Guira, who is associated with the sleep-inducing *dikki* herb.[2] Lastly, the presence of the spirits may be inherent to phenomena such as thunder and lightning, earthquakes, gales, or the raging fire that burns the newly cleared swiddens.

Thanks to the knowledge that has been carried over from preceding generations, people know the most prominent spirits by name. The most important ones even have several names. The creator, Dakkara, a male, is also called Rabuga, Dakgipa, or Nokgipa. Nokgipa translates as 'master', or owner, and is a term that Christians use for God.[3] Risi, as mentioned above, is female, the spirit of the *kram* drum. Lesser spirits are typically not known by proper names. Instead, they are referred to in relation to the object that the spirit is associated with, such as 'the spirit of the rice storage vessel' (*rong'dikni mitde*), or, more generally, the 'spirits of the house' (*nokni mitde*) or the 'spirits of the jungle' (*burungni mitde*). In everyday life, people generally avoid calling spirits by their proper names since that would be disrespectful (the same applies to naming persons; see section 3.2). Moreover, uttering a spirit's proper name means invoking them. Doing so is best avoided unless they need to be called, as in the context of a sacrifice.

The spirits are believed to be a primordial presence that already resided on Earth before any humans, animals, or plants existed. The creator Dakkara-Rabokka made life. How he did this is narrated in the *dani*: a highly stylized, lengthy epic. It is chanted during the Songsareks' Wangala celebrations conducted at the village level. (I discuss the Wangala festival in detail in section 4.6.) The *dani* is then chanted by the man who officiates as priest. It begins as follows:

> Before during Wangala, long ago during Wangala
> Deep under the surface, deep under the water
> All the spirits were beneath the surface, they were all beneath the water ...
> The Earth was unstable, the anvil stood wobbly ...
> The Earth was in twilight. Long, long ago, it was like that.
> *Da'si duriba'ua, mini wanbibaua.*
> *A'ni ku'kimracha, chini bakchatracha.*
> *Miti a'ningrara, katchiba chiningrara. ...*
> *Gul-rokrekana, silkamni til'ekana. ...*
> *A'ni simsamgasam, da'si dakmitingo*
> (An excerpt from the *dani*, recited by Biki Mangsang Sangma[4])

Biki, a senior man who was highly respected for his knowledge of Songsarek chants and rituals, explained to me that the very first time the spirits had celebrated Wangala, Dakkara-Rabokka had hammered on an anvil, creating plants, animals, and men. In those days, land and water were still mixed; there was only mud. The life that he had created could not thrive in mud, so, to separate land from water, Dakkara-Rabokka created the wind. A later section of the *dani* chant narrates:

> The Earth was like an eyelid without lashes, its fontanelle was soft
> A daughter was born, a son was born
> Then the eyelid darkened, the fontanelle became hard.
> *Mani mikilsimjana, pildiin taru rakjana.*
> *Digipaku ba'isa, chiratangko neng'isa.*
> *Maniba mikilsimbajok, pildiba taru rakbajok.*
> (An excerpt from the *dani*, recited by Biki Mangsang Sangma)

Biki explained that as long as the vegetation that had been created could not grow, the Earth had remained 'an eyelid without lashes'. The wind was a child of Dakkara-Rabokka. It was at once his daughter (Balira) and his son (Balsisa). Once the wind had solidified the earth ('the fontanelle became hard'), the vegetation, animals, and humans were able to multiply ('the eyelid darkened'). The *dani* chant describes the creation of life analogously to the birth of a baby, and Songsareks maintain that life continues to depend on Dakkara-Rabokka. The process of creation continues whenever plants sprout, or animals or children are born. In birthing rituals, therefore, Songsareks explicitly acknowledge Dakkara-Rabokka as the progenitor of every new-born baby.

Despite people's fragmentary knowledge of the spirits, there is no doubt about one of their attributes: all of them can prey upon people. Spirits crave blood, which they can obtain by 'biting' (*chika*) people. Like the spirits themselves, such bites are invisible. Depending on the spirit responsible, being bitten may cause minor discomfort, such as toothache or a swollen eye, or can be so extreme as to result in death. Different spirits cause different illnesses, so the nature of a sufferer's complaints is key to diagnosis of the spirit involved. For example, earache is caused by the spirit Kompru Atop, migraines by the spirit Ganolma, and being bitten by Risi results in the 'hot and cold' fever (*sin'na-dinga*) that is very common in Garo Hills.

When people suspect that someone has become ill from having been bitten by a spirit, it is essential to ascertain which one is responsible. The identification of a spirit (*sma channa*) that is causing harm requires the performance of one or another diagnostic technique. Someone who has the skills to do that is referred to as a *kamal*, which is the term used for persons who can conduct any kind of Songsarek ritual. For one diagnostic technique, the patient or their representatives must provide a handful of uncooked rice grains. The person conducting the diagnosis drops these one by one into a glass of water while whispering the names of the spirits suspected of biting. The behaviour of the rice grains, as the various names are mentioned, reveals which spirit is involved. If two rice grains float to the surface and touch each another, this indicates the biting spirit's identity. Alternatively, a diagnosis can be conducted by means of a small bow (*pongsi*), the bent bamboo stave of which is dipped into rice grains taken from the house of the person who is ill. The man diagnosing (I have only ever seen this done by men, and have never heard of a woman doing it) then lifts the bow by its string with his index finger, balancing it on the tip of the upturned finger. With just a few grains remaining on the bow stave, he utters the names of the spirits suspected of biting. When the name of the spirit responsible is mentioned, the bow begins to swing (Figure 4.1). These kinds of diagnoses serve not only to reveal the name of the spirit, but also the nature of the sacrifice that might cure the patient.

Figure 4.1 Oldap diagnosing spirit-induced illness with the use of a *pongsi*. Mentioning the name of the spirit responsible, made the bow tremble.
Video still: Erik de Maaker, 2001.

A biting spirit is thought to have attached itself to its victim. To tempt the spirit to let go of the afflicted, a sacrifice must be performed in order to 'change the bodies' (*mangsrea*). This means offering the spirit a sacrificial animal as a substitute for the person being bitten. Spirits that only cause minor discomfort may be satisfied with the sacrifice of an egg, but those whose biting is life-threatening demand a chicken, duck, pig, goat, or even a cow or bull (Figure 4.2).

A sacrifice to a spirit (*amua*) tends to involve extensive invocatory chanting—chants that the person conducting the ceremony knows by heart. The sacrifice is made at a temporary 'altar' (*kimindam*), which is constructed from tree branches and fresh leaves from the forest, including a specific kind of bamboo (*wa'ge*). The design of these altars differs according to the spirit they are prepared for. The sacrifices are often made in front of the house of the person who is ill, some ten to fifteen metres away from it, at a dedicated spot. New altars are placed in front of old ones. Altars that have been made and used 'belong to the spirits', and Songsarek households often have a whole

Figure 4.2 Gatjeng sacrificed a chicken to the spirit Risi, as part of a healing ritual (*amua*) intended to bring about the release of his nephew Gotjen.
Photograph: Erik de Maaker, 2000.

cluster of disintegrating altars at that place. For certain spirits, sacrifices need to be made at other locations, such as inside the house, at a water source, at a crossroads, or in the forest. The more ferocious spirits are not easily incited to give up their victim and successive sacrificial rituals may be required, offering ever larger and more valuable animals. This is particularly often the case with Risi, for whom three distinct sacrificial rituals of increasing gravity are known.

Sadolpara and the surrounding area continues to be home to a substantial number of Songsareks, including many men and women old enough to remember the days when the community religion went virtually unchallenged. Many of the men spent their teenage years living in a collective bachelors' house (*nokpante*) and are well versed in Songsarek ritual skills. The last of these bachelors' houses in Sadolpara was abandoned during the early years of my research. These days, young men stay in individual bachelor's houses that they build for themselves close to their parents' homes, which makes it more difficult for the next generation of Songsareks to become acquainted with the ritual skills and techniques that used to be central to village life.[5] With the gradual decrease in the number of youth who have not converted to Christianity, middle-aged and elderly Songsareks continue to support each other both in making sense of the world around them and in the various (ritual) techniques that are required to engage with it. In quite a few of Sadolpara's neighbouring villages, there are now so few people with the requisite knowledge that it has become difficult if not impossible to find men or women who are able to diagnose spirit-induced illnesses, or who know how to conduct the sacrifices required to treat them, or indeed are able to lead any of the celebrations associated with the community religion (de Maaker 2013a). Nonetheless, even as the ontological influence of the Songsarek spirits wanes, their presence continues to structure the relationships that people maintain with the land they live on, which constitutes their most important resource.

4.4 Occupying the Land

Several senior persons were keen to tell me what they knew about the historical foundation of Sadolpara, and their versions of the story varied slightly. Biki told me that the village had been founded hundreds of years ago by Daknem Bolwari Marak and his wife Sadol Mangsang Sangma. Daknem and Sadol were a young couple who had come from Dadenggre, a village (which has since grown into a small town) four miles to the north of where Sadolpara is now located. Dadenggre was large and the founders of many villages in the region are said to have originated from there. The village founded by Sadol and Daknem took its name from Sadol, while 'para' (or 'bra') is a common suffix for 'village' in the region.[6]

It is not unlikely that the establishment of Sadolpara involved the displacement of earlier residents of the area. According to Oldap, who had heard such stories when he was young, one of the Garo headmen from Dadenggre had fought with a group of Koch living at the place that then became Sadolpara, which ended with the Koch 'leaving for the plains'. These days, Koch are a minority community in Garo Hills, and primarily resident in the plains belt. Meji, Jiji's younger sister, had heard another story. She denied that any fighting had taken place. Rather, she had heard that the Koch had caught and eaten a big tortoise. This was a serious transgression that had triggered an earthquake, which had swallowed half of the village. The surviving Koch were afraid and had fled to the plains. Comparable legends and myths telling of previous Koch settlement in Garo Hills are cited by Majumdar (1985: 183).

The establishment of Sadolpara required eight heavy boulders to be brought from a stream near Dadenggre. In fact, every Garo village that was founded in the times when the community religion dominated has such a cluster of boulders. Each boulder was about half a metre long and at least twenty-five centimetres thick. They were 'planted' (*gi'a*) in a cluster near the founding couple's home. Any such cluster has a main boulder, the *kusi*, which is surrounded by a few supporting ones. The *kusi* boulder is the tallest. It was (or is) a seat of the spirit Guira. Unlike other spirits of the community religion, Guira had initially been human—a valiant warrior—but transformed into a spirit upon his death (Sangma 1960: 152).[7] Guira's human past is the reason why he rarely bites people. Even if he does, his biting only causes mild complaints such as a scratchy cough or pain in the feet or stomach. Moreover, it is said that Guira can offer people who live in the vicinity of the *kusi* boulder protection from the ferocious spirits that dwell in the depths of the jungle. These spirits never come near *kusi* boulders; they stay far away from them, so Guira is evidently somehow able to keep them at bay. Nonetheless, Guira's presence cannot protect people from the countless other spirits that can bite and induce illness. With the planting of the *kusi* boulder, its custodians claimed the forest surrounding it as land to be used exclusively by themselves and the people of their village. In Sadolpara, the boulders are still located in the vicinity of the village head's house, although that is no longer located were the founders initially settled. Over time, the *kusi* boulder has been moved within the village, while new supporting boulders were added by subsequent generations.

The House founded by Sadol and Daknem was reputedly continued over hundreds of generations, although nobody could tell me their successors' names. Then, for some unknown reason, the House came to an end. In its place, the House of Bilka Chambugong Marak and his wife Maji Mangsang Sangma came to be acknowledged as that of the founders of the village. According to some people, the latter House may well have 'branched off' from that of Daknem and Sadol, meaning that Maji was a daughter of the House of Sadol, but no one knew for sure. Bilka and Maji replanted the *kusi* boulder, which might have toppled over, or perhaps they decided to shift it to a new location. The replanting required them to 'sacrifice for the village land' (A'songtata), by way of which they also asserted that their House had founded the village. Biki and Jiji, and others too, told me that they had heard this had involved the sacrifice of a man whose head had been buried under the *kusi* boulder. No one knew for certain who the man had been, but they presumed that he had either been a Garo from another village or someone abducted from the plains. By positioning their House as custodian of the *kusi* boulder, Bilka and Maji acquired the concomitant claim to the village land surrounding it.

After their deaths, Bilka and Maji were replaced, allowing their House to be continued for nine more generations. Several people remembered the names of each of these. Assuming that each generation could have lasted anywhere between twenty and fifty years, Bilka and Maji must have occupied the house in the early 1800s, if not before that. One of the couples that succeeded them shifted the *kusi* boulder and three of its supporting boulders, and thus the centre of the village, about a mile to the south. This is believed to have happened in the 1920s or 1930s. Some of the supporting boulders remained at the earlier location, where they can still be seen. Physically moving the *kusi* boulder was undertaken by men closely affiliated to the House of the custodians. Malsin, a very old and withered man, told me: 'Anyone else would have become blind or lame.' This replanting of the boulders demanded enactment of A'songtata once again.

Many years later, the replanted *kusi* boulder toppled over, probably due to termite activity. Its re-erection again called for A'songtata. Based upon the number of generations that have been part of the House since the couple who headed it at that time, I estimate that this last re-erection probably took place in the 1950s. Jiji, who had been young at the time, described her memories of the event to me. Each House of the village had contributed a vessel of rice beer to the celebrations. A man beheaded a dog with a sword and dappled its blood onto the *kusi* boulder. That was a substitute for the sacrifice of a man, which would have formerly been required. The dog's head was laid in the pit that had been dug for the *kusi* boulder and the boulder was planted on top of it. Facing the boulder, men affiliated to the House of the custodians performed a war dance (*grika*) with swords and shields. The custodians slaughtered a bull and offered beef curry and rice to everyone who had gathered. Some of the Houses closely affiliated with the custodians contributed bulls as well. There was enough meat and rice beer for many days of drinking, eating, and dancing, as Jiji fondly recalled. By participating in A'songtata, people expressed their connection to Guira, as well as their affinity to the House of the custodians of the *kusi* boulder (Figure 4.3).

Going by this historical account, initially only the custodians of the *kusi* boulder established a claim to the land of the village (*a'king*). Yet even if the custodianship formally rests with one specific House, all the other Houses of its matrilineal group also share in the right to live on the *a'king* land. Among

Figure 4.3 The *kusi* boulder of Sadolpara, standing in between two supporting boulders. A third supporting boulder has fallen over, and is lying in front.
Photograph: Erik de Maaker, 2001.

the members of a matrilineal group, custody over stretches of land can be transferred. Land can be offered as a funerary gift. Alternatively, it can be sold from one matrilineal group to another, even if the groups are located in different villages. Going by the memories people shared with me, the transfer of *a'king* land seem to have been fairly common in the distant as well as more recent past. In Sadolpara, over time, these mechanisms have enabled custody of land to be (re-)distributed among Houses. Nevertheless, a few Houses hold title to a great deal of land, while others have much smaller holdings.

If the custodians of a *kusi* boulder convert to Christianity, the religious rituals that the *kusi* used to call for will no longer be performed. But that does not mean that the *kusi* boulders will no longer be acknowledged. Even in villages where all the residents have been Christians for generations, *kusi* boulders continue to be treated with respect, which suggests that their erstwhile religious connotations have not entirely lost their significance. The boulders are often located in an 'old village' (as mentioned in section 1.1), and everyone knows that they are not to be disturbed. Hence, such places tend to be densely forested, and may sometimes be designated a 'forest reserve' by the villagers themselves. In a Christian or secular context, the *kusi* boulders continue to mark and substantiate claims to village land. They provide physical evidence that the rights to place of the people who currently live there are a continuation of claims that have been made by their predecessors. The boulders' significance in the context of the traditional community religion thus serves as a reminder that such claims are deeply rooted in history.

The continuing relevance of the *kusi* boulders is also demonstrated by a new set that was erected in Tura in 1997 to commemorate fifty years of Indian independence. The huge central *kusi* boulder is sealed in masonry and concrete, as befits a modern monument, and is located on a hill in the central Ringre area, just above the main road (Figure 4.4). Its placement in the centre of Tura town underscores the ongoing capacity of *kusi* boulders to express claims to place.

When Garo Hills was conquered by the British, its village heads became subject to the authority of the colonial state. Shortly afterwards, in the late 19th century, the British began claiming large tracts of 'forest reserve',

Figure 4.4 The *kusi* boulder at Ringre in Tura, with plaques inscribed in both Garo and English. The plaque reads: 'We, the citizens of Tura, erect this stone today, the 15th of August 1997, to commemorate 50 years of independence of India.'

Photograph: Erik de Maaker, 2010.

often infringing on existing claims to land (Das 1990: 14; Sinha 2003: 200). Following the protests led by Sonaram Sangma in response to this (see section 2.3), and the subsequent commission of enquiry headed by Arbuthnott, the colonial government set out to register the *a'king* land that was claimed by each village (Arbuthnott Report 1908; Karlsson 2011).[8] The topography of the hilly land made the surveyors' task challenging, so only relatively simple 'boundary' maps (*delim* maps) were created. These maps show the limits of each village's *a'king* lands, as marked by rivers, streams, ridges in the landscape, or occasionally by large trees or boundary stones (Figure 4.5). No cadastral survey of the hill areas has been conducted since then, and there are no government records regarding the surface area of the hill land. The Garo Hills Autonomous District Council (GHADC) still keeps and refers to the boundary maps that were drawn up in the 1920s. Before the mapping exercise, *a'king* boundaries had not necessarily been clearly defined, but

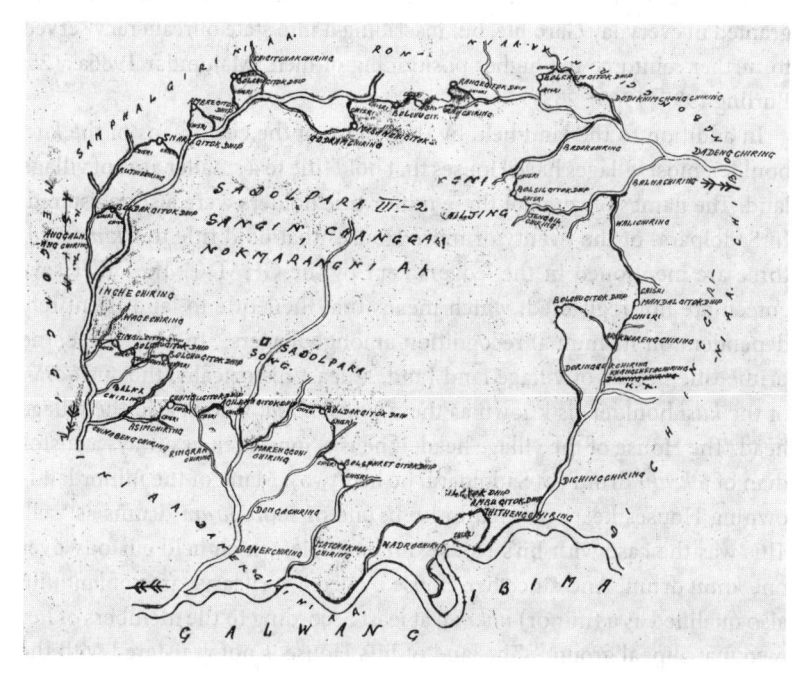

Figure 4.5 Map showing the boundaries of the land belonging to Sadolpara, finalized on 15 June 1926 by the administrators of what was then Garo Hills district.

Courtesy of Garo Hills Autonomous District Council.

the surveying changed that. In some places, claims to land were disputed between villages at the time of mapping, and in the years—or sometimes decades—that followed, such disputes became subject to litigation, first by the colonial district authorities, and later by the GHADC (Kar 1982: 32; Das 1990: 14; Burling 1997 [1963]: 269–271).

Houses that hold a claim to *a'king* land do so not exclusively, but also on behalf of the matrilineal group to which they belong. The Houses constituting such a matrilineal group are dependent on, support, and empower the House with which the claim rests. Consequently, every member of the group has a right to the usufruct of the land (Majumdar 1976: 16). When the boundary maps were created, the names of the couples who were the custodians of *kusi* boulders were also registered by the authorities since they were the main title holders to land in each and every village. Although land belongs to the matrilineal group of the wife, and the custodianship formally rests with her House, for all practical purposes the husband was acknowledged as the main title holder. This patriarchal bias is more or less taken for granted in everyday Garo life, but inscribing it into state bureaucracy served to further reinforce the higher positioning of men (Majumdar 1986a: 125; Burling 1997 [1963]: 233).

In addition to the land held by the House of the custodians of the *kusi* boulder, most villages have Houses that hold title to a smaller area of village land. The names of some of these minor title holders were also registered. In Sadolpara, of the twenty or more Houses that hold title to *a'king* land, three are mentioned in the ledgers kept by the GHADC. The other seventeen are not registered, which means that their title to land is entirely dependent on its mutual recognition among villagers.[9] In any village, the prime title holder of village land (and, at least historically, the custodian of the *kusi* boulder) is known as the *a'king nokma*, who is also the village head. The House of the village head, if he is a Songsarek, is always a custodian of a *kram* drum (in Sadolpara, he had two). Many of the minor landowning Houses keep, or used to keep, one or more *kram* drums as well. This was the case with Jiji's House, for example, which held custody over one *kram* drum. And since her House owned a very large area of land, Jiji also qualified as a (minor) *nokma*, at least according to the members of her own matrilineal group.[10] The land of Jiji's House is not registered with the GHADC, but her uncles, sons, and sons-in-law maintain that they know the exact location of each and every plot. So far, other villagers have never disputed their claims, but it is obvious that land rights that are not officially registered are vulnerable. No matter how willingly the village head may acknowledge such claims, the risk remains that they might not be upheld in GHADC court cases.

The creation of the land records, in the 1920s, fundamentally transformed the position of the village heads. Until then, a village head's authority would have depended primarily on his ability to ward off any intrusions upon village land, if necessary by means of violence. His role also required him to make sacrifices to the spirits for the benefit of the village as a whole (Burling 1997 [1963]: 295). In the past, if a village head was seen to fail to deliver in these respects, and thus as a leader, he could have been challenged. His most likely contender would have been a son-in-law who was more successful both in a political and a religious sense (Burling 1997 [1963]: 230). The registration of village heads (or, more accurately, village head couples) by the GHADC resulted in their position becoming one that was endorsed by the state. No longer exclusively dependent on the acknowledgement of the members of his matrilineal group, a village head's position came to require recognition from civil servants as well. Village heads are not the sole owners of the land registered with their House since that belongs to their matrilineal group as a whole (Majumdar 1986a: 125; Das 1990: 15). Yet with the bureaucratic registration of land rights, village heads acquired signatory powers that far exceeded the customary mandate they had borne hitherto. This also meant that a village head who failed to deliver, or failed to act in the interests of the (most influential) villagers, could no longer be ousted without the endorsement of the state. From that time on, therefore, it became essential for village heads to maintain good relations with the relevant civil servants, and (after the creation of the GHADC) their political bosses.

A'king land, the land which can be used for shifting cultivation, is the collective property of a matrilineal group. Houses subsidiary to a senior House that holds the land title have the right to use the land for shifting cultivation; a right that is also extended, albeit to a lesser degree, to other Houses within the same village. Shifting cultivation is done on fields that are cultivated for one or two years at a time and then abandoned to revert back to forest. Fields cannot be cultivated for more years at a time because the soil is too poor to continue to sustain crops' growth. Once fields have been abandoned, the land should ideally be left fallow for fifteen to twenty years if it is to fully recuperate (Roy 1981: 218). If *a'king* land is left undisturbed for such a period of time, the trees and shrubs that were cut in order to make a swidden can grow back, restoring the fertility of the soil. The long-term viability of shifting cultivation therefore depends on the availability of sufficient land to allow enough time to be left for the forest to regenerate in between cycles of cultivation.

Going by the available literature, as well as by what people told me based on their own experiences, it is evident that over the course of the previous century the duration of the fallow periods has been severely reduced throughout West Garo Hills.[11] Where at the beginning of the 20th century the fallow period is estimated to have indeed been around twenty to thirty years, by the 1970s it had been curtailed to an average of four to five years (Roy 1981: 217; Bhat 1988: 370). This was mainly due to population increase. Since the 1980s, the area of land available for shifting cultivation has gradually reduced further due to the increasing cultivation of cash crops in permanent orchards.[12] Continuing to do shifting agriculture with drastically shortened cycles of cultivation does 'damage the soil permanently' (Saha 1970: 220). Villages such as Sadolpara had relatively large amounts of land and substantial areas remained available for shifting cultivation. This may be an explanation for why people there have been so dedicated to sustaining the traditional Garo community religion, which cannot be practised without the swidden crops. These crops cannot be grown, according to Songsareks, if the rituals of the community religion are not conducted.

4.5 Landed Responsibilities and Religious Stature

Songsarek Houses that hold title to *a'king* land bear a greater responsibility to negotiate relationships with the spirits than that borne by landless Houses. This is most clearly manifested in the possibility for *a'king*-owning Houses to maintain one or more *kram* drums. Having a *kram* drum proves that a House holds title to *a'king* land. Housing a *kram* drum facilitates a privileged relationship with Risi that enables—and obliges—the drum's caretakers to take on a prominent role in the rituals that relate to the annual agricultural cycle of the swidden crops. These rights and obligations make maintaining a *kram* drum a costly enterprise, which is probably why some minor landowning Houses have never kept one. That would be out of the question for the custodians of the *kusi* boulder, however. For that House, the husband being the village head, maintaining at least one *kram* drum is mandatory.

I was told by senior men such as Biki and Oldap that a *kram* drum could only be acquired if the head of a House dreamed that the spirit Risi ordered him to obtain one, and this corroborates with Burling's account (Burling 1997 [1963]: 227). *Kram* drums are chiselled out of hardwood (preferably *gambari*), and can last for many generations. I was told that the chiselling is a man's job. Presumably, the danger of angering the spirit in the process is too great for women to risk it. With the gradual increase in the number of Christian converts and the concomitant decrease in the importance of the community religion, no new *kram* drums have been made for decades. In Sadolpara, a good number of *kram* drums are still maintained, but all of them were made a long time ago.

Due to its association with Risi, a *kram* drum is treated as though it were alive. Jiji once recounted how a House had acquired a new *kram* drum during her childhood. When it was ready, the drum had been brought into its new house. A turban was wrapped around its top end, and the man who brought it carried it tied on his back, like a baby. Jiji also told me how her sister had once borrowed her *kram* drum as well as the smaller *natik* drum that accompanies it, because she had needed them to perform a healing ritual. When the ritual was over, someone had brought back the *kram* drum, but forgotten the *natik*. That night, Risi had visited Jiji's sister in a dream. Risi looked like an ordinary woman, and wore a turban, as is typical among Songsareks. Risi had asked Jiji's sister where her child was, and told her she was missing it. Jiji herself had also seen Risi in her dreams, as had many other people.

An owner of a *kram* drum maintains a personal relationship with Risi, which creates a dedicated channel of communication that becomes crucially important if Risi causes illness. Given Risi's infamous craving for blood, she often bites people.[13] This results, as mentioned in section 4.3, in an illness called *sin'na-dinga*. The healing rituals that need to be performed to cure this vary according to the severity of the biting. Usually, the first attempt to entice Risi away from her victim is the performance of the Risi Denchokola ritual, which involves the sacrifice of a chicken. If this fails to achieve the desired effect, the more elaborate Risi Srenggata ritual needs to be performed, which includes the sacrifice of a goat. If the biting continues, that ritual should be followed up by an extended, day-long version of Risi Srenggata. In addition to another goat, a cow or a pig should then be provided as well. Any of these last two sacrifices require a *kram* drum to be taken to the House of the person who is ill. For this reason, any Songsarek House that does not have its own *kram* drum needs to be in a good relationship with a House that does, in order to be able to conduct such sacrifices in times of need. Houses of a single matrilineal group tend to relate to a single *kram* drum, and within that group the House of the *kram* drum owners is attributed the greatest seniority. With one *kram* drum per matrilineal group, historically at least, the ties that Houses maintained to the *kram* drum through which they engaged with Risi shaped their matrilineal group. *Kram* drums thus underpin the hierarchical relationships that are maintained among Houses. Being a 'tamer' of a *kram* drum both marks and upholds the position of a House as senior within its matrilineal group, providing physical evidence of its entitlement to land, and thus securing its high status.

Although Risi can pose danger to the inhabitants of a *kram* drum-owning House, since she can bite them for no apparent reason, the close relationship maintained with her through the *kram* drum also provides a certain degree of protection. Risi guards the property of *kram* drum owners: people explained to me that she would bite anyone who tried to steal from them. What is more, the site of a house in which a *kram* drum is kept becomes a 'strong house plot' (*nokkap raka*).[14] Even if the house is rebuilt at a different location, as any house may be from time to time, the particular plot continues to be associated with Risi. Should anyone else later attempt to build a house there, I was told, Risi would bite them. Risi is also said to pass on some of her powers to the owners of the *kram* drum, enabling them to control tigers, elephants, and other kinds of animals that are dangerous to people. Such abilities are most strongly attributed to the *a'king nokma*—perhaps because his House is the most prestigious anyway—and are represented in wood carvings depicting biting, stinging, and otherwise dangerous animals on the main crossbeam above the entrance to his home. A House that maintains a *kram* drum is also able to keep other rare potent objects, such as swords or gongs associated with particular spirits.[15] Finally, *kram* drum ownership also translates into judicial authority: any such House is entitled to have a thick Y-shaped pole (*tilta*) in front of it. During a kin trial, the accused can be tied to the pole, to prevent them escaping justice. This tying rarely happens nowadays, and I have never seen it done, but some of the poles remain standing as a reminder of the *kram* drum owners' right to settle disputes relating to their own matrilineal group, and to administer punishment if deemed necessary.

In addition, and probably more significantly, the social networks forged by affinity to a *kram* drum oblige the Houses associated with a *kram* drum-taming House to support the latter in the context of sacrificial rituals. This includes the obligation to help the *kram* drum-owning House when it needs to enact healing rituals for illnesses attributed to Risi, or when it needs to perform rituals in relation to the growth of the swidden crops (section 4.6). Furthermore, *kram* drum owners have to reaffirm their relationship with Risi each time they renew the roofing of their house. This is done by means of an extensive and costly celebration, Den'bilsia, which requires the slaughter of a goat, four to five cows or bulls, and five or six chickens. The *kram* drum owners bear the majority of the expenses, but subsidiary Houses have to contribute as well, by providing animals, rice beer, rice, and money.

As I have already mentioned, to be a tamer of Risi is not without risk. If a House that has a *kram* drum fails to provide sufficient offerings to Risi, the likelihood that she will bite its members increases. Risi is known to be not only unpredictable, but also to have an insatiable thirst for blood. Risi can cause illness in a House repeatedly, resulting in multiple deaths. The sacrificial animals required, time and again, if such illness occurs, can easily reduce a House to poverty. In desperation, or out of sheer anger, people may be driven to break or burn their *kram* drum in order to disempower a particular manifestation of Risi associated with it. This is extremely risky: destroying or burning a *kram* drum may anger Risi so much that she bites the persons responsible until they are driven insane or simply die.

I was told about a man, Jongan, who had destroyed his *kram* drums in the recent past. Jongan belonged to a prestigious House that maintained two *kram* drums. In a relatively short period of time, several members of the House died, and Risi was held responsible. Jongan made numerous expensive sacrifices to her, but all to no avail. When Jongan himself was killed by Risi, his wife's uncles and brothers decided to destroy both the *kram* drums. The drums were taken at night to Jongan's swidden and placed in the small hut that served as a place to take rest when working the fields. The men set the hut alight, and the drums were consumed by the fire. Oldap, who saw the fire at the time, commented: 'To get rid of them like this was the right thing to do.' To terminate the relationship with the particular manifestation of Risi associated with a *kram* drum, the drum must be destroyed intentionally. If it is simply left to rot, that relationship may continue to exist, I was told.

This burning of the drums by Jongan's relatives most probably took place sometime in the 1980s. Since then, with more and more people turning away from the traditional Garo community religion, the power of the spirits appears to have waned. In the early 2000s, one *kram* drum-owning House in Sadolpara was headed by a widow called Noab. The *a'king* land owned by the House was located in a neighbouring village (Megonggre), where Noab and her then husband Jing had originally lived. In addition to land, their *a'king* right also related to a deep pool (*wari*) in a river. The pool was known to be the seat of a spirit who controls the rains. Noab and her husband Jing were therefore responsible for maintaining a good relationship with that spirit, which meant they had to provide it with offerings annually: at the very least an egg or a chicken, but in times of erratic rainfall the spirit could demand a goat, a bull, or even a human being. On one occasion, people in Megonggre insisted that a bull should be offered to the spirit of the pool. When Noab and Jing refused to do so, they were told that if they didn't have a bull, they should 'give' a family member instead. Jing threatened them with a gun, saying, 'If you don't go away, I'll shoot you.' No cow, bull, or human life was lost, but the atmosphere in Megonggre remained tense, which ultimately led Noab and Jing to seek refuge in Sadolpara. They were able to do so because the Houses of Noab and of the village head of Sadolpara belonged to the same matrilineage. Jing died within a few years, but was not replaced, and Noab lived as a single widow. As long as she maintained custody over the pool, she was obliged to continue to provide offerings to its spirit every year. That was a burden for an aged woman living alone. Her matrilineal kin were initially reticent but eventually agreed to her request to abandon custody of the pool. By then, the perceived importance of the spirit had apparently diminished, and, as far as I know, no other House has come forward to become its custodian. The annual sacrifices are simply no longer conducted. Like the spirit of the deep pool, the powers attributed to Risi herself also appear to be waning. When Noap died in the early 2000s, her relatives did not want to keep the *kram* drum maintained by her House. But rather than deliberately burning her *kram* and *natik*, they simply let them rot inside Noap's abandoned house, which eventually collapsed with the drums inside it. In Jongan's story, Risi had evidently shown herself to be very aggressive, hence it had been decided that the drums would have to be burned ritually in order to end the relationship conclusively. It seems likely that the indirect destruction that was apparently sufficient for Noab's drums would have been considered too dangerous some decades ago, but nowadays—as fear of Risi wanes—has become an acceptable way to end a relationship with Risi without risking harmful consequences.

When the House of Jongan relinquished its *kram* drums, it also shed many of its former socio-religious responsibilities. Houses of its matrilineal group that had been dependent on its *kram* drums and the dedicated relationship with the particular manifestation of Risi that they had channelled, subsequently shifted their allegiance to other *kram* drum-owning Houses. The House of Jongan had been the second most senior House in the village, junior only to that of the *a'king nokma*. After it lost its *kram* drums and the corresponding religious responsibilities, it gradually lost that status. Other Houses gained precedence, which eventually resulted—at least for all practical matters—in a reinterpretation of the genealogical relationships traced between Houses. While relationships traced among Houses are perceived and described in terms of a genealogical model, their respective rankings are at least partly dependent on Houses' relative capacities to fulfil religious and social commitments—and the prestige, rights, and responsibilities that these bring. If a House fails to meet such religious commitments, the genealogical model recognized within a village becomes prone to adjustments that bring it in line with the prevailing configurations of power. While the examples above demonstrate this kind of flexibility in a Songsarek context, such modifications are also possible among Houses that no longer identify with the traditional Garo community religion. The main difference is that prestige and rights in non-Songsarek contexts are more or less directly associated with wealth and economic success.

If the owners of a *kram* drum get baptized, they have no choice but to destroy or abandon their drum. I have been told several stories about *kram* drums that were 'taken away' by missionaries, who reportedly either broke them or burned them. Some that were not completely destroyed have found their way into ethnographic museum collections.[16] Since entire matrilineal groups of Houses are associated with a single *kram* drum, the decision to convert is often taken by a whole group collectively. Doing so allows them to stay together in a religious, social, and even political sense. If a House from such a group that does not have its own drum chooses to remain with the community religion, its inhabitants are required to reshuffle their alliances to build a relationship with an alternative *kram* drum-owning House. Conversely, if some people from a group of Houses affiliated with a certain *kram* drum get baptized, and therefore stop contributing to the collective Songsarek sacrifices and celebrations, it becomes increasingly difficult for the *kram* drum-owning House to continue to fulfil its religious obligations. This means that people belonging to a group of Houses affiliated with a single *kram* drum either encourage each other to stay with the community religion, or, if there is a strong inclination to get baptized, to all do so at the same time.

4.6 Negotiating the Growth of the Crops

For Songsareks, cultivating swidden is inextricably linked to the spirits. Certain actions must be taken, and others avoided, to ensure that the fragile relationship between humans and spirits is sustained on favourable terms in order to secure a good harvest. Every year, new fields need to be made in the forest. Villagers know which House owns each and every patch of forest that can be used for shifting cultivation (*a'king* land), but that does not give the owners an exclusive right to use that land. Usage rights to *a'king* land are always vested with all the Houses that belong to the matrilineal group of the one that owns it. Moreover, albeit to a slightly lesser degree, these usage rights extend to all the inhabitants of a village.

The process of making a new field starts with laying claim to it. This 'claiming' (*kanga*) can only be done by married men, who each claim on behalf of the members of their House. As a woman, Jiji could not claim her own field; a son-in-law had to do so for her. Every year, the location for the new fields is chosen in a meeting called by the village head. Next, Songsareks need to seek an omen that will indicate what kind of harvest the spirits are likely to grant. One spring, I accompanied Chekjing (Jiji's eldest son) when he visited his prospective field. The land was covered by shrubs, and he used his sizeable Nepali-style knife (*kukuri*) to cut his way through them. He made a small clearing (*den'pata*) in the middle of his proposed new field, cutting down the brushwood that had grown there. Then he cut a stick of about a metre long, hammered it into the ground, and split its top end. He squeezed some bundled up leaves into the split, placed a few lumps of earth on top and murmured: 'This is for the *marang* (pollution). I have seen the land, give me a dream, show it to me in a dream!' ('*Ia marangna ia. Ha nia, jumangsi, jumang nik*').[17] Then he left the jungle. With this 'leaves in the split' (*samsepa*) invocation, he had requested an omen from the spirits. The omen is expected in a dream in the following night. The next morning, when I asked him whether he remembered what he had dreamt that night, he said: 'I saw . . . a white cow. . . . I just saw a white cow and I saw cotton-bearing fruit on the swidden.' ('*Nikjok, matchu gipokku nika anga. . . . Matchu gipokkuhan nika aro a'bacha kil nanganiko nikjok anga.*')[18] These images were part of a known repertoire: the cow and the cotton are familiar symbols in this context. Chekjing explained that if the dream shows a white cow, that is said to predict abundant cotton but a disappointing rice harvest. The dreams come with relatively few variations, the interpretations of which are fairly standardized. An earthen pot, new and empty, forecasts an overall meagre harvest. If the dream shows lots of fish, abundant rice and millet can be expected. A black cow indicates that the swidden will have more weeds than can be dealt with. If the dream shows a broad river that one can cross, the weeds will be manageable.

The content of the dream is expected to influence whether people actually cultivate the field they have claimed or not. I am not sure whether everyone attached that much importance to it, but in the days and weeks that followed the first day of claiming new fields, quite a few people reconsidered and ultimately made them at locations different from those initially selected. Chekjing changed his mind twice. He performed the same ritual at each prospective field. He finally settled on the third field, relinquishing his claims towards the first two fields. I regret that I forgot to ask him what he had dreamt in relation to the third field. Quite apart from the various omens, I am sure that other considerations played a role as well. It is important that the soil has a good capacity to retain moisture. Ideally, people want their fields to be located no further away than one hour on foot, and people normally prefer to make their fields on land owned by a House of their own matrilineage.

Fields for shifting cultivation are made on land in the jungle. In the weeks after the new fields have been claimed, the plots are cleared of shrubs and small trees. Large trees are spared, although all their branches are chopped off to ensure that they will not compete with the swidden crops for sunlight and water. When the first storm clouds gather in March at the start of the rainy season, the cut branches and leaves, which by then are dry as a bone, are set alight. Everyone who lives within the confines of a village does this together, irrespective of their religious orientation. Once lit, the fire rages, with flames shooting up ten to fifteen metres high. It is dangerous and difficult to control. Many glowing embers are airborne and people sit ready with buckets of water on the roofs of the houses nearest to the blaze to prevent any thatched roofs catching fire.

The fire is required to clear the new fields of all the dried up branches and leaves, and its ash fertilizes the ground in the process. Yet the violence of the fire, and the potentially lethal threat it poses, is also 'polluting' (*marang*). *Marang* is associated with violence, blood, and death. Sites of houses in which someone has died a 'bad' death, such as a mother who died in childbirth, are known to have *marang* (as mentioned in section 1.1). *Marang* is also associated with the putrefaction of the corpse. But *marang* is not only unavoidable, it is also a prerequisite of life.[19] *Marang* emerges in childbirth in the blood that flows, and in the afterbirth. It is also associated with war, the violence of which may be necessitated in order to defend oneself against a greater threat. And yet, objects or places that 'have' *marang* can cause death, so it is crucial to contain and purge it.[20] *Marang* is dangerous, contagious, and polluting, not only for the practitioners of the community religion but also for Christians.

The *marang* that the fire generates is purged in the morning following the burning of the new fields. According to the community religion, if this was not done, hill rice (*mi*) and other crops would not grow on the new swiddens. That day is known as A'galmaka (*a'gal*—blackened earth). At the break of dawn, the villagers go to their new fields. There, they offer an egg and chant a short invocation in order to remove the *marang*. Then they demarcate the boundaries of the new fields with tree branches, and scatter a mixture of seeds for crops such as millet, aubergine, pumpkin, white gourd, melon, and chillies. The part of A'galmaka that takes place in the fields is concluded with offerings of fish curry, cooked rice, and rice beer to the spirits Saljong[21] and Rokkimi, who are the ones credited with making the crops grow. Sitting next to the small altar that each family constructs in their field, people eat the rest of the rice and curry, and then leave for their homes (Figure 4.6). They may not return to the fields until A'galmaka has been concluded.

The celebration of A'galmaka continues in the village. In the days that follow, the practitioners of the community religion 'lead Saljong around' (Saljong *rodila*) by 'drinking rice beer from house to house' (*chu ringjola*). In Sadolpara, each of the three matrilineal groups organized their own round. Starting at the most senior House of the matrilineal group (the House that keeps the *kram* drum and holds the titles to *a'king* land), people gathered to drink rice beer provided by that House. Next, the other Houses of the group were visited, in order of seniority. Houses that owned a *kram* drum hosted the party twice, at the beginning and end of the drinking 'from house to house'.

The owners of each house that is visited place gongs on the floor of the main room. These are 'common' gongs that are not very valuable. Precious

Figure 4.6 On the morning of A'galmaka, a family has ritually cleansed their new field of *marang*, and is now preparing to have rice beer and food. At the right, the small altar at which they offered an egg.
Photograph: Erik de Maaker, 2001.

ones are not displayed during festivals nor are they ever shown except when they are offered as gifts at funerals (section 5.6). The men of a party that is going from house to house carry large wooden drums (*dama*).[22] Unless the House being visited is a *kram* drum-owning House, they also carry the *kram* drum that the House they are visiting relates to. Men sit in the main room of the house; women gather in the kitchen and on the rear veranda (Figure 4.7). Every now and then, for about five to ten minutes at a time, the men play the *dama* drums and the gongs in synchrony. When food is served to the guests, the hosts first offer curry, rice, and rice beer to the spirit Risi on the *kram* drum. People should not begin to eat or drink until the *kram* drum has been fed.

Rice beer is prepared in earthen vessels that are large enough to hold several kilograms of fermented rice. It takes several weeks to brew. To make the 'beer' (*chu*) drinkable, water is poured onto the fermented rice, producing a whitish draught. As the first rounds of water are added, the rice beer has substantial alcohol content and a strong taste, but it becomes gradually weaker in both senses as more and more water is poured over it. Hosts

Figure 4.7 Neighbours drinking rice beer together with Jiji's daughter Waljak (second from left) on the rear veranda of her house at A'galmaka. Plying one another with rice beer is an enjoyable way to strengthen social bonds.
Photograph: Erik de Maaker, 2001.

normally offer more than one vessel of rice beer, which are drunk one after the other. Since it can take anywhere between thirty minutes and two hours to empty a vessel, each visit to a single house can last several hours. The free-flowing alcohol loosens people up, which results in lively chatting and snappy wisecracks. The joking and jesting creates a relaxed atmosphere that allows people to experience each other as equals, challenging and defying everyday hierarchies and the tension these create. Often, hosts also provide tasty snacks, such as beef liver fried with salt and chillies. And hosts who want to be extra hospitable even serve their guests a full meal of rice and (preferably) beef curry. Once the rice beer stocks of one house have been exhausted, the group moves on to the next house. The party continues to move from house to house, until all houses that want to take part have been visited. Particularly at night, men and women sometimes dance to the rhythmic beat of the *dama* on the area of beaten ground near the house that is hosting the party at that moment.

I attended the A'galmaka celebrations in Sadolpara twice and on both occasions the 'drinking rice beer from house to house' (*chu ringjola*) continued without pause for four days and three nights.[23] At any time, the party comprised between twenty and forty people, mostly men. Some of them stayed with the party for just a couple of hours, others participated for twenty-four hours or more. Every now and then, additional people would join, or some who had been taking part for a while might leave. They either had other things to do or were too drunk and exhausted to continue. New people joined in when the party called at the houses of their close relatives, neighbours, and friends. Women also participated, although they generally spent less time with the group than men did. Christians were obviously never part of these celebrations, unless—as occasionally happened—they were in the process of reverting back to the community religion.

In the weeks following A'galmaka, people sow crops such as rice, maize, pulses, vegetables, and tubers on their swiddens, as well as cash crops such as cotton and ginger. From then on, frequent rain is needed if the seeds are to sprout. If it only rains intermittently, the seedlings wither in the hot sun. And even if a House has enough seed grains for a second sowing (which is often not the case), there may by then be insufficient time left for the plants to produce a good harvest. According to popular belief, at least among Songsareks, droughts occur if a spirit 'withholds' the rains. Such spirits are located in deep pools in rivers, and require annual offerings, which can be really demanding for the custodians of such pools (see section 4.5, for the struggles of Noab and Jing that such custodianship led to).

If there is sufficient rain, the weeds grow as fast as the crops that are being cultivated, and throughout the growth season villagers spend a major portion of their time weeding. A swidden yields many different crops and one of the last to be harvested is hill rice. Hill rice is highly valued for its unique flavour. For Songsareks, it is also the preferred food for use in rituals, and it is the kind of rice that should be given to the dead (Christians prefer to give paddy rice to the dead). The growth of hill rice is central to most of the agricultural rituals of the traditional Garo community religion. In some of the chants, hill rice is represented as a living being, sometimes a mother, while its harvest is referred to as a murder (Marak 2018: 11).[24] Hill rice grows on steep slopes, in relatively dry soil. Up until a couple of decades ago it was a good crop, which could be relied upon for a substantial harvest. In recent years, most probably due to the shortened fallow periods and resulting reduced fertility of the soil, yields have become almost negligible in terms of quantity—but not in significance.

According to the traditional Garo community religion, nobody should consume the harvest from the swiddens until the 'first fruits' have been offered to the spirits. Failing to adhere to this would 'go against *niam*', as I was told repeatedly, and this particular transgression can trigger deadly sanctions. For example, people might be bitten in their fields by venomous animals such as snakes, millipedes, tarantulas, or scorpions. Jiji's sister Meji told me how her daughter Sta had once, at a time when harvesting swidden crops was not yet allowed, picked sorrel from her swidden. Sorrel grows wild, including on swiddens, and is therefore not subject to the 'first fruit' related restrictions. But when Sta picked the leaves in her field, a small but lethally poisonous *gram* snake curled itself around her arm. That proved to be a warning since the snake did not bite. Meji surmised that the snake would have bitten Sta had she harvested any of the swidden crops that had been deliberately sown or planted. First fruits such as maize, white gourd, ginger, onion, tubers, and rice need to be offered to the spirits by custodians of *kram* drums in a series of religious ceremonies.

The village head has explicit ritual responsibilities with respect to the germination, growth, and carrying of hill rice. Biki told me that the ancestors had obtained the first rice from the spirit Saljong. Two sisters, Sisi *mikgri* ('blind Sisi') and Balmi *ja'gri* ('lame Balmi') had run out of food. They were starving. In desperation, they burned the resin of a pine tree inside their house. The strong smell attracted the spirit Saljong. He came into their house and gave them the first rice seed grains. They would never have to go hungry ever again, because they would always be able to produce more rice by sowing the seed. Saljong told them to burn resin every year after harvesting their swidden rice. He promised that if they did this, he would renew his gift. This myth is at the core of the annual celebrations that mark Wangala, which is by far the most extensive religious festival of the community religion.

Wangala is held at the time of transition from the wet season to the dry season, by the end of September or early October. Each village head fixes his own date for the festival, which makes it possible for Wangala to be celebrated on different dates in neighbouring villages. In principle, Wangala is a festival that anyone from 'outside' should be able to attend. Historically, this would have been confined to neighbouring villages. More recently, with increased communication facilitated by the extension of mobile phone networks to rural West Garo Hills, it has become fairly common for at least some people from Tura to attend Wangala in Sadolpara. Garo ethnic activists in particular, as well as other people with an interest in Garo traditions, are keen to experience Wangala (and drink rice beer, although that is formally a sin for Christians). Sometimes even an entire coachload of college students arrives to join the celebrations. Christians from the village itself do not actively take part in any of the celebrations. As the number of Songsarek Houses continues to diminish with ever more religious conversions, this inevitably places a strain on the remaining Songsareks, who are left to prepare all the rice beer and provide all the food required for hosting.[25]

In the early 2000s, the Wangala celebrations I attended in Sadolpara were inaugurated with offerings made to the spirits in the last remaining bachelors' house. The building was no longer lived in but was kept for these kinds of ceremonies. The next day, early in the morning, groups of five to eight Houses each slaughtered a bull or cow that they had bought together and fattened in the preceding weeks. Custodians of *kram* drums offered some of the cow's blood to Risi on their drums, as well as to the other spirits in their houses, for whom they smeared the blood onto the interior crossbeams and pillars. Everyone, whether they had a *kram* drum or not, decorated the insides of their houses with a white paste made from rice powder (*wanchi*) and water. Some people told me that this was done because the rice powder was 'eaten by the spirits', but others said it just showed that 'everyone is happy'.

That same day, the main Wangala celebrations were conducted by the village head. In Sadolpara, he lived in a huge house that could accommodate a large number of people. As for most Songsarek celebrations, dozens of men gathered in the main room, where gongs and drums had been placed. The women gathered in the kitchen part of the house and on the rear veranda. Malsin, an old man who classified as a son-in-law of the village head, started the ceremony. He made an offering to the spirits at the pillar (*manjri pillar*) that stands at the front of the main room. There, he gave white gourd, ginger, onion, and tubers to the spirits: first fruits that could not yet be eaten by humans. As the men rhythmically pounded *dama* drums and beat gongs, creating a deafening sound, Malsin then offered some freshwater crabs[26] at the pillar. Pouring rice beer over them, he chanted:

> Saljong ...
> To the father of millet
> To the good Saljong
> For all the months of the year
> For all seasons
> Making a promise
> Sworn at the smoke
> Till the cotton tree buds like charcoal
> Till the *mandal* tree blooms
> Making a promise
> Sworn at the smoke
> Saljong ...[27]
> Saljong ...
> Appa Misina
> Nama Saljongna
> Ja'bilsinaha
> Ja'karinaha
> Ku'manchietonga
> Wal'du kaetonga
> Bolchu anggal su'una
> Mandar tekkauna
> Ku'manchietonga
> Wal'du kaonga
> Saljong ...

Pine resin burned ('burning *sa'sat'*—*sasatsu'a*) on glowing charcoal produced a dense white smoke. I was told that the smoke provides a good omen if it rises in a single column to the roof of the house, moving from there along the ridgepole towards the rear of the main room, then returning along the same ridgepole to the front of the room. This shows that next year the spirit Saljong will once again be willing to give rice and other crops and that next year's harvest will be abundant. By burning the resin, the village head fulfils the promise he had made during last year's Wangala festival. In the chant, Saljong is promised ('sworn at the smoke') that if he makes the crops yield in the year to come, the resin will be burned again at next year's Wangala. The year I attended the ceremony, the smoke behaved approximately as desired, but not entirely, producing a somewhat ambiguous omen. While people observed the omen with interest, they did not seem too concerned about it. The ceremonies were observed, but I did not get the impression that anybody seemed to believe Saljong was the only force responsible for crop growth.

Once the resin had been burned, as the ceremony came to its climax, people began to dance inside the house. Then, one after another, men and women came out of the house ('coming out one by one', '*jol onkata*'), onto the area of beaten earth in front of it. There, they danced the beginning of life, the story of creation. Malsin led the dance, holding leaves in front of him that had the burning charcoal, and chanting the story of creation (*dani*) (section 4.3). As they danced, the men cast large amounts of cooked rice onto the ground, presumably to feed the spirits. Women mocked the men by playfully pushing at the turbans of those playing the *dama* drums, so that the men's hair came loose.

These celebrations were repeated, although much less extensively, in many of the houses that had *kram* drums. Only the House of the village head had the right to burn the resin. The chanting of the *dani*, and the dancing out of the house onto the ground in front of it, however, also took place at Houses that were attributed slightly less seniority. All *kram* drum-owning Houses, such as Jiji's, offered the first fruits and the freshwater crabs, but the Houses affiliated to them could not do so. People of affiliated Houses were expected to support the ones in which the more extensive rituals were performed by supplying food as well as by participating in the rituals.

The unequal distribution of ritual responsibilities reflected and reinforced the hierarchical relationships between Houses, and—at least historically—the ritual tasks that Houses took on, or perhaps gave up, seem to have been accompanied by corresponding reinterpretations and modifications of inter-House relationships. This would have played out in much the same way as maintaining or abandoning a *kram* drum did, as discussed in section 4.5. For the custodians of *kram* drums, the performance of these kinds of rituals validated their status as landowning Houses, senior to those of their affiliates. Now, with ever more people converting to Christianity, the impact that shedding ritual responsibilities has on the relationships traced between Houses is decreasing. Nevertheless, followers of the community religion continue to attribute great importance to the rituals and celebrations, not only for their religious content, but also for the feasting and extensive sociality associated with occasions like Wangala.

Returning to my personal experiences of Wangala: Over the next couple of days, up to a week, Sadolpara's Songsareks visited each and every house participating in the celebrations to drink rice beer, joke and laugh, and play the *dama* drums and gongs. Their movements followed a pattern roughly similar to that of A'galmaka, or any of the other major religious festivals. But what distinguishes Wangala is that, unlike during other annual religious celebrations, visitors from neighbouring villages and 'outsiders' more generally are welcome to join. This provides unmarried men and women who live in different villages with an opportunity to meet, dance, drink, chat, and more, which makes the festival a worthy prelude to the marriages that will be conducted during the 'marriage season' in the months that follow. Marriages are preferably arranged during the dry and cool season, which lasts from October to March. During these months, there is little work to be done in the fields, and it is relatively easy to travel along the dry paths and roads. After the main harvests, people also have more abundant food stocks and cash than during the wet season, so it is a good time to host guests.

Although Christian Garo do not perform the rituals of the traditional Garo community religion, they do celebrate Wangala—albeit in new contexts and in a rather different format, which is by and large disassociated from the community religion. Since 1976, the large-scale 'Hundred Drums Wangala' festival has been celebrated annually (except for a few years when it could not take place due to lack of funds). 'Hundred Drums Wangala' was initiated by influential Garo from Tura, all of whom belonged to the educated Christian elite. The motivation for creating the festival is explained in a brochure produced in 1993: 'In the face of modern civilisation, due to the impact of foreign cultures, the good-old customs and practices of the Garos can be seen on disappearing trends and (are) not without the risk of vanishing away from the society. . . . it is high time to preserve and promote the cultural heritages like the Wangala festivals and thereby to keep alive the cultural identity of the Garos' (Marak 1993: 1).

The annual 'Hundred Drums Wangala' festival brings crowds of people together from towns and villages, and over the years, it has gained recognition as a kind of Garo 'national' celebration (de Maaker 2013b). The festival's key event is a competition between ten dance troupes, each of which is made up of more than twenty members, with roughly equal numbers of men and women. The men carry and play *dama* drums. With each of the competing groups bringing at least ten drums, the festival mobilizes (at least) a hundred *dama* drums, hence its name 'Hundred Drums Wangala'. The dance troupes may be made up of villagers, or of students from one of the colleges. Despite the students' best efforts, the trophy tends to go to one of the villagers' groups, who 'know the rhythms best', as I once heard a judge remark. Sadolpara's dance troupe has been very successful over the years, and has won the first prize several times.

The 'Hundred Drums Wangala' festival is organized with financial and practical support from the Meghalaya state government. The festival is typically opened by Meghalaya's governor (so far always a non-Garo), who wears a turban with cock's tail feathers for the occasion. This is the archetypal headdress of (Songsarek) Garo Wangala celebrants and all the dancers at 'Hundred Drums Wangala' are dressed in the traditional attire of practitioners of the Garo community religion. The 'Hundred Drums Wangala' is well publicized and promoted by the Meghalaya Tourism Department, and each year it attracts tourists and journalists from elsewhere in India, and from across the world. In many respects, the festival is like a smaller version of the much more renowned but more recently initiated 'Hornbill Festival' that showcases 'Naga culture' (Kikon 2005). Hornbill has been celebrated annually since the year 2000 in Dimapur (Nagaland).

In line with the tendency to essentialize 'tribal' culture that often prevails in South Asia, Wangala has received recognition as a hallmark of Garoness in multiple ways. As mentioned in section 2.5, the day that 'Hundred Drums Wangala' is celebrated is an official holiday in the state of Meghalaya, which means that government offices, schools, and banks across the entire state (in which the Garo are a minority community) are closed. In addition, Wangala-style dance performances are often staged as cultural entertainment at functions organized by the state administration on other occasions as well as at political rallies. And as I have discussed elsewhere, Garo Wangala has made it onto India's national stage at least twice: when it was included in the cultural programme of the 2008 New Delhi Republic Day parade and when Wangala drummers participated in music composer A.R. Rahman's performance in the opening ceremony of the 2010 Commonwealth Games (de Maaker 2013b). On both occasions, the troupe included dancers from Sadolpara, who, as noted above, are rated among the best Wangala dancers and drummers.

The need to appease the spirits of the community religion in order to secure the growth of the swidden crops is not felt by Christian Garo. On the contrary, Christian priests make a point of insisting that converts publicly break taboos relating to the spirits of the community religion. If such acts do not trigger sanctions, that can be taken as evidence that the taboo was either unfounded, or (as the priests are more likely to argue) that the Christian divinities the convert now 'obeys' are more powerful than the spirits of the community religion. Particularly in the latter interpretation, breaking taboos becomes a way to put one's religious loyalty publicly to the test and to attempt to convince others (and oneself) that one has made the right choices. This is a proven missionary strategy, which is used by proselytizing movements the world over. Duncan, in his analysis of the conversion strategy adopted by the New Tribes Mission among the Forest Tobelo of Halmahera (Indonesia), notes that 'the consistent violation of taboos . . . without any repercussion' contributed significantly to the Mission's presentation of Christianity as a superior faith (Duncan 2003: 312). In Sadolpara, Christians made a point of harvesting and eating white gourd before Wangala, going against the dictates of the community religion. I remember Ratmi, Jiji's youngest daughter, who had by then been baptized, proudly telling me that she could now eat white gourd before Wangala since she was 'no longer afraid of the spirits'.

In rural West Garo Hills, Christians do acknowledge the cultural relevance of the annual agricultural festivals, but they do not normally take part in them. Even their participation in A'galmaka is limited to the sowing of the first seeds on the morning after the fields have been burned. After all, the festivals all involve rice beer, the drinking of which is more or less unavoidable if not compulsory for those celebrating. As mentioned already, the consumption of rice beer is taboo for Christian Garo. Even though Roman Catholics are more lenient in this respect, they generally also refrain from active participation in the 'drinking from house to house'. Consequently, as less and less Houses follow the community religion, the number of people who take part in collective festivals is also decreasing. Crowds on such occasions are gradually becoming thinner, and older—it is the youth who are generally the first to convert.

Garo Christians have carried some of the elements of Wangala over into the way they celebrate Christmas. Throughout Garo Hills, Christmas has become the most important annual religious festival, and it is celebrated lavishly. In West Garo Hills, in villages as well as in towns, a number of Christian Houses join forces to buy a bull or pig some weeks before Christmas, as they would in preparation for Wangala. The animal is fattened and then slaughtered on Christmas day, producing plenty of meat for several days. In addition to attending church services, on Christmas Day a meal is cooked and shared among the Houses that bought an animal together. Celebrations also include extensive visits to neighbours and friends, where tea is served with fried doughnuts made from glutinous rice (*pita*). At night there is dancing, to the rhythm of a large drum (*drim*) and a harmonium. Christians are not allowed to play traditional Garo drums because of their association with the spirits of the community religion.

Although Songsareks consider the spirits omnipresent, in practice there appear to be certain realms that they have no impact upon. Significantly, the spirits are not seen to influence crops that are not grown through shifting cultivation. In addition to swidden, many Songsarek Houses also have at least some 'level' fields that they use to cultivate paddy rice (wet rice). Paddy rice, grown in small valleys between hills, brings a much higher yield than swidden rice. It can therefore be very important as a subsistence crop. Yet as far as the community religion is concerned, paddy cultivation is not 'regulated' by any ritual mechanisms: no practices are required 'to awaken' the seeds, nor do any stipulations dictate how and when the harvest may be consumed. As Jiji's sister Meji explained, this is because wet (paddy) rice does not derive from Saljong. 'He doesn't 'give' it', she told me. Paddy rice is thus not conceptualized by Songsareks as a living entity, the 'life' of which can be 'taken' away, as hill rice is. Majumdar notes that paddy rice was not cultivated in the upland areas of West Garo Hills until the 1950s or 1960s (Majumdar 1978: 23). As a relatively recent addition to the economic repertoire, its cultivation never became incorporated into the community religion, which by then was probably already starting to lose its former pre-eminence. Nor are the spirits credited with 'giving' the fruits of orchard crops such as areca nut or cashew. With ever larger sections of village land getting taken over by such orchards, people are dedicating more and more time to caring for their trees. Because paddy rice and orchard crops grow and produce without their cultivators needing to maintain good relationships with the spirits, Songsareks' religious practices are gradually losing their economic relevance, even for Songsareks themselves.

In a rather general sense, Christian Garo attribute the rains and the growth of crops to God or Jesus, and—perhaps in return—many offer a share of their paddy yield to their church, once a year after its harvest. This share is referred to as a 'gift' (*dan*) to God and the quantity given is not fixed but varies from House to House. Churches sell the rice that they receive and use the proceeds to finance the large-scale celebrations they hold at Christmas, Easter, and on other occasions.

These days, despite becoming more and more economically dependent on crops that do not derive from the spirits, Songsareks continue to value the communal celebrations linked to the annual cycle of shifting cultivation.

Perhaps this testifies to the importance that people attribute to the social aspects of the festivals. Going by my own observations, Christians like to drink tea, but they don't enjoy it in a way that is even remotely comparable to the pleasure Songsareks express when having rice beer. And whereas rice beer drinking can go on for hours, as long as sufficient vessels are available, drinking tea rarely sustains more than a few rounds. As mentioned before, the consumption of factory-produced distillates is acceptable to most Christians, but they are expensive, and they cause a much more rapid and violent sort of intoxication. Conversion to Christianity means relinquishing celebrations fuelled by rice beer, which may partly explain the determination of the remaining Songsareks to stay with the community religion as long as that is even remotely viable.

At a different level, the celebrations related to the growth of the swidden crops link relationships to land with inter-House relationships. For instance, they provide opportunities for *kram* drum-owning Houses like Jiji's to emphasize their ownership of *a'king* land, which is essential when the titles have not been registered with the GHADC, as the members of Jiji's matrilineal group are painfully aware. In other words, offerings and celebrations in relation to the spirits also retain their relevance because they facilitate the assertion of social positionings through religious, political, and economic responsibilities. Thus, even if the religious dimension has lost some its former hold in terms of beliefs or cosmology, it continues to legitimize and support claims in the political and economic sphere. Such claims underlie hierarchical relationships among Houses. Agricultural ceremonies provide occasions for such relationships to be expressed, but it is at funerals that they prove most open to negotiation and redefinition, as the following chapter will show.

5
Engaging the Dead

5.1 The Religiosity of Funerals

In rural West Garo Hills, news of any death spreads quickly. Close relatives of a deceased person inform the people who they believe should attend the funeral by calling them on their mobile phones or by sending someone as a messenger. If the deceased person was elderly or belonged to a politically and economically influential House, the news is likely to travel far, and dozens if not hundreds of people will attend the funeral. The funeral of an infant, by contrast, may draw just the closest kin.

People who decide to attend a funeral abandon their work for the day more or less immediately to go over to the village ward and the house in which the dead person is kept in state. They bring gifts for the person who has died, which also serve to 'help' her or his close relatives. Everyone who attends a funeral needs to be given food, and the most appreciated and appropriate meal on such an occasion is beef curry with rice. Depending on the number of people attending, huge quantities of meat and rice may be required. Since no single House can provide such amounts, to host a large-scale funeral the close relatives of the deceased person need the support of their guests. The more cows, bulls, and rice the hosts receive, the more lavish the meals they can provide, and the more prestige is earned by the House in which the death occurred as well as those that are closely related to it.

In rural West Garo Hills, Garo funerary rituals are conducted according to either a Songsarek or Christian protocol. The character of a funeral depends on the religious positioning of the person who died, as well as on that of their closest kin. Songsareks are unable to take part in most of the rituals performed at a Christian funeral, and Christians can only participate to a limited extent at Songsarek funerals. For instance, at a Songsarek funeral women cook a meal for the ghosts, but Christians cannot do so. Likewise, at a Christian funeral, Songsareks do not pray alongside Christians for the deceased person. These conventions do not prevent people from attending funerals conducted according to the protocol of a religion other than their own, which indicates that the obligation to honour social relationships takes priority over any such differences. Irrespective of whether they are Songsareks or Christians, funeral guests bring gifts for the deceased person and take part in the extensive socializing that makes up a significant part of any funeral.

Christians cannot lead a Songsarek funeral. If the children of Songsareks have become Christians, the children are unable to arrange their parents' funerals. This situation is not uncommon, and I have experienced several occasions when elderly Songsareks were encouraged to convert when their death was imminent. This was what happened, for instance, a few weeks prior to Nangseng's death. Nangseng proudly upheld a strong reputation for his stamina in drinking rice beer, and he was also revered for being skilled and knowledgeable concerning the traditional Garo community religion. But during his lifetime, his two daughters and two sons had become Baptists, and just weeks before his death Nangseng himself got baptized. Jengda, his wife, did the same. Nangseng was severely ill at the time, unlikely to live for more than two weeks, yet it was imperative that their marriage was registered under Baptist law. Otherwise, according to the Baptist tenets, they would have lived together in sin.

Songsareks and Christians in rural West Garo Hills tend to consider their respective ritual practices to be mutually incompatible. Songsareks are preoccupied with all the guidelines, restrictions, and prohibitions that regulate practices in order to maintain good relationships with the spirits. Christians do not acknowledge the spirits, but instead relate to the Christian divinities and revere the absolute truth of the Bible. Yet while Songsareks' and Christians' explanations differ regarding who or what 'gives' life or causes death, they all share the assumption that, upon birth, people are infused with a soul, which leaves their body when they die. Hence, irrespective of religion, all Garo funerals have many features in common. Whether Christian or Songsarek, funerals are about the dead, and it is in relation to the dead that people position themselves in relational terms, either as matrilineal kin or as affines. Due to the moiety division among Garo, this binary applies to any Garo person who attends a Garo funeral, even if their relationship to the deceased is far too distant to be 'traceable'. This positioning is critical, because if a person who has died was married with the consent of his or her matrilineal kin, and is leaving behind a widow or widower, then their matrilineal kin needs to arrange a replacement for them—or, at very least, they should state their intention to do so.

5.2 Souls and Their Wanderings

Jiji became frail in her old age and regularly suffered prolonged periods of illness. For days or weeks at a time she would be down with 'body ache' (*be'en sadika*), frequently in combination with 'hot-cold' (*sin'na-dinga*). During these periods of illness, she did not move about but stayed at home. If she did not feel like eating or drinking she simply did not do so, and the people who looked after her never insisted that she should. The treatment provided by her close kin aimed to first identify the spirits responsible for her illness, and then to perform the sacrificial rituals required to stop the spirits' biting. In addition, every now and then relatives and friends brought her herbal medicine, which consisted of rather expensive herbal pastes and powders prepared by specialized healers (*sam A'chik*, see section 2.2). Equally popular, at least among Jiji's friends and relatives, and often cheaper, were the medicines that people bought for her from itinerant vendors at the weekly market. Such salesmen (I have never seen a woman in this role) were referred to as 'doctors of the market' (*bazalni doctol*) and suggested appropriate medicines based on the rather unspecific descriptions of symptoms recounted by their customers, individually tailored to their available budget.[1]

Jiji patiently underwent the sacrificial rituals, accepted the herbal compresses, and swallowed the biomedical pills and capsules that people bought for her. In my observation, she experienced illness primarily as something that had to be 'waited out' and she appeared rather resigned towards any of the remedies. As long as she felt ill, she did not leave her house. Jiji was a very strong woman. More than once, when people apparently began anticipating her impending death, she veered back to life. People realized that she was on the mend when she once again became grumpy and impatient with her next of kin, cracking impertinent jokes that made people burst out laughing.

Death, as conceptualized among Songsareks, is what happens when one's soul (*janggi*) is abducted by one's deceased predecessors. Once, when Jiji had been severely weakened by weeks of fever and stomach pains, she told me that in her dreams the ghosts (*mi'mang*) of her deceased relatives had gathered, ready to take her to the afterworld. In her dreams, the ghosts had appeared as ordinary people, although she said that in earlier dreams she had seen them as putrid corpses. Some of the ghosts were familiar to her, while others were unknown. Ghosts try to encircle a person who is ill and weak, to take hold of them in a manner similar to the abductions that are common in the context of Songsarek marriages (section 3.3). The passage from the world of the living to the world of the dead is thus undertaken in a manner that is comparable to the transfer of a spouse upon marriage. In both cases, it is preferable for people to be abducted. This suggests, in a normative sense, that the agency determining the transfer rests with the relatives, rather than with the person concerned. The ghosts are threatening, but Jiji said that if one manages to get hold of a broom, a drinking gourd, or a rice cooking stick, the utensil can be used to chase them away. In addition, if somewhat at odds with the chasing strategy, she told me that one should not argue with the ghosts or attempt to ward them off, but instead keep still, uttering 'Hmmmmmm'—perhaps so as to avoid communicating or cooperating with them.

Both Songsareks and Christians in rural West Garo Hills assume that a person consists of a physical body (*bimang* or *mang*) and an immaterial soul (*janggi*). A man named Bimsing elaborated: 'The soul is invisible. It is like wind. That is why it is often called *baljanggi*.' *Balwa* means both 'wind' and 'breath'. As long as people breathe, their soul is connected to their body, hence they are alive. When someone stops breathing, the soul ceases to bond with the body and transforms into a ghost (*mi'mang*). Strong gusts of wind and gales are therefore dangerous since they can take someone's breath along with them, leaving the person dead. According to Songsareks, strong winds are associated with certain spirits but can also represent the ancestors.

Like a soul, a ghost is usually invisible. Yet, as is evident from Jiji's account above, ghosts are sometimes seen in dreams. Ghosts are associated with corpses, with bones left over after cremation and more generally with any material objects associated with the dead. Quite a few people told me that they had heard ghosts talking and rummaging around in the graveyard at night. Christians bury their dead, and in the last few decades that has become common among Songsareks as well. Despite being invisible, ghosts can leave traces that can be seen and smelled. Songsareks offer food to the dead at funerals, as well as in the weeks, months, and years that follow. Meji told me that if a ghost touches cooked rice, the rice turns black. Similarly, uncooked rice touched by a ghost becomes slimy. Rice beer turns sour.[2] The rot and decay of food touched by ghosts suggests that they continue to be associated with putrefaction even after becoming separated from their own corpses.

Songsareks say that ghosts dwell in an afterworld named Balpakram. People I spoke to in rural West Garo Hills did not seem to locate this afterworld on Earth, even though there is a tableland called Balpakram in the distant south-eastern part of Garo Hills. The tableland cannot be seen from West Garo Hills, and none of the Songsareks I spoke to had ever travelled anywhere near it. The ghosts' Balpakram is a shared imaginary that nobody can state anything about with certainty. Some of the more authoritative accounts derived from people who had travelled to Balpakram in their dreams but had managed to return to wake up alive (see also E.C. Sangma 1984: 181–182). Based on such accounts, and on other stories that have been passed down, most people assume that the afterworld closely resembles the world of the living. The entrance to Balpakram is guarded by Bang-Nawang, an ogre-like spirit who threatens to devour the ghosts who try to pass, as described in the lament chanted by 'mothers' (*grapmangtata*) who sit with the corpse when it is laid out.[3] The ghost can distract Bang-Nawang by throwing into his mouth some of the metal earrings that Songsareks wear, or some of the coins that are placed on the corpse when it is kept in state (section 5.4). All ghosts come prepared with these items, and, I was told, none of them are ever swallowed by the spirit. In Balpakram, ghosts need to work swidden in order to survive. They have to work 'just as hard as those who are alive', as Jiji's daughter Ratmi once explained to me, when she had not yet been baptized.

Far more intimidating visions of Balpakram also circulated in Sadolpara, largely thanks to the efforts of Christian preachers like Father Theodore in the early 2000s. Father Theodore, who had come from Kerala in South India, was a regular visitor to Sadolpara during the early stages of my fieldwork and was eager to win new converts. Fuelling villagers' uncertainties and fears about death, he declared that 'there is nothing' in Balpakram. According to him, it was a place of 'hunger and drought' where ghosts were doomed to 'wander forever'. With proselytizing zeal, he contrasted the desolate state of such ghosts with the far more attractive—in his eyes—fate of Christians who could look forward to life after death in heaven, 'next to Lord Jesus'. Father Theodore was not alone; it was common practice among Christian preachers to equate Balpakram with hell, a place where the dead were doomed to 'burn' forever (as mentioned in section 2.2).

Going by what people like Jiji told me, as well as by what the death rituals imply, a Songsarek who dies is guided by their own deceased relatives to Balpakram. Funeral attendees therefore bring cooked food for these ghosts, as well as for the deceased person, who continues to receive such offerings at regular intervals. People also give seed grains and water storage gourds to the deceased person to equip them for their existence in the afterworld. As already mentioned, this existence is remarkably similar to that of the living, as Jiji's younger sister Meji explained: 'As a ghost, one is born in Balpakram, in the House of one's mother. There, one grows up, marries, and has children.' Someone else confirmed: 'A man is reborn in the House of a mother.' These remarks indicate a perceived continuity: after death, souls remain associated with the same matrilineal group as before, which means that matrilineal groups encompass both the living and the dead. A ghost is not only likely to be born into the same matrilineal group as that in which it had lived on Earth, it even retains its former personal identity and gender. Marriages among the living, it seems, can be reunited after death. For example, Meji's husband Wantsang died many years before she did. Meji assumed that he had since been born in the afterworld, grown up, and married. She did not mind about that marriage, since 'A man should not live alone.' Yet she also made it clear to me that after her own death, she expected to marry him once again. These remarks all indicate that the afterworld is expected to resemble that of the living to such an extent that the Houses on which people depend in the 'real' world are equally important in the afterworld.

Ghosts are personifications of deceased persons, but as personalities they lack individual desires, longings, or preferences. At least, that was the general assumption that emerged in conversations, but people also expressed a great deal of uncertainty about it. With the rare exception of people who have visited Balpakram in dreams and woken up alive, no one 'knows' or 'has seen' what awaits them after death, as people readily remark. It is not known how long ghosts remain in the afterworld, but Songsarek eschatology suggests that eventually all ghosts are reborn among the living. By then, the souls that are reincarnated seem to have become anonymous and cannot normally be linked to identities from previous lives. Even so, people can suffer misfortune related to transgressions committed by their soul in a former embodiment.[4] While it is said to be possible for a ghost to be reincarnated as an animal such as a pig or a tarantula, most ghosts are reborn as humans. Jiji told me: 'When a child begins to move inside the womb, a ghost dies in Balpakram.' This ghost that 'dies' is then transformed into a soul. When the soul attaches itself to the foetus, the foetus gets the hiccups. This indicates that the soul is bonding with the infant, which happens weeks if not months before it is born. Ideas vary about how this entrance or bonding of the soul takes place; another woman told me that it first enters the baby at birth, 'like the wind', inciting it to start breathing.

Whereas Songsarek interpretations of death emphasize the circulation of souls, Christians proceed from the assumption that death results in the permanent relocation of the dead in heaven and thus their departure from society. Christian and Songsarek perspectives might seem incompatible in this sense, but in practice Christians continue to acknowledge the presence of the dead among the living in many ways. One example of this is the popularity of the annual celebration of All Souls among Garo Catholics, which provides a dedicated occasion for people to be with and connect to their dead (*The Shillong Times* 2017). And even though the dead are not reincarnated according to Christian eschatology, they continue to substantiate matrilineal relatedness, as will be shown below. Ideas and practices derived from the realm of the traditional Garo community religion thus continue to shape the ways Garo Christians deal with death and the dead, even if, for them, heaven has replaced Balpakram.

5.3 Anticipating Death

In rural West Garo Hills, people are not shy to anticipate the death of elderly persons. On the contrary, in the time I spent there, jokes about impending death typically generated a great deal of laughter. More formally, deaths could even be pre-emptively announced, as in the 'washing the sling' (*debra su'gala*) ritual that Songsarek Garo, as adults, sometimes performed in honour of their ageing mothers. This pre-death ceremony is never held for men. A sling (*debra*) is a piece of cloth the size of a large shawl, in which infants are carried from the time the umbilical cord drops until they reach about three or four years of age. With its arms and legs spreadeagled, the child's chest is in constant contact with the back of the person carrying it. For the child and the parent, the bodily contact is reassuring, and a child tied in a sling rarely cries. Although men also frequently carry their children in slings, as do older siblings, 'washing the sling' is a way of explicitly acknowledging motherhood.

The person who arranges a 'washing the sling' ceremony gives their mother a new sling.[5] After her subsequent death, this new sling (as well as others she had received previously) will be given to her relatives who qualify as close 'mothers'. Each of them will then wear the sling that they receive tied over their left shoulder. This means that when they return home after the funeral, they are able to carry the ghost of the deceased woman with them. By contrast, when a baby is carried in a sling, the sling is always tied over the right shoulder. The pre-death ritual of 'washing the sling' thus anticipates the eventual reconnection of the deceased woman's soul to the Houses of its 'mothers'. Analogous pre-death funerary rituals in Japan, according to Suzuki, bring elderly persons and their kin together for a social event that is similar to a funeral but allows for the (living) participation of the person celebrated (Suzuki 2013: 102). In the Garo context, the sling ritual provides the one who is soon to die with a tangible link to the matrilineal group, explicitly inviting her to remain part of the group. Christian Garo do not formally acknowledge the reconnection of the ghost after death and therefore do not perform 'washing the sling.'

A person who performs 'washing the sling' has to provide a bull for slaughter,[6] which is expensive, but also brings a great deal of 'good honour' (*rasong nama*). Senjak invited me to attend when she conducted 'washing the sling' for her mother Sisi, who was one of the oldest women in Sadolpara at the time. Over the years, Sisi had lost much of her ability to engage in life. She had stopped working the fields and could no longer earn her own livelihood. She had lost her eyesight, her hearing, and her mobility, and had all but stopped eating. Except for a couple of hours a day, when she would warm herself in the sun, she spent her days inside, mostly sleeping.

Sisi's House derived some of its prestige from being closely affiliated with that of the village head. Yet her House had been newly established at the time of her first marriage, and the prestige that it had accrued was mainly thanks to Sisi herself and her two successive husbands. Sisi's current husband Dising, who was several years younger than she was, had worked for many years as a dealer of the subsidized rice that is sold through the Public Distribution System to low-income families (he had a 'fair price shop'). This can be a profitable business, and it had made him into an important and influential person. Even more significantly, he acted as a middleman for politicians seeking support in their election campaigns (see also section 7.1). But like Sisi, Dising no longer worked. He was suffering from tuberculosis. No longer able to provide for themselves, for years the couple had been living on food brought by their children, especially by Senjak, the daughter who now wanted to perform the ceremony. Obviously, Sisi and her husband had previously looked after their children, including Senjak. 'Washing the sling' confirmed the reversal of this relationship of care.

Sitting next to her mother, Senjak said to me unabashedly, 'She will soon be dead.' Sisi reacted resignedly: 'Yes, I won't live much longer. I am old and blind, what should I live for?' Senjak elaborated: 'I am alive due to the rice that mother fed me in the past. I am grateful for that, and so I want to offer her some meat. Once she has died, she cannot eat it anymore. That is why I offer this meat to her now.' Senjak's offering of 'washing the sling' implicitly put pressure on her siblings to do the same, but most of them were unwilling or unable to do so. At the time, I was in the early days of my research, and a bit naïvely perhaps, I rather brazenly asked Sisi's eldest son whether he was going to offer 'washing the sling' as well. He answered rather bluntly, 'No, I cannot provide a bull for slaughter.' None of his relatives believed this, and his elder sister later confided: 'He was not speaking the truth, he is just stingy.' She herself and another of her brothers had already performed the 'washing the sling' ritual for their mother. 'Washing the sling' bestows honour upon the mother to whom it is offered, but given the—conspicuously—high costs involved, it also results in prestige for the person who offers it, or rather, the House to which that person belongs.

5.4 Death's Demands

When someone stops breathing, death is imminent. For both Songsareks and Christian Garo, this indicates that the soul, which is synonymous with 'breath' or 'wind', is becoming detached from the body. If death is caused by the biting of spirits, it does not pose much danger to other living people. But that is not the case when someone dies due to a contagious disease,[7] a traffic accident, suicide, or is killed by a snake or other kind of wild animal.[8] These are all causes of violent death that emit dangerous levels of *marang*. Historically, the worst kind of death in this respect was when someone died after being attacked by a tiger.[9] Most Garo, irrespective of whether they are Songsareks or Christians, assume that some people transform into tigers in their sleep. Those tigers are thought to be searching for their (human) relatives, which suggests that deaths caused by tigers might actually be brought about by relatives in disguise. Moreover, if a tiger kills someone, or has attempted to do so, more attacks on members of the same House are likely to follow.[10]

Violent deaths do not occur without reason. One myth tells of two men, Asi and Malja, who went to their field on a day when, according to *niam*, they were not allowed to do so. They committed an additional transgression by harvesting some of their crops although the first fruits had not yet been offered to the spirits (see section 4.6). This double transgression proved fatal for both of them: 'Asi was bitten by a tiger, and Malja taken by a water spirit' ('*Asiko matchaa chikka, Maljako buga ra'a*'), as the proverb goes. People frequently cite this proverb as a reminder and warning of the violent sanctions that disobeying *niam* can bring about.

One morning while I was staying in Sadolpara, a particularly tragic death occurred in a neighbouring village. Nagal, a young woman, died from a snakebite. She had been weeding her swidden, carrying her six-week-old twins on her back. For her midday break, Nagal went to her field house—a thatched hut that offered shelter against sunshine and rain. As she stepped into it, a lethally poisonous 'pig-dung coloured cobra' (*gram wakki*) bit the sole of her right foot. Nagal knew that she was in serious trouble, but she managed to carry her two babies to the safety of the village. Herbal medicine was applied to the wound, but she died soon after. A couple of weeks later, I was with Jiji in her field. At some point we decided to take a rest, and as we headed for Jiji's field house, I was the one to enter it first. When I hesitated at the entrance, Jiji laughed. She said: 'There's no reason to be afraid. Snakes never bite at random. Only people who transgress are bitten.' I took advantage of the opportunity to ask her about Nagal's death. She replied that Nagal had almost certainly been at fault, even though she herself might not have been aware of it. Sometime later, I discussed Nagal's death with an old man who was highly regarded for his knowledge of *niam*. He confirmed: 'No one is bitten by a snake unless *niam* has been violated.'

Nagal's violent death gave rise to excessive *marang*. Fearing that this could lead to subsequent fatalities, people took significant measures to contain and purge the *marang* that had been released. The most important way of purging *marang*, at any (Songsarek or Christian) funeral, is by ensuring that the corpse is disposed of appropriately. When I first came to Garo Hills in the early 2000s, it was already usual for Songsareks to bury their dead. Going by the available literature, that was a relatively recent development since cremation had apparently been the norm until a few decades before (Eliot 1799: 28; Playfair 1909: 107–109; Burling 1997 [1963]: 338). Nagal's dead body, however, was cremated, after a consensus was reached among her close kin that cremation, as 'old *niam*' or 'real *niam*', would be more effective than burial in purging the intense *marang* unleashed by her death. Cremations are also conducted for people of great social standing, with 'old *niam*' representing a way to show respect. Cremations are not without risk, however: the funeral pyre upon which a body is burned is thought to attract many ghosts who are eager to connect to the ghost of the newly deceased person. In such large numbers, ghosts also pose a danger to the living. Christians never cremate the dead; among Garo the practice is exclusively associated with the community religion. Yet Christian funerals do involve practices concerned with containing and purging *marang*, as is evident from the caution Christians exercise when handling the corpse.

I have attended at least a dozen funerals in rural West Garo Hills, conducted by both Songsareks and Christians. A funeral typically lasts two days. On the first day, the corpse is kept in state inside the house in which the deceased person lived, usually to be disposed of at sunset by either burial or cremation. If many of the relatives who want to attend live far away and are unable to come at short notice, the interment or cremation may be delayed until the second day of the funeral. This is, since it is essential that close relatives who want to see the corpse get the chance to do so, so that they can ascertain for themselves that the deceased has truly died and has not simply gone into a coma to be buried or cremated alive. This latter possibility is a widespread cause of concern. Seeing the dead body also allows people to make sure that there has not been any foul play regarding the cause of death.

Songsarek funerals include many practices that are not part of Christian funerals. According to Songsarek *niam*, soon after the death of a married woman, one of her close sisters should break the rice storage vessel (*rong'dik*) in which the deceased kept the rice for her family to eat (Figure 5.1). Cooking rice, which is synonymous with feeding the family, is a married woman's responsibility. When a married man dies, one of his wife's senior male kin should break an earthen rice beer vessel (*dikka*) from the dead man's House.[11] Both of these vessels symbolize—or embody—the ability of a man and a woman to host guests. Breaking the vessels marks the death of the person who cooked rice or served rice beer. Perhaps even more significantly, the person who breaks such a vessel at a funeral pledges their commitment to ensuring the replacement of the deceased. On the second day of the funeral, the broken vessels are thrown away—into the jungle.

Figure 5.1 The vessel in which Sisi used to store the rice she cooked. It was broken at her funeral to disconnect her from the house she had lived in.
Photograph: Erik de Maaker, 2001.

Soon after a death, close relatives of the deceased person wash the corpse. They do so inside the house in which the person had lived, which is where the corpse will be laid out. Songsareks display their dead without clothes, whereas Christians dress the dead body. In either case, the corpse is placed on a sleeping mat and covered with large pieces of cloth. All the other clothes, bedding, and other personal belongings (sandals, comb, and toothbrush) of the dead man or woman are put aside. I was told that these items cannot be kept, since the dead person's ghost would be likely to attack anyone who dared to use them. Later, the personal belongings will either be cremated with the corpse or placed on or in the grave. Songsareks use some of the deceased's clothes to dress an effigy of the person (section 5.8). Any other possessions left over after the burial or cremation are thrown into the jungle.[12] Next, heirloom objects are placed alongside or onto the corpse, such as jewellery or—in a prosperous House—a gong, which will later be given to relatives who attend the funeral. Gongs are only rarely displayed, since doing so is likely to encourage matrilineal relatives to demand a gong as a gift, as discussed in section 5.6.[13] The corpse of an adult man should always be accompanied by a sword (*mil'am*), which may be supplemented by a wooden shield (*spi*) or a bamboo shield (*danil*).

5.5 Engaging Gifts

At a Garo funeral, people are called upon to express their relationship to the deceased person, to the House that she or he belonged to, and to the larger matrilineal group with which that House is associated. The gifts that people may offer and the roles they can assume vary, depending on whether they trace these relationships through matriliny or affinity. By presenting certain gifts, and taking on certain roles, people relate themselves in specific ways towards the deceased person. These relationships are understood in terms of kinship, and it is important to reiterate that in a Garo context kinship is not restricted to biological relationships, but is always categorical, and can be open to interpretation. Sometimes the relationships invoked are well established and mutually accepted, but funerals can also provide opportunities for new kin ties to be foregrounded, or—if people refuse to take on certain roles—the refusal of relationships previously acknowledged. The degree to which people show their commitment and allegiance, initially by deciding whether to attend a funeral, then in providing or withholding certain gifts, depends significantly on the prestige of the House in which the death has occurred, as well as on the strength of the emotional attachment felt towards the deceased.

During the whole time that the corpse is kept in state in the main room of the house, women who classify as 'mothers' of the deceased maintain a wake. This involves chanting a lament (*grapmangtata*) that describes in detail the journey of the soul of the deceased to the afterworld (see this Chapter, note 3). During the wake, the women fan the corpse with sticks of about half a metre long that have a plume of cocks' tail feathers tied to them. According to Jiji, these are for keeping flies at bay, but the feathers also seem to be able to grasp or direct a sort of ephemeral presence of the ghost: at a later stage of the funeral, the sticks serve to guide the ghost from the graveyard or cremation ground back to the house in which the deceased person used to live. Christians also fan the corpse, but they use flags made of coloured paper rather than cocks' tail feathers, and the women who do the fanning do not lament (Figure 5.2).

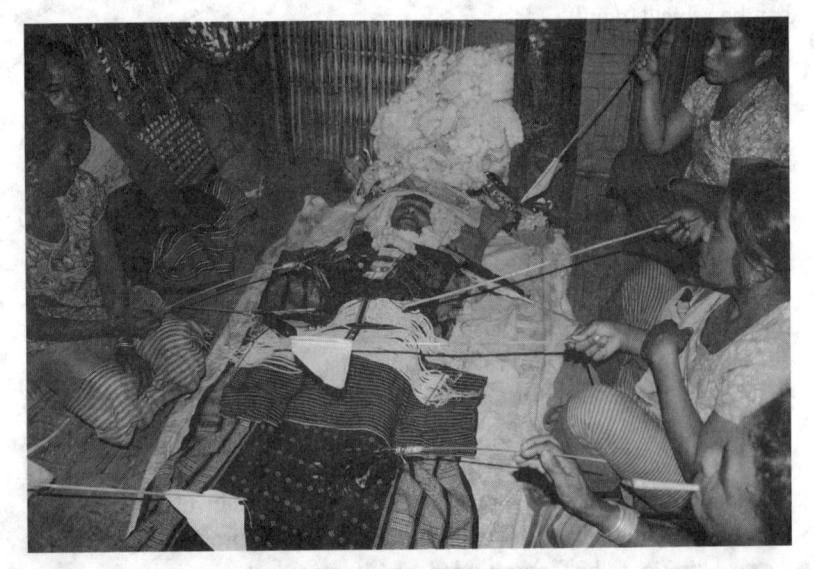

Figure 5.2 At Jiji's funeral, Songarek women fanned the corpse with cocks' tail feathers and Christian women did so with white paper flags. Heirloom jewellery and coins were displayed on her chest, and guests had placed the unginned cotton wool that they had bought for her near her head.
Photograph: Kriten Marak, 2015.

I got the impression that it is not considered appropriate for people attending a funeral to express sorrow if they are not in the vicinity of the corpse. They may gather in front of the house, in its gazebo (*kachari*), or in houses nearby, where they drink rice beer and chat cheerfully. Once the corpse has been disposed of, it becomes even more unusual to see expressions of sorrow, to the extent that it seems almost taboo to do so. The rice beer drinkers move to the house in which the dead body had been kept, and if the funeral has attracted a large number of guests they will often drink and chat well into the night. As on any rice beer drinking occasion, men occupy the main room of the house, while the women sit in the kitchen and on the veranda at the back. Young people gather in the gazebo in front of the house to throughout the ensuing night play cards, or board games until dawn (Figure 5.3).

Every woman who comes to a funeral brings a basket with some 'rice on the ear' (*michikang*) and some unginned cotton wool. These gifts for the deceased are to be used as seed grains by the ghost in the afterworld. Many women also cook 'food for the ghost' (*mimi'mang*).[14] According to Jiji's sister Meji, '*Mi'mang*s do not like the curry made with dried fish that people eat.

Figure 5.3 After Genna's funeral, young men and women stayed up all night playing cards in the gazebo near the house in which she had lived.
Photograph: Erik de Maaker, 2000.

They like egg. For them, egg is like beef.' The food is not only intended for the deceased person, but also for the ghosts who will guide them to the afterworld. Cooked 'food for the ghost' is placed on either side of the corpse's head. Christians do not cook 'food for the ghost' but instead place a bag of uncooked rice near the head. The greater the number of people who attend a funeral, the larger the heaps of rice ears and cotton wool, and the more packets of 'food for the ghost'. Or, at a Christian funeral, the more sacks of uncooked rice placed near the corpse. The quantity of these gifts visually attests to the reputation of the deceased and of the House he or she belonged to.

The representatives of a House in which a death has occurred have to provide a meal of meat curry with rice to everyone who attends the funeral. This is the same for both Songsarek and Christian funerals. Eating food that others have cooked implies that one trusts them. This is particularly relevant in rural West Garo Hills, where suspicions of fatal poisoning (*snaka*) are not uncommon.[15] Nobody who attends a funeral may leave before they have been served food, and eaten it. To do so would insult the House in which the death has occurred. The representatives of the hosting House have to ensure that all guests are offered as much meat curry and rice as they can eat. In rural West Garo Hills, it is more or less compulsory to serve beef. Beef is the most prestigious meat, but pork or even chicken can be served in addition (see also Chapter 2, note 29).

The House of the deceased person should offer at least one bull for slaughter.[16] In addition, more bulls, cows, and pigs are brought by people who attend the funeral. These animals are brought for 'slaughter out of love' ('*ka'sae den'a*'). The more cows and bulls provided, the greater honour that is bestowed upon the deceased person. More than forty cattle were slaughtered when Malsin, the closest son-in-law of the village head of Sadolpara, died in 2003. Jiji's death, as the inhabitant of another important House, also saw the slaughter of more than forty cattle and at least twenty-nine pigs. Funerals, whether Christian or Songsarek, are primarily compared and remembered with reference to the number and kinds of animals slaughtered, rather than to the number of attendees. Cows and bulls are valuable, hence large numbers of animals are only slaughtered for important persons who belong to major Houses. If a child dies, close family may consider it sufficient to slaughter no more than a chicken.[17] Funerals for children are also sharply curtailed in other ways, and what follows in this section primarily applies to the funerals of married women and men.

According to *niam*, a person who heads a House is expected to offer a bull or a cow at the funeral of a father, mother, sibling, son, or daughter. Since these designations refer to categories of kin rather than to specific persons, people may find themselves faced with this obligation very frequently—at least in theory. Rich Houses might own up to twelve or fourteen cows and bulls, while poorer ones may have just one or two, or even none at all. Given that the number of bulls and cows that a House owns serves as a measure of its prosperity, people do their best to only provide one when doing so is either unavoidable or deemed likely to strengthen relationships that they consider worthwhile. Less critically, because rice is less valuable, people who attend funerals are also expected to bring baskets of uncooked rice, which further help the House in which the death has occurred to feed its guests.

Women and men from a single locality tend to come to a funeral as a group. The women bear the heavy loads of rice in baskets secured by a tumpline. Men carry lighter loads, or nothing at all. If the party is bringing a cow or a bull, the animal is driven ahead of the procession, and the group is then permitted to have young men or boys beat a *kram* drum, play a gong, or blow a hollowed-out buffalo horn at intervals as they walk along (Figure 5.4). The instruments are played in a unique rhythm explicitly associated with death, which announces that a bull or a cow is being offered for the person who has

Figure 5.4 Men driving a small bull ahead of their relatives, as the group from Sadolpara walks together on their way to attend a funeral. A boy playing a *kram* drum is walking between them and the rest of the party.
Photograph: Erik de Maaker, 1999.

died ('to act for the ghost'—'*mi'mang dakenga*'). This expresses respect for the deceased and at the same time bestows 'good honour' upon those providing the animal.

Some of the men who attend a funeral bring heirloom swords, which they use to hack at the old altars in front of the house in which the corpse is laid out. They also use their swords to hack at the doorposts of the house's entrance. Both the altars and the doorposts are strongly associated with the spirits. People never normally touch the altars, nor do they sit in the doorways. The men yell loudly as they hack at the altars and the doorposts, shouting defiant proverbial sentences known as *turia* (Figure 5.5). If a man has died, they may shout: 'Even if a father died, a child is gone. We are not defeated, we're not completely lost.' ('*Apa sia, angde bon'o. Chon'tokkuja, gimatokkuja.*')[18] Or, if the deceased was a woman: 'The matrilineage is alive. A mother has died, but it's not the end. The empty place has been filled up.' ('*Chatchi sitokja. Ama bon'o bon'tokja. Da'ohana damhana datanga.*')[19] They repeat these actions when the corpse is taken out of the house for burial or cremation. As we watched a video recording that I had made of this taking place, a villager explained to me: 'This is being done in anger. The spirits have bitten that man to death.' ('*Ua mitian ia sianggipa mandiku mitin chiki*

Figure 5.5 At Sisi's funeral, one of her uncles uses an heirloom sword to hack at the posts of the entrance door of her house.
Photograph: Erik de Maaker, 2001.

siatahani giminsa, uku ka'unangskae dakahan ong'jok uadi.') Another viewer added: 'The spirits cannot be seen. Even so, guessing where to hack, they can be chased away' (*'Mitiko nikja nikjauba andaso rikigala'*). Hacking at the spirits is thus an act of defiance in the face of death. But it also expresses commitment towards the matrilineage, and specifically (if the deceased was married) to the replacement of the person lost, to ensure the continuation of the House affected. Only men who belong to Houses that are matrilineally related to the deceased person can bring swords and hack at the altars and the doorposts. For a married woman, or for her unmarried daughters and sons, these are her uncles, brothers and nephews; for a married man, men married to his aunts, sisters and nieces are eligible. The larger the number of men that hacks at the altars and the doorposts, the stronger the commitment they express towards the House in which the death has occurred.

In addition to all this, people who attend a funeral also give money to the close relatives of the one who died. This money is given 'to help' (*abisi*; in full: *'abisi migimin'*—'sharing cooked rice among sisters'). People refer to it as 'money that is forced onto the ghost' (*'mi'mangko tangka gua'*). The money is 'forced' rather than 'given', which means that the recipient is unable to refuse it. To this end, the giver folds the notes, concealing their value, and with a quick movement slips them into the hands, the shirt pocket, or under the shirt collar of the person they are giving to. This should be done as unobtrusively as possible, since the giver should avoid even the faintest suggestion that he (or, much more rarely, she) is taking pride in offering the gift. The recipient, in return, often responds with a semi-surprised 'Why this? What are you doing?', making it clear that the gift was not expected, even though such gifts are very much part of the protocol. Attempts to refuse the money given result in tussling and scuffling, with people trying to shove folded paper money back and forth into each other's hands, shirt pockets, and so on.

Like the other funeral gifts, the amount of money given 'to help' depends on the nature of the relationship the giver traces to the deceased person and the significance they attribute to that person's House. If someone poor from an insignificant House dies, people are unlikely to offer more than INR 10 or 20. The death of a member of an important House will easily raise gifts of INR 50–100 or more. People's willingness to provide this kind of support is also influenced by the kind of help that they have received at past funerals that they themselves hosted. Gifting animals, notably, is embedded in reciprocal arrangements: people offer bulls or pigs to Houses from which they have received those at previous funerals, or from which they expect to receive such animals on future occasions. Reciprocation may balance out within a short period of time, but it can also be drawn out across decades. Since all these gifts have a bearing on the one who died, failure to meet obligations to reciprocate is also interpreted as a lack of commitment towards the deceased, and the Houses that they belong(ed) to. This is all the more important in the context of a Songsarek worldview, in which such connections are likely to continue to be of relevance beyond death.

5.6 Acknowledging the Source

In rural West Garo Hills, representatives of a House in which a death has occurred have to distribute gifts to the Houses of the deceased person's female matrilineal relatives. The most important of these gifts is *ma'gual* (literally: 'valuables that are forgotten', *ma'a*: 'valuables', *guala*: 'to forget'). Ideally, *ma'gual* should be given in the form of a brass gong, heirloom jewellery, or a sword.[20] A gong attributes the most honour, and receiving a gong means being acknowledged as a close and important relative. But since gongs and other heirloom objects are precious and rare, *ma'gual* is often given as money instead. In practice, such monetary gifts are enabled by the money 'to help' that was given by the funeral guests. Handing out *ma'gual* as money has the added advantage that its exact value can be more precisely adjusted, not only by the giver but also by the receiver, who may turn down an amount deemed inappropriate. The value of *ma'gual* can vary from a gong worth several thousand rupees to just INR 10 or 20 in cash. A precious object or large sum of money honours a close relationship, while a small sum of money is more of a token reference.

Ma'gual is typically handed out by men, to men whose wives are matrilineal relatives of the deceased person. The matrilineage of the deceased person thus defines which Houses qualify for *ma'gual*. If a woman has died (or an unmarried man), the Houses belonging their own matrilineage qualify for *ma'gual*. At the death of a married man, Houses belonging to the matrilineage in which he was born (or adopted) are set to receive *ma'gual*. Whereas *ma'gual* in the form of money is primarily offered to men (albeit on account of the relationship that their wife traces to the deceased), women may also be given slings (if a woman has died) or the 'silver' one-rupee coins that had been placed on the corpse (of a man or a woman). Both slings and coins are only ever handed out to women. Giving a sling shows appreciation of a close relationship, but the coins can also be given to distant 'mothers'.

Ma'gual as money is highly valued, but the actual banknotes themselves are not imbued with any special significance and can subsequently be put into normal circulation. Heirloom objects obtained at death, such as gongs or jewellery, become an asset of the House that receives them. When such a recipient House hosts a funeral at a later date, these heirlooms can be given as *ma'gual* gifts. The only restriction is that an heirloom should never be returned to the House from which it had been received as *ma'gual*. Jiji explained that an heirloom that is given as *ma'gual* at a funeral represents the 'bones' (*greng*) of the deceased person. She made this connection explicitly when she received a gong at the funeral of a man whom she regarded as her younger brother. She told me that the gong was 'like bones of my younger brother' ('*angni angjongni greng*'): for her, the gong came to represent the deceased man. As time passes, people are likely to continue to remember the funeral at which they received a certain heirloom, but the object's long-term history is generally unknown, which effectively renders anonymous any deceased person with whom it has previously been associated. This means that gongs can eventually return to Houses that have kept them previously, despite that being theoretically unacceptable. Handing down heirlooms such as gongs and jewellery at successive mortuary rituals associates the objects with a cumulative number of dead. The heirloom objects thus represent the dead as a general category, rather than as deceased individuals. Oral histories state that the founders of Sadolpara brought the first heirlooms with them from their village of birth. Some villagers even suggested that those objects had originally been brought from Tibet, where they said the forefathers of the Garo had come from, thousands of years ago. The deep-rooted history that is attributed to the gongs implies that they have been transferred at funerals since time immemorial (Figure 5.6). Apparently contradicting this, people also told me that until recently gongs, heirloom jewellery, and weapons had been made by Bengalis from the nearby plains.[21] Nowadays, this production has ceased, primarily due to the decrease in the number of Songsareks. Christians attribute less value to heirlooms than Songsareks do, although they do occasionally continue to give them as gifts at funerals (Majumdar 1978: 125). For the urban affluent in Tura, the gongs also serve as decorative objects. Displayed in studies and living rooms, they represent 'traditional' Garo culture. As such, gongs and other heirloom objects are also included in the collections of local ethnographic museums.

Sharing out *ma'gual* is not easy. The task falls upon men who were closely related to the deceased person (traced along the female line), or who are

Figure 5.6 Large stacks of gongs, representing great wealth, kept in the storeroom of the house of a village head in Madhupur (Bangladesh).
Photograph: Erik de Maaker, 2008.

married to one of his or her close female relatives. *Ma'gual* must be given to the representatives of all the Houses that qualify for it. Sharing out *ma'gual* is a precarious balancing act: on the one hand, sufficiently valuable *ma'gual* must be offered if the House is to uphold or even boost its reputation. On the other hand, the resulting loss of wealth can lower the status of a House. This means that the men handing out *ma'gual* must exercise restraint when it comes to giving heirloom objects such as gongs or jewellery, and even in sharing out larger sums of money. Since a House is expected—according to *niam*—to make the maximum possible effort to provide *ma'gual* generously, its representatives exhaust themselves in lamenting the limited means at their disposal. This necessarily involves a good deal of posturing. The men sharing out *ma'gual* take pains to understate the actual extent of their House's possessions, since revealing that would oblige them to give everything away. No one but the widow or widower and their closest kin has access to the storeroom of the house (*kompa*), which is where heirloom valuables are kept, so outsiders are typically unable to verify the (lack of) possessions claimed by those distributing *ma'gual*.[22] At one funeral, a man who was sharing out *ma'gual* as money after he had distributed three of four gongs said apologetically: 'If there were more gongs, we would give more gongs.... We wouldn't share out this paper money that can be obtained anywhere.' ('*Rang dongudi, rangku on'pangming... Dangga rekka man'winniamangmangkudi sualjapang ini.*')[23] Since only the people most closely involved with the House in which the death occurred can judge whether such a statement is truthful, and since everyone is aware of the conflicting pressures facing those distributing *ma'gual*, people who do not belong to this inner circle are not necessarily inclined to believe such words.

At Sisi's funeral, her husband Dising waited for the arrival of a man named Rengteng before he started to offer *ma'gual*. Rengteng was Sisi's 'biggest grandfather' (*atchu dal'gipa*); he headed the House that was most senior to that of Sisi. Rengteng had to come from a neighbouring village and only arrived late in the afternoon. His party drove a bull and was accompanied by boys playing a *kram* drum, gong, and horn. Soon after Rengteng's arrival, widower Dising offered him a *narikki sil* gong ('earring metal' gong). This type of gong is worth relatively little. Rengteng refused the gift politely, saying: 'It is really not necessary to give anything to me.' Rengteng knew that he was considered Sisi's 'biggest grandfather' and that no one else could be offered *ma'gual* until he had accepted his. Widower Dising correctly understood Rengteng's refusal of the *narikki sil* gong as a demand for a more valuable gift. I observed how, following the refusal, Dising went to his storeroom and brought out a much more precious *kasamati* gong. When he placed this gong in front of Rengteng, it was readily accepted. Rengteng's gentle refusal of the *narikki sil* gong was—for those who understood the language of the funeral gifts—a straightforward demand for much more substantial *ma'gual* (Figure 5.7).

People who accept *ma'gual* formally acknowledge that they are like 'a mother' to the one who died. If they refuse *ma'gual* that is offered to them,

Figure 5.7 A valuable gong being presented as *ma'gual* by widower Dising (second from right) at the funeral of his wife Sisi.
Photograph: Erik de Maaker, 2001.

or as long as they persist in doing so, they reject that relationship. A man who was trying to share out *ma'gual* at the funeral of his sister-in-law, but whose gifts were not accepted, expressed his disappointment with the words: 'If you all act like this [refusing *ma'gual*], she won't have mother and father.' (*'Iadi ama appain dongjawamo na'ongni indakjokode.'*)[24] The closest 'mothers' of the deceased person should receive the most substantial *ma'gual*. Distant 'mothers' can be satisfied with much smaller amounts. Again, kinship designations refer to categories of people. People's willingness to accept *ma'gual*, relative to the value of what is being offered to them, or their persistence in refusing it, indicates their perception of the proximity and importance of the relationships traced.

Diran's parents died when he was still a young boy, and he grew up in the House of his elder sister Janji. Janji became his stepmother and her husband Singgat as his stepfather. When Diran died, as an old man, the House in which he had grown up was headed by a man named Arseng. Arseng had entered the House following the death of Singgat, by marrying Singgat's widow Kanjak. Kanjak had married Singgat, after Janji had died, replacing her. During adulthood, Diran had been an influential man. When Diran died,

Arseng slaughtered a cow for him near his own house and then came to the funeral accompanied by boys playing a *kram* drum, gong, and horn. At the funeral, Diran's heir Ratjen made several attempts to offer *ma'gual* as money to Arseng, but he refused to accept it. Since Arseng had to accept *ma'gual* (because he was a stepfather to Diran and had slaughtered a cow and arranged for the boys to play the instruments), his refusal of the money could only be understood as a demand for an heirloom. Annoyed, a grandson of Diran remarked: 'He [Diran] is a son of his [Arseng's] House. . . . Therefore, at his death, he [Arseng] wants this [he pointed at a gong]. . . . He [Arseng] has seen his son [Diran] die in poverty. . . . We will need to fulfil his wish, although he [Arseng] is behaving badly' ('*Ua chragipa bini nokuni dipanti. . . . Uni gimin atchuni siani ja'mano anga iko man'a nanggen bia aganenga. . . . Bini chra-dipantini dilrureng bon'chichonakuba nikanga. . . . Chu'sokatna nanggen changhaudi, bia namjauba.*)[25] It was unclear to me whether Diran had really died as a poor man or not. As far as I knew, the House owned quite a few cattle, an important sort of wealth. By stating that Diran had died 'in poverty', the grandson was arguing that Arseng's demand was unreasonable. Arseng was behaving 'badly' because, together with other men, Arseng was responsible for the continuation of the House of Diran. From that perspective, it was not appropriate for him to make demands that would drain the House's resources and hence threaten its continuity. Nevertheless, Arseng persisted in his refusal, and a gong was finally offered to him on the second day of the funeral, just hours before the event came to a close.

Months later, I discussed Arseng's demands with some of the people who had been present at the time. One of them explained to me that at the funeral, some time before Arseng rejected the *ma'gual* money offered to him, a woman named Jangmi had received a gong. Jangmi was the current head of Diran's House of birth, which was not the House in which he had grown up. I concluded that Arseng, as Diran's stepfather, had then expected to be treated equivalently to her. When he finally did receive a gong, it raised the status of Arseng's House, since he had received *ma'gual* similar to that provided to Jangmi, even though the House she headed was senior to his.

People who offer *ma'gual* have to gauge the proximity of relationships between the deceased and each of the persons they are obliged to give to. These assessments involve weighing up many different factors. It can be compulsory for someone to accept *ma'gual*, or acceptable for them to refuse it, or a refusal may even be expected. At the funeral of a man named Miknang, when a woman refused to accept *ma'gual* money that had been offered to her, one of the men distributing asked his kinsmen: 'The one who refused, will she come back and remind us of our duty?' ('*Da'ode ikude jinang rike ra'pilkunauama ra'gijagipade?*')[26] He was uncertain whether she had refused because she wanted to be offered more valuable *ma'gual*, or because she truly did not want to accept any. At the same time, those who stand to receive *ma'gual* have to assess and reconsider the relationship that they themselves trace to the person who has died. People who reject *ma'gual* that is offered to them are likely to justify their refusal, publicly, by playing down the gifts 'to help' that they themselves brought for the deceased person. This is because it would be shameful to accept *ma'gual* if one has not been able to provide an appropriate amount of 'help' to the House in which the death occurred. One woman who was offered *ma'gual* replied: 'If I am not able to help you, but accept a gift, how can that be in compliance with *niam*?' ('*Angan dakchakna man'jaongode, da'oba anga ra'angpilode mai niam ga'aka ia.*')[27] And a man who probably felt that he had given too little 'to help' the House of the deceased person refused *ma'gual* with the words: 'I couldn't give anything, so how can I accept it? I won't take it. It would be shameful' ('*Anga on'a man'jaode, anga mai dake ra'gen? Dat ra'jawa. Mangri solmangri.*')[28]

The tragic death of Nagal due to a snakebite (section 5.4) gave rise to an emotionally intense funeral in Gambaregre that drew many attendees, including people from the surrounding villages. Rikseng, a close matrilineal uncle of Nagal who had married into Sadolpara, went to the funeral accompanied by many people from Sadolpara (including Nandini and myself). With so many guests, Nagal's close relatives had to share out *ma'gual* to many of the visitors. Some of these people were so closely related that they simply had to accept *ma'gual*. But in other cases, acceptance was by no means a foregone conclusion and the close relatives of Nagal (primarily her brother Waling and her stepfather Wiljeng) had to make great efforts to convince people to accept the *ma'gual* they offered.

Among the many people who attended the funeral of Nagal were Rengji and Jingmi. They were mother and daughter, and belonged to Nagal's matrilineal group. Rengmi, a woman in her early sixties, had given INR 20 to Nagal's widower 'to help.' Considering that at least four of the people who attended the funeral had given a bull or a cow, and many others had provided large sums of money, this was a modest contribution. In the afternoon on the first day of the funeral, both women were sitting by the side of the gazebo in front of Nagal's house. The brother of Nagal who was making most of the gift offerings to the guests held out some folded notes to Rengmi, saying: 'Take this Grandma, take this. . . . How can you refuse it? To do so would go against custom.' ('*Ha iku na'ambi ra'angbo. . . . Na'ong niamgri-tiamgri ong'ja?*').

Rengji looked up, but otherwise remained impassive. She kept her hands in her lap. With a quick move, Nagal's brother slipped the folded notes under one of Rengji's arms. Wiljeng, an in-law of Nagal who was supporting her brother, said: 'Even if you take this, we are not free. If you refuse it, we aren't free either.' ('*Ia ra'anguba jokja, ra'angjauba jokjaba.*'). Rengji picked up the notes, which she unfolded and counted. Adding weight to the gift of money, Nagal's brother added: 'To you, a gong should have been given. If we had had one, if we had been able to give . . . a *narikki sil* ['earring metal' gong] would have been given. But we don't have one, and can only give you something small.' ('*Nang'nadi, na'ongnadi rangkun on'pangba, na'ongnadi. . . . silkuba on'etpang, dongja.*'). He stepped back, increasing the distance between himself and Rengji, thus making it more difficult for her to hand the money back, and said: 'This is just something small.' ('*Alamala.*'). From inside the gazebo, someone added: 'If she had died having lots, being able to give, we would have stabbed (a pig) for you.' ('*Dongi, niki gambrii jakkrai siudi su'i.*'). Nagal's brother said to Rengji: 'When you die, we will accept a gift. (After all) she is your grandchild.' ('*Nang'ni sijokoba ra'pilbanabaokana. Nang'su ong'in.*') Wiljeng added: 'Are we asking you to take [accept] from a stranger? Even if others . . . are afraid to accept [*ma'gual*], you should still do so.' ('*Jawaniku inkunama, jawani 'Hut rang'ja' inuba kenoba.*'). Nagal's brother continued: 'Why would you be scared? Is it because she was bitten [by a snake]?' ('*Nang'ni aganani aganjok iadi ma'naba kenkuna, chikaniku cha'aniku inkunama.*'). Wiljeng delivered a final argument: 'She is equal to someone of your own House!' ('*Noktang mandi, iadi!*')[29] As the men walked away, Rengji made no attempt to return the money, which indicated that she had accepted it.

The dialogue above shows that the representatives of the House of Nagal categorized Rengji as a grandmother of Nagal. They stated that Nagal had been a 'grandchild' of hers, so close that Nagal was 'like someone of your own House'. The men explained Rengji's reluctance to accept the money offered to her not so much as a denial of the closeness of the relationship traced, but as an expression of fear of the deceased Nagal, because she had 'been bitten'. They implied that Rengji might be afraid that the excessive *marang* brought about by the snakebite could be contagious. While Nagal's brother did not claim that such a fear was unwarranted, he suggested that it should not take precedence over the closeness of the relationship traced. Emphasizing the reciprocal nature of the relationship, Nagal's brother added, 'When you die, we will accept a gift.' In other words, when Rengji herself died, he promised, one of Nagal's close relatives would accept *ma'gual* in turn, acknowledging their relationship to Rengji. In addition, the men made statements that bestowed honour upon Rengji. Nagal's brother maintained that Rengji deserved a gong, a gift that is only ever presented to the closest relatives, saying they would have given her one if they had had one. Someone sitting inside the gazebo reinforced Wiljeng's and Nagal's brother's persuasive arguments by stating that Rengji was so important that, had one been available, a pig would have been 'stabbed' for her. Relatives can be honoured by providing them with beef or pork from an animal slaughtered especially for them. By adding, 'even if you take this [money], we are not free', Wiljeng downplayed the value of the *ma'gual* offered. While the representatives of the House of Nagal had to ensure that someone as important as Rengji accepted *ma'gual*, they insisted that they were unable to offer her the kind of gift that her position commanded. Waling and Wiljeng thus humbled themselves in an attempt to convince Rengji that they respected her as an important matrilineal relative of Nagal and that she should therefore accept the monetary gift that was being offered to her.

Refusing *ma'gual* implies refuting the existence of a close relationship to the one who died. Conversely, someone who accepts *ma'gual* acknowledges their relationship to the deceased person, while also indicating that they consider the 'help' (money, rice, animals) they have provided to be appropriate and sufficient. The latter implication of the acceptance of *ma'gual* can put distant relatives who have only provided modest 'help' in an awkward position. If they are offered *ma'gual* as money, they can resolve the dilemma by negotiating to accept an amount lower than that initially offered by the House of the deceased. That way, they acknowledge their relationship to the deceased person, but avoid giving the impression that they are so proud as to think that they have provided sufficient 'help'. In this case, they state that they themselves should have provided more substantial 'help' but regrettably lacked the means to do so. According to this same logic, offering people more substantial *ma'gual* than is warranted by the generosity of their gifts 'to help' serves to humble them. It can even be a way to demand additional 'help', which is sometimes given retrospectively.

The distribution of *ma'gual* is guided by *niam*. *Niam* defines the ritual conventions that need to be followed, and as the examples above have illustrated, these are flexible enough to accommodate the intentions of both the person offering and of the intended recipient. Offering *ma'gual* serves to acknowledge the matrilineal kin of the deceased person, while assessing, ranking, and testing the strength of these ties. Since the nature and quantity of the resources that the House of the deceased person has at its disposal is never revealed, people who receive *ma'gual* can only guess at whether the *ma'gual* presented to them is appropriate relative to the wealth of the House. And since *ma'gual* is offered at least partly in response to the gifts made 'to help', its value is also relative to whatever help the House of the deceased has received, or had expected to receive from the funeral guests. Offering *ma'gual* can therefore be a way to bestow honour upon an intended recipient, but it can also be an ostensibly indirect way to humiliate them.

Ma'gual is offered to the 'mothers' of the deceased person (or rather, to their husbands). It is a gift to the source, an acknowledgement of that person's origins, and an important way of sustaining and renewing kin ties. The capacity of *ma'gual* gifts to express, evaluate, and rank matrilineal relatedness derives from their association with the dead. The prized heirloom objects that circulate as *ma'gual* are related to anonymous dead predecessors, and they can move across the boundaries of matrilineal groups and even moieties. By encompassing relations to the dead, and taking account of exchanges conducted at previous funerals, ongoing relationships can be proposed, challenged, or rejected. This enables *ma'gual* (as well as other gifts given according to the same pattern, such as slings and coins) to validate current relationships by anchoring them in the past. These relationships, and the 'social order' in which they are embedded thus reflect, but are also reinforced by, the various gift transactions (Bloch and Parry 1982: 6). The importance attributed to *ma'gual* shows that the status of a deceased person both influences and is then retrospectively remembered in terms of the value of the gifts received and given at their funeral. But funerals also give rise to other important forms of offering and reciprocation, which I discuss in the section below.

5.7 Vouching to Slaughter a Cow

In addition to gifts 'to help' and *ma'gual*, funerals also occasion the handover of gongs or small sums of money as part of dedicated exchange relationships that are typically maintained over a number of years, or even several generations. The gong or amount of money transferred in such an exchange is referred to as *ukam*. Like *ma'gual*, *ukam* is offered by close relatives of the deceased and is considered important by both Songsareks and Christians—at least in rural West Garo Hills. Irrespective of an *ukam*'s value, and whether it is given as a gong or as money, accepting it obliges the recipient to slaughter a cow in honour of the deceased person. As Bimsing told me, 'even if five rupees are accepted as *ukam*, a cow will need to die' ('*gong'bonga ra'angoba matchu mangsadi sina nanggen, ukamdi.*')[30] An *ukam* exchange is initiated when an *ukam* gong (typically a relatively inexpensive one) or *ukam* money (just a small amount) is handed out by the representatives of the House of a deceased person to someone attending the funeral. *Ukam* offered is seldom accepted because doing so commits the recipient to a very costly reciprocal exchange. The *ukam* gong or money continues to be owned by the House that gives it, and it can be returned to the House that provided it whenever a death occurs in the House that has accepted the *ukam*. But the gong or money is of far less value than what it represents: an *ukam* is a pledge.

The word '*ukama*' means 'to call,' both in the sense of 'to announce' and 'to summon'. If someone dies, and their House has previously 'taken' *ukam*, their House can summon the House from which the *ukam* had been received, announcing that the time has come to collect the *ukam*. Bimsing explained this, referring to *ukam* that had been accepted at a funeral in Sadolpara by someone from a neighbouring village: 'If someone dies at his [the taker's] house, like his wife or a child, he will have to send for the people from here [Sadolpara], and return the *ukam* money. . . . Ukam taken from here, can be got back there' ('*Aro bini jikgipani siuba ba dipanti didrangni siuba bia inuniko mandi rikbana nanggen, nokchi sijokodi. Ua Ukam ra'anggipa tangkaku on'pilskana nanggen. . . . Inuniko ra'anga I'chakuba man'baskagen.*')[31] In other words, when a death occurs in House A, someone attending the funeral from House B can accept *ukam*, a pledge. With the acceptance of the pledge, people belonging to House B are expected to slaughter a bull or cow in honour of the person from House A who died. That is, they commit themselves to doing so, usually soon after the funeral. When a death subsequently occurs in House B, its representatives can summon people from House A to collect the *ukam*. The pledge is thus returned to House A. If people from House A do indeed collect their ukam, they are expected and obliged to slaughter a bull or cow in honour of the recently deceased person from House B. Summoning Houses that have previously given *ukam* to collect it at the time of a funeral is a way for a House in which a death has occurred to induce the slaughter of *ukam*-related cattle. This bestows honour upon the person who died, and the House to which he or she belonged.

Once an *ukam* exchange has been initiated, the *ukam* gong or the *ukam* money is spoken about as a debt that rests with the House that has accepted the *ukam*. If it has been given in the form of a gong, that same gong should later be returned to the House from which it derived. If the *ukam* is money, the same amount of money as initially taken will have to be given back. The negotiations of offering, refusing, or accepting *ukam* are primarily conducted by men, just like most transactions involving cattle or money.

Ukam exchanges are—according to *niam*—not restricted to specific categories of kin, but can be taken on by anyone, whether matrilineal or affinal kin. People who qualify for *ma'gual* are first offered *ma'gual* and then *ukam*. Those who are not eligible for *ma'gual* are only offered *ukam*. Given the costly commitment that accepting *ukam* involves, the people sharing it out are unlikely to be offended if anyone refuses to accept it. On the contrary, it is even considered inappropriate for closely related relatives to accept *ukam*, since they are expected to provide cattle 'to help' to feed funeral guests anyway, without the need for a pledge to secure the eventual reciprocation of the cow provided. At the same time, very distant relatives are unlikely to accept *ukam*, since doing so is unlikely to yield much in terms of strengthening relationships, while slaughtering a cow is always an expensive affair. Accepting 'new' *ukam* translates into 'good honour', but *ukam* exchanges are most likely to be engaged in by Houses that are not closely related but both stand to gain, in an economic and political sense, from more solid relations.

Nekjing was a man in his fifties, who had white hair but a boyish sense of mischief. He had come to the funeral of Nagal with Nagal's biological elder brother, who was his neighbour in Sadolpara. Nekjing was not eligible for *ma'gual* since his wife Misha did not belong to Nagal's clan or even to her moiety. She was a Mangsang Sangma, and Nagal a Raksam Marak. Nekjing himself was a Chambugong Marak. On the first day of the funeral, in the afternoon, Nekjing was sitting in the gazebo in front of Nagal's house when Waling (one of Nagal's brothers) tried to give him some money. With a skilled move of his hands, Waling tried to shove some folded paper money under Nekjing's shirt, saying: 'Hey you, matrilineal uncle, how come (you haven't accepted anything yet)?' ('*Mamaba na'a badakiha. Iaa aksamai gisik ra'rimangbuda?*') Nekjing laughed, knowing that he was not eligible for *ma'gual*. This meant that Waling was not offering him a 'gift' (which *ma'gual* would be) but was trying to impose *ukam* upon him, and accepting it would oblige him to slaughter a cow. Nekjing caught hold of the folded banknotes and deftly slipped them under the collar of Waling's shirt. Waling did not resist but reacted as if taken aback. He said: 'At least one of you should acknowledge us. How come all of you matrilineal uncles are behaving like this? Accept at least a little bit from us, you people.' ('*Aia na'adi mamasongdi indaka na'ongdi? Iaa akkisa mai na'ong mandi.*'). Waling used a kin term to address Nekjing respectfully, even though Nekjing only very remotely classified as a matrilineal uncle. They were both of the same clan (Marak) but not the same matrilineage within that clan (Raksam rather than Chambugong). Downplaying his own status, Nekjing said: 'I simply came along, just roaming', then added, mischievously, 'Did you get one, father of Sima?' ('*Angadi indinba indinha i'pabai rua.*' . . . '*Sima pagipaina man'alamana?*') This was clearly intended to poke fun at Waling. By addressing him as 'father of Sima', Nekjing was implying that Waling had slept with Sima's mother, who happened to be Waling's mother-in-law. If Sima's father died, Waling would indeed be eligible to marry his widow, so the relationship was one worth cracking jokes about. Moreover, 'did you get one' worked as a pun to insinuate that Waling had a girlfriend in addition to his wife. While playing on Waling's virility, addressing him as 'father of Sima' also expressed respect. Sima's actual father headed a large landowning House and was also an important maternal uncle to both Nagal and Waling. In response to the remark, Waling grinned and said: 'Listen, this is just teasing and mocking. Mixing truth and lies. Maternal uncle, really recognize us and take it. . . . Though Rika [Rikseng] is a younger brother to us, he is your father-in-law, am I right?' (Waling: '*Hotchala. Iaba kal'akrurae siningrurai donga gita; bu'a bibi pakha, hat, mama gisik ra'bibiangbuda. . . . Angde-angjong Rikakudi na'achingdi; o'bitihajok?*')[32] Here, Waling was referring to a relationship that could indeed be traced, albeit rather remotely. Yet he presented it as a close relationship to support his attempt to convince Nekjing to accept the *ukam* he was offering. Nekjing was nonetheless persistent in his rejection, and refused to accept any of the money.

An *ukam* exchange is initiated to be resolved. When a death occurs in a House that has taken on an *ukam* debt, members of that House decide among themselves whether or not to notify (*ukam rika*—reminding of *ukam*) the people from whom they have taken *ukam*. This enables them to influence which of their dead will have *ukam* cattle slaughtered for them, and which not. By not sending out 'reminders' at the deaths of members of their House who do not have a high social status (such as infants), people who have given out *ukam* can try to ensure that their most important dead will receive large numbers of cattle. The option for people to choose when to 'remind' of *ukam* or not often leads to long time spans elapsing between the initiation of an *ukam* exchange and its resolution. In theory, this should not reduce the chances of an *ukam* exchange eventually being fulfilled, because the debt does not rest with an individual person, but with the House of the person who accepted it. It is not unusual for *ukam* to ultimately be resolved by a different man than the one who initially took it on.

For *ukam* to grant Houses prestige, fulfilling an *ukam*, once initiated, should be experienced as compulsory. Likewise, failure to comply with the obligations that *ukam* triggers should be experienced as shameful and even socially damaging. If this were not the case, taking *ukam* and making attempts to resolve it would not have much impact on inter-House relationships.

As mentioned in section 5.6, in his prime, Diran had been an important man in Sadolpara. He had married into a very wealthy House. Some people claimed that the House possessed up to a hundred gongs, or enough gongs to fill five large gong-baskets (*jengkoks*). This large number indicates very substantial wealth. Throughout his adult life, Diran lived up to the status of his House. He and his wife frequently hosted other people, offering rice beer, meat curry, and rice. Diran provided bulls or cows 'to help' at many funerals, and took *ukam* more than once. However, people told me, he was not very prudent economically. Rather than funding these activities from the income he generated, he consumed the wealth of his House. 'Diran has sold [the heirlooms] and eaten.' ('*Diran pali chajok*'), Jiji told me, with some disapproval in her voice. 'Eaten' here meant 'used up'. But even that had been insufficient for him to fulfil all the commitments he had taken on. After his death, it emerged that on several of the occasions on which he had taken *ukam*, and thus committed himself to slaughtering a cow, he had never actually done so. The obligation to slaughter the first of the two cattle that an *ukam* exchange demands cannot be carried over to a successor, which means that an *ukam* exchange 'fails' if someone who has taken on a new *ukam* dies before he has slaughtered the pledged cow or bull (once the first commitment to slaughter has been fulfilled, *ukam* can be completed by the successors of the ones who have initiated it). People explained to me that such a failure is—posthumously—very shameful for a man, rendering him, as they contemptuously put it, 'like a dog' (*a'chak ji'a*). Likening a man to a dog expresses disgust. Dogs are said to scavenge on offal and dirt, waste and rotten food, and are hence regarded as beings without shame.

Some years before his death, Diran and his wife Chengjak had attended the funeral of the head of a nearby village, a man named Jonggan. There, Diran had accepted INR 10 of *ukam* and thus taken on the obligation to slaughter a cow in Jonggan's honour. He did not intend to do so immediately upon returning from the funeral, which is why Chengjak also accepted a butchered hind leg of a cow and some cooked beef liver. They cooked the meat at home, and together with the liver it allowed them to feed the ghost of Jonggan inside their house, as is customary. Had they slaughtered the *ukam*-related cow immediately upon their return, its meat would not only have provided food for relatives and neighbours but also for the meal to be offered to the ghost of Jonggan. Accepting the hind leg thus enabled them to postpone the slaughter of the first *ukam*-related cow or bull. But when Diran himself died, a number of years later, he still had not slaughtered it. Even though unmet *ukam* obligations should not be passed down to a man's successors, Diran's close relatives felt obliged to at least attempt to annul the *ukam* exchange, by returning the money and meat that Diran and Chengjak had taken at the funeral of Jonggan. Diran's representatives therefore sent a messenger to Jonggan's heir to inform him that Diran had died. Jonggan's heir had other pressing obligations, or perhaps he did not want to attend, so he asked his son-in-law (Gongsin) and his daughter (Nalji) to go instead. At Diran's funeral, a man named Awara offered Gongsin INR 10 *ukam*, which he accepted. After all, that was the amount that Diran had taken from Jonggan's relatives all those years ago and now it had been returned. Later that day, when Nalji and Gongsin were about to go home, close relatives of Diran put a bull's rear leg and a large-folded leaf with cooked beef liver into Nalji's carrying basket. Nalji did not feel comfortable about accepting the meat, since her father had not mentioned it, and she wanted to refuse it. But Diran's widow Chengjak explained to Nalji that she should take the meat, since all those years ago she herself had brought a hind leg and some liver from Jonggan's funeral: 'I carried and brought it myself!' (*'Anga holbaok da'ning!'*)[33] Her words convinced Nalji to take the joint and the liver. Gongsin was not present during this conversation and only came to know about it once he and Nalji were on their way home. Gongsin feared that they were being tricked by Diran's successors into accepting meat that did not relate to the former *ukam* exchange. If this was the case, they would be accepting new *ukam* in the form of the hind leg and the liver. Therefore, Gongsin and Nalji decided to hand back the basket with the meat to one of Diran's grandsons, who they met as they were leaving the village. The grandson carried it back to his grandfather's house, to the men responsible for sharing out *ukam*. Realizing what had happened, one of them responded angrily: 'Now it will remain here forever!' He pointed at the basket with the meat and said, 'According to the debt ... she should have taken this.' (*'Bisongha iun dongaigen pangnan!... gru gitan ... bia ra'angna nangamingba iko.'*)[34] The failure of the representatives of the House of Diran to complete the *ukam* exchange was particularly discomforting since it meant that they had not managed to compensate for the honour lost by Diran's failure to slaughter a cow in the first place.

This was not the only *ukam* exchange to fail at Diran's funeral. When he died, his close relatives had also taken care to inform a man named Baljeng, who lived in the nearby town of Dadenggre. Neither Baljeng nor his wife were directly related to Diran and Chengjak. On the morning of the funeral, one of Diran's close relatives told me: 'The one who died [Diran] took *ukam* when his [Baljeng's] wife died. So, he [Baljeng] has been sent for. Baljeng will come here to collect his own money.' (*'Ia bini mandini sianiku ia da'u sianggipa ukam ra'bajok. Ra'baani gimin ia rikangjok. Bia an'tangni danggaku ra'na i'bagen, Baljeng.*')[35] Apparently, that was what Diran's representatives expected to happen. But although Baljeng received the news, he did not come to the funeral. His absence made Diran's heir angry, and for months he claimed that Baljeng was so ashamed of himself that he had not dared to come to Sadolpara since. A couple of years later, I met Baljeng in Dadenggre and asked him why he had not come for Diran's funeral. He remembered the situation very well. He told me that he had previously lived with his wife in Marakapara, a village close to Sadolpara. At his wife's funeral, he told me, Diran had taken *ukam*. But after he had moved to the nearby small town of Dadenggre, Baljeng's relationships with people in Sadolpara had weakened. When Diran died, Baljeng had decided not to collect his *ukam* and slaughter the requisite cow or bull for Diran, preferring instead to keep his savings 'for the education of his children', as he himself put it. Baljeng did not believe that by not fulfilling the *ukam* he had damaged his relationship with Diran's relatives. Rather, the *ukam* debt had simply remained open, to be collected by him, or one of his heirs, when a subsequent death occurred. Baljeng even told me that he had gone to Sadolpara and visited Diran's heir in the months following the funeral. He rejected the assertion of the latter that he was ashamed to have failed to resolve the *ukam*. When I asked him afterwards, Diran's heir strongly disagreed with this and insisted that Baljeng was not speaking the truth. As everyone knew, Baljeng had become a Christian when he moved to Dadenggre. Although people generally maintained that conversion shouldn't affect obligations such as *ukam* exchanges, it did perhaps play a part in Baljeng's rather flexible interpretation of his commitments. Regardless of which account was most accurate in this particular case, the story illustrates that *ukam* exchanges are framed in terms of honour and shame, which are always interpreted within the contexts in which people find themselves. Baljeng's move to Dadenggre had not only increased his physical but also his social distance from the people living in Diran's village. His decision to prioritize his children's education when allocating his household resources may have increased that distance further, but also shows that he didn't have much to lose. Apparently, Baljeng did not fear the social repercussions of failing to fulfil—or postponing fulfilment of—his commitment towards Diran and the representatives of Diran's House.

The *ukam* exchanges that I have been able to learn about took place between people of influential Houses, belonging to distinct clans. Once, at a funeral, a man who was trying to share out *ukam* reacted to its refusal with a disgruntled: 'If no one accepts it . . . no more marriages will be initiated.' ('*Dongnap-atchian dongjajok.*')[36] Indeed, exchanging *ukam* is often referred to as 'tying groom givers and takers' (*nokchame ka'a*), suggesting that it can help to create the kind of inter-House relationships that can be secured with marriages.

Although *ma'gual* and *ukam* are very different modalities of exchange, if they are handed out as folded banknotes, they look alike. Hence, it is not always clear to recipients what is being thrust upon them. At the funeral of a man named Nangseng, one of his wife's younger brothers was sharing out money. He approached a man named Junan, and after some pushing and scuffling, he managed to shove some paper money into Junan's shirt pocket. When I asked Junan later what he had received, he said: '*ma'gual*.' But when I put the same question to the son-in-law of Nangseng who had done the sharing out, he told me it had been *ukam*. From subsequent discussions with people who were familiar with the kinds of situations described above, it became clear that this sort of ambiguity is not entirely unavoidable. The recipient of such an ambiguous offering will almost certainly try to refuse the money being thrust upon them, as Junan had. But even though Junan maintained that he had received *ma'gual*, he returned the money a short while later, most probably because he did not want to take even the slightest risk that the younger brother of Nangseng's widow had actually meant to give *ukam*.

Ukam creates a connection between funerals and marriages. Initiating *ukam* serves to strengthen relationships and may potentially lead to the offering or taking of grooms. It encompasses a pledge to future mutual commitment, which is why failure to fulfil the obligations taken on is met with contempt. Once initiated, *ukam* exchanges are compulsory, yet failure to fulfil them on a particular occasion can always be understood as postponement to a later date. Obligations can thus remain pending interminably, even as the likelihood that they will ever be fulfilled diminishes.

5.8 Putrefaction and Presence

A funeral facilitates the dissolution of people's ties to the deceased, but at the same time it allows for reconnection in multiple ways. The dead are ghosts and can potentially harm the living. This is particularly true of ghosts that are dissatisfied. But if ghosts have been given a proper send-off and established themselves well in the afterworld, maintaining connections with them can bring benefits. Doing so can earn prestige for the people involved and can emphasize and cement relationships between Houses. All the more so if the deceased person had had a high social status and if the living have provided substantial and conspicuous gifts (such as a bull) in the context of the funeral.

One important way for Songsareks to reconnect to the dead, after the funeral, is by providing them with food. Ghosts are known to be fond of cooked rice with meat (preferably beef, and especially spleen) as well as rice beer. Close relatives of the deceased are expected to provide such a meal near the house in which they used to live, once or twice a day, starting as soon as the dead body has been disposed of. Likewise, people who have given a bull or a cow for the deceased person, either 'to help' or as part of an *ukam* exchange, are expected to feed the ghost at least once after returning home from the funeral.

The ghost of the deceased person maintains a close association with the dead body. People consider a corpse *marang*, as evidenced by its swelling, the oozing out of bodily fluids, and the stench emitted. In the heat and humidity that characterizes the weather in Garo Hills for much of the year, putrefaction starts almost immediately. To limit the extent to which people are exposed to this, the corpse should ideally be disposed of on the day of the death itself. This is preferably done at sunset, a liminal time between day and night. Cremations and burials are essential acts of transformation; conducive of the deceased person's passage to the afterworld.

Graveyards and funeral pyres are strongly associated with ghosts. Cremations are only conducted by Songsareks, and nowadays only rarely, as mentioned in section 5.4. Sadolpara's graveyard is a dedicated stretch of jungle, located at some distance from the nearest clusters of houses, which is divided into a Songsarek and a Christian part. It is a place where ghosts are known to roam about, especially at night. A cremation forges associations between the ghost and the funeral pyre, with its fire and smoke, and then later to the ashes and the charred remains. The morning following a cremation, people collect some charred pieces of bone and bury them in front of the house in which the deceased person had lived (Figures 5.8 and 5.9). At the same spot, a repository is made for seed grains to be used by the deceased person in the afterworld. These seed grains—rice grains and cotton seeds—have been contributed by people who attended the funeral (section 5.5). The repository is a largish box woven from split bamboo. The pieces of bone,

Figure 5.8 The morning after Sisi's cremation, Nenchi and Nokmi collect pieces of bone from among the ashes of the funeral pyre.
Photograph: Erik de Maaker, 2001.

Figure 5.9 Oldap discovered the imprint of a tiger's paw among the ashes of Sisi's funeral pyre. Distant kin of the deceased, who can transform themselves to take the form of tigers, are known to visit the funeral pyres and graves of their deceased relatives at night.
Photograph: Erik de Maaker, 2001.

buried beneath the box, continue to represent the deceased person, allowing its ghost to access the repository.

People also associate the ghost with the deceased person's personal belongings (as mentioned in section 5.2), particularly those that have been in close contact with the body and its sweat (clothes), saliva (toothbrush), or hair (comb). None of these items will normally ever be used by anyone else since it is feared that doing so would trigger the ghost's wrath. Christians bury these personal belongings together with the corpse, or leave them in a bag or tied in a blanket on the grave.

At a Songsarek funeral, the deceased person's best clothes are used to dress a wooden effigy (*kima*) that is carved from a thick tree branch 'to the likeness of the person' (*mande dakgipa*). Such an effigy is about twenty centimetres thick and about two metres long. As I was told, 'Its flesh [the wooden pole] is made to resemble that of the deceased person' ('*Sigipani be'enku banairiknajok.*').[37] The day after the burial or cremation, a man with woodworking skills carves a head into one of the ends of the pole. Using blood from one of the slaughtered bulls or cows that is mixed with soot or with crushed carbon from an old battery, he paints eyes, ears, and a mouth onto the effigy. He also places numerous dots all over the face of the effigy, to indicate 'that this person has died', as one man told me as he painted. Despite a carver's best efforts, an effigy can only approximate the appearance of the person who died, and observers tend to be frank with their criticisms. Passing judgement on Nagal's effigy, one woman commented: 'The eyes did not turn out well at all.' Another woman added: 'Her nose is crooked.' One of the men who had carved the face agreed, 'One eye is skewed, isn't it?' ('*Gingtingin gonggiahajok ia. . . . Iaa mikgronba namsrangsrangja. Mikgron samha gongbengana, mo?*')[38]

The effigy, once carved, is planted into the earth, next to the entrance of the house in which the deceased person had lived. Several people told me that the association between an effigy and a deceased person is so strong that the ghost is able to animate its effigy. At night, or sometimes in dreams, people had seen effigies 'moving around' or even 'dancing between the houses'. When the effigy of Nagal was given a carrying basket of the type that is used for daily work in the fields, Jiji expressed her disapproval: 'It makes her restless, always wanting to go here and there. (The basket) charges the effigy with an urge to work.' The effigy creates a new embodiment of the deceased person and enables people to give food and rice beer to the ghost. That the effigy is treated as a person is also apparent in other respects: according to *niam*, theft from an effigy is as serious as stealing from a human being. To hack at an effigy with a bush knife or a sword—as men sometimes do when they

Figure 5.10 Jiji posing with the effigy of her daughter Waljak, who had died in her fifties.
Photograph: Erik de Maaker, 2014.

are drunk—is, according to custom, no less reprehensible than an attempt at murder, as became clear when a man who had committed such an offense received a hefty fine from the village court (Figure 5.10).

An effigy, once created, is never touched up or repaired. As a new or perhaps alternative embodiment of the deceased person, it is subject to a slow and delayed process of putrefaction (de Maaker 2015). It is exposed to rain, sunshine, and wind. Even more destructive are the insects, such as the omnipresent termites, which eat the wooden pole from the inside out. Nothing that drops from an effigy is ever put back onto it. Within just a few weeks after the funeral, it begins to shows signs of decay. After a few months, the clothes have already been colonized by fungus, rotted, and fallen off. The same goes for umbrellas, cups, and bags put on the effigy. As insects consume the wood, the face's features gradually fade, and eventually the wooden pole disintegrates (Figure 5.11). Six to ten years after its creation, an effigy has completely disappeared. Yet for as long as it exists, even if only as a remnant of a wooden pole, people continue to associate it with the deceased person it

Figure 5.11 An effigy after one or two years: the face has disappeared, and most of the clothes in which it was initially dressed have fallen off.
Photograph: Erik de Maaker, 2003.

represents. In other words, as long as their effigy remains, a deceased person has a material presence among the people with whom he or she once lived.

An effigy may only be made if one or more bulls or cows have been slaughtered for the person who died, since the man who carves the effigy is entitled to a hind leg of beef. Dead for whom no cattle are slaughtered, usually those who had lived in poverty and/or were relatively insignificant socially, receive a much simpler effigy. A proxy effigy, as I call it, consists of no more than a bamboo pole, the top end of which represents the head, although no face is carved into or drawn onto the pole. 'Shoulders' are made by tying another fairly short bamboo pole across the main one. Like a full-fledged effigy, the proxy is dressed in the clothes and non-heirloom jewellery of the deceased person, and is planted in the earth close to the house in which they lived. One such proxy effigy was made for Genna, a young woman who died in her early twenties and had belonged to a House with a fairly low status.

At large-scale funerals for important people, Songsareks may also plant additional poles to represent the bulls and cows that have been slaughtered. A *kimbrong* pole has three notches hacked into its top end. It may be planted by people belonging to the House in which the deceased person lived, or by members of other Houses that have provided a cow or bull. When a *kimbrong* pole is made, the crown of the skull (*mikking*) of the cow or bull is tied to its top end, and both are rubbed with the animal's blood, creating a strong association between the pole and the cow or bull. Planting such a pole also enables those who do so to maintain a connection with the deceased, since it becomes a place where rice beer and food can be offered to them. *Kimbrong* poles are cut from hardwood, which is able to withstand the elements for twenty years or more. This means that the poles can last much longer than the effigies made for the dead. Moreover, *kimbrong* poles that topple over may be replanted. And when a house is rebuilt at a new location, the poles can be moved with it. Thus, *kimbrong* poles can support a relationship with someone who has died over an extended period of time, enabled by the slaughter of a bull or a cow at that person's funeral (Figure 5.12).

Planting a *kimbrong* pole earns its planters prestige by conspicuously testifying that a House has been wealthy enough to provide a bull or a cow for a funeral. Yet, even people who are entitled to do so often choose not to plant such a pole, since that could—as I was told—make them appear to be boasting about the status of their House. Once, Jiji's son-in-law Rancheng

Figure 5.12 The size of a cluster of *kimbrongs* near a house gives an indication of its inhabitants' capacity to offer cattle for their own dead, as well as for the dead of other Houses.

Photograph: Erik de Maaker, 2001.

had the right to plant a *kimbrong* pole after he had slaughtered a cow for the funeral of a matrilineal relative. But he refrained from doing so. When I asked him why, he said: 'Because my House is only that of a son-in-law.' Rancheng felt that planting a *kimbrong* pole might be interpreted by others as a claim to a higher status for his House than that which he himself, as well as other people in his matrilineal group, considered justified. In contrast, after managing to obtain a gong at Diran's funeral (section 5.6), Arseng added a new *kimbrong* pole to the cluster that was already in front of his house. He was keen, it appeared to me, to display a publicly visible reminder that he had been able to provide a cow for Diran.

5.9 Separating, Distancing, and Reconnecting

People face a twofold challenge in relation to the dead. On the one hand, they have to ensure that the deceased become detached from their former social location, and established in the afterworld. On the other hand, they have to ensure, more or less at the same time, that ghosts reconnect to the living. First of all, the ties of the deceased to their former existence must be severed. Should this be unsuccessful for some reason, for instance, because of a failure to appropriately dispose of the deceased's personal belongings, a ghost may be left pining for its former life, and therefore stalk and harass its close relatives. This is dangerous because ghosts can bite and cause further deaths. To avoid such a situation, a series of measures are taken. First and foremost, the initial separation of the ghost from the living is accomplished by the disposal of the dead body, which allows people to 'direct' the ghost to the afterworld, as well as to contain or purge the excessive *marang* that a death inevitably releases. The dead body represents the deceased person, but in the process of burial or cremation it loses much of its significance. Instead, its material presence is substituted by a variety of objects and places. These include the grave or the funeral pyre, the remains (such as charred pieces of bone), effigies, and objects that in the course of the funeral have made contact with the corpse (heirloom jewellery, slings, and coins), or been kept in its vicinity (gongs, sword, and shield). In addition, the deceased person is represented by clothes and other objects imbued with their bodily fluids, which are put on the effigy, or items (such as cattle) that they have been offered. The placement of (traces of) these objects at various sites creates a number of locations associated with the deceased. These various presences of the dead shape memories of the deceased person over successive time frames: some representations disintegrate relatively quickly, others remain prominent for much longer periods of time.

Engaging with the various representations of a deceased person provides people with a context for (re-)tracing their relationships to the House that he or she had belonged to, as well as to other associated Houses. As they accommodate relationships with the dead, relationships among and between Houses may gain new meanings or weight. For the living, in other words, the dead are instrumental to the establishment and maintenance of the relationships between Houses that structure matrilineal groups, as well as of the relationships between such groups. The dead can symbolically represent and affirm these relationships, as *niam* links specific kinship designations to the various transacted items and performative acts. People distinguish between Songsarek and Christian *niam*, although in many respects the two are similar. Both versions of *niam* include guidelines as to what is morally appropriate conduct, which is why people invoke *niam* whenever they advance claims, challenge others, or more generally reposition themselves within their relational networks (de Maaker 2012). In the context of funerals, *niam* allows people to strategically consider potential social gains and losses as they evaluate their degree of commitment towards someone who has died, as well as towards the people through whom they are related to the deceased. Individual transfers of money, goods, and animals at a single funeral are never individual affairs, but are always conducted in relation to transfers that have taken place at past funerals, while anticipating those that may be undertaken at such events in the future. Frequently, reciprocation patterns stretch across multiple generations, securing long-term inter-House relationships.

Funerals are attended by relatives, neighbours, and friends of any religious (or ethnic) background, who participate to the degree allowed by the custom that they follow. While Songsareks may attend the funerals of Christians, and vice versa, Christians never make effigies or plant *kimbrong* poles. Nonetheless, for Christians in rural West Garo Hills, the provision of bulls and other animals 'to help' remains an important practice. Acknowledging relatedness, whether matrilineal or affinal, comes before religious divisions.

According to the classic Durkheimian perspective, as interpreted by Bloch and Parry, funerals facilitate the separation of a deceased person but also pave the way for the eventual regeneration of life among the living. Life is often regarded as a limited good: unless people die, new life cannot emerge (Bloch and Parry 1982: 9). Funerals typically include measures to control the dead, to make their actions predictable, to ensure that they will contribute to the regenerative processes envisioned (ibid. 12). Garo funerals—particularly those of Songsareks—include practices that serve to contain and purge *marang* ('death pollution'). Yet *marang* is also inevitably released when children are born, or when people enact violence (which can be socially acceptable if it is justified). The dangers of dealing with *marang*, and the 'presence' of the dead, make funerals very intense and symbolically charged events, which bring key social interrelationships to the fore and call for them to be reiterated, transformed, or even refuted.

Based on the extensive research that he conducted on the relevance of funerals among the Tangans of Melanesia, Foster concluded that rather than posing a devastating threat to the collectivity, death is 'the reciprocal condition of human reproductive capacity, not external to human sociality but inevitably constitutive of it' (Foster 1995: 140). In other words, Foster identified the occurrence of death, or rather the ways in which humans conceptualize and engage with it, as essential to the definition of the kind of mutualities, commitments, and identifications that make up the fabric of society. In Garo contexts, when death takes away a living person, the matrilineal group is weakened. To counteract that, *niam* calls for Houses to be continued. Negotiating how continuation is to be achieved in each case is done with reference to the dead, hence the dead are central to the renewal and reconfiguration of Houses. The dead, in their many presences, which transcend temporalities, not only demand the continuation of Houses, but also provide substance and structure to the matrilineal groups within which Houses are embedded.

In West Garo Hills, land titles are held by Houses and are therefore inextricably linked to a House's relative political influence and (among Songsareks) religious responsibilities. The death of a married man or woman therefore poses a threat to the very social, economic, and (among Songsareks) religious structures that people depend on for their existence. It is in the interest of all who in one way or the other depend on a House affected by a death, especially one that owns land or otherwise controls assets, to ensure that the House continues to exist. A House is supported by the male matrilineal relatives (uncles, brothers, cousins) of the wife at its head. Acting on behalf of their niece, sister, or aunt, these matrilineally related men share the responsibility for the assets of the House. Junior Houses also help to keep senior ones going by contributing resources and labour, and participating in any decisions taken with respects to the senior Houses' assets. In other words, Houses cannot exist on their own.

The *niam* that guides conduct at funerals in rural West Garo Hills is considered authoritative. Even though the ways *niam* is enacted varies across religious orientations, these variants share the core principles of mutual support and complex patterns of gift transfer. While these transfers of rice, cattle, money, slings, heirloom objects and so on are focused on the newly deceased person, they also encompass the ancestors in a more general sense, as well as relatives traced along both matrilineal and affinal lines. Funerary *niam* is specific yet flexible, allowing for compliance, ambiguity, or rejection of its stipulations. As people engage with *niam* in the context of funerals, they may reiterate or subtly reinterpret the position of their House, and themselves as individuals, within their relational networks. In rural West Garo Hills, funerary *niam* not only transforms and relocates the deceased person (in the afterworld, as well as among the living), but also, inevitably, the people who relate to him or her—closely or more distantly.

6
Claiming Relationships, Spaces, and Resources

6.1 Replacing Baka

Once, when I asked Jiji at what age she had married, she pointed to a girl of about ten or eleven years old who was sitting nearby, and said: '(I was) like that.' Close matrilineal kin of Jiji had decided to 'give' (*onna*) her to Baka, her husband-to-be. Baka was much older than her at the time. Initially, Jiji told me, she had been very unhappy and had run back to her parents' home whenever she could. But her relatives did not give up; they kept bringing her back to Baka and eventually she agreed to stay. In those days, in the 1950s or 1960s, marriage for women at such a young age was reportedly fairly common. Now, in 2020, it is still not exceptional. It is usual for Songsarek marriages to be initiated by the close matrilineal kin of the bride and the groom. This is the case for marriages that create a new House, and even more so for marriages that replace deceased spouses. In the past, girls had little choice but to accept the marriages chosen for them, Jiji told me. Although it is difficult to ascertain retrospectively, men seem to have had more influence upon their own destinies, although attempts certainly were made to force them into marriages against their will. In the more recent past, men's agency has clearly increased, as illustrated by the repeatedly unsuccessful attempts to replace Baka after his death, which failed due to the proposed husbands' unwillingness (discussed below). When Jiji became Baka's additional wife (*jikgite*), she joined his first wife, a much older woman named Dajap. Dajap was one of Jiji's maternal aunts. Dajap herself had been a widow when Baka married her to replace her deceased husband, and according to Songsarek custom this 'entitled' him to a second wife who was much younger, and had not been married before. Dajap's first husband, Tujen, had been a maternal uncle to Baka, so Baka was Tujen's nephew.

When Jiji first came to live with Dajap and Baka she was 'like a daughter' to the two older spouses, helping out with daily household chores such as drawing and carrying water, cooking food, and cleaning dishes. According to what used to and continues to be customary, once Jiji started to menstruate, or at most a few years after, the marriage would have been consummated. I am not aware that Dajap and Baka had any children, but Baka had eight children with Jiji. Of these, one died as an infant and the others grew up into adulthood. Going by the age of her oldest child, it is likely that Jiji first became pregnant at the age of 16 or 17. Again, even today this is by no means unusually young—and it would have been even less so when Jiji was a teenager. Baka died at a ripe old age in the early 1990s, at least ten years before I first came to Sadolpara. Jiji proudly showed me a photograph that had probably been taken in the 1980s, which showed her dancing together with Baka within a group of people during Wangala (Figure 6.1). It was one of her most treasured pictures, which she kept with her other photographs securely wrapped in a plastic bag and a cloth, to protect them against humidity, heat, and xylophagous insects. The many stains on the dancing picture suggest that it had been taken out and shown around during quite a few rice beer drinking parties.

Baka's death, I was told, had given rise to a large-scale funeral that was attended by many representatives of subsidiary and affiliated Houses. Baka

Figure 6.1 Jiji's cherished picture of herself and Baka dancing at Wangala, which was most probably taken in the 1990s.
Photograph: Erik de Maaker, 2001.

had been a well-respected man, who was said to have always lived up to the ritual responsibilities that came with his House's custody of the *kram* drum. Moreover, he and Jiji had managed to extend their *a'king* land, increasing the economic assets of their House. Garo marriages ideally bring together partners from different clans, and this had been the case for Jiji and Baka. Jiji was a Sangma, Baka a Marak. Furthermore, Jiji belonged to the Mangsang matrilineage, hence her surname: Mangsang Sangma. Baka was of the Mrong matrilineage; he was a Mrong Marak.

Baka, Jiji, Tujen, Dajap, and their predecessors had all been married into the House at the instigation of their respective matrilineal groups. Both these groups, therefore, were obliged to provide *a'kim*, that is, to after his or her death replace the spouse who had been their own matrilineal kin (see section 3.3). Baka's death, consequently, created a debt for his matrilineal group (the Mrongs) to Jiji's matrilineal group (the Mangsangs), which could only be redeemed by the Mrongs providing a new spouse to replace Baka. Given that Baka was much older than Jiji, the eventual need for his 'replacement' (*onsonga*) had already been anticipated during his lifetime. Chekjak, the fourth of Jiji and Baka's eight children, had married a man named Gongring a couple of years before Baka's death. Gongring classified as a matrilineal nephew of Baka, and although neither Gongring, Chekjak, Baka, nor Jiji ever stated it in public, it was generally assumed that if (as he probably would) Baka died before Jiji, Chekjak and Gongring would 'enter' the House. Gongring would then take over Baka's responsibilities and rights, while Chekjak would become Jiji's 'heir' (*nokkrom*).[1] Yet such a succession also meant that Gongring would have to—at least formally—become Jiji's husband as well. This kind of a marital constellation is quite common, with a man being the husband of two wives, who are at least in a classificatory, if not biological sense, mother and daughter. That does not necessarily make such arrangements easy. Depending on the age difference between the partners, there may be issues in relation to the consummation of the marriage. For instance, a husband may make demands upon a younger wife who does not appreciate them, or an older wife may make demands upon on unwilling younger husband. Furthermore, living together in a single household can place a lot of stress on the mother–daughter relationship. The older woman might try to boss around the younger one, or the other way around.

As it happened, the idea that Chekjak and Gongring would become the heir couple fell apart soon after Baka's funeral. Gongring had not wanted to live with Jiji after all, I was told. In addition, it had transpired that he did not want to be a farmer, but saw himself as a businessman, which was incompatible with the kinds of responsibilities that heading a House like Jiji's would bring. Emotions are said to have run high, and even though Gongring and Chekjak already had a daughter together, Gongring divorced her in a formal 'kin trial' (*mahari bichel*). When he left, he stopped supporting his daughter. Chekjak was in her early twenties at the time of the divorce, and her daughter was an infant. It was not an easy situation for Chekjak, but fairly soon after Gongring's departure she entered into a relationship with a man named Pongjan. Without formally marrying, they simply started to live together, creating a household of their own. Pongjan quickly made a good impression on Chekjak's sisters, brothers, and other close kin. He proved to be pleasant, reliable, caring, and hard-working, and was also accepted by Jiji. Chekjak and he raised several children together, including the daughter she had had with Gongring. But living with Pongjan made Chekjak unsuitable as a potential heir to Jiji. Pongjan did not belong to the same matrilineal group (Mrong Marak), as Gongring and Baka. Pongjan was a Chambugong Marak. As a matrilineal group, the Mrong Marak held the right to provide *a'kim* replacement for Baka, which meant that—at least in principle—Pongjan could not become Baka's heir. That is, in the years immediately following Baka's death, the Mrongs were not open to the kind of solution which they would eventually settle for (which I will discuss shortly).

After Gongring divorced Chekjak, Baka's matrilineal relatives (the Mrongs) made several attempts to provide Jiji with a new husband. Their first choice was Mingnan, who was still a teenager. He was abducted several times, but he escaped repeatedly and made it very clear that he did not want to stay. Next, the Mrongs chose a young man named Disen, but from the moment of his initial abduction, he made his unwillingness clear. The plan was quickly abandoned when Jiji's eldest son once again tried to persuade him to stay, only to be threatened by Disen with a knife. The Mrongs gave up on Disen, but months—or perhaps even years—later they proposed a young man named Sal. He also refused. By the time I was told about all this, many years had passed, and it was difficult for me to get a clear picture of why all the men had so determinedly refused the marriage. One reason might have been that Jiji had dependent children, and marrying her would have meant sharing in the responsibility to raise them. Many men believe that it is not good to have to bring up children who have been fathered by someone else, even though this happens frequently, and Garo are generally—certainly compared to other South Asian communities—very accepting of children who have been born out of wedlock. The men's reticence may also have been due to the status of Jiji's House. As a landowning and *kram* drum-taming House, it faced many relatively costly religious commitments. Any man who came to head the House would have had to live up to those obligations, particularly as both Jiji and her close matrilineal kin were clearly unwilling to accept a change in the religious status of the House. That could have been achieved by converting to Christianity, which would have required the destruction of the *kram* drum. Lastly, there was another issue, which was perhaps the most important of all: Jiji had a strong personality and she would never have allowed a younger man to dominate her. Consistent with prevailing understandings of gender relations in the wider region, married men tend to assume that it is their role to 'head' a House. This assumption is reflected linguistically: as mentioned before, in everyday speech, a married man is referred to as the *nokgipa*, or the 'one who heads' the House.

Once Sal had also clearly expressed his unwillingness to live with Jiji—and, potentially, her youngest daughter Ratmi, who would most probably have become his second wife, since Chekjak was already married—Baka's matrilineal kin made no further attempts to replace Baka. Having put forward four successive men, no one could deny that the Mrongs had taken their *a'kim* debt seriously and thus honoured their obligations to Jiji, her House, and the Mangsangs. The repeated failure of their attempts gave Baka's matrilineal kin grounds to—at least implicitly—blame their lack of success on Jiji and her family, although no one would have ever voiced such a view directly. After the series of failed attempts, Jiji herself made it known that she did not want the Mrongs to propose any further men, effectively confirming that the Mrongs had indeed done all they could in relation to their *a'kim* debt.

For the rest of her life, Jiji remained without a partner. When I first got to know her she was living with Ratmi, who was unmarried, and a mother to two children born out of wedlock. A couple of years later, when Ratmi was in her early twenties, a husband was found for her who agreed to being abducted. He was a Baptist. At the time, Ratmi was a Songsarek, but she had already expressed her intention to get baptized. Mijeng, the abductee, subsequently explained that as he was not a Songsarek, he was not obliged to fake resistance. He simply liked Ratmi and had no objections to the marriage. Like Pongjan, Mijeng was a Chambugong Marak, and hence also unsuitable to become Baka's heir. Moreover, he was a Baptist, and Ratmi was to become a Christian soon after the wedding. Ratmi and Mijeng therefore could not become 'tamers' of the *kram* drum. Nonetheless, they made their house next to Jiji's, and for the rest of Jiji's life they provided her with tea, food, daily chats, and otherwise took care of her. Such care was also extended by the households of some of Jiji's other daughters and granddaughters, many of whom lived close by. Her two sons, who also lived nearby (which was unusual), as well as the husbands of her daughters and granddaughters, took care of the annual maintenance of the house, and did 'typically male' chores for her such as weaving baskets, or fitting handles onto knives and sickles. Each year, Pongjan claimed a new stretch of swidden for Jiji, another task that she could not do herself as a woman (section 4.6). Jiji and Baka had depended entirely on shifting cultivation for their subsistence. As Jiji grew older, she gradually lost her strength and could no longer cultivate her field, and therefore became entirely dependent on her children, her grandchildren, and their respective partners. Despite his illiteracy, Pongjan, the husband of Jiji's daughter Chekjak, made a tremendous effort to tackle bureaucracy and managed to secure a pension for Jiji of INR 200 per month under the 'Indira Gandhi National Widow Pension Scheme' (IGNWPS) from the office of the Sub-Divisional Officer in Dadenggre. That was enough to buy about 15 kilograms of 'fair price' rice per month, which meant that she could—if needed—contribute rice to the households of the children who cooked for her and would always have enough to eat. Even I, who had been 'adopted' by Jiji as a son, pitched in by topping up her monthly pension as long as she lived.

For Jiji, managing her day-to-day affairs included trying to live up to the responsibilities of her House. This meant, for instance, that at funerals hosted by closely related Houses, whenever appropriate, she was expected to offer money 'to help', or sometimes even a bull or cow. Baka had taken *ukam* on several occasions and those obligations needed to be honoured. Jiji told me that not long after Baka's death she had become unable to offer the kind of support that people had previously received from her House. Moreover, since the House kept a *kram* drum, it had religious obligations to meet that were much more comprehensive than those of Houses without *kram* drums. For example, at least once a year, at Wangala, *kram* drum-owning Houses have to feed Risi cow's blood and beef curry. Cattle are an important source of wealth, but when I first met her, Jiji hardly had any. She had become poor, and behind her back people who did not belong to her matrilineal group used to mock her for being needy. It was even rumoured that Jiji had adopted me in the hope of receiving support from the (comparatively) well-off foreigner that I was. Obviously, I cannot entirely rule out that there may have been some truth in the allegation. But as I mentioned in the introduction, in all the many years that we knew each other, Jiji never once asked me for support nor did any of her close kin.

Jiji was the head of an important House, and quite apart from their emotional attachment to her, supporting Jiji and thus sustaining the House was in the interest of her daughters and sons and their various spouses and children. After all, substantial land titles were vested with the House, which all the members of Jiji's matrilineal group stood to benefit from. They shared the rights granted by these land titles by virtue of their affiliation with the House of Jiji, and that was a strong incentive to work towards the perpetuation of the House, so that it could continue to exercise its rights in relation to the land. Along the same lines, maintaining the *kram* drum was not just a matter of religious importance for Jiji and her matrilineal group. It was also a source of pride. And at the same time, it substantiated the claims to land vested with Jiji's House, since only landowning Houses can maintain a *kram* drum (as mentioned in section 3.1). After all, the land titles of Jiji's House had not been acknowledged by the Garo Hills Autonomous District Council (GHADC), and the people of her matrilineal group were all too aware that this meant that even locally, at the village level, recognition of the land titles of Jiji's House could not be taken for granted (as mentioned in section 4.4). Moreover, the House's custody over the *kram* drum verified its status as long-standing and important in terms of inter-House relationships, which added to its political weight in the local context.

On 16 November 2015, at half past three in the morning, I was woken up by a phone call. I was at home in the Netherlands, far away from Garo Hills. When I picked up the phone, I heard the voice of Chekjing, Jiji's eldest son. He said: 'Erik, mother is dead.' ('*Iruk, ama sijok*'). I heard the silence at the other end of the line after he had spoken those words, and I felt awful and powerless, incapacitated by distance. I had been to Sadolpara a couple of months before on what had become a rather emotional visit. Jiji had been in low spirits. She had lost her appetite (and, by then, all of her teeth), was generally not feeling well and barely set a foot outside of her house. As I was departing, she had told me with the directness that I had grown used to in rural West Garo Hills: 'You will not see me again. I am going to die.' I had disagreed and assured her we would meet again. But in my heart, I knew that she was probably right, as indeed she was. Chekjing did not just call me up in the middle of the night out of kindness. According to *niam*, it was compulsory for him to do so. Jiji's relatives felt obliged to inform me about her death immediately, so that—at least theoretically—I would be able to attend her funeral. Had they not informed me, I would have had reason to be angry with them for denying me the opportunity to see the corpse before its interment or cremation, and for depriving me of the chance to attend the meeting (*toma*) at which her replacement would be discussed. Even if I was unable to make it in time for the funeral, it is possible to give gifts 'to help' afterwards and even *ma'gual* can be accepted months later. 'Are you going to come over?' asked Chekjing over the phone. But of course he knew that the journey would take me several days and be very expensive, and that with my multiple other obligations it was more than unlikely that I would be able to travel at such short notice.

When I did return to Sadolpara, two and a half months later, I was told that Jiji's funeral had drawn a massive number of attendants and had seen the slaughter of at least forty cattle and twenty-nine pigs. That was a very impressive amount, even for Sadolpara. It indicated that Jiji, and her matrilineal group, were doing well. The large number of animals showed that many local people had acknowledged their relationships to Jiji, to her House, and to her matrilineal group. In addition to her local networks of relatives and acquaintances, in the last decade of her life Jiji had become friends with numerous people from Tura who had visited Sadolpara to experience 'real' Garo culture (see section 1.1). Jiji had always been open, friendly, and inquisitive towards the student leaders, dignitaries, and tourists (to name a few) who came over to meet her every now and then. She was so highly respected, both at the village level and in the eyes of people from 'outside', that her body was cremated, which by that time was only undertaken for very important people, or those whose death involved severe *marang* (see section 5.4). One of her friends from Tura, who had come over for the funeral, recorded the cremation on his smartphone and posted the video on Facebook. The text of the post read 'The last rites of Ambi ['grandmother'] Jiji Mangsang Sangma, a Model Lady of Sadolbra Village who always lead the Wangala Troupe during Harvest Festival' (Figure 6.2). For me, to watch her cremation on Facebook, from my home in the Netherlands, once again underscored that Songsarek practices had become a marker of Garoness for middle-class Garo. Facebook posts in English are only accessible to Garo who have received enough education to read them and can access internet, which basically only applies to the urban middle class. Lack of language skills would already exclude most residents of Sadolpara, and in 2015, few villagers had smartphones anyway.

On the visit to Sadolpara some months after Jiji's death, I was told about the customary meeting between senior men—and a few women—of the matrilineal groups of Baka (Mrong Marak) and Jiji (Mangsang Sangma) that had taken place at Jiji's funeral to arrange her replacement. Jiji's matrilineal kin had proposed her daughter Chekjak as her heir after all, even though Chekjak's husband did not belong to the right matrilineage. Since there was no viable alternative to Chekjak and Pongjan at the time, Baka's matrilineal group had agreed to accept Pongjan as a kind of adoptive relative (see Figure 3.3, p. 62). That meant that he was symbolically 'born as our

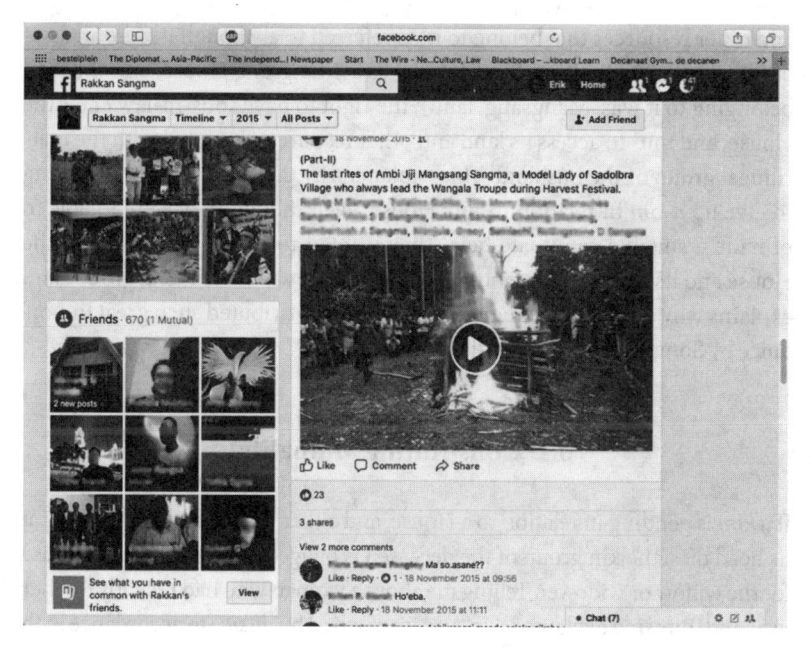

Figure 6.2 The Facebook post dedicated to the cremation of Jiji, displayed on Rakkan Sangma's Timeline.
Screenshot courtesy of Rakkan Sangma, 2015.

child' (*angde ba'a*) into the matrilineal group of Baka. Pongjan remained a Chambugong Marak; he did not change his matrilineal affiliation nor did the Mrongs give up their *a'kim* claim to what had been the House of Jiji and Baka. The principle of being 'born as our child' is well established, and it was a pragmatic choice. I did not understand why the Mrongs hadn't accepted that option years before, but it probably would have made little difference to the lives of Jiji, Pongjan, and Chekjak even if they had. The adoption of Pongjan as 'a child' by the Mrongs ensured that the House continued to exist, safeguarding the custodianship of its *kram* drum. Chekjak and Pongjan were Songsareks, like the vast majority of Jiji's close kin, and showed no inclination to get baptized. As is evident from the difficulties posed by the replacement of Jiji and Baka, increasing Christianization is making it ever more complicated to continue Houses that have custody over *kram* drums.

The great importance attributed by people to *a'kim* relationships indicates that the continuation of Houses is not just dependent on, but actually induced by the two constituent matrilineages. While a House (and the land

and other resources that belong to it) is referred to as though it were an asset of the wife's matrilineage (Jiji's House was a 'Mangsang House', and the land belonging to it was 'Mangsang' land), the right to have sons-in-law enter the House, and thus to access its land and other resources, is vested with the matrilineal group of the husband. This explains why the Mrongs were unwilling to give up *a'kim* in relation to Jiji's House, even though they were unable to provide a suitable candidate heir. They wanted to retain their stake in the House and its assets. Such mutuality characterizes all matrilineal groups and explains why *a'kim* replacement continues to be attributed such great importance by Songsareks and Christians alike.

6.2 Constituting Mutuality

If *a'kim* is pending in relation to a House, and either the husband or the wife at its head dies, the kin group of the deceased is obliged to arrange a new spouse for the widow or widower. Telling me about a woman who had recently lost her husband, Bimsing explained: 'They were married by *du'sia* [in accordance with Songsarek custom, see section 3.4]. Since the man died before the woman, the kin group of the man incurred a debt (*gru*). To redeem it, they needed to send a person, which is called *a'kim*. If the woman had died first, an *a'kim* debt would have rested with her kin group. . . . To provide an heir or heiress to replace a deceased person fulfills *a'kim*.' ('*Do'sia, do'siani gimin da'odi ia do'siiming skang mi'asa sijok, mi'asa siani gimin Mrongodi gru nangjok mandi watna uan a'kim ong'a. Me'chik skang siudi Mangsang maharini a'kim ong'a . . . A'kim o'e, a'kim ong'a maina sianggipani palo nokkrom watakon ukon a'kim jia ini agana.*')[2] A matrilineal kin group that faces such a debt is not only obliged to redeem it, but actually has the exclusive right to do so. Pongjan could not 'enter' the House of Jiji and Baka without the consent of Baka's matrilineal kin, who eventually agreed to adopt him 'as a son', which made Pongjan Baka's heir.

A'kim replacement undergirds Garo Houses, enabling them to continue to exist for a potentially infinite number of generations. This entails the inheritance of kinship designations and subsequently the creation and continuation of hierarchical relationships among Houses. For example, as discussed in section 3.3, a young girl who replaces a deceased elderly woman can become a categorical 'mother' or even 'grandmother' to her own biological sister. Because kinship designations always refer to categories of people, rather than to individuals, *a'kim* replacement ensures the succession of 'mothers' by 'daughters', and of 'uncles' by (matrilineal) 'nephews'.

An *a'kim* alliance comes into being when a couple marries with the consent of their respective and distinct matrilineal kin groups (see section 3.4). For Songsareks, such a marriage involves the groom being abducted and brought to the home of the bride and the consultation of oracles within the *du'sia* ceremony. For Christians, it means a marriage that is prearranged and settled with a shared meal and tea drinking. If a couple comes together of their own volition, rather than having been brought together by their kin, the obligation to provide *a'kim* does not apply—neither for Songsareks nor Christians. Nonetheless, if such a couple manages to acquire assets during their lifetime that are worth inheriting, *a'kim* will usually be arranged for. Clearly, the respective matrilineal groups will always stand to gain from adopting a share in the responsibility for—and rights to—any assets that belong to a House.

If a death creates an *a'kim* debt, its settlement should be negotiated in a meeting that is held at the funeral itself. This meeting brings together senior male representatives of both matrilineages. Elderly women are also present but remain in the background and generally do not assert themselves. To be able to attend the meeting, people need to first participate in the funeral. They should provide 'help' to the close relatives of the deceased, and they should take on dedicated ritual tasks such as the vigorous hacking of the altars and the doorposts with a sword, or the breaking of the rice storage or rice beer vessel. In addition, those who are eligible for *ma'gual* should accept it from the representatives of the House in which the death has occurred, thereby confirming their commitment to the fulfilment of *a'kim*. Most importantly, *ma'gual* should be accepted by the parents, uncles, and aunts of the one who is chosen, or likely to be chosen, to replace the person who died. At Nagal's funeral, an onlooker explained to me: 'They [the matrilineal kin of the girl chosen to replace Nagal] have chosen to get her [the chosen replacement] married, they have kept the [*ma'gual*] gongs'. ('*Jawani kimna jia, rangna chan'a.*') Here, 'keeping the gongs' ultimately means taking custody of the assets of the House, and, by implication, of its inhabitants as well.[3] If people accept *ma'gual* but fail to replace the person who has died, it is said that '*ma'gual* has been forgotten' (*ma'gual guala*). Since the most valuable *ma'gual* is supposed to be given to the person closest to the deceased, that person comes under the most pressure to ensure that a 'new person' (*mande gital*) is provided. Ideally, according to custom, the 'new person' should be a close relative of the deceased. Whether or not that is feasible depends on the availability and inclinations of a suitable candidate. The larger the number of people who attend a funeral, and the more shares of *ma'gual* that can be handed out, the greater the pressure that people who are close to the House in which the death has occurred exert upon the close kin of the deceased person to make an effort to ensure replacement.

Alternatively, the settlement of an *a'kim* debt can be initiated by the surviving spouse, which deviates from the modes of replacement discussed so far. Like other nuptial ties that are initiated by the spouses concerned, such a resolution is considered a 'catch and stay with' (*seki donga*) marriage. As long as the replacement spouse belongs to the matrilineal group of the deceased, objections are unlikely to be raised. However, if the replacement spouse belongs to a third matrilineal group, 'catch and stay with' replacement is problematic. After all, the matrilineal group of a deceased person is not only obliged to provide *a'kim*, but has an exclusive right to do so. This right is not upheld if the replacement spouse comes from a third matrilineal group.

The process of replacing a deceased spouse varies according to their gender, the religious orientation of the surviving spouse, and the kinds of demands asserted by the latter. Songsarek custom treats men and women unequally when it comes to marriage: a man can live with more than one wife, but a woman may never have more than one husband. A couple can propose heirs in advance of their eventual succession, but whether or not those heirs will actually succeed them only becomes clear after one of them has died. If the wife dies before her husband, it is not possible for the widower to marry the heiress. It would be incestuous for a man to marry his own daughter (whether adopted or biological). Moreover, if the daughter is already married, she is ruled out anyway, because women cannot marry more than one man.

When a married woman dies, her widower can demand that her relatives provide him with a new spouse. He does not have to, however, and a young widower is much more likely to do so than an elderly man is. In the latter case, widowers often indicate that they would prefer to remain alone than take a new wife. This makes it possible for the heir couple to informally take care of the House, in cooperation with the widower, without taking over formally until after his death.

If, on the other hand, the husband is the first of an elderly couple to die, the man who has been proposed as his heir can marry the widow. She then becomes his senior wife ('big wife', *jikpangma*), while her (classificatory, and perhaps biological) daughter, who the heir had already married previously, becomes his junior wife ('additional wife', *jikgite*). Whether such a replacement proves satisfactory for all concerned, or results in quarrels and conflicts, depends on the personalities involved.

I have attended several meetings at which replacement was discussed and—at least formally—settled. Generally, these meetings took place on the first day of a funeral, on the rear veranda of the house in which the death had occurred, immediately after the body had been buried or cremated. At Diran's funeral, the meeting took place before his burial. The number of people present on these occasions ranged from ten to forty, depending on the importance attributed to the House affected by the death. Seated in a circle, senior men representing each of the matrilineal groups involved spoke in a highly erudite register of language, rich in metaphors. The aim of such meetings is to express respect for the other matrilineal group and to reach an agreement (*melia*) that settles the *a'kim* debt. The immediacy of death, and the social significance of these negotiations lends these gatherings a charged atmosphere. Speakers express their respect for the strength and defiance of the matrilineage of the bereaved in the face of death, even as they mourn.

Prior to such a meeting, it would be inappropriate for an heir couple to publicly state that their succession as heirs had been arranged. This is not just because of uncertainty regarding how the replacement will ultimately be resolved, but rather that such a statement would imply a lack of respect for the authority of the kin seniors. People expressed disdain for a man who pre-emptively claimed that he was the heir to his father-in-law. One critic remarked: 'Who takes pride in it, when one's (father-in-law) is still alive? No one talks like this.' ('*Sa maiba tangarongu rasong daksuua. A'gilsakba indakidi wekja mo.*')[4] Evidently, it was disrespectful of the man to anticipate the death of his father-in-law and to assume that his kin seniors would decide in his favour. Nonetheless, in the case of Diran and his wife Chengjak, it was commonly known that they wanted their youngest daughter Minjak to become their heiress. Minjak had married Ratjen, a nephew of her father. Ratjen and Minjak had been taking care of the elderly couple for years. At Diran's funeral, I sought Ratjen, whom I had never met before. When I asked a man to point out 'the heir' to me, he chuckled and replied: 'As yet, there is no heir.' That was his way of reminding me that the man who Diran and his wife had chosen to be Diran's heir could not yet be considered as such. It was up to the decision of the kin seniors, who in turn would have to formally obtain the consent of Diran's widow. When I asked the man about the heir's whereabouts, the meeting to settle Diran's replacement had not yet been held.

That evening at Diran's funeral, some thirty men gathered on the wobbly rear veranda of the house in which he had lived with his wife. Widow Chengjak, her daughter Minjak, and son-in-law Ratjen were present at the meeting. A senior man spoke on behalf of Diran's matrilineal group to ask

Chengjak whether she agreed to Ratjen being 'put in the place' of her deceased husband. If Ratjen replaced Diran, that would make him Chengjak's husband. Chengjak answered: 'I will stay put and eat along with them. What choice do I have? Where shall I eat?' ('*Garikari cha'paarinajok batchaba maidakkun? Batchaba ma'bai cha'kuna?*'). Once she had consented in this way, the same man asked Chengjak's daughter Minjak: 'You there, niece, will you care for your mother?' ('*Na'a awa, ah, namchik aksaba nang'mako mittanginaokma?*') One of her uncles interjected: 'Speak up, say: "I will care!"' ('*Aganetbuda: "Mittanggen!", ini*'). But Minjak kept quiet and said nothing. Perhaps she was too shy to speak in front of all the senior people gathered. One of the men came to her rescue and said: 'Say it later.' ('*Ja'man aganetaibujok.*') Another man added: 'Yeah, it's enough.' ('*Im, ong'aijokba ia.*'). The man who had been doing the questioning then turned to Ratjen and said: 'Your matrilineal kin is proposing you. My granddaughter [Minjak], your wife, and your mother-in-law [Chengjak] say: "We are willing to live with him, whether he cares for us or doesn't care for us, whether he sacrifices to the spirits or not." Are you willing to take care of them?' ('*Na'a angsutanga, ah, nang'jikongde, nang'ni maniongde: "Chingade gaari i'ari cha'najok mittanguba, mittangjuba, hamuba, hamjauba inonga," Na'ara nang'ma nok, nang'ma nokgri dona gitan na'aba mittangnajokma?*'). Neither Chengjak nor Minjak had made any such comprehensive statement; this was the speaker's interpretation. Ratjen did not say anything either but remained quiet, also probably too shy to speak up. A voice surmised: 'It's enough.' ('*Ong'jokba ia.*') Another confirmed: 'This is it.' ('*Iaba kakketha*'). And another man observed: 'Is there anything else to ask? There's nothing more.' ('*Ia ma'ku weni-kon'i sing'ani dongjajokba ia.*') One of Diran's senior male matrilineal relatives concluded: 'If they, mother and child [Chengjak and Minjak] say: "Let's pound together and eat, live together and eat." If they say: "Let's pound in one mortar, in one wooden block", then they have agreed to it.' ('*Bisong ma'ningha, pawaha: "Su'grimi cha'na, donggrimi cha'na." Nang'ni inagita: "Cha'am dotsainku, bola dotsanku su'na," inudi bisong ku'rachaki ra'jok*'). Again, neither Chengjak nor Minjak had said anything of the sort, but the words spoken on their behalf were meant to reflect their supposed sentiments. I understood the 'pounding together in one mortar' as a metaphor for domestic harmony: it requires perfect synchronization for two people to pound together in a single mortar, each using their own pestle, one descending when the other is raised up. The man who had led the meeting brought it to an end: 'There's nothing more to say, we all seem to be content.' ('*Dongjajokba, kusiongjokba na'achingbamo.*')[5] Chengjak, Mingjak, and Ratjen had kept quiet throughout, but by being present, and by not publicly objecting to the arrangement proposed by the kin seniors, they had given their consent. For the settlement of an *a'kim* debt, it is important that the people involved agree to the replacement in public, or at least do not disagree or run away (which is not unusual), so that its validity cannot be challenged at a later date.

At these meetings, kin seniors express respect for the matrilineage of the 'other side', while playing down their own importance. At one funeral, a man speaking on behalf of the widower addressed the widow's kin as 'wise and reputed ones'. At the same time, he was self-effacing. Referring to himself, he said: 'I don't know and I don't understand . . . I am not wise and not sharp-witted.' (*'Angnaba u'ijauba-ma'sijauba . . ., anga seng'jaoba matjauba.'*)[6] Similarly, a senior relative of Diran emphasized his own humility, saying: '. . . I am not a wise person, I am not knowledgeable, I can't speak well and I cannot comprehend.' (*'Maina angadi ku'paba man'ja, mandiba seng'ja, u'iaba u'ija-ma'siaba ma'sija, katta aganna man'ja, gisik u'isoknaba man'ja.'*)[7] It is also customary to play down the attributes of the person put forward as a replacement for the deceased. At one such a meeting, a proposed heir was described as 'foolish' (*'jada'*), as 'someone who cannot till land, someone who is unable to build a house to live in' (*'dangi cha'ja, riki dongja'*). On another occasion, an heiress was characterized by one of her male matrilineal kin as 'unable to cook rice or draw water' and 'unwilling to weed swidden'.

Arranging replacement becomes more complicated if a widower demands a spouse to replace his deceased wife even though an heir couple has already been (albeit informally) planned, or if a death occurs in a House for which no heirs have yet been arranged. In such cases, close matrilineal kin of the deceased are expected to propose a replacement spouse during the meeting that is held at the funeral, within hours of the announcement of the death. Ideally, men of the matrilineal group to which the House belongs (that is, of the widow or deceased wife) should abduct this 'new person' and bring them to the house of the widower or widow on the evening of the day that the corpse is disposed of, or soon after.

Songsarek custom stipulates that a man who is single and marries a widow as a replacement spouse has the right to have an additional young wife as well. She should classify as a daughter of the widow, and in the context of the marriage becomes 'attached' (*chapa*) to her.[8] A woman explained to me that the younger woman is 'given [to the man] for the same place as the elderly one', because 'an old woman cannot give birth to children, cannot weed fields, and cannot carry heavy baskets'. The junior wife thus compensates for capabilities that the senior wife lacks. Often, when a man marries a widow, the additional wife is not arranged for at the same time. In fact, it can take years before the widow's kin arranges the second wife, and men who have married a widow often express dissatisfaction about the apparent lack of effort made to provide them with an additional young wife. While Christians do not allow men to have additional wives, both Songsareks and Christians practice *a'kim* replacement. Arranging *a'kim* can demand the cooperation of kin across religions divides, which are often accompanied by distinctions of class.

Miknang was a Songsarek who died as an old man. He was poor and no heirs had been arranged before his death. His widow Migat was in her sixties. In the meeting that was held at his funeral, Miknang's matrilineal relatives arranged for a young man named Ningsen to become Migat's new husband. Ningsen, a nephew of Miknang, lived in the nearby town of Dadenggre, where Miknang had originally come from. Not only was Ningsen accustomed to the practical comforts of small town life (such as running water and electricity, which weren't available in Sadolpara), he was also a Christian and had attended school, at least for a couple of years. Migat was a Songsarek, who had no desire to get baptized. From the outset, it seemed unlikely that Ningsen would be willing to move to what was at the time a predominantly Songsarek village, even though nobody involved admitted such doubts publicly. Five weeks after Miknang's death, I accompanied some of his in-laws from Sadolpara to Dadenggre to visit his matrilineal kin. This visit was referred to as 'leading the ghost' (*mi'mang dila*), a ritual to invite the ghost of Miknang to reconnect to the House in which he had been born. Burling mentions that when they 'led the ghost' in the 1950s, the representatives of a deceased man used to carry a gong, tied in a sling, to the House from which the man had originated (Burling 1997 [1963]: 155). But on the day we visited Dadenggre there was no gong. Moreover, no one made any mention of Miknang. The get-together in Dadenggre was cheerful and, to my surprise, even Ningsen's move to Sadolpara was only referred to in passing. Somehow, I had expected Migat's relatives to bring it up explicitly, since it seemed to me that it was taking a long time for the marriage to come into effect. On our way back home, I asked when he was likely to move. The people I was walking with told me that he would come in about five months' time, 'after Wangala'. A couple of months later, I once again discussed the replacement of Miknang with one of Migat's maternal uncles. He offered his view of the relatives in Dadenggre who had chosen Ningsen: 'They know that he [Ningsen] is not willing to work, not duty bound, does not do tilling and will not fit in. It's to pretend to give to mother and niece. We do not consider that sincere. Just to make a statement they have said: "We give so-and-so's son."' (*'Indiba kamdi gong'ja a'seldi chikja dangidi cha'ja rikidi dongjawa. Amana namchikna chingan on'misia gita ong'gen. Chingadi buria-bikdipa gita ong'aigen piniki: "Nionga agani nionga amikkani bi'sako," iniming agana.'*)[9] As it happened, Ningsen never did move to Sadolpara. In terms of both religion and class, it would not have worked out. His relatives from Dadenggre had put forward his name to indicate their willingness to meet their *a'kim* obligations. Yet, for them, Sadolpara was far away, and Migat's House did not own land or any other assets. Apparently, Miknang's kin assumed that nominally honouring the *a'kim* alliance would suffice as a gesture towards the relatives of Migat. Miknang's relatives were not genuinely motivated to ensure the continuation of the House affected by his death, and since their reasons for this were widely understood, they must have assumed that their lack of effort would not really damage the reputation of their matrilineal group. According to *niam*, *a'kim* should always be provided, but the lengths to which kin are willing to go to actually realize replacement can vary significantly, especially when the religious loyalties and social class of the people involved diverge.

Religious affiliations are not always homogenous within a single matrilineal group, and since the obligation to provide *a'kim* is faced by the group as a whole, arranging it can require cooperation within matrilineal groups yet across such lines. Although both Songsareks and Christians practice *a'kim* replacement, in certain respects Christian custom (*'rurini niam'*) and Songsarek custom (*'mandeni niam'*) differ significantly. Some contexts bring these differences, in terms of 'rights' and 'obligations', explicitly to the fore. While Songsareks allow or prefer polygamous (re)marriages, Christians do not. For Christians, the replacement of a deceased man can result in a new spouse either marrying the widow or the heir daughter. If the 'new man' marries the heir daughter, the widow cannot become his wife as well, but ends up being 'looked after' (*mitanga*) by the heir couple. And if a widower is 'provided' with a woman who has been previously married, such as a widow or a divorcee, under Christian *niam* he does not have the 'right' to an additional wife. Songsarek *niam*, by contrast, would grant the man with the right to an additional wife who had not been previously married.

Nangseng and Jengda had designated their youngest daughter Netjak and her husband Rajeng to become their heirs. Nangseng was at least ten years older than his wife, which made it quite likely that he would die before her, which would allow their heirs to 'enter' the house. Nangseng and Jengda were Songsareks, but about two weeks before Nangseng's death, they converted to become Baptists (as mentioned in section 5.1). I can only presume that Rajeng and Netjak had convinced them to do so. Like Nangseng and Jengda's other children, Rajeng and Netjak had become Baptists some time before, and would have quite simply been unable to organize a Songsarek funeral for Nangseng. Since he was a Baptist at the time of his death, he could be given a Baptist funeral. At the funeral, one of the schoolteachers who was posted in the village read out Nangseng's obituary, which made explicit reference to the faith he had so recently embraced: 'Having physical ailments for many days . . ., God has taken him into his kingdom, to life's everlasting dwelling place, which God has prepared [for him] to rest.' ('*Aro adita salrangna be·enni an·senggijaniko man·e . . . Isolni song-nokona neng'takchina, Isolni dakgimin biapona rimangako man·aha.*')[10]

Within hours of Nangseng's burial, representatives of the two matrilineal groups that bore *a'kim* held the formal meeting to discuss the 'appointment' of the heir couple and to define the couple's future relations with the widow. Since the widow had been a Songsarek until very recently, her kin apparently felt the need to address her future relationship to the heir explicitly. Junan, an uncle of widow Jengda and himself a Baptist, said: 'Some time ago, when he [Nangseng] was close to bubbling over [close to his death], he became a Christian. And his wife became a Christian as well, am I right? Nangseng's wife will have to understand . . .' ('*Unigimin da·odi, mijao mineo biaba sina gittu-katna ja'pango. Ruri ong·aha. Unigimin, ia rurini ong·anio jikgipaba ong'paama? . . . Nangsengni jikgipa u'ina nanggen . . .*'). Digat, another of Jengda's uncles, added: 'She will need to!' ('*Nanggen!*'). Junan continued, putting into words (his version of) the way Jengda should see the situation, '"I am a Christian, that is my husband's wish. There can't be two wives, he [Rajeng—the heir] can't weed two fields."' He clarified: 'It would lead to quarrelling and create trouble for the *chra*s [Jengda's uncles]. So, now is the time to know and to understand.' ('"*Anga ruriha, angsini dakdilanga. Jikgnikudi dongjanawa, a·gnikudi dangjanawa.*" *Ja'manu kengkang daknawa-kangkang daknawa. Chrana nidikani ong·a, ja'mano. Uni gimin, da'uin u'ii ma·sii ra'bu.*'). Tajak, a mother of Nangseng, added: 'You [Jengda's uncles] have the power to tell, don't you?' ('*Aganna pawal donga mo*'). Junan elaborated further: 'You can serve him [Rajeng] rice to eat, . . . but you cannot sleep with him. . . . You should only take care of the grandchildren. Eggs cannot be laid in your stomach, your breasts cannot feed. . . . You should not wriggle and worm for that. Such is the law and custom of the Christians, such is our culture. Do you understand, or don't you understand?' ('*Miku on'i cha'na man·a . . ., kimi chuna man'jajok. . . . Na·a diba'rikari su·songdilari* *dongpaaniha. Oko bitchi'na ong'ja, chelo bimik nana ong'ja. . . . Una gitekanigujronani dongja. Rurini law custom gita. Ah, an'chingni biwalba, indakiha. U'iama u'ija mo.'*) Widow Jengda replied: '(I) do not want to marry and hold him' (*'Kimpanadi keppanadi gong'janawa'*). Junan: 'Yea, this is it, it's up to you to decide. . . . You have said it' (*'O'e i'kun, iadi nang'ni gisikha. . . . Nang'ni kattaha'*). Siljon, an uncle of Nangseng and Rajeng, responded: 'These words are enough . . . ' (*'Iadi ong'jok kattadi . . . '*) Junan concluded: 'So, we have reached an agreement. A'gitok [Nangseng's matrilineage] has redeemed its debt.' (*'Unigimin da'o na'song kanbaen ong'aha. A'gitoknoba gru dongjajok.'*)[11] Jengda was in her sixties, and long past childbearing age, but this degree of clarity was apparently required in order to ensure that later on neither Jengda nor her matrilineal kin would be able to contest the validity of the fulfilment of *a'kim*. Christian custom does not allow second marriages, and although this results in the formal remarriage of widows becoming increasingly rare, the example shows that solutions are found to enable the continuation of Houses and the inheritance of kinship designations nonetheless.

A'kim replacement, at the core of Garo *niam*, defines relationships among Houses with reference to the dead. When a spouse dies, in a House for which *a'kim* is pending, the constitutive matrilineal groups need to act to prove their commitment. If *a'kim* pertains to a House that holds substantial property, rights, and claims, the right to provide *a'kim* constitutes a valuable asset. In addition to providing support and accepting gifts at the funeral, it is crucial that the matrilineal group of the deceased spouse acknowledges its obligation to provide a replacement for them. Even more than the actual fulfilment of this debt, publicly announcing one's commitment to do so substantiates relationships among Houses. Relationships among Houses are also honoured by humbling oneself, while attributing wisdom and strength to the representatives of the Houses one connects to. Conversion to Christianity redefines certain aspects of Garo *niam*, but the principle of *a'kim*, and its capacity to define relationships among Houses, holds strong.

6.3 Showing Commitment, Acknowledging Debt

A matrilineal group that fulfils an *a'kim* commitment honours the person who has died, as well as the matrilineal group to which they belonged. People state that according to *niam*, *a'kim* replacement should always be provided. In reality, the amount of effort that is made for a particular House depends on the importance attributed to it and the personal commitment that people feel towards a particular deceased person and their relatives. If *a'kim* replacement were always provided, all Houses would be continued for an indefinite number of generations—but that is evidently not the case. In my experience, villages typically count a small number of Houses that are believed to have existed since the village's foundation, one of which is usually the House of the village head. A few other Houses will also be known to be 'old', but the genealogy of the majority of the Houses is likely to be relatively recent. Many Houses are not continued for longer than one or two generations, even if there are *a'kim* obligations pending, which indicates that replacement often fails.

Historically, Houses that maintained *kram* drums or held custody over *kusi* boulders were unlikely to be short-lived. After all, the relationships that these objects enabled people to maintain with the spirits could not be simply neglected or abandoned—that would have been expected to incite retaliation from the spirits. In the days when Songsarek custom and religious practices went uncontested, these safeguards seem to have been quite steadfast. I was told about one particular House that had held and continues to hold custody over a *kram* drum. About sixty years ago, the husband and the wife heading the House both died within a very short period of time. When their respective matrilineal groups failed to replace the couple, the two youngest children were taken into the care of their elder sister, who was already married. She stored most of her parents' valuables (such as gongs and swords) in her own house, except for the *kram* drum. People say that because of its relationship to Risi, a *kram* drum may not be moved to another house. A couple of years later, the abandoned house collapsed, destroying the *kram* drum. But since the drum had not been purposefully destroyed, the relationship with Risi did in those days not come to an end. Despite the House lacking a physical presence such as a building, or people, its titles to land continued to be respected. Like the land titles of Jiji's House, those of that particular House were not registered with the GHADC. It took at least fifteen years for the constituent matrilineal groups to arrange a new heir couple. When they did, the new couple built a new house and had a new *kram* drum made, thus re-establishing the House physically. These days, it would be impossible to revive a relationship in this way because new *kram* drums are no longer produced. Moreover, with the waning of the Songsarek presence, and the consequent decline in the fear inspired by Risi, the gradual phasing out the relationship of a House to Risi has become feasible (as mentioned in section 4.5).

The Houses of village heads, as well as other Houses that are registered as landowners with the GHADC, are the least likely of all to be discontinued. Benefits from the claims, titles, and assets of registered landowning Houses filter down to Houses that are subsidiary or otherwise dependent on them, which is a strong incentive for the latter to invest in their continuity. If a House owns valuable assets it will almost certainly be continued through *a'kim* replacement. This is not only the case in rural West Garo Hills, but in urban environments such as Tura as well. If someone there dies who belongs to an important House, the deceased person's kin group is expected to arrange a spouse to replace them. And even in Tura, property continues to be passed on in the female line, within Houses that are constituted by the matrilineal groups of both the marriage partners.

It can nonetheless be difficult to arrange a suitable person to take the place of someone who has died, or who agrees to become an additional wife. Providing *a'kim* is an obligation, but it also constitutes a right. I have often heard senior men say that according to custom they had the right (and the duty) to 'appoint' a replacement spouse, and they therefore expected the person chosen to 'listen' to them. It is not uncommon, however, for the young person selected to respond with defiance rather than obedience. Someone who has been chosen to be 'given' in fulfilment of *a'kim* can be put under intense social pressure, but they are not without agency. Due to the current coexistence of different strands of Garo *niam*, the degree of agency is most probably greater nowadays than it was some five or six decades ago, when Jiji's kin chose her to marry Baka (section 6.1).

Among Songsareks, a replacement marriage is initiated by forcefully guiding the 'new person' to the House he or she will be married into. Young men from the matrilineal group of the House that requires the new spouse go to the chosen person's home, surround them, and bring them to the widow or widower. As with any other marriage by abduction, the abductee is expected to try to escape (see section 3.5). If the 'new person' makes it clear by repeatedly escaping that he or she is truly unwilling, the marriage lapses, and the *a'kim* debt has not been redeemed. The matrilineal group facing the debt must then propose another person, as happened when a replacement was sought for Baka. Reflecting the gender inequality that shapes many aspects of life, abducted women are put under much greater pressure to comply than abducted men are. Women are expected to obey their uncles. If they refuse to do so, they may need to resort to rather radical measures to get their way. Kin seniors not only exert pressure on the man or woman who has been chosen, but also on that person's parents and others responsible for their 'release'.

Nagal, who died of snakebite, left behind a husband and five young children. The youngest two of these, two-month-old twins, were cared for by Nagal's sisters and cousins after her death, but the older children remained with their father. No one doubted that he needed a replacement wife if his household were to continue to function. When Nagal's replacement was discussed at the meeting held at her funeral, her kin decided on a girl aged about twelve years, Bilmi. She lived in Nagal's village, and soon after the meeting she was abducted and married to the widower. I saw her once, shortly after the news had spread that she had been chosen, and she looked simply defiant. From the outset, Bilmi made it clear that she did not want to live with the widower. But as a girl, she was not granted a say in the matter, and in the weeks that followed she was abducted time and again. Each time, she fled from the house of the widower as soon as she could. But even if she wanted to hide, she had nowhere to go and kept returning to her parents for food and shelter. One evening, I was sitting near the widower's house when Nagal's elder brother once again brought Bilmi to the house and tried to persuade her to go inside. The abductions involved some degree of physical force, but it was clear to him that Bilmi ultimately had to be convinced to accept the marriage. I heard him say: 'This is now your house. Why don't you go into it? You don't have to feel shy. Let's go to the rear veranda, it has a nice fresh breeze.' Nagal's eldest daughter, who was around eight years old (just a few years younger than Bilmi), and a neighbour's daughter of a similar age encouraged Bilmi: 'Come, come in', gesturing to invite her into the house. Even though it was obvious that Bilmi did not want to become the widower's new wife, as long as her own matrilineal kin refused to heed her objections, she remained the one designated to replace Nagal. As the weeks went by, uncertainties were voiced among the relatives of the widower regarding the degree of commitment of Nagal's kin. If they had truly chosen Bilmi, were they doing enough to convince her to accept the marriage?

The repository dedicated to Nagal's ghost, which contained seed grains and utensils for her to use in the afterworld, was taken apart and its remains set alight some three weeks after the funeral. This burning of the repository (*delang su'a*) is preferably done at dusk, the time of day most favourable to the ghost. It signals the end of the (ideally) daily feeding of the ghost, which increases the distance between the ghost and the people who have cared for it. This transformation of the relationship with the ghost calls for a modest celebration and on this occasion Nagal's elder brother, her mother, Bilmi's parents and one of her grandfathers, as well as the widower gathered at Bilmi's parents' house. Nagal's mother had brought a vessel of rice beer. In the light of a kerosene lamp, people sat near the entrance of the house and talked about the replacement of Nagal. In order to facilitate an omen, a chicken was slaughtered and its large intestine 'read' by Bilmi's grandfather, a common

Songsarek practice (see section 3.4). After examining the amount of dung in the intestine, the shape of the two protrusions in its lower part, and the direction in which these were pointing, he concluded: 'The intestine is in agreement. It is in agreement. It is even full of dung.' (*'Du'bikba ku'mongaanming. Ku'de ku'monganming. Ki'ba gapasokaming.'*) The two protrusions were facing forward, and the entire intestine was solidly stuffed with dung. It was the second chicken intestine that day to provide a favourable omen regarding the replacement. Bilmi's father sighed and remarked: 'I am getting angry at this person [Bilmi]' (*'Hatch, anga mandi iku anga ka'uba nangpilongahajok.'*) Her grandfather commented: 'If the one [Bilmi's father] releasing doesn't truly release her, everyone will say: "This is a very serious offence!"' (*'Watgipa'a i'na watjaode: "Darang-marang mingnoa!" iniha.'*) Although he had not named anyone specifically, it was obvious that he was referring to Bilmi's parents and uncles. Bilmi's father was quick to put the blame for his daughter's unwillingness on Nagal's elder brother, Bilmi's uncle. Bilmi's father said: 'I told her uncle earlier: "Just be here for a while, to tell her all" . . . I wanted him to slap her a little bit, but not too much.' (*'Anga da'anoba, ian mamagipa: "Da'o okkisa innode, dongsukubo, gimiko aganangi donnade." . . . Inan dokangkan inni alamala agani donangna am'aming inni.'*) Nagal's elder brother reacted with resignation, blaming Bilmi, rather than her parents: 'What can be done, after you [Bilmi's father] have truly released her, and she refuses to stay with her husband?' (*'Na'ong kakket bibi wato dongjajokode ma'dakkunua?'*) Nagal's grandfather chimed in, rejecting this attempt to absolve Bilmi's parents of their responsibility: 'You [Bilmi's parents] must act in earnest. I agree with others who say: "This is embarrassing for our matrilineal group as a whole."' (*'Kakketo dakbibinaba nangan nangakini. Jani innagita: "Dol gimikni kraba cha'ba cha'an."'*). But then, with his gaze lowered to the ground, he continued: 'I am full of shame, and feel I lose my honour. But if the one chosen is unwilling, a man can't be forced, nor can a woman.' (*'Kracha'oba rasi chonoba. Gong'gijakode gong'gija, me'asakoba man'ja, me'chikhakoba man'ja'*). Another man agreed: 'Not even by the clan as a whole.' (*'Chatchi gimikming.'*)[12] It seemed to me that Nagal's kin had proposed Bilmi because she had been their best available option at the time of the funeral itself. None of the people present when the conversation took place seemed to truly doubt Bilmi's father's intentions. Rather, as I understood it, Nagal's relatives hoped to indirectly convince the widower that they were committed to providing him with a new wife. The main hindrance at this point was Bilmi's unwillingness to cooperate. The widower took the cue and said: 'We [Bilmi and I] will whisper while sleeping at the swidden.' (*'A'ba chusuo tiltalna innoa.'*). The widower's remark hinted at consummation of his marriage with Bilmi. People spend the night in field houses so they can protect their fruit-bearing crops from being eaten by animals such as elephants or wild boar, but field houses are also reputed for the privacy they offer to couples. Rather than expressing his conviction that Bilmi would become his wife, I understood the widower's remark as an acknowledgement of the commitment of Nagal's kin. Since it was becoming obvious that Bilmi would never comply, the widower was trying to lighten the mood with a joke. Bilmi's father chuckled, but said: 'I may be laughing, but I feel like dying of shame.' ('*Anga bu'oba, siongjok da'ning.*')[13]

In the weeks that followed, Bilmi's uncle continued to pressurize her to accept the marriage. He came to her parents' house on several occasions. Whenever she saw him coming, she tried to hide. Bilmi's parents made it clear to anyone willing to listen that Bilmi was beyond their control; she did not 'obey' them, she was 'ill-mannered' and 'disrespectful', her father would complain with a deep sigh. Bilmi came out of hiding each time her uncle left, and she slept and ate in her parents' house, like every other member of the household. That she was a Baptist, or intended to become one, whereas Nagal's widower was a Songsarek, was probably to her advantage. As I understood the situation, this justified her resistance to the marriage to Nagal's widower in a way that may have appeared legitimate to many people. No one ever said so explicitly since that would have implied doubting the commitment of her parents (who were Songsareks), and of the matrilineal group as a whole, to providing an appropriate replacement. People assured me that 'Of course she would have to adopt the religion of her husband.' But in the context of the wider decline of the community religion, an involuntary conversion in that direction would have been most unusual. Bilmi's religious orientation made it even less likely that she would ever actually replace Nagal. In the end, after many more weeks spent trying to make her accept the marriage, Bilmi's matrilineal kin group gave up. Instead, they chose another girl of about the same age, Najak. Najak was a Songsarek and showed no inclination to get baptized. She more or less readily accepted becoming Nagal's widower's new wife. Even though it had been clear for quite some time that Bilmi was unwilling to replace Nagal, her uncles and other kin seniors could not have given in sooner, since that could have been seen as giving in to the disobedience of a young girl.

In other cases, girls or young women were put under even more pressure to accept much older men as their husbands. Dolmit, a teenager of fifteen or sixteen, was chosen by her kin to marry a man the age of her grandfather. Wilson, a widower, was in his sixties. Initially, Dolmit gave in to the pressure exerted by her parents and uncles and agreed to live in Wilson's house. She cooked food, drew water, and worked the land, but she refused to sleep with him. Other youth told me that she had confided to them that she was very unhappy with the situation. One morning, a couple of weeks after the marriage had been initiated, Dolmit disappeared. Rumours circulated that she had previously threatened to commit suicide and had now most probably hung herself. After a couple of days, Dolmit's father came to the place where I was living with Nandini and Sengjrang and asked us to come to help search for her. He presumed that our video camera might be able to find her, as a kind of scanning device, which was unfortunately not the case. He told us that she had been working as a day labourer on the rubber plantation that Meghalaya's Department of Soil Conservation had made in Sadolpara. Someone had asked her why she was working there, and she had answered that she did so 'to earn money to buy clothes'. The person who had posed the question had then asked: 'Does your husband refuse to provide you with money to buy clothes, or is he unable to?' Wilson, her new husband, was very poor. Apparently humiliated, she had run away from the plantation and had not been seen since. Dolmit's father looked very worried. Nobody knew where to search for her, and it seemed best to wait a while, in the hope that she would show up again.

Six days later, in the early morning, all the physically fit men of Dolmit's matrilineal group held a meeting near Wilson's house and proclaimed that they would search every bit of the vast jungles and fields surrounding the village. The men formed several search parties, one of which I joined. We walked through the fields and forests for a couple of hours, but we also took a long break in one of the field houses. According to me, the search was not conducted very thoroughly, as though it was no more than a formality. By noon, the search was declared over and another meeting called, which was attended by representatives of the matrilineages of both Wilson and Dolmit. After some discussion, a written statement was drawn up and read out, which held Dolmit responsible for her own presumed suicide. Wilson absolved himself of any liability for her death, which he underlined by divorcing Dolmit. The next day, news spread that Dolmit was alive and well. Desperate to escape the marriage with Wilson, she had not killed herself but had taken refuge with relatives in a village some two or three hours by foot from Sadolpara. Her parents deplored her behaviour to anyone willing to listen, and one of her male cousins went to bring her from the place where she had sought refuge. About two weeks later, Dolmit had returned and moved back in with her parents. For the next couple of months, she hardly came out of the house. But after those months of seclusion, she began to behave like any other local teenager again. Wilson was very angry with Dolmit's parents, whom he considered partly to blame for her rejection of the marriage, and I can only presume that he felt deeply humiliated by the whole affair. He did not ask for another replacement wife but lived alone for the rest of his life. Considering the lack of determination with which the search party had gone about its task, it is likely that at least some of the men suspected that Dolmit's disappearance was a ploy to enforce a divorce, which Wilson would never have agreed to otherwise.

For *a'kim* replacement to work out, not only does the one chosen as a replacement need to accept their fate, but the widower or widow also has to accept the person who has been chosen as their new spouse. Even this cannot be taken for granted, as became clear when Sisi died (I referred to her earlier in section 5.3). Dising had replaced Sisi's first husband sometime in the 1980s, according to my estimations. Sisi was probably in her fifties by then, and Dising in his twenties. Sisi had had four children with her first husband but did not have any more with Dising. In accordance with Songsarek custom, a younger wife had been arranged for Dising as well, but she had died soon after the marriage. Sisi's relatives replaced the deceased younger wife, but that did not work out because Dising did not like her. Sisi's kin then arranged for another woman, but after she became deaf, Dising divorced her. By the early 2000s, when we had come to live in Sadolpara, Dising had married his fourth younger wife, Ralmi, who was a younger sister of the one who had become deaf. By then, Dising was an old man. About fifteen or sixteen years old, Ralmi agreed to draw water, cook rice, and work the land, but she refused to sleep with him. Dising was unhappy about that. He suspected Ralmi's parents of secretly encouraging her to refuse him, but they vehemently rejected any such allegations. One of Ralmi's in-laws told me: 'Ralmi should give birth to Dising's child; such is Songsarek custom.' Nonetheless, it was generally assumed that Ralmi would become Dising's main wife after Sisi's death. He was against the idea, however, because of her refusal to sleep with him. When the meeting was held to settle Sisi's replacement, Oldap, one of Ralmi's senior uncles asked her: 'Do you accept Dising fully, as a wife? That is, to cook for him, but also to sleep with him?' Ralmi refused to answer and left the meeting in tears. From then on, she slept next door to Dising, in her parents' house, but she continued to fetch water for him and work his fields. Her parents told anyone who stopped to listen that they were ashamed of their daughter, but they could not refuse her a place to sleep. After a while, Dising divorced Ralmi and requested that Sisi's kin provide another wife.

A few half-hearted attempts were made to abduct another woman, who immediately made it clear that she was not willing to live with him. Eventually, Dising accepted that no woman would ever bear a child of his, as he stated at yet another meeting about the pending *a'kim* debt. This relieved Sisi's kin of the obligation to propose any further replacement wives for him. Ralmi agreed to continue to fetch water and cook for Dising, but she would no longer stay in his house.

I maintain that, over the years, effectuating *a'kim* replacement has become increasingly complicated due to a gradual decline of the authority of senior male matrilineal kin. These men continue to play a dominant role in society, with their authority resting, to a good degree, on the importance attributed to Houses and hierarchical inter-House relationships. Yet the more resources become tied to individual Houses, rather than to the larger collectives of matrilineal groups, the more viable it becomes to resist the authority claimed by kin seniors. In an ideological sense, Christianity also contributes to the erosion of seniors' authority, by favouring harmonious marriages between consenting individuals over formalized unions initiated by abductions of men chosen by the larger matrilineal group. Currently, economic developments are transforming relationships among Houses across rural West Garo Hills. New modalities of ownership and control of land are emerging, which are not necessarily rendering former management regimes obsolete, but nonetheless can have a major impact on the status of Houses and the kinds of relationships that Houses maintain among one another, as I shall show below.

6.4 Rural Workers, Rural Entrepreneurs

The men were thin and their possessions few. They lived under a large stretch of plastic sheeting that had been tied between a couple of trees, a couple of metres above the ground. It was their job to harvest four to five metres long, wrist-thick bamboo poles from a grove that had been left untouched for at least three or four years. Each of the bamboos that they cut and carried through the dense and steep forest to the roadside collection point earned them one rupee. Working flat out, a man could thus earn up to INR 150 in a day, which was more lucrative than the INR 50–100 per day that was the going daily rate for agricultural work in the early 2000s.[14] The men had very few belongings: some blankets, a couple of pots in which to cook rice, a kettle and mugs to drink tea, all of which they kept in their makeshift tent. There were at least twenty of them, but they hardly ventured beyond the perimeter of their roadside labour camp. They were all Bengali Muslims who had been contracted from a densely populated riverine village in the nearby plains of the Brahmaputra river, some 40 kilometres away. The villages they came from were all located on Indian territory, and none of the men was known to have come from across the border with Bangladesh. Selsen had contracted them. He was a young Garo who lived as a caretaker in a semi-abandoned office of the local government in the village of Rongchugre, not far from Sadolpara, and could speak elementary Bengali because he had attended school for a couple of years. He had a motorbike, so it was easy for him to travel to the villages where he recruited the workers. Sometimes Garo men worked in such groups as well, but middlemen like Selsen preferred Bengalis because 'they work hard, and make very few demands'. Once the harvest had been completed, the workers would take their pay, pack up their meagre belongings, and be taken back to their villages by truck. Selsen would use the same vehicle to transport the bamboo to Phulbari, a nearby town on the bank of the Brahmaputra river. There, he could sell the bamboo to traders, who in turn would take it further into the plains where there was (and still is) a strong demand for such materials. Today, these kinds of work parties are still a common sight, and ethnic Bengali continue to be brought into the 'interior' part of Garo Hills to work and live under conditions that most Garo would consider unacceptable.

In the densely populated riverine plains that surround Garo Hills, there is an unlimited demand for natural building materials such as timber and bamboo. Logging has been severely restricted in Garo Hills since 1996, when a 'timber ban' for the entire North-Eastern region came into effect (Nongbri 2001). Ever since, 'legal' timber has become very expensive, if it is available at all. Illegal logging is not uncommon, but transporting illicitly harvested trees can be risky, as forest rangers or the police may apprehend such shipments. Bamboo grows fast and it can be harvested every three to four years. Better still, bamboo is not affected by the timber ban, and with the increasing scarcity of wood, demand for it has sharply increased (Laine 2012). Traditionally, bamboo has been the most important building material in Garo Hills. In the past, people used bamboo that grew on their own land for their own use. It is only in the last few decades that bamboo has become a commodity that can be harvested and sold for cash.

Throughout rural West Garo Hills, and all across rural Meghalaya, the network of roads suitable for motor vehicles is steadily being expanded. Even roads that are initially no more than dirt tracks make it possible for trucks to transport bamboo, firewood, and other produce to and from what were formerly inaccessible locations. In addition, the availability of motorized transport such as a trucks or pickups is gradually increasing. Young men like Selsen were eager to make use of these opportunities. I have never seen women in rural West Garo Hills engage in the kind of trade that Selsen was pursuing, which leaves these kinds of ventures to men. Unlike most Garo villagers, who neither spoke Bengali nor had their own means of transport, village-based entrepreneurs like Selsen could easily travel to the nearby plains and communicate with the Bengali-speaking traders there. Moreover, and probably more significantly, many Garo villagers are still illiterate, and fear being cheated by Bengali traders.

Selsen's business benefitted not only himself, as an entrepreneur, but also the village head and his close affines. Selsen had been born in Sadolpara, into one of its more influential Houses. This meant he could draw on influential, trusted kin relationships. He also knew which resources the village could offer access to, and how those resources could be monetized in a cash market. The village head, as one of the largest owners of *a'king* land, had granted Selsen the right to harvest the bamboo grove. In exchange, it was rumoured, Selsen had paid him INR 30,000 as a share in the profits. I was unable to get this confirmed: such deals are always confidential, and the amounts involved are never made public.

The House of the village head held title to the *a'king* land where the bamboo grove was located, but according to the local interpretation of *niam*, all the Houses subsidiary to that House have a share in that claim. This should have entitled them to a proportion of any returns from that land. Relationships between Houses are traced down the female line, but transactions of this sort are negotiated almost exclusively by men. The village head, I was told, had brokered the deal with Selsen with the help of some of the head's closest allies, who in turn had received a decent share of the money. Other men who, based upon their House's relationships, also considered themselves entitled to some of the profits, had only been offered token amounts of INR 100 to 500. In the row that ensued, some of those men refused to accept what they considered a ridiculously small amount. The village head and his close allies put forward a different interpretation. They claimed that the bamboo grove was exclusively theirs, hence they did not need to share any proceeds from it with representatives of subsidiary Houses and had only chosen to do so out of generosity. The conflict created serious discord, and a couple of weeks later, when the village head was drinking rice beer together with some of the men who felt they had not received their due, it all came out. A heated argument erupted and other men present had difficulty preventing them from starting a fight. The men who felt betrayed never got any additional money, and from what I understood, the whole affair left a scar. It was the kind of dispute that flared up time and again, souring relationships between people who were not only closely related but also mutually dependent.

The digging of coal used to present a comparable source of potential conflict. In and around Sadolpara, the most important mineral resource is low-grade coal. This coal is located in shallow subterranean deposits that were identified, most probably in the 1980s or 1990s, by government surveyors. A House that owns *a'king* land has the first right to any subterranean resources like coal but shares that right with its subsidiary Houses, which are constitutive to the *a'king*-owning House. Informal mining probably began in the early 1990s and continued until about 2014.[15] In the days when coal was mined in Sadolpara, it was bought by Bengali traders, who transported it to Assam or Bangladesh. Mining and selling coal was profitable and appreciated as a valuable source of income. Before any coal deposit was mined, it was first divided into sections that were each wide and long enough for a tunnel (*jul*) to be dug (Figure 6.3).[16] These were allocated so that each House that obtained such a section or 'tunnel' became the owner of all the coal that was

Figure 6.3 A man from Sadolpara mining coal on village land. The coal-bearing layer is close to the surface, and mined using a pickaxe.

Photograph: Erik de Maaker, 2003.

dug from it. Since the deposits were often not very large, they could usually only accommodate a small number of tunnels. People told me that tunnels ought to be assigned to subsidiary Houses according to the nearness of their relationship to the House of the *a'king* owners. This meant that the Houses 'nearest' to that of the *a'king* owners were most likely to obtain tunnels, while others that were considered more distantly related might well receive none.

I was told how on one occasion, when coal had been about to be mined from a deposit located on land of the village head's House, some of his sons-in-law had not received a tunnel. 'There weren't enough shares', one of them told me. His statement sounded neutral, and by explaining it to me in this way, he avoided addressing the question of why others had received a tunnel but he had not. But I learned later that a great-grandson of the village head, who was a more distant relative than the son-in-law, had obtained a share. Years later, when coal was mined from the *a'king* land of a House to which the great-grandson's wife was distantly related, the same man obtained another share, which this time was justified by his being a grandson-in-law of the titular owners of the coal deposit. Given that the grandson of the village head was one of the village's young entrepreneurs, owned a truck and knew how to deal with the Bengali traders to whom everybody eventually had to sell their coal, it seemed likely that the division of shares was not only worked out in accordance with kin relations, but that more pragmatic considerations played a role as well.

When it came to sharing out tunnels to dig coal, relatedness mattered, but so did personal interests and capacities. These politics of sharing often enabled villagers who were already relatively well-off to gain further benefits. This contributed to a widening of the economic disparities that have gradually arisen between Houses that, in principle, all share rights to the same *a'king* land. The new trading opportunities generated by the expansion of transport routes, and the growing demand for the kind of commodities that rural Garo Hills can produce, have altered the ways land is being used and valued. Holding title to *a'king* land is as important as ever, but the ways this shapes inter-House relationships is changing, as new strategic relevancies come to the fore.

6.5 Accessing Swidden

In rural West Garo Hills, shifting cultivation continues to be important both socially and economically, as it is in many other hill regions of North-East India. Currently, a 'shifting field' or swidden is cultivated for one, or at most two, successive years.[17] The first year, people grow subsistence crops such as rice, millet, tubers, and vegetables, as well as cash crops like ginger, chillies, and cotton. If a field is cultivated for a second year, which is becoming increasingly rare in this part of Garo Hills, it is entirely dedicated to rice. Quite a few elderly people told me that in their youth, hill rice used to yield very good harvests, enough to provide their staple for much of the year. But harvests have sharply declined over the last couple of decades. Villagers have noted that the yield of rice cultivated on the second-year fields in particular has fallen far below what it used to be some four to five decades ago, which is why few people still bother to cultivate it. They attribute this change mainly to reduced rainfall, with an observed decrease in both the length of the rainy season and the intensity of the rains. In addition, environmental scientists such as Tiwari claim that the fertility of the land has diminished due to the steady decrease in the number of fallow years between cultivations (Tiwari 2003: 168–169). If fields are left fallow for about eight to twelve years, the forest has enough time to grow back to a considerable extent, which replenishes the nutrients in the soil. Roy even mentions that 'in the past' fallow periods of twenty to thirty years were common across Garo Hills (Roy 1981: 217), which reportedly guaranteed very high yields. Garo Hills saw a sharp rise in population in the course of the 20th century, which has increased the demand for land. In addition, the amount of land available for shifting cultivation has been greatly reduced, mainly due to the creation of orchards (next section). Nowadays, Sadolpara's fallow periods last an average of five to seven years, although in some cases they may be much longer. Fields also lose fertility due to the selling of tree branches and logs as firewood after the fields have been burned. Formerly, villagers only collected firewood for their own use, and many branches and logs were left on the fields to decompose as an organic fertilizer. The sale of firewood by the truckload is a relatively recent development, facilitated by the new roads and tracks that enable trucks to reach previously inaccessible locations. In the 2000s, one pile of firewood (one *kaman*, approximately half a truckload) fetched approximately INR 850; the figure had increased to INR 1,500 by 2019. Across the region, demand for firewood continues to grow. Many people, including those living in towns, like to use firewood for at least part of their cooking, not only for what it allows in terms of slow cooking, but also because LPG gas cylinders are relatively expensive and can be difficult to obtain.

In Sadolpara and the villages nearby, new swiddens are made every year. At the beginning of the dry season, in the month of November, people discuss the location and size of the plots to be made. This involves decisions that have an impact on all the *a'king* land of a village and should therefore ideally be made collectively. To this end, the village head calls a meeting, which should be attended by all the men who head a House and want to make a new field. The meeting is attended by Songsareks and Christians alike. Women cannot take part. I was told that this is because the meetings end with participants heading out into the jungle to claim their new fields, which is taboo for women. Presumably, this is because the jungle is known to be home to spirits, including very fierce ones, which should not be confronted by women. This taboo is evidently based in Songsarek ontology, but Christians heed it nonetheless. Single widows who intend to make a new field have to ensure that a (married) male relative represents them—when Jiji used to still cultivate a swidden, her son-in-law Pongjan claimed a new field for her each year. The first objective of the meeting is to reach an agreement regarding the locations of the new fields. These locations will usually cover *a'king* land owned by different Houses, the representatives of which should agree to the use of their land. As mentioned before, while ownership is formally vested with a particular House, the right to its *a'king* land extends to the larger cluster of Houses that are subsidiary to it. People who can claim a close relationship to such a House consider themselves entitled to use its land to make swidden, and usually put pressure on its 'head' to allow them to do so.

The meeting is presided over by the village head, an important responsibility of whom it is to ensure that every resident of the village who wants to cultivate a field can claim one. I attended several of these sessions when I was living in Sadolpara for my doctoral fieldwork, and they typically proved lengthy, complicated, and rife with conflict. The village head was charged with the responsibility of mediating decisions while taking multiple interests into account, but the men gathered barely acknowledged his authority. At the first meeting that I attended, the village head proposed that all the new fields be made on land belonging to his own House. The hillsides he suggested had not been cultivated for over twelve years and were covered with thick forest. Once cleared and burned, the soil would be fertile. However, the land was far away from the main village—at least an hour on foot—which many people objected to. Some of the men went against the village head and decided amongst themselves to make their new fields on *a'king* land that was closer to their homes, which the owners of that land consented to. Their defiance made the village head very angry, not least because their proposal would result in the year's new fields being spread across different locations rather than situated together on one single or at least several large contiguous areas (*cha'rimsa*). This dispersal of the fields would complicate future field rotation, since it meant that the fallow periods would come to vary within a single area. This was all the more problematic because some people intended to eventually transform their fields into orchards, so they would continue to occupy part of the land rather than leaving it fallow after swiddening. (Making orchards to cultivate cash crops has over the years been actively encouraged through a variety of government programmes, with saplings being provided to farmers either for free or at a subsidized rate—as discussed in the next section.) This discord contrasts with the mood of such meetings in the past, when—according to what people told me—there was generally consensus regarding which large contiguous areas were to be cultivated. The rotation cycle of these contiguous areas used to be fixed to the extent that people referred to it to state their age. Someone might say, for instance, that he or she 'had eaten around five times' (*cha'changbonga*). This meant that during that person's lifetime, each of the areas where swiddens were made had been cultivated five times, translating to an age of twenty five years.

During that first meeting which I attended, it became clear that even though the village head was supposed to be in charge of the claiming of the new swiddens, he was unable to impose a decision if several men in unison chose to go against him. In the end, it took three meetings that year, spread out over at least a fortnight, before it was established who would make which new fields and where they would be located. At those successive meetings, the men gathered discussed the qualities of the land at each of the potential locations. I noted how every slope, hilltop, and stream was known and had a name, which allowed people to discuss the locations in great detail. The men talked about the soil, and how that in combination with rainfall and heat would influence the harvests that could be expected. Shifting cultivation is entirely dependent on rain and sunshine. The rains are typically abundant from April to August, after which they completely cease. Once the clouds are gone, the sun is unshielded and the days become extremely hot. All this influences the growth of the crops. A plot at the top of a hill retains less rainwater and is relatively dry and hot, which is good for growing cotton; at the foot of a hill the soil retains more moisture and is therefore better for rice. In addition, some of the men mentioned that certain places had 'strong earth' (*a'a raka*), which meant that cultivation should be avoided in order not to anger the fierce spirits located there.[18] Christians are not supposed to heed these kinds of beliefs, but even among Songsareks it was unclear to what extent they ultimately dissuaded people from cultivating certain fields.

As they evaluated the potential new fields, the men discussed possible boundaries, referring as they did to small streams, ridges in the landscape, large trees, boundary stones, and the remnants of paths. Even if an area had not been used for ten to twelve years, the men knew which House had previously cultivated it. A former field is referred to as 'an eaten one' (*cha'a*). People can attempt to reclaim a field that their House has previously made, and it seems that they have precedence over others to do so, but it does not necessarily happen. Often, they will want to change the size of their new field in accordance with the labour that is currently available to their family. Obviously, Houses that no longer exist cannot reclaim their former fields, while couples who have created a new household since the previous cultivation cycle do not hold any previous claims. Hence, it is necessary to adjust the borders between the various plots, also in order to avoid patches of jungle being left uncultivated between fields. Such patches could provide shelter to wild animals that feed on the crops, which is of course undesirable. It is considered bad practice for people to claim more land than they can work—that would be greedy, hence shameful. Lastly, no field should stretch across *a'king* land that is owned by more than one House since that would blur the boundaries between the *a'king* of the different landowning Houses.

Hierarchical relationships among Houses determine the order in which fields can be claimed. In principle, the representative of the House that owns a particular stretch of *a'king* land has a first right to choose their own new field, followed by the representatives of Houses that are closely related. Once these men have announced their claims, others can do so too. Hence, it is advantageous for people to work the *a'king* land of their own House, or from one they are closely related to, since that provides them with the best opportunity to get the kind and size of field that they want. As mentioned before, Jiji, as a widow, could not claim her own new field (Figure 6.4). Following Baka's death, she made her field together with her daughter Chekjak and her son-in-law Pongjan. Pongjan claimed fields that were large enough to accommodate Jiji's swidden as well as his and Chekjak's.[19] If new fields were being made on *a'king* land owned by Jiji's House, as a close son-in-law he was always among the first to extend a claim.

Most households work their swiddens themselves. Additionally, people who have the means to do so may employ others, who need cash, to work for them as daily wage labourers. People who are poor can easily acquire debts during the 'lean' months (March to June), if they have to borrow rice or money from wealthier villagers in order to survive. These months are lean because by then the previous year's harvests have been more or less exhausted, but the new crops have yet to yield. One man who was relatively well-to-do within Sadolpara, and thus able to loan money or rice to those who needed

Figure 6.4 Jiji returning home after a day in the fields, carrying a heavy load of cotton on her back and a bundle of tapioca stems in her hands.
Photograph: Erik de Maaker, 2000.

it during the lean months, was Jetsin. The fields that he and his wife claimed each year were always much too large for them to manage themselves, so they hired fellow villagers to work for them. On swiddens, the weeds grow as fast as the crops. Weeding is very labour-intensive, and it is crucial for a good harvest. Since the fields are sown with a mixture of crops, some of which initially closely resemble weeds, weeding is not only arduous but also demands a great deal of skill. When the time came each year to weed the fields, Jetsin summoned his debtors to work for him to repay the money or rice that they owed him. This arrangement put the debtors at a disadvantage, since working someone else's fields reduced the amount of time they could spend on their own fields. As a result, their own yields would be poorer, while the harvest of those who could employ labourers increased. The practice of employing labourers or being employed as such thus served to exacerbate economic inequality (Burling 1997 [1963]: 202). In the early 2000s, a day's work on the field was considered worth 3½ kg of rice, or approximately INR 50. As mentioned in section 6.4, the rate has now gone up to about INR 150, which, disregarding inflation, indicates that available monetary wealth has slightly increased.

Residents of villages like Sadolpara have exclusive access to the land that belongs to their village domain, contingent on the matrilineal group in which they were born, or (for men) which they marry into. The land located within a village domain belongs to several *a'king*-owning Houses, as mentioned in section 4.4. All the Houses that constitute a single matrilineal group tend to more or less jointly manage their land, with access to that land, at least in principle, being allocated according to matrilineal relatedness. This means that married men have access to land that is held by their wife's matrilineage. In addition, as a secondary right, men are often able to claim land belonging to the matrilineage of their mother. Both of these rights apply to land for cultivation, for building a house, or for extracting other resources such as coal. Most of the *a'king* land in Sadolpara is owned by Mangsang Sangma Houses, while a smaller part is held by Mrong Marak and Chambugong Marak Houses. A Mrong Marak man, married to a Mangsang Sangma woman (and thus belonging to a Mangsang Sangma House), should therefore make his house or field on Mangsang Sangma land. In addition, or alternatively, he might also be able to use Mrong Marak land, because he is a son of the latter matrilineal group. People decide among themselves how land is to be used and how it is to be divided among residents. In these decision-making processes, the relative seniority of Houses matters, as does the status of the individual persons involved. The right to reside in a Garo village is dependent on one's relationships to its senior Houses. Since land is associated with matrilineal groups, and land titles are inherited in the female line, the right of women to reside on land where they were born is taken for granted. The same applies, albeit to a lesser degree, to their brothers. This is why Jiji's two sons can reside in her village and cultivate its land. Men who belong to other matrilineages cannot move in unless they enter into a relationship with a woman who belongs to the particular village. Outsiders who have an independent income may be welcomed (such as school teachers or anthropologists), but those who have not are unlikely to be able to settle in a Garo village, which explains why the rural 'interior' of Garo Hills remains more or less exclusively inhabited by Garo. The village head of Sadolpara explicitly brought this up when he agreed to our prolonged stay, cautioning us not to 'depend on the village for our rice' (section 1.3).

Kin relations are thus fundamental to the negotiation of access to land among the residents of a village. With marketization bringing ever more opportunities to accumulate capital, people who are well positioned in kin networks can not only obtain the best plots of land, but are also likely to be able to pay for labour, so they can capitalize on its returns, which in turn increases their investment capacity. The result is that the contrast between people who are poor and those who are well-to-do within a village is becoming increasingly pronounced.

6.6 From Rotating Swiddens to Permanent Occupation

Until a couple of decades ago, fields worked for shifting cultivation in rural West Garo Hills would have been abandoned after a maximum of two years. By the early 2000s, cultivating fields for a second year had become rare, and as far as I am aware it is hardly done at all any more. In the days when the cultivation of second-year fields was still common, Songsareks used to—customarily—release and abandon their fields at the time of the Jamegapa festival. The festival started with a brief sacrificial ritual conducted on each of the second year's fields, which was concluded by tossing one or more bundles of rice straw from the centre of the field into one of its furthest corners. This tossing of the bundles ritually ended the claim that had been made on the field when cultivation began (section 4.6). Once people stopped farming their fields for a second year, the rituals relating to the Jamegapa festival were shifted to the first-year fields. This meant that Jamegapa came to be conducted on fields where quite a few crops were still growing, so the rituals no longer marked the fields' release. Whether or not a field would eventually be released at the end of the season came to depend on economic decisions made by the person who had claimed it. Christians never ritually marked the release of their fields.

If a field that has been used for shifting cultivation is abandoned, it reverts back to being 'common land' (*a'a ramram*). Common land typically has shrubs, bamboo, and forest growing on it, and it supports the wide variety of plants, insects, and animals that characterize Garo Hills as a 'biodiversity hotspot' (Kumar, Marcot, and Patel 2017). Once a field has become common land, anyone is free to harvest the self-seeded swidden crops that continue to grow on it, such as ginger, aubergine, chillies, and tubers. People also visit common land to forage for wild plants such as tubers (*ta'a narot, ta'a steng*), fruits (such as Indian gooseberry or banana), and vegetables (such as sorrel), while it also provides materials such as wood, bamboo, cane, and thatch, which are used to make implements and baskets or for construction. The land also provides many kinds of leaves, roots, and tree barks that are valued for their medicinal properties (de Maaker 2013a). If someone has purposefully planted trees or bushes on *a'king* land belonging to a House of their matrilineal group, those are excluded from this common usage of *a'a' ramram*. These might be fruit trees such as mango or citrus, thatching grass, or the kinds of bamboo that can be sown. Common land also provides a habitat for wild animals such as deer, wild boar, wild buffaloes, wild cats, and elephants. In the dry season, men armed with muzzleloaders and spears hunt some of these animals, but hunting wild cats or elephants is taboo.[20] In the rainy season, people collect edible grasshoppers (*gukmittim*) as well as large frogs (*bengbong*).[21] Rivers and streams are also for common usage, and their water is used for washing, and at times for drinking and cooking. Fishing is popular in the dry season.[22]

Common land in and around Sadolpara is now becoming increasingly scarce, due to the creation of orchards (*bagans*). Since the 1990s, people have been planting areca nut trees and cashew saplings on their fields in addition to the swidden crops. These trees provide harvests for a decade or more, so once an orchard has been created, the land it stands on is permanently occupied (Figure 6.5). In effect, it becomes inaccessible to the owners of the *a'king* land. Their title does not formally cease to exist, but they lose access to the land for as long as the orchard is maintained. Land thus becomes permanently occupied when a House that claimed a plot of land for a swidden simply never releases it. In the more densely populated Tura region, the trend towards permanent occupation of land began as early as the 1960s, or even before, which has transformed a rural economy that used to be primarily based upon shifting cultivation into one that is almost fully dependent on orchard-based cash crops (Saha 1968: 1695; Saha and Barkataky 1968: 230; Goswami and Majumdar 1972: 75). Even in Sadolpara, the surface area that is occupied by orchards is increasing year by year, making it ever more difficult to find forest that can be used for shifting cultivation. Nonetheless, compared to other Garo villages, Sadolpara still has quite a lot of available land, and so far people are managing to accommodate both orchards and shifting cultivation.

The most common orchard trees, areca nut and cashew nut, do not require much labour once they have been planted. Periodical clearing of undergrowth and harvesting of the crops are the main tasks. Consequently, households can maintain large orchards with relatively low effort, which makes the trees all the more attractive. But even if orchards are not very demanding in terms of labour, people are careful to keep watch over them. While the trees are

Figure 6.5 An orchard of areca nut trees. The undergrowth is cleared regularly so that it does not disturb the trees' growth.
Photograph: Erik de Maaker, 2016.

saplings, they are at risk of being eaten by wild animals or freely roaming cattle (as was the fate of Nagon's areca nut saplings, section 4.1). And once the trees mature, their owners like to keep an eye on the progress of their fruits. Hence, it is an advantage to live fairly close to one's orchards. Because the orchards are spread out across the *a'king* land, people are increasingly building their houses further away from what traditionally used to be the centre of the village. In order to manage both orchards and swiddens, people prefer the latter to be located near their homes too, especially if they intend to convert the latter into orchards in the future. This explains why it is becoming ever more difficult for people to agree on common locations for the new swiddens. Previously, before orchards became a major factor, people used to more or less live in the field houses on their swiddens during the growth season. This allowed them to protect their crops from marauding elephants or other potential assailants, without having to walk long distances back and forth to the village. The increasing economic importance of orchards is thus transforming not only patterns of agricultural land use but also of residence.

Shifting cultivation has been condemned by many policymakers and administrators as 'economically unviable and environmentally destructive' (Pant, Tiwari, and Choudhury 2018: 2). A high-ranking official of the Government of Meghalaya told me in 2019: '*Jhumming* [shifting cultivation] is a bad practice, and it should be stopped. In whatever way we look at it, it means destruction of the forest.' Environmental scientists have long supported a much more nuanced perspective, arguing that shifting cultivation can actually make a major contribution to the sustenance of biodiversity.[23] Farmers in and around Sadolpara do not share the negative convictions voiced by the government officer either, and even those who invest heavily in orchard cultivation continue to make swiddens as well. Young entrepreneurs like Selsen are no exception. According to villagers, shifting cultivation provides people with invaluable food crops such as local vegetables, tubers, and hill rice. Such items are rarely available from the market, even for those with money, so the only option is to cultivate them oneself. Moreover, it provides people with a certain degree of independence from market forces, thus ensuring food security, however limited. Also, cultivating swidden includes keeping land fallow, which can be harvested for 'wild' crops, and nurtures animals that can be hunted. Although the Songsarek rituals relating to shifting cultivation are becoming less crucial as more and more people convert to Christianity, shifting cultivation continues to bring people together in collective effort, for example, when burning the fields or sowing the first seeds (section 4.6). All villagers take part in these events, irrespective of their religious orientation. Shifting cultivation constitutes a shared livelihood that demands cooperation and sustains a village community, which may be one of the reasons why people in Sadolpara and neighbouring villages are continuing to practise it as far as conditions allow. People seem to cherish shifting agriculture for what it yields, not just in terms of produce, but also socially.

The mechanisms by which common land, once claimed, becomes permanently occupied, do not appear to be a recent innovation. In addition to their temporary swiddens, many Houses have permanent wet 'paddy' rice fields (*a'pal*), as mentioned in section 4.6. West Garo Hills is very hilly, but the wet rice fields are located on flat land in small valleys between hills, and typically receive—at least during the rainy season—a steady supply of water from a river or brook. Wet rice is highly valued, since its cultivation provides much better returns than that of hill rice. Once claimed, wet rice land is never released, but cultivated year after year. In Sadolpara, going by what villagers say, all the land suitable for the cultivation of wet rice had already been claimed by the 1960s. As with all fields, wet rice fields and orchards can be located on land that is not owned by one's own matrilineal group. Given the distinction between owning land and holding a claim to fields that are made on it, such wet rice fields or orchards can even be sold or given away without the owners of the *a'king* land having a stake in the transfer. In practice, nonetheless, almost all such transfers take place between people who live in the same village and thus among kin. The sale or gift is then of the claim to the field, not of the title to the land on which it is located. In practice, however, the permanency of the usage right renders the underlying land title all but redundant.

Fields that become permanently occupied in this way do not necessarily get registered with the GHADC. The District Council can grant a title deed (*patta*) that relates a specific plot to an individual occupant, but the procedure requires a 'No Objection Certificate' (NOC) to be issued by the village head. An NOC is a formal statement that certifies his agreement to the registration of a dedicated plot of land as *patta*. Once an NOC has been issued, the House that owns the *a'king* land on which it is located no longer has usage rights to that particular plot of land. In principle, this is analogous to the situation I outlined earlier, whereby fields once claimed continue to be occupied. The difference is that in the first case, the alienation of fields is not endorsed by the state authorities, and therefore remains—at least in theory—potentially reversible. So far, the village head of Sadolpara, apparently with the support of most villagers, has been reluctant to share out these kinds of 'individual' titles to permanent plots. Elsewhere in Garo Hills, particularly in the urban areas, such title deeds have become very common, and in many places, all the erstwhile *a'king* land has already been permanently occupied.

The only persons accepted by the GHADC as lawful signatories with the authority to validate NOCs are the village heads listed in its registers. This fails to take into account that, according to the customary land rights that operate in villages like Sadolpara, the village head is no more than a representative of the matrilineal group he has married into, rather than a titular owner as an individual person. As far as the District Council is concerned, the representatives of Houses that are directly subsidiary to that of the village head formally have no say in affairs relating to the land that is owned by their matrilineal group. Any owners of *a'king* land whose land titles have not been recognized by the District Council are rendered equally invisible in the eyes of the administration. This situation is unfortunate since the mandate of the District Council, which operates under the Sixth Schedule of the Indian Constitution, is to enable customary land management at the village level. Rather than achieving this, it is imposing a rather skewed interpretation of custom that fails to offer the scope for negotiation among villagers that customary procedures would allow.

Making village heads the sole signatories of NOCs has given rise to many problematic land deals across Garo Hills.[24] In Sadolpara, Jiji's matrilineal group owns *a'king* land that has not been registered by the District Council. But at least vis-à-vis other villagers, the group's maintenance of its *kram* drum serves to validate its claim since *kram* drums can traditionally only be maintained by Houses that own *a'king* land. In a similar way, the significant efforts made to replace deceased spouses of *a'king* land owning Houses, even when their ownership is only recognized at the village level, demonstrates the great importance that is attributed to these (unregistered) land titles by the matrilineal groups constitutive of such Houses.

The GHADC creates *patta* with reference to a sketched map of the plot in question, which is produced by one of their surveyors. Since no comprehensive cartographical surveys have been made of villages' *a'king* lands to date, these maps are not geographically precise, but merely indicate the location and size of the plot. To keep the *patta*, once created, its holder is required to pay an annual land tax (*kazina*) of approximately INR 30–40 per bigha[25] to the District Council. Technically, *patta* can be sold, but so far this has yet to happen in Sadolpara or the surrounding area. Villagers told me that for such a sale to take place, it would most probably have to be agreed upon by close kin, and transactions would be likely to remain confined to within the matrilineal group.

Garo *niam* associates property rights with women, but *patta* nevertheless tends to be registered in the name of men. According to me this is more reflective of the overall patriarchal bias of Indian state bureaucracy than of a fundamental change in Garo custom. Currently, as mentioned in section 3.3, a married man's property is inherited in the female line, and cannot be passed onto a son. Accordingly, *patta*, registered in the name of a man, is inherited by his daughter and her husband.

In Sadolpara in the early 2000s, a number of men managed to register some land as *patta*. One reason for doing so, I was told, was that it enabled them to take out loans from the State Bank of India (SBI), which required a security deposit. One of Jiji's neighbours told me that he wanted to obtain such a loan in order to buy areca nut saplings for an orchard. According to the SBI's directives, *patta* can serve as security for loans, because it constitutes a permanent land right. In theory, this means that *patta* could be forfeited if a debtor failed to make their loan repayments. But these were 'soft' agricultural loans, offered by the SBI as part of a Government of India rural development package, and bank staff assured me that such a penalty would never actually be imposed in rural West Garo Hills. So far, then, the commodification of land in Sadolpara has only been partial, and land ownership continues to be anchored with the matrilineal groups that are its traditional owners.

People were not eager to talk to me about who had made *patta*, or whether they themselves had done so or not, which I take to indicate that making *patta* is seen critically: as a way of gaining private property at the cost of the larger collective. To weaken the matrilineal group in this way is something that no one would like to stand accused of. Moreover, making *patta* has a further antisocial taint, since it reputedly involves the payment of substantial amounts of money under the table to the people who process the documents. I have not been able to verify this, but it does indicate that at least in the public imagination, making *patta* is only an option for those who have considerable monetary assets. And whereas money brings prestige, holding on to it, or investing it to increase one's own wealth, in theory goes against the traditionally respected use of wealth to host—or contribute to hosting—large-scale celebrations, thus redistributing it. In fact, people in Sadolpara were much more keen to tell me how they had jointly decided to resist the creation of *patta*, fearing that it would result in the dissolution of their communally held land than to talk about transfers that had taken place.

Nevertheless, the gradual, often partial, commodification of land is changing the ways in which people can access it: annual negotiations to create new fields, shaped each year anew by current relationships traced among Houses and the status of the people involved, are slowly giving way to permanently privatized access. Fields claimed once and then converted into orchards effectively become private plots, even without formally being redefined as *patta*. As selling cash crops to people from outside the village economy becomes increasingly lucrative, there is ever more incentive to—at least partially—commodify land. Despite going against the *niam* that prioritizes managing Houses' interests with the benefit of whole matrilineal groups in mind, given the current economic developments, exclusive ownership clearly has advantages. This is leading to a gradual weakening of the mutual dependencies that hold such matrilineal groups together.

6.7 Living on the Land

Jiji grew up at a time when people in Sadolpara and the surrounding villages depended primarily on shifting cultivation for their livelihood. In those days, people lived in wards of between five and fifteen houses, which typically comprised a senior House and its subsidiary Houses.[26] The senior

Houses were often, but not necessarily, custodians of a *kram* drum. People described such wards, rather androcentrically, as the House of a grandfather surrounded by those of his sons-in-law and grandsons-in-law. Since the Houses were interrelated in the matrilineal line, they could theoretically just as well have been referred to as the House of a (grand)mother and those of her daughters and granddaughters. The houses of a village ward were typically arranged around the top part of a low hill, with their entrances facing towards the centre. A village's various wards were thus spread across several conjoining hills. Villagers kept an area of at least five metres around their homes free from grass and shrubs in order to avoid providing cover to leeches, snakes, or other unwanted creatures in the rainy season. This created large open spaces of adobe-coloured beaten earth between the houses. To this day, Sadolpara is still made up of several such village wards, each of which has a good number of houses. This imbues the village with the 'traditional' character that warrants its classification as a heritage village by government administrators (section 1.1).

The house in which Jiji lived used to be central to one of these wards, where she was surrounded by her daughters, granddaughters, and even a son. As mentioned in section 3.1, Jiji lived in a 'Songsarek house' (*nok mande*), a 'traditional' Garo house, which was initially built entirely of natural materials: wood, bamboo, and thatch. Every winter, her sons-in-law, grandsons, and sons spent several hours patching up the roof and the rear veranda, but the condition of the house gradually deteriorated nonetheless. After Jiji's death, as mentioned in section 6.1, her daughter Chekjak and son-in-law Pongjan became the heirs. When they took the 'places' once occupied by Jiji and Baka, they inherited the house and the *kram* drum as well as its other assets. Pongjan and Chekjak, and the people of their larger matrilineal group, continued to attribute religious importance to the *kram* drum. Maintaining it also substantiated their claims to the land owned by the House. Because a *kram* drum is a seat of the spirit Risi, it cannot be kept in a house that is unsuitable for the sacrifices that Risi demands. During the annual Wangala celebrations, the tamers of a *kram* drum need to rub the pillars, posts, and rafters of their house with the blood of a bull or cow that they slaughter for the purpose (section 4.6). This can only be done in a 'traditional' Garo house that has been ritually initiated for Risi.[27] Chekjak and Pongjan did not live in such a house, so they could not take the *kram* drum to their own house. Moreover, while it was all right for the *kram* drum to stay for a couple of weeks or even months in Jiji's uninhabited house, that was not a long-term option. If Risi were to be left alone, she was liable to become dissatisfied and bite her custodians (section 3.1).

In the first few months after Jiji's death, the matter remained unresolved. Anyone could see that the building in which Jiji had lived would not hold out much longer. A new 'traditional' Garo house would have to be built, in accordance with the requirements of Risi. Moreover, her 'tamers' would have to live in that house—and this was where the situation became complicated. Chekjak and Pongjan lived in a 'new' village ward, about two or three kilometres from the 'old' village. For years, they had invested in orchards and wet rice fields, both of which were located close to their house. The fields were essential for their livelihood and abandoning them was out of the question.

In the locality where Chekjak and Pongjan lived, families maintained close neighbourly contact, which created a good atmosphere. People visited one another in the mornings and evenings to drink tea and chat about everything under the sun, as is common in rural Garo Hills. However, most of the families living there were Christians. Taking the *kram* drum to this locality would mean that it would be isolated, with no one to relate to it except Chekjak and Pongjan, as well as one of their daughters and her husband. Nonetheless, that is what they intended to do.

Jiji's sons objected. One of them told me that he was against the idea of rebuilding Jiji's house in the relatively distant village ward. He argued that as the main house of their matrilineal group, the one with the *kram* drum, it had to be at a place where there were many Songsareks. The main house could not be located in a place where there were 'no *mande*', he said, meaning 'no Songsareks.' He was also opposed to the move because the original location of Jiji's house had been relatively easy to reach by car, whereas the road to the new location was in an appalling condition. It was no more than a track, and included a river crossing with steep slopes and large boulders that posed a serious challenge to even the most experienced driver. During the rainy season the water level rose, which, combined with the fast current, made it impassable in those months, even for four-wheel drive vehicles. Some of the politicians, student leaders, and other dignitaries from Tura who had become friends with Jiji, her sons, and their larger matrilineal group used to visit every now and then by car. If the house were rebuilt in the 'new' village ward, it would become difficult for them to reach it. Moreover, both of Jiji's sons had earned themselves a reputation as committed and knowledgeable Songsareks, and to move the house that had their *kram* drum to a location outside the 'old' village, in a ward dominated by Christians, did not sit comfortably with that image.

One year later, when I had another chance to visit Sadolpara, I found that Chekjak and Pongjan had indeed built their new house at the location of their choice. They had taken the decision, and at their instigation, men of Jiji's matrilineal group had dismantled her old house so that they could use some of its hardwood posts and girders for a new, albeit much smaller, 'traditional' Garo house in the locality where most of the families were Christians. The new house was well built and attractive, but it was too small to accommodate the large numbers of people that had come together regularly for rice beer drinking sessions in Jiji's home. Other remnants of Jiji's house had been left at the original location, and Pongjan told me that they intended to use its biggest hard wooden pillars for a much larger house that they would eventually build.

The ward in the old village where Jiji's house once stood, as well as those of her daughters and granddaughters, is now virtually empty; many of its former houses have been dismantled. Quite a few of its residents moved their houses elsewhere after Jiji's death, and now, like Pongjan and Chekjak, live in wards that are some distance from the old village, but close to their orchards. From other 'old' wards as well, more and more families are gradually shifting their houses to newly emerging outlying wards. While the primary impetus for this relocation is economic, as was the case for Chekjak and Pongjan, it is obviously facilitated by the shift towards Christianity. Songsareks depend on the *kram* drum of the most senior House of their matrilineal group in order to communicate with Risi (section 3.1), and members of a matrilineal group need each other's support for the performance of Songsarek sacrifices and celebrations in relation to healing, death, or the annual agricultural cycle. Christian worship does not require subsidiary Houses to maintain such a close connection to the main House of their matrilineal group. It creates a more generalized and less kinship-oriented religious framework, which is able to operate within a less tightly structured residential space.

In Sadolpara and the villages nearby, many people are trying to hang on to the community religion as long as they can, since they are convinced by its underlying premises, and value the rituals it offers to facilitate interaction with the spirits. In addition, its frequent and often costly rituals and celebrations bring people together, demanding the sharing of food (most importantly, meat) and rice beer with everyone who attends them, thus redistributing wealth. This stands in stark contrast to the exacerbation of economic disparities between Houses that is being driven by their increasing participation in the market economy, by the privatization of land titles, and by Houses' unequal access to the subsidies and contracts offered by the various government bodies active in the region (discussed in the next chapter). For Songsareks, in order to maintain good relationships with the spirits, kin must be strongly committed to one another. Christians do not face as many mutual religious obligations, but are nonetheless dependent on resources shared among kin. In rural West Garo Hills, land continues to be the most important of these resources. Access to land is anchored in *niam*, which provides people with good reasons to uphold it, even as they interpret and adapt it to the changing conditions of the environment they live in.

7
Customizing Traditions

7.1 The State as a Resource

It was barely eight o'clock in the morning. The sun, still gaining strength, was trying to drive away the chill of the short upland winter. In Jiji's ward, people had just got up. Men huddled around small fires on the adobe-coloured beaten earth in between the houses, either squatting or standing, warming their arms and hands over the flames. Women were making tea and cooking rice and dried fish curry. The quiet of the morning was disrupted by the distant hum of a Maruti Gypsy. The unevenness of the track forced the vehicle to move in first gear, at a snail's pace, its engine roaring. Even for a car this powerful, it took time to scale the steep and rocky slopes that interspersed the short smoother stretches of the rough dirt road. The torrential rains, so frequent in the hills during the six-month-long rainy season, had etched deep ruts along and across the road.

At this hour of the day, the sound could only mean that a visitor from 'town' was approaching: most likely a government officer or a politician. I had just woken up and was in the kitchen of our house. As the sound of the car's engine grew gradually louder, I heard the rasping cough of Dising. Tall but emaciated, his skin dark and leathery, Dising was one of Sadolpara's most senior and respected men (see sections 3.3, 5.6, and 6.3). He was a close 'grandson' of the village head, although the latter was many years his junior in age. At the frequent kin trials held to resolve conflicts between spouses, relatives, and neighbours, Dising was acknowledged as one of the men who best knew the guiding principles of *niam*. His cough was due to his suffering from 'T.B.-illness', as he never failed to remind me. His physical condition prevented him from working the fields, and for the many years that I knew him, Dising spent most of his time in and around his house. Even though he suffered from frequent pain in his chest, his wit seldom failed him. Cracking naughty jokes brought a mischievous twinkle to his eyes: his body was weak, but his spirit unbreakable (Figure 7.1).

When the dark red Gypsy finally came into sight, Dising called out: 'It's Tuna! I knew he would come!' 'Tuna' was the nickname of Metrona Marak,

Reworking Culture. Erik de Maaker, Oxford University Press. © Oxford University Press 2022.
DOI: 10.1093/oso/9788194831693.003.0007

Figure 7.1 Dising was highly respected as a figure of authority due to his extensive knowledge of *niam*.
Photograph: Erik de Maaker, 2003.

a politician affiliated with the Nationalist Congress Party (NCP). The NCP had been founded in 1999, as a breakaway from the Indian National Congress (INC), the party that had once led India to independence.[1] Tuna had previously belonged to the INC, but had followed senior Garo politician Purno Sangma in leaving the party.[2] At the time of that morning visit, Tuna was one of the sixty Members of the Legislative Assembly (MLAs) of the state of Meghalaya, which forms the government that rules the state. Tuna represented the Rongram constituency, a rural area spanning at least 30 kilometres across and encompassing approximately sixty villages. With at least 1,600 inhabitants in the early 2000s, Sadolpara was the largest of those villages, and was thus home to a good number of voters.

Somewhat nervously, Dising began to ask around whether anyone could spare any milk. He knew that Tuna would come to him, and he wanted to give his guest tea with milk. 'Red tea', as tea without milk is called, would look like a poor man's offering. When it became clear that there was no milk on offer, he changed his strategy, and asked whether anyone could spare any liquor. The small bottle of Old Monk rum that I had at home made a modest but appropriate contribution. A little later, the car hobbled up to us and came to a standstill near Dising's house. As the news of Tuna's arrival spread, men from various parts of the village gathered. In his usual jovial manner, Dising ordered me to join them. As a 'white skin' (*bigil gipok*) I added to his status, and I suppose that he wanted to show Tuna that I was his friend. For my part, I did not resist. I had little doubt that the meeting would prove interesting, since people often talked with some degree of admiration about Tuna. Tuna visited the village frequently, and people from Sadolpara often stayed at his house when they needed to be in Tura.

Tuna himself had not come 'empty handed' (*jak rara*—'with only his hands', as is a common expression); he had brought a couple of bottles of liquor as a gift for Dising. Seated around the central hearth in Dising's house, the rum was served in tea glasses, undiluted. Given the early hour, it was likely that at least some of the men hadn't had breakfast yet, and neither had I. The men quickly loosened up, cracking the usual sharp and mildly sexually insinuating 'name jokes' (section 3.2). The favourite, as in any other setting, was to call a man by another man's name, implying that he has had sex with that person's partner. The joking, eliciting tumultuous laughter, was interspersed with bragging, but also with serious talk about the prices of cash crops or even just plain politics. I did not feel like drinking, but was urged to do so, and my glass was topped up frequently. After several glasses of rum I had a splitting headache and left the house. The other men had more stamina, and continued drinking and chatting for a long time. Their gathering was concluded with a meal of rice and chicken, cooked by one of Dising's granddaughters. Tuna, who also seemed to handle the alcohol well, left soon after.

Sometime later, Dising dropped in at our house. He chuckled as he told me that Tuna had promised him a contract for the construction of a 'spring chamber'. A 'spring chamber' is a concrete casing built around a shallow spring. It allows spring water to collect in such a way that it remains free from leaves and cannot be contaminated by cattle. Sadolpara had no pipe water distribution system at the time, and people depended on springs for drinking water, as well as for cooking, bathing, and washing dishes and clothes (bathing and washing was also done in rivers and streams). Contracted out for approximately INR 15,000, the spring chamber was a small project for the MLA, yet—certainly in the early 2000s—represented a substantial sum of money within Sadolpara's economy. Dising told me that Tuna had granted comparable contracts to some of the other men who had been present that morning, such as money to improve parts of the stretch of uneven dirt road that connected our village ward to the main road, which was so difficult for vehicles to negotiate. Projects such as these were very profitable for those who took them on, since they could be completed in such a way that a good portion of the funding remained with the person contracted. Tuna was in a position to assign such projects. As an MLA, he was responsible for the implementation in his constituency of the 'Special Rural Welfare Programme', locally known as the 'MLA scheme'. Small projects of up to INR 100,000 funded through this programme were not subject to auditing, so those who received money to execute them were relatively free in their use of the budget. In disbursing these funds, Tuna proved to his constituents that he was connected to the wealth and authority of the state and able and willing to let them benefit from his connections. It was obvious to all that the contracts were shared out as favours and no one in Sadolpara saw reason to condemn that. In everyday experience, people were used to authority, influence, and wealth being personalized. Addressing the perceptions and expectations of villagers, politicians who themselves have grown up in similar social contexts personify a state administration that never presents itself as neutral or anonymous (A. Gupta 2012: 105).

At the time of that early morning visit to Dising, Tuna was serving his second five-year term as MLA. He depended on men like Dising to help him connect to his voters, particularly with the next rounds of elections in sight. Despite what is claimed in populist critiques of democracy in India, there is no way for politicians there to literally 'buy' votes (Björkman 2014: 617). Politicians can attempt to woo voters, but they can never be sure that their constituents will actually choose their name on the day of the ballot. Tuna could not be certain of votes, nor was it within the power of men like Dising to create a dependable 'vote bank'. This is another term often used in relation to elections in India, which implies that citizens tend to choose their political allegiances collectively rather than as individuals (Björkman 2015: 194). Other candidates, affiliated to different political parties, also made visits to Sadolpara, hoping to encourage people to vote for them. Nonetheless, Dising did act as a middleman for Tuna, who expected Dising to advise people to give their vote to him, as the candidate who 'gave' the most. This giving materialized in lucrative contracts handed out to men in significant positions; men who in turn might share some of their profits with people who depended on them. Conspicuous giving was also seen when politicians hosted free meals for anyone who wanted to partake in them. Such a meal, which inevitably involves the slaughter of a large bull, bestows prestige and thus 'good honour' upon the host. In this respect, it is analogous to the meal that is provided to guests at a funeral, or one that is served by the followers of the community religion to conclude an important healing ritual, or to some of the collective meals served during Wangala.

Tuna had also come over to Sadolpara that morning to discuss the celebration of Republic Day, two weeks later (26 January). Republic Day is celebrated annually across India with parades and festivities to commemorate the day on which the Indian Constitution replaced pre-independence legislation (de Maaker 2013b). That year, Tuna was going to ceremonially open a new primary school in Sadolpara on Republic Day, and offer a meal of beef curry and rice to all who attended (Figure 7.2). In preparation for these celebrations, he had bought a large bull from Dising (for the curry), had acquired a large gunny bag of rice from someone else, and made arrangements for the meal to be cooked on the day. Tuna could never be sure that this would result in the votes he needed to be re-elected, but it would certainly show his generosity. When election time came around, other campaigning candidates would host free meals too.

The account above derives from my first and longest stay in Sadolpara, in the early 2000s. As I write this in 2020, neither Dising nor Tuna are among the living. Tuna was voted out of power in 2003 and passed away in 2009,

Figure 7.2 Meltrona Marak ('Tuna') giving a speech at Sadolpara during the award ceremony that concluded an Independence Day football tournament.
Photograph: Erik de Maaker, 2001.

soon after suffering a stroke. Dising kept faithfully taking the antibiotics that he received from the 'TB' (Tuberculosis) hospital in Tura, but only survived Tuna by one year, passing away in 2010. Their places have since been taken by others, but from the stories I've heard since, it is evident that the mechanisms through which residents of the rural areas connect to representatives of the state, and vice versa, have barely changed.

All the residents of Sadolpara have—according to government assessments—an income that is 'below poverty line' (BPL). This means that they qualify for central government schemes, such as subsidized rice and kerosene, which are intended to raise the standard of living of the rural poor. Funding for rural development is not only available through the MLA scheme but also through a number of departments of the state of Meghalaya, as well as through the Garo Hills Autonomous District Council. Most of the schemes are ultimately implemented by the lowest administrative division of the district, the 'Community and Rural Development Block', the office of which is locally referred to as the 'Block Office'. In addition to funding for the improvement of roads or wells, the Block Office also allocates projects intended to diversify and improve individual families' sources of income (by digging fish ponds, making terraces or dams for wet rice cultivation, distributing teak tree saplings, and so on). The Block Office also implements national schemes to support the rural poor, such as the provision of corrugated iron sheets (cast galvanized iron (CGI) sheet) for people who live in houses with thatched roofs, which Jiji also benefitted from. The same office is responsible for distributing grants to build small houses for ageing widows and widowers as well as for implementing the major national scheme that guarantees 100 days of paid work per year to each rural household that is categorized as 'Below Poverty Line'. This latter scheme, the Mahatma Gandhi National Rural Employment Guarantee Act (MGNREGA), locally referred to as the 'Job Card' scheme, has been underway in West Garo Hills since 2006. Every village has its own Village Development Board to implement the scheme. This board collaborates with the Block Development Office to enable people to do work that is thought to benefit the larger collective, such as improving village roads, or constructing a 'playground' (a sports field that can also be used for village events). People who do such labour are paid according to the number of hours worked, which are registered in a dedicated booklet called a Job Card.

The Block Office in the town of Dadenggre (Sadolpara's nearest town) is located in a bungalow at the centre of a small compound by the side of the main road. The office has a field in front of it with a flagpole. The field is used when state functions are celebrated; otherwise it is the place where the officials who work there park their cars. Within the compound are the quarters of the office staff, many of which look rather dilapidated. In fact, quite a few of them are not in use. Hardly any of the office staff stay in Dadenggre for more than a couple of days a week. The same holds for the staff of the other large office in Dadenggre, that of the Civil Sub-Division. Responsibilities of the latter office include the allocation of subsidized rice through the Public Distribution System to dealers like Dising (section 3.3), as well as issuing the official certificates required to claim benefits from many of the government schemes.

Over the years, whenever I met with staff of either the Block Development Office or of that of the Civil-Sub Division, I noted that most of them were from Tura, where they generally had their houses and families. The distance of approximately 50 kilometres along a narrow and winding road resulted in a commute of about two hours by car or motorcycle. On days that staff came to Tura, they left home early. No one liked to travel after dark, presumably because they were keen to avoid freak encounters with elephants, or with young men who might in one way or another be affiliated with the underground. This latter concern posed a genuine threat to the more affluent office workers; for as long as the militants were active in Garo Hills, hold-ups were not uncommon and even kidnappings occasionally took place (section 2.5).

The office staff I encountered were educated middle-class people, more often men than women, who had studied to undergraduate level at least. With most government jobs in Meghalaya reserved for members of the Scheduled Tribes, nearly all these positions were held by Garo. In addition to reading and writing in Garo, most staff also had knowledge of languages such as Bengali, Assamese, or Hindi. Many of them had a good command of English as well, which is the official language of Meghalaya. Office staff were paid according to government salary rates, which made them rich in comparison to villagers. So, in terms of educational background and income, they were markedly different from the inhabitants of villages like Sadolpara. Hardly any villagers had a regular cash income and most had to do substantial physical labour for every hundred rupees they ever obtained. The villagers were almost without exception illiterate or at best semi-literate. Many people could not write their own names but gave their thumbprints by way of signature. Jiji was not even able to read the numbers printed on banknotes, and she was by no means exceptional in that respect. She recognized the value of paper money by its colour and size. The contrast was stark in other ways as well. Working the land was exhausting and involved enduring mud, insects, heat, and sweat. Government employees, by contrast, worked at desks. As well as being far less physically demanding, their work left their clothes clean and their hands and feet free of callouses.

The distinction between the educated and the illiterate, between office worker and farmer, between salaried and self-producing, between being (relatively) well off or 'Below Poverty Line', created a glaring social gap. At times, this produced mistrust. Sometimes, office staff would refer to villagers rather disparagingly as 'these people', who were 'cunning', or sometimes even 'dirty' or 'drunkards'. Conversely, villagers might describe office staff as 'unwilling' or 'greedy', and sometimes felt they were being subjected to abuse as they struggled with the complex bureaucracy of state-funded programmes. Rumours circulated that certain officers tended to share out benefits to people with whom they maintained particularly good relationships or who were connected to people who they in turn were dependent on. For instance, a man who lived in Sadolpara who had a reputation for being very smart and had influential relatives in Tura, once proudly told me that for four consecutive years he had managed to obtain, free of charge, a bundle of corrugated iron roofing sheets from the Block Office (each bundle comprising seven sheets of approximately three metres in length). An influential man, a matrilineal relative of his, well placed within the state administration, was responsible for the favourable treatment he had received from the Block Office. In principle, a single household should only have been able to obtain one bundle once under the scheme. By applying under a different name each time—which his contacts in the office had made possible—the man had been able to get a bundle each year for several years. While this had enabled him to collect enough sheets for the roof of the large house he was planning to build, other villagers had traipsed time and again to the Block Office, only to return empty-handed, having been told by the people in charge that no more roofing sheets were available. Knowing that the office staff were in a position to give, or not give, while the villagers as recipients depended on them, no doubt contributed to the sense of inequality that already pervaded in other respects.

Accessing the Garo Hills Autonomous District Council (GHADC) in Tura involved similar hurdles. The District Council office is located in the centre of Tura, at the top of a tree-covered hill that commands great views over lower-lying parts of town. The District Council not only maintains land records but also collects taxes, facilitates rural development, and has courts where (mostly land-related) disputes are settled. The GHADC is governed by an assembly comprised of elected members (Members of the District

Council, abbreviated to MDCs). For the purposes of the GHADC, Garo Hills is divided into twenty-nine constituencies, which are much smaller than the constituencies of Meghalaya's Members of the Legislative Assembly. Unlike the government of Meghalaya, which obtains significant funding from 'the centre', as the Indian federal government is often referred to, the GHADC has to make do with relatively meagre means. It is supposed to generate much of its income from the land it governs. Officers of the District Council repeatedly state that its mandate is to ensure that the collective customary management of landholdings in Garo Hills is upheld, but under the current arrangements, land that is privately controlled (as *patta*) is far more lucrative for the District Council in terms of revenue. *Patta* land calls for annual payments of several hundred to thousands of rupees, depending on the quality and size of a holding. By contrast, communally managed *a'king* land that is not registered as *patta* only draws a 'house tax', which is levied per household, and currently stands at INR 50 per year. Generally speaking, the GHADC has little to offer in terms of funding for rural development, or at least nothing comparable to the amounts of money that are channelled through Meghalaya state. Nonetheless, the District Council is the prime authority in Garo Hills with respect to land records as well as the appointment of village heads, which makes people from villages like Sadolpara truly dependent on it (section 4.4). The GHADC's registers state, for each village domain, who is legally recognized as village head, who are recognized as 'minor' owners of *a'king* land, and who owns *patta*. The files are maintained by hand and can only be accessed by visiting the office itself.

For people from villages like Sadolpara, dealing with the District Council in Tura is even more trying than visiting the government offices located in Dadenggre. Since very few people have their own means of transport, most have to travel by bus (section 6.4). At the time that I started my research, in the early 2000s, the main road that passes Sadolpara had one daily direct bus to Tura and one a day in the opposite direction. In recent years, this service has been suspended. Now the journey to Tura starts with an hour's walk to a bus stop at the road junction near the village of Chibonggre. There are two buses a day from there to Tura: one in the morning and one in the afternoon. The buses are old and not very fast; when they break down there may be no service for a day. The road is steep and narrow, with many sharp bends, and the journey is not without danger. The road has a very low traffic density, and hours can go by without any vehicle passing, so hitching a lift is not a viable option. For people from Sadolpara, the bus timings are such that it is often impossible to return home on the same day.

Instead, people who travel to Tura tend to end up staying for a night, for instance, in the house of their MLA or MDC. Politicians are used to that, and many keep a room available as overnight accommodation for their constituents, whom they also provide with a simple meal, usually free of charge. Some residents of the rural areas go to Tura quite often, but some may have never once visited the town in their entire lifetimes. In villages like Sadolpara in the early 2000s, it was not difficult to find people who had never travelled that far from home.

The GHADC staff are in a position to take decisions that affect people's access to land. The 'Acts, Rules and Regulations' (GHADC 2007), which guide the District Council's operations are mostly written in English, and given rural people's extremely limited knowledge of that language, or any written language at all, they have to rely on the explanations of District Council staff. Consequently, the GHADC is experienced by villagers as a highly personalized administration, where it is essential to maintain good relationships with the 'right' officers if things are to get done. It is rumoured that at least some of the District Council officers sometimes abuse their positions of power to demand personal monetary favours from the people who depend on their services (Sangma 1998: 136). For people from rural Garo Hills, then, this underscores the point which I have already made in relation to Tuna: that the state is by no means perceived as an anonymous entity, but is personified by individual people who exert its authority, interpret its laws, and channel its wealth.

Sadolpara and other, similar Garo villages are self-governing to a good degree in terms of day-to-day affairs, given that these are overseen by the village head, and village residents settle inheritance, marriages, divorces, and minor conflicts among themselves with reference to their own interpretations of Garo *niam*, without interference from higher authorities. Yet villagers are nonetheless keenly aware of their dependence on the many government bodies that make their presence felt in the area in relation to other legal matters, and in their regulation of access to the many development schemes they implement. People expect their MLAs and MDCs to advance their voters' interests, and the performance of these representatives is primarily evaluated in terms of how well they deliver access to the various government schemes. At the same time, elected officials need the votes of villagers, while administrators depend on the latter in order to meet the targets set for the schemes they are responsible for. While these relationships are characterized by extreme structural inequality, a certain mutual dependency incentivizes cooperation across social and economic divides.

Year after year, funding continues to be sanctioned from one or another government fund for the improvement of the dirt road that connects the village ward where Dising and Jiji used to live to the main road. Each year, during the dry season, people work to improve it, and over time it has gradually been widened from a very uneven track into a small road. But the torrential rains and thunder storms of the next wet season invariably wash away parts of the road. People in Sadolpara are nonetheless convinced that improving the road will advance the 'development' of their village. They are convinced that better access for motorized transport will create new economic opportunities, resulting in better marketing of village produce and higher standards of living. Regardless of how much the road has actually improved over the years, work on it has facilitated a consistent channelling of state funding from politicians and administrators to middle-men at the village level. Given the fairly limited sums of money circulating there otherwise, this constitutes a substantial resource. This means that those who are able to receive and distribute these funds at the village level, and perhaps siphon off some part in the process, stand to gain wealth, power, and prestige.

7.2 Reinterpreting Status, Wealth, and Prestige

To this day, most followers of the community religion live in houses made of wood and bamboo like the one Jiji used to live in (sections 3.1 and 6.7). Inside, such houses are somewhat bare, furnished with some drums, traditional weaponry (spears, shields, swords), a chair, some low stools, sleeping mats, clothes, and household utensils. Anything that is considered really valuable is kept out of sight. Heirloom gongs, jewellery, and money are kept in a small storeroom, which is only accessible to the 'heads' of a House. Similarly, rice and other food stocks are stored in a granary, the door of which is kept closed. Even cows, wandering embodiments of wealth, are generally herded away from the village. For Songsareks, much more than for Christians, prestige is gained by *giving* rather than *having*. If support is requested from people who are known to 'have', then support must be provided, otherwise the House will risk gaining a reputation of 'stinginess' and lose face. Being able to give translates into honour, but that comes with an obligation to actually give when called upon to do so.

One of my vivid fieldwork memories is of an incident that occurred one time when I was together with Jiji and Ratmi in the field (a swidden) that they—at the time—worked together. Two women passed by—distant acquaintances of Jiji. They asked her if they could harvest some tubers from the field. Jiji didn't hesitate to welcome them to do so, and the two women made their way onto the field, where they filled an entire basket with tubers. Ratmi kept quiet, while Jiji was clearly proud that she had been able to make the women happy. Afterwards, when the women had left with all the tubers, Ratmi vented her anger. She could not understand why Jiji had given so much food away for free, whereas Jiji had done what mattered most in her view: to give, when one is able to, and to enjoy the 'good honour' that giving translates into. Ratmi had two young children to feed, and it was the time of the year when food was scarce. My understanding of her reaction was that she not only belonged to a generation for whom sharing had become slightly less of a priority, she also felt that the two women who had filled their basket had taken advantage of Jiji's generosity. Indeed, the prestige which Jiji earned during her life was evident from the grand send-off she received following her death (see section 6.1).

Those who are unwilling to share what they have risk gaining a reputation for being 'stingy' or even 'bad persons'. To avoid being cast in such a light, it is not uncommon for Songsareks to hide their wealth, or at least not conspicuously show it, in order to reduce the potential social pressure to give. One man who was known to be very wealthy, whenever he was asked to provide support of one kind or another, used to pull the empty pockets of his trousers inside out, cheerfully proclaiming that he was a poor person with no possessions who was simply 'unable to give'. It was clear to all that this was a white lie, which added a sense of mischief to his performance. Needless to say, people like Jiji considered him a bit of a cheat, but he did not seem to mind about that. Other people's pronouncements of their alleged poverty were less elaborately staged, but their intentions were similar. Hiding wealth from view, and claiming that one had 'nothing' even when that was obviously not the case, were strategies that everyone deployed to some degree to limit how much they would have to give. In villages like Sadolpara, especially for Songsareks, the number of occasions that arise that potentially oblige one to support others exceeds by far the capacity of any House to do so. At the same time, the brazenness with which the man mentioned above turned his pockets inside out exemplified the well-established strategy of publicly declaring one's poverty in order to be able to accumulate wealth.

Even though people in Sadolpara and its neighbouring villages have long participated in a cash economy, money played a relatively minor role in their lives until recently. Having food, for instance, did not necessarily involve cash as long as harvests sufficed for people's subsistence. Ginger and cotton, cultivated on the swiddens, have long been cash crops, but in the past, the money earned was directly spent on necessities such as knives, pottery, and other items that villagers could not produce themselves. This changed in the latter part of the 20th century, when areca and cashew nut cultivation, as well as coal mining, began to bring much more significant amounts of cash. As the swidden harvests declined, people became increasingly dependent on buying staples from the market (including rice sold at a subsidized rate through the Public Distribution System, see section 3.3). More recently, the amount of cash in circulation has been rising further with people increasingly working as day labourers, either for fellow villagers, or, for instance, through the MGNREGA 'Job Card' scheme (section 7.1). Households that have gained access to monetary wealth have typically invested it to buy saplings to extend their orchards, to arrange for paid labour to work their land, as well as to pay for their children's schooling. Recently acquired wealth has also been invested in brick houses with roofs made from corrugated iron, cell phones, and sometimes a television, motor scooter, or pickup truck. Christians are typically at the forefront of market-oriented economic activities, but many Songsareks are also entrepreneurial. However, some of these new forms of expenditure are not so compatible with the traditional Garo community religion. For example, the new brick buildings that are increasingly replacing 'traditional Garo houses' are not suited for the celebrations that are central to the traditional community religion, and most of the people who build such houses are Christians. A brick house is referred to as a 'Christian/outsider house' ('*nok ruri*') or 'Nepali house' ('*nok Nepal*').

Households with access to cash also utilize it to pay for their children's education. Currently, in 2020, the vast majority of people living in Sadolpara and the surrounding area are illiterate. They are well aware that this puts them at a disadvantage in their dealings with the state in its various guises, and with the world beyond their immediate surroundings. It is taken for granted that anyone who has a salaried job must have attended school. Jiji referred to such persons as 'studied ones' (*poraigipa*—people who have been to school), or (to the men among them) as 'the ones who wear long trousers' (*longpingagipa*). On an everyday basis, and certainly in the rainy season, villagers do not wear long trousers but shorts or sarongs. Long trousers would quickly get full of mud, and make it difficult to spot leeches that may try to climb up one's legs. In town, or anywhere with paved ground, there are no leeches. Those who were illiterate, like Jiji's son-in-law Pongjan, clearly felt vulnerable in environments in which literacy was called for. I mentioned earlier (section 6.1) that Pongjan had managed to open an account with the local branch of the State Bank of India, but he could not read what was written in the bank book. He had to ask the bank employees what it said, and more than once he suspected them of cheating him. In order to prevent their own children facing such difficulties, Pongjan and Chekjak prioritized investing in their education. This was costly, not in terms of fees, but because it meant years of managing without their children's labour. All the time that the children spent in school or doing homework, they were unable to contribute to the family income by working the fields, providing a good reason for Pongjan and Chekjak to invest in orchard crops (see section 6.6). Just as significantly, gaining education was liable to make them reluctant to work the fields, since the knowledge and attitudes conveyed in school would prepare them for anything but a farmer's life.[3] At least two of Pongjan's and Chekjak's children successfully completed primary school. They went on to attend Garo medium school in a neighbouring village, but even after repeating classes many times they did not manage to pass the main 10th standard exam ('matriculation', a national examination). This reflected the poor quality of the tuition they received and was in no way exceptional. Even so, compared to their parents, the younger generation were much better able to deal with government services, banks, mobile phones, and the like.

In the early 2000s, Sadolpara, which was then home to about 1,600 inhabitants, had one single government-funded lower primary school. The school was in a small brick building on one side of the large field at the centre of the village. The school's teacher lived in Tura. He came to the village on his motorbike, staying for perhaps two or three days a week. During the rainy season, when the road dissolved into slippery mud, the school sometimes remained closed for several weeks at a time. When classes were on, he taught for two to three hours a day. Any longer would be ineffective, he claimed, since the students were unaccustomed to sitting still for so long. It was a 'lower primary' school (Class I to IV), but with only one teacher, students from all standards had to take lessons together. To help their teacher out, the students maintained his areca nut trees, which were close to the school building. The teacher's irregular presence combined with his rather disparaging attitude towards the students did not help them to learn, and it proved very difficult for them to progress from one standard to the next.

The government school did not charge tuition fees, but pupils were required to wear school uniform. This was rather a burden on the poorer households, but all of them made the effort. Then, soon after I started my doctoral research, the Garo Student Union (GSU) opened an additional primary school in Sadolpara, and a couple of years later two more primary schools opened. These latter two were run by the Baptist and Catholic missions respectively. The teacher of the GSU school was committed and gave regular classes, but the two later schools quickly earned themselves an even better reputation. To my surprise, the monthly tuition fee of about INR 150–220 (in 2006) charged by these latter schools did not deter parents; again this showed that people without much money to spare were convinced of the importance of investing in their children's education. More affluent households even sent their children to the boarding school of the Catholic 'Little Flower Mission' in Dadenggre, or to the reputedly even better schools in and around Tura. More recently, Sadolpara has also gained a middle school (Classes V–VIII), which provides tuition to children who have completed primary school. The strong attendance of this school provides further evidence of villagers' belief in the value of education.

The contrasts between rural and urban spheres, introduced in section 2.1, can be stark. Tura, the political, commercial, and administrative centre of Garo Hills, is home to—among others—an affluent middle class. Due to the preferential discrimination that applies to Garo in the state of Meghalaya, elite Garo families dominate the administrative and political bodies of the four Garo Hills districts. With relatively few Garo active in trade, and almost no industry in the region, government jobs are highly sought after. Holding an important position in the local administration has enabled quite a few Tura families to acquire large houses, multiple cars, paddy fields and orchards, and more. Rumours claim that such jobs often go to those who have the 'right' contacts or, alternatively, make under-the-table monetary payments. It is said that sums of up to several thousand rupees are sometimes required just for a letter of application to be taken into consideration by a recruitment committee. If there is truth in this, higher-ranking officers in particular would be in a position to increase their income in underhand ways, which in turn would make government jobs all the more attractive. I am unable to assess the degree to which clientelism pervades the administration, but I do note that many people are eager to express their dissatisfaction with it. While these rumours clearly feed distrust, I have also heard stories of people gaining jobs as the result of apparently transparent assessment procedures.

In Tura, the houses of the rich are surrounded by high walls with tall gates. Burglary, almost unheard of in a village setting, poses a real threat. As further evidence of increasing economic inequality, Tura now has beggars, though their numbers are negligible in comparison to other parts of India. Begging is a phenomenon unknown to villages like Sadolpara, where anyone in need of food or shelter can make demands on relatives, who simply cannot ignore them. In these villages, disparities of income and wealth do exist, and always have done, but among the followers of the traditional Garo community religion, the frequent sacrifices and hosting constitute a strong redistributive mechanism whereby wealth raises social status—when it is shared. In places like Tura, social and religious practices have been reconfigured quite dramatically. Redistributive mechanisms continue to operate, for example, with people belonging to a single matrilineal group being expected to help one another, or politicians making efforts to display their generosity, but these do not normally affect the distribution of wealth in the long term.

Politicians in Garo Hills, as elsewhere in India—and in democracies the world over—are expected to show that they represent the interests of their constituents. The late Purno Sangma, a prominent politician who was a minister in various cabinets of India's union government and also served for two years as the Speaker of its Lok Sabha (the 'lower house'), understood this very well.[4] Purno Sangma secured (financial) support for many of the large-scale projects that have been undertaken in Garo Hills (particularly in Tura) over the last five decades. This resulted in Tura acquiring a large government hospital (Civil Hospital, or the 'hundred bed hospital'), the Nehru sports stadium, one of the tallest TV towers of the North-Eastern region, a large shopping complex, the very extensive Tura campus of the North-Eastern Hill University, an extension of the Indian railway network to Garo Hills (to Mendipathar), and even the (not yet functioning) Baljek airport. Negotiating such projects earned him a reputation as a politician who could deliver to his voters in the region and saw him repeatedly re-elected until his untimely death in March 2016.

Tura is governed under the Sixth Schedule of the Indian Constitution, and formally most of the land it occupies continues to be *a'king* land that is registered with a number of villages and thus theoretically within the purview of several village heads. However, all the *a'king* land in Tura and its peri-urban area has been converted into *patta*, so there is effectively no longer any 'common' land left (section 6.6). The *patta* plots can be traded from one Garo to another Garo and in that sense have become a commodity. According to the land laws of Meghalaya, such plots can be transferred between any of the state's Scheduled Tribes, but no sales of Garo land to Khasi or Jaintia have taken place so far. Everyone I have asked about this told me that selling land to non-Garo would not be socially permissible.

Among Garo, the transfer and trade of land is fairly common. House plots can be and are sold or rented to people who are not related to the owners of the *a'king* land, and may not even consider themselves relatives of the person selling or leasing out. As a consequence, in Tura and the surrounding area, where all the land has been converted into *patta*, neighbours are not necessarily close relatives. Even more remarkably—from a 'village' perspective—neighbours may have little contact with one another. Tura has grown from a small town to its present size of more than 75,000 inhabitants in just over thirty years, and living close to 'unknown' others is a relatively new development in Garo patterns of residency. Job postings, particularly for the increasing number of civil servants employed in the administration of Meghalaya state, may take people to towns and villages (even if only temporarily) where they have no close kin, resulting in middle-class people living more dispersed across Garo Hills than they did a few decades ago. While this allows for a certain degree of anonymity, which some people may welcome, it can also lead to people feeling uncertain about the interpersonal environment in which they find themselves. I have argued elsewhere that, perhaps as a side effect of this development, suspicions of witchcraft are becoming increasingly common in the peri-urban areas of Garo Hills (de Maaker 2009, 2013a). While experiences relating to witchcraft are grounded in ideas and practices that are deeply rooted in the Garo traditional cultural and religious repertoire, they seem to be gaining ground in contexts in which the mutual trust that used to be taken for granted in interactions structured by kinship can no longer be relied upon.

In rural West Garo Hills, people who live in a single village ward tend to be related as matrilineal or affinal kin. Usually, these relationships primarily connect the women, but they may also include some of their sons or grandsons. In Tura and the surrounding area, people also prefer to live with (close) matrilineal kin—and many do so. This is often all the more convenient because of relatives' access to nearby land, and it appears to me that even if the sale of *patta* plots has led to far more mixed residential environments than used to be common, many people continue to live on land that, as *a'king*, would be held by the matrilineage of the married woman at the head of a House. In this sense, matrilineal relatedness continues to shape patterns of residence.

Nonetheless, the reconfigurations of residential space that are taking place in the Tura area, combined with a growing tendency of Houses to adopt a slightly more 'nuclear' orientation, are posing challenges to the authority of kin seniors. Household economies are becoming increasingly focused on prioritizing their own members, in contrast to the strong emphasis on inter-House relationships in villages like Sadolpara. In response to these changing conditions, '*mahari* associations' have emerged in the urban and peri-urban areas. The term *mahari* refers to both consanguineal and affinal kin. *Mahari* associations are organized rather formally, with membership, a chairperson, a treasurer, and so on. Their objective is to unite matrilineally related Houses, as well as uncles, nephews, and sons (*chras*) who all belong to the same matrilineal group. In many ways, this is a formalized way of encouraging the solidarity within matrilineal groups that is more or less taken for granted in villages like Sadolpara, although *mahari* associations typically encompass a much larger number of people who often live dispersed across a far greater area.

Mahari associations are intended to facilitate the provision of mutual support among their members. In and around Tura, Houses continue to function as units of property. Upon marriage, men often (but not always) move to live with their wives and inheritance continues to be passed on in the female line. Because importance is attributed to the continuation of Houses, *a'kim* replacement needs to be arranged whenever the obligation to do so arises. Unlike in villages, where it is fairly easy to maintain an overview of the members of a matrilineal group from which partners could potentially be selected, in urban or peri-urban contexts, members of a group may live dispersed across Garo Hills, or even as far away as Khasi Hills (Meghalaya), Goalpara (Assam), or Mymensingh (Bangladesh). In villages, there are often quite a few people who are at once matrilineally related to one group and affinally to another. These people are very important as go-betweens, since they can act on behalf of both matrilineal groups and may be able to mediate should conflicts of interest arise between them. In urban and peri-urban contexts, by contrast, marriages may be conducted between partners whose matrilineal groups do not have many people in common. In addition, the increasing social stratification among Garo may be weakening the informal mechanisms (such as the fear of losing face) that used to pressurize people to take responsibility for the obligations of their matrilineage or matrilineal group. For all these reasons, organizing more formal structures to foster solidarity within matrilineal groups is proving fruitful, as the great popularity of *mahari* associations indicates. Providing a replacement spouse can be a complex task (sections 6.1–6.3), but in many cases it is nonetheless successfully accomplished—even among the urban middle class.

Garo *niam* primarily governs marriages, death, replacement, and inheritance. It is experienced as definitive, even though there are differences in interpretation between its distinct religious orientations (Songsarek, Catholic, Baptist) (Figure 7.3). While people value *niam* for being traditional and steadfast, it clearly needs to be able to deal with the changing resource base in Garo Hills. From temporary usage rights of land, anchored with Houses that strive to maintain good relationships with the spirits in order to secure ample harvests,

Figure 7.3 A Tura marriage, celebrated in style.
Photograph: Erik de Maaker, 2017.

the emphasis is shifting to land that is permanently occupied by crops that grow or fail independently of the spirits. From subsistence agriculture towards the production of cash crops and an increasing dependency on the whims of the market. And from close-knit, almost self-governing local communities, towards the utilization of and partial reliance on funding from 'outside' in the shape of small-scale development initiatives and grants, designed by distant bureaucrats to supplement meagre rural livelihoods. In the light of these major transformations, which have already had dramatic impacts in Tura and the peri-urban area and look likely to soon affect rural West Garo Hills in similar ways, disparities of class and income have emerged among Garo of a magnitude that would have been inconceivable just a couple of decades ago.

7.3 Polarities and Convergences

Garo living in the Tura area, who are all Christians, express strong nostalgic sentiments about 'village culture', which they associate with a Songsarek cultural 'past'. Many people decorate their homes with drawings and paintings (rarely photos) that show Songsarek men and women dancing at Wangala, working swiddens, or weaving wicker baskets. Such scenes, set in an apparently timeless past, provide anchors for a Garo cultural history. In addition to pictures, objects that originate from village environments also feature in home decoration. These include the ubiquitous small-scale bamboo or wooden model of a field house made in a tree (*borang*), a construction that in its original form provides cultivators protection at night from elephants as well as from the mosquitos that are omnipresent in the fields during the rainy season. Other popular decorative objects include (often miniaturized models of) domestic utensils that are part of village life, such as carrying baskets or drinking gourds.

Affluent middle-class living rooms often also display 'real' objects that relate to—supposedly past—Songsarek practices. These could be anything from highly valued *dama* drums (used for Wangala dancing) to traditional heirloom jewellery or even the gongs that are such prized gifts at funerals in villages like Sadolpara (section 5.6). I have never come across a *kram* drum in a private collection, which leads me to suppose that quite a few Christians would feel uncomfortable to have a drum in their house that, in the context of the traditional Garo community religion, is the seat of a spirit that can cause severe illness. *Kram* drums are to be found, however, in the collections of a number of ethnographic museums, as are many other highly valued heirloom objects. The objects are displayed alongside various utensils used in quotidian village life, comprising presentations of what middle-class Garo living in the peri-urban areas have learned to recognize as 'past' village culture.

The omnipresence of such depictions and artefacts relating to everyday Songsarek village life indicates that they are considered aesthetically pleasing, perhaps even comforting. Christian missionaries from 'outside' (Europe, Australia, the United States, or South India) have long vilified the traditional Garo community religion, and some continue to do so wherever potential converts are yet to be convinced (section 4.2). Garo Christians may feel superior to the followers of the traditional Garo community religion, yet at the same time they often express a lot of empathy for them, as well as (as I have shown) continue to share common ground in an ontological sense. Perhaps there is a sense, more widespread than most Garo Christians would be willing to admit, that zealous 'outsider' missionaries have taken away rather more Garo cultural heritage than they should have.

Conversely, Songsareks are not generally dismissive of Garo Christians either. While I have had numerous conversations with Songsareks who expressed concern and regret about the increasing number of youth converting to Christianity, conversions did not normally lead to conflicts within families. Moreover, the strong association of education with Christianity does not deter parents who follow the traditional community religion from sending their children to school, even though they are aware that doing so will almost certainly result in them opting for religious conversion. It is not unlikely that Sadolpara and the surrounding area has remained a Songsarek stronghold for so long because, until relatively recently, schools were all but non-existent there. More problematically, the standardized syllabi of formal schooling make it difficult for even the most engaged teachers to incorporate and foster pride in local knowledge and skills that have been carried over for generations. I am by no means an advocate of 'salvage ethnography' and I have never wanted to frame my research in such terms, but despite my convictions it has at times been difficult for me not to experience the waning of the traditional community religion as a cultural loss. The traditional Garo community religion fosters engagement with an animate earth, while it inspires strong redistributive social networks, and creates room for egalitarianism, gaiety, and joy. Yet associating conversion with cultural loss, is a sentiment far more seldomly expressed by Songsareks themselves than by Garo Christians, or even by outsiders like myself. Perhaps it has been more important for Songsareks that conversions do not usually significantly affect people's relational networks.

The first Christian conversions in Sadolpara took place in the 1960s, according to what people have told me, and by the time I started my research, the village had already been a multireligious environment for several decades. Since the 1960s, or perhaps even earlier, the 'traditional' Songsarek worldview—according to which the world is populated by innumerable spirits with whom humankind is obliged to negotiate its existence—has become entangled with ideas that derive from Christian as well as secular contexts. Whereas cultivating swidden crops—for Songsareks—requires the enactment of numerous rituals in order to keep the spirits benevolent and to secure good harvests, no ritual practices have ever been necessary for the cultivation of paddy rice or orchard crops (section 4.6). This implies that by the time these latter forms of permanent cultivation became established, the absolute power formerly attributed to the spirits had already begun to wane, and with it the degree of faith in the potency of taboos and the authority of customs associated with the spirits that had been passed down from previous generations.

In missionary discourse, religious conversion is often presented as a watershed event, a key moment when converts abandon ideas and practices that were integral to their former non-converted selves and embrace new ones, culminating in a spiritual rebirth (Rambo 1993). Numerous anthropological studies of religious conversion have convincingly shown that baptism, regardless of the convert's willingness or reticence, is rarely actually experienced as such a complete transformation. The convert continues to hold onto past cultural memories and typically continues to be part of the same relational networks that they related to before conversion (Marshall-Fratani 1998; Buckser and Glazier 2003). Hence, rather than constituting a singular life-changing event, religious conversion is often drawn out over a number of stages, characterized by varying intensities of commitment. Based upon her work among the Angami Naga, Vibha Joshi identified 'a series of overlapping acts of conversion and changing church membership, of competition between churches, and of conflict between burgeoning Christianity as a whole and important aspects of animism' (Joshi 2012: 9). I have made similar observations relating to Garo conversions. In the following section, I give three examples, based on arguments I have made previously, to show that there is more continuity between Garos' various religious ontologies than might appear at first glance.

The first example refers to peoples' approach to the environment. Christians do not consider it necessary to perform any dedicated ritual actions in order to secure the growth and productivity of the swidden crops. In their view, swidden or any other crops grow when provided with soil, water, and sunlight, all of which have been created by the Christian God. This God also created paddy rice, areca palm trees, cashew trees, and even human life itself. Every year, Christians offer some of their rice harvest to the church (as *daan*) to acknowledge that it is a gift from their God. This *daan* is always paddy rice, perhaps to avoid connotations of the strong symbolic association of rice from the swiddens with the community religion. But rather than denying that the Songsarek spirits exist, Garo Christians generally seem to assume that they have been silenced (de Maaker 2013a: 150). My understanding is that the Christian God is believed to have overpowered the spirits, which have lost much of their influence as a result, but may nonetheless still maintain a presence. This perspective is mirrored by that of some Songsareks who include the Christian God (Isol) and Jesus among the innumerable spirits that they recognize. The difference is that Songsareks continue to see the 'traditional' spirits of the community religion (such as Risi) as the most powerful, which is why they 'obey' them. Likewise, Christian Garo continue to respect the *kusi* boulders (section 4.4), at least in rural West Garo Hills, suggesting that their ontological realm is similarly open to accommodating multiple sources of inspiration and authority (de Maaker 2021b: 145-147).

Second, when it comes to the treatment of illness and the identification of its causes, it becomes even more evident that Garos' ontological realms tend to be shaped by both the community religion and Christianity (as well as 'secular' medical science). If someone is unwell, Songsareks have access to dedicated diagnostic techniques and sacrificial rituals based upon Songsarek understandings of illness (section 4.3). In addition, Songsareks often take biomedical treatments as well. Songsareks sometimes refer to these as 'Jesus' medicines' (*Jesuni sam*), identifying them as something associated with Christianity and/or with the kind of knowledge communicated in schools. All Garo medical doctors are Christians, and many dispensaries and hospitals are run by church-based organisations. Conversely, Garo Christians' approach to illness is not limited to the biomedical. Particularly when it comes to mental illnesses, interpretations often extend into the realm of the community religion, with the spirits held to be capable of inflicting great harm. Remedies for such often very serious conditions, as well as for more common ailments, are sought by Christians and Songsareks alike in 'Garo medicine' (*sam A'chik*). The principles underlying 'Garo medicine', as mentioned in section 2.2, are derived from the traditional Garo community religion (de Maaker 2013a: 152).

My last example refers relates to the position of the village head, which has dramatically changed as a result of religious conversions. In a village with a predominantly Songsarek population, a village head's political power would have rested upon his capacity to meet the religious responsibilities associated with his position as the most senior grandfather of the dominant matrilineal group of his village. If he failed to live up to that role, he would risk losing his authority. When Jiji was a teenager, sometime in the 1960s, the collective ceremonies linked to the annual cycle of shifting cultivation used to involve nearly all the Houses of Sadolpara. The village head conducted the main rituals and hosted extensive rice beer parties. His central role in all these ceremonies emphasized his privileged relationship to the spirits and his concomitant crucial responsibilities on behalf of all the Houses that cultivated swidden. He earned prestige by acting as a mediator between spirits and men.

The pre-eminence of a village head at that time thus depended first and foremost on his House's subsidiary Houses, which belonged to the same matrilineal group. They empowered his House by providing support, and in return they shared in its claims to *a'king* land, benefitted from its mediation with the spirits, and participated in the celebrations it hosted. From the early 20th century, the position of village head also became a matter of bureaucracy, with the registering of heads' names by the district administration, in an attempt to integrate Garo *niam* into the colonial state's structures of governance. Once Garo began converting to Christianity, a village head's religious responsibilities towards his village started to become less crucial. But his position was nonetheless secured in the registers of the GHADC, which had taken over following independence as the administrative body that was meant to continue to govern in accordance with *niam*. Moreover, written entries in the GHADC's registers were not subject to a village head's performance; he could not normally be overthrown or replaced if a group of villagers were to reach a consensus that he was failing to meet his duties. In recent decades, the Indian state has become a source of numerous development-oriented schemes, most of which need to be approved by the village heads. By enabling these schemes, and thus being seen as a conduit for government funds, village heads have acquired a new way to 'give' and thus to earn prestige. In this sense, their role is similar to that of politicians who are seen as brokers of the wealth of the state and who are judged by their voters to a good degree by how well they channel some of that wealth to them (section 7.1). Village heads thus continue to act as mediators between villagers and greater powers or authorities that are difficult for the villagers to access themselves, yet ultimately provide or withhold essential resources.

8
The Modernity of Garo *Niam*

8.1 Cherishing Tradition

One night, in Sadolpara, I was woken up by a deafening sound. It was pitch dark. In the early hours of the morning, Jiji had come over to the house where I was sleeping and was banging with her flat hand on the closed hatch of one of its windows. She called me, in her usual commanding manner: 'Iruk, come and have rice beer, our relatives have come over!' (*Iruk, chu ringen, mahari sokbajok!*). I didn't want to get out of bed and had no desire to drink rice beer in the middle of the night. I knew that our neighbours had been called as well when I heard the typical screeching sound of a woven bamboo door being opened nearby and then another similar sound from a little further away. Clearly, they had agreed to heed Jiji's call. I had had an exhausting day and couldn't muster up the energy to live up to Jiji's expectations. I went back to sleep. When I did get up, at around six o'clock in the morning, Jiji repeated her invitation. The guests, who were distant relatives, the neighbours, and many others were still socializing in her house. This time I gave in. Soon after I entered the main room, a new vessel of rice beer was opened for everyone to share. Several vessels had already been emptied, and the jokes and laughter made it clear that everyone was having a good time. People would simply compensate for the short night later on, I knew, by sleeping for a couple of hours during the day. The food and drink that Jiji served were from her own supplies, while some of her daughters and granddaughters who lived nearby had also contributed vessels of rice beer. Jiji wanted to be welcoming to the visiting relatives, but the get-together also cemented relationships between neighbours and other close kin. The night-time and early morning party revolved around drinking rice beer, something which—at least in principle—only Songsareks do. Christians abstain from it, and although it would be technically possible for them to drink tea while others have rice beer, that doesn't happen often. Attending a rice beer party as a Christian would invite suspicion that one is 'drinking' on the sly. Christians therefore only rarely join rice beer parties, and on this particular morning, all those present were Songsareks.

Reworking Culture. Erik de Maaker, Oxford University Press. © Oxford University Press 2022.
DOI: 10.1093/oso/9788194831693.003.0008

Visits like the one described above do not need to be announced in advance. They can occur any day, at any time of day or night. When visitors arrive, depending on the importance attributed to them, relatives and neighbours who want to join the gathering, or feel obliged to do so, stop whatever they were doing and change their plans for the day. Christians are also hospitable to their relatives, but they only serve them tea, which does not loosen people up the way the mildly alcoholic rice beer does. In my experience, the inclusive sociality created by having rice beer together is what people who have resisted religious conversion are so reluctant to relinquish. They really appreciate the long hours of shared cheerfulness, which make life enjoyable and provide entertainment, while at the same time reinforcing and renewing relationships with neighbours and kin. For people who have stayed with the traditional Garo community religion, being Songsarek evidently brings benefits that are important enough to make them hold on to it as long as that is even remotely viable.

Throughout Garo Hills, people tend to refer to the followers of the community religion as 'traditional' Garo, since their ontology and its associated religious practices precedes that of Garo Christians. But 'traditional' here also refers to a way of life that primarily centres on shifting cultivation, based on vernacular knowledge that has been passed down from earlier generations. Christianity, conversely, has come to epitomize the 'modern', which encompasses biomedicine, formal education, and is linked to 'Western' global Christianity.

Unpacking this rather oversimplified opposition of the traditional and the modern, I have shown that Songsareks keep to certain traditions, but this has not prevented them from being pragmatic and adaptive in embracing 'new' economic opportunities such as selling bamboo or timber, mining coal, or cultivating orchard crops. Their ideas, attitudes, practices, and *niam* are by no means frozen in time but flexible enough to incorporate the modernization of economic practices and to adapt to changing political contexts. In Sadolpara, the followers of the traditional Garo community religion are well aware what is required of them if a documentary film producer asks them to enact the practices of 'real *niam*' (*niam chongmot*, section 1.2).[1] In everyday life, however, people of a village such as Sadolpara have collectively converged upon a 'modernized' *niam* appropriate to their current circumstances, even if they are quick to state that it is a toned down version of the 'real *niam*' that used to be practised by the 'old grandfathers and grandmothers'. Living what they cherish as a 'traditional' life does not prevent the practitioners of the community religion in West Garo Hills to adapt and change.

8.2 How *Niam* Facilitates Social Change

Shifting cultivation, historically the main source of subsistence throughout Garo Hills, makes specific demands on social relationships. Since swiddens are impermanent, and vary in size and location over a rotational cycle of multiple years, land titles cannot be fixed to specific plots. Rather, ownership titles and usage rights referring to larger areas of land are held by Houses that are hierarchically related to one another. Relationships among these Houses are traced—among Songsareks—with reference to religio-political responsibilities. Shifting cultivation has gradually become less profitable in recent decades, but neither Songsareks nor Christians are willing to give it up. Not only does it continue to provide essential crops, it also forges a sense of commonality that people are keen to sustain. In villages like Sadolpara, everyone is related to everyone in some way or another, and they all live on the land that is their main resource. Staying together and maintaining unity, particularly as a matrilineal group, but also as a larger village community, cannot be taken for granted; conflicts of interest can easily arise. Songsarek rituals and ceremonies, in responding to the demands made by the spirits and the dead, also occasion the expression and renegotiation of relationships between Houses. At the same time, they encourage the redistribution of wealth, which can, at least to some degree, serve to counterbalance inequalities produced by the cumulative acquisition of individualized (or, perhaps better, 'nuclearized') wealth.

Customary titles to *a'king* land, some of which are only recognized at the village level and have not been registered with state authorities, have facilitated the use of land for income-generating activities like coal mining and the harvesting of bamboo. While the exploitation of such resources has been negotiated on the basis of the titles of senior Houses to *a'king* land, the distribution of resultant revenues has tended to be limited to the most prominent players involved, rather than encompassing all the members of an entire matrilineal group who—according to *niam*—share in those land titles. In addition, the procedures and taboos that guide how land is allocated for shifting cultivation have served to facilitate the creation of permanent orchards. Even without the creation of permanent *patta* land titles, the ongoing occupation of a former swidden plots results in the de facto privatization of land. Within village communities, some members have been much quicker and more successful in occupying land in this way than others have, so the shift towards orchard cultivation has exacerbated previously existing social and economic inequalities. The shift from temporary to permanent occupation of plots has reduced the mutual interdependency of Houses, at least in economic terms. Customary land arrangements, applied and adapted to new ways of utilizing land, have thus facilitated the intensification of structural disparities between Houses.

8.3 Reworking *Niam*

In this book, I have explored how culture is experienced among the Garo, one of the ethnic 'indigenous' communities of upland North-East India. I have located the Garo historically, politically, and ontologically, in order to explore and explain how cultural normativities are lived and enacted, shaping everyday life. I have focused on practices that are deemed traditional and shown that people can mobilize such practices (often referred to collectively as *'niam'*), perceived as customary, deep-rooted, and authoritative, to (re-)negotiate the relationships that they maintain with one another, as they share but also compete for the resources they depend on in everyday life.

Garo *niam* becomes manifest, first and foremost, in relationships among people, which are primarily structured through matrilineal groups. The matrilineal group determines who belongs, needs to comply, or can make demands, while kin seniors expect their authority to be respected by kin who are junior to them. The acknowledgement or initiation of certain relationships and the neglect of others, continually reshapes kin networks. Being part of a matrilineal group should provide one with support in times of need. That assumption is taken for granted in villages in West Garo Hills, but it is also the premise underlying the *mahari* associations that operate in urban and peri-urban areas. Although it is common to hear people complain that their relatives do not provide sufficient support, kin networks continue to create fundamental social texture, as is clear from the narratives that I have recounted.

Garo *niam* is encompassing; it defines social principles that transcend divisions of religion and class. At the same time, people practise *niam* in different ways, according to their social location. In rural West Garo Hills, for example, understandings and enactments of *niam* differ significantly between Songsareks and Christians, but also between Garo Christians living in rural West Garo Hills and middle-class Christian residents of Tura. Interpretations of *niam* specify what it means to provide and share, when providing and sharing are required and when this can be tactfully avoided. *Niam* is invoked when people define what kinds of actions are honourable, shameful, antisocial, or taboo. Irrespective of how people position themselves, maintaining and honouring kin relationships is at the core of Garo *niam*. The obligations, rights, and commitments this involves come markedly to the fore at funerals, when people are required to express acknowledgement of the deceased and the wider kin groups that he or she lived among. The gifts provided, offered, accepted, and rejected are tangible symbols in the articulation, negotiation, and reinterpretation of kin relationships. The most significant among these obligations is *a'kim*: the replacement of deceased spouses. Although *a'kim*-related commitments differ between Songsarek and Christian interpretations of *niam*, reformulations and reinterpretations make it possible for them to be honoured across religious divides (section 6.2).

In rural West Garo Hills, the administrative designation of village heads as the only signatories authorized to approve land transfers has unquestionably strengthened their position vis-à-vis the other representatives of their matrilineal group. Houses close to that of the village head, as well as savvy local entrepreneurs, have consequently been better able to profit from opportunities to engage in new kinds of market transactions (bamboo, coal), from the shift towards permanent land occupation (orchards), and from the emergence of the state as a substantial financial resource (access to development schemes). People who have been successful in tapping into such new sources of income have been able to build themselves 'modern' brick houses and acquire consumer goods such as mobile phones, televisions, motor scooters, or pickup trucks. Such wealth was previously almost unheard of in rural areas, and it is now redefining what it means to own and share as a member of a matrilineal group. Garo *niam* is thus being reinterpreted in line with the changing nature of the resources that people depend on for their livelihood. But as long as *niam*, as the epitome of Garo cultural ideas and practices, continues to be perceived as traditional and long-standing, it will continue to be attributed the authority to define the relationships and commitments that shape the lives of people.

Notes

Preface and Acknowledgements

1. Research conducted at the Research school CNWS, Leiden University, while affiliated with the North-Eastern Hill University in Shillong. Dissertation 'Dynamics of Death. Mortuary Rituals and Social Transformation among the Garo, North Eastern India', funded by a four-year Individual Project Grant from NWO/WOTRO (1999-2004) and a Cultural Exchange Scholarship funded by ICCR and NUFFIC (1999-2001).
2. Research project 'Markets, Ethics and Agency: Changing Land Utilization and Social Transformation in the Uplands of Northeast India', funded by NWO and ICSSR. This research project explored the strategies employed by upland farmers in North-East India to increase their engagement with markets and the state. Substantial investment by the Indian state into the North-East and the region's expansion of commercial activities such as mining have fuelled rapid development in terms of infrastructure and connectivity. Conducting in-depth multidisciplinary and empirical research into the hitherto overlooked agency of upland farmers and their complex and changing relationships with markets and the state, the project highlighted the dynamic changes that upland indigenous communities are encountering.
3. The research project 'Postcolonial Displacements: Migration, Narratives and Place-Making in South Asia' (funded by Leiden University, focus area Asian Modernities and Traditions). This project explored the multiple ways in which migration in South Asia contributes to the imagining, questioning, subverting, and reframing of territories, nations, and communities. Examining a range of historical and contemporary sociopolitical contexts, the project foregrounded the contested fringes of the politically divided South Asian subcontinent to investigate how people in South Asia engage with, resist, and reaffirm the arbitrary borders that divide, define, and delineate the states of the subcontinent. The research included studying how cultural imaginations, narratives, and claim-makings are shaped by histories, memories, and experiences of mobility and migration.

Chapter 1

1. Historian Willem van Schendel coined the term 'Zomia' to refer to the contiguous uplands of South and South East Asia that stretch across India, Myanmar,

Bangladesh, Thailand, China, and Vietnam (Van Schendel 2002). It was his intention to show that areas of study can be delineated in multiple ways, and that scholars should not necessarily limit themselves to working in accordance with political boundaries. Zomia brings together a broad range of communities of 'Zo' uplanders, who often have more in common with each other culturally and politically than they do with the lowlanders of the plains. Although Van Schendel's intention was to challenge the delineation of areas per se, rather than just creating a new one, Zomia has been enthusiastically adopted among scholars. Scott popularized the concept in *The Art of Not Being Governed: An Anarchist History of Upland Southeast Asia* (2009), while Sheiderman (2010), for instance, proposed redefining the boundaries of Zomia in a way that would include Nepal and Tibet.
2. Garo Hills is part of Meghalaya, one of the twenty-nine federated states of the Republic of India. Each of these states has its own state government, which is formed based on elections that are held every five years. While many policies and laws are defined by the union government in New Delhi (often colloquially referred to as 'the centre'), states have a certain degree of autonomy. Laws can vary from state to state. State budgets can be substantial, and states are significant employers in North-East India.
3. The 'Proposal for developing Sadolpara—Ethnic Garo village as a tourist attraction' was written by the Sub-Divisional Officer (Civil) of the Dadenggre Sub-Division (which Sadolpara is included in), in order to attract INR 25 lakh (roughly $35,000) in funding from the Tourism Department of the state of Meghalaya. The funding was to be used for the construction of a bachelor's house (historically the joined residence of unmarried adolescent men) and a tree-based field shelter. And, in order to enable tourists to spend cash in the village: a cafeteria, an interpretation centre, and a small museum coupled with a souvenir shop were to be created as well (Office of the Sub-Divisional Officer (C) 2010).
4. Early colonial travellers noted that the Garo community was characterized by great ethnic permeability. In 1838, Robert Montgomery Martin wrote: 'a Garo man or woman, that has connection with a person of a different nation, is not liable to excommunication; and any person who chooses to live among them, and follow their manners, may obtain the rights of a free man' (Martin 1990 [1838]: 94).
5. My doctoral fieldwork was made possible by a four-year Ph.D. grant awarded by the Dutch Research Council (NWO). In addition, I received a two-year ICCR Cultural Exchange Fellowship, which allowed me to register with the North-Eastern Hill University in Shillong. In the many years that followed, my research has been supported by Leiden University, NWO, and the Indian Council for Social Science Research (ICSSR).
6. The village territory Sadolpara encompasses two smaller domains, that is, Sadolpara (hence Sadolpara 'proper') and Mangdugre. In 2001, the latest Census of India data indicated that the village territory in its entirety had 1,672 inhabitants in

167 households: 125 in Sadolpara proper (1,089 inhabitants) and 42 in Mangdugre (583 inhabitants). According to the 2011 census, the number of households had risen to 150 and 63 respectively, while the number of residents had fallen to a total of 1,070 (742 and 328 respectively). See: https://www.census2011.co.in/data/subdistrict/1963-dadenggiri-west-garo-hills-meghalaya.html (accessed 29 January 2020). This latter sharp decline in population does not correspond with my observations, and I am under the impression that in 2011 the census takers were unable to account for all the residents of the Sadolpara village territory. As a conservative estimate, it is reasonable to assume that the village territory has at least 1,700 inhabitants, and most probably more than that.
7. The processes by which erstwhile communally held land is privatized, and rural economies become more market oriented, are apparent throughout the uplands of North-East India. In *The Politics of Swidden Farming: Environment and Development in Eastern India* (2018), Debojyoti Das analyses how in Nagaland the hills have over the past couple of decades transformed 'from their ideal beginnings as self-sustaining "little insular barter economies" into timber and cash-crop plantations that sustain export to urban and regional markets on the plains' (2018: 4). Combining ethnographies with critically used historical sources, Das explores discourses and narratives of a dominant policy paradigm floated by transnational environmental non-governmental organizations (NGOs) and institutions, as well as the micro-policies of the swidden farmer's life worlds, and argues against negative stereotypes that unjustly frame shifting cultivation almost exclusively in terms of inefficacy and under productivity.

Chapter 2

1. According to the census taken in 2011, Tura's population at that time comprised 74,858. It has continued to rise since then (Directorate of Census Operations 2014: 36).
2. As of 2019, these districts were West Garo Hills (created 1976), East Garo Hills (created 1976), South Garo Hills (created 1992), North Garo Hills (created 2012), and South-West Garo Hills (created 2012). The newer districts were created by dividing up existing ones, with the argument that creating additional district headquarters (in Williamnagar, Baghmara, Ampathi, and Resubelpara) would spread government agencies across Garo Hills, thus bringing structures of governance 'closer' to citizens. Processes of administrative fragmentation, common throughout India's North-East, have the advantage of creating numerous government jobs, which are always in high demand.
3. In the vicinity of the towns Nongalbibra and Siju (East Garo Hills district) there are many small-scale coal mines. These mines are mostly worked by Nepali,

Bengali, and Bihari men under dangerous conditions. When the coal mining ban was imposed, in 2015, quite a few of them left (Mcduie-Ra and Kikon 2016: 266). They gradually returned when it became clear that the state government was not making determined efforts to close all the mines, and in the summer of 2019 the high court revoked the ban altogether (Sitlhou 2019).

4. According to the Census of India (2011), the three districts that made up Garo Hills at the time (West, East, and South Garo Hills) had a population of 1103,542 in total, of which 913,426 or 83% were Garo. In West Garo Hills, of 643,291 persons, 474,009 or 74% were Garo. East Garo Hills had a total of 317,917 persons, of which 305,180 or 96% were Garo. And with 142,334 inhabitants, South Garo Hills had 134,237 or 94% Garo (Singh 2015: 82–83).

5. When I first came to Sadolpara, in 1999, hardly any of its residents used latrines. People defecated in the forest. I remember one of our neighbours telling me that latrines were not good: 'Songsareks don't defecate inside a house, that is not in accordance with *niam*.' But when the International Fund for Agriculture Development (IFAD) rural development programme took on Sadolpara a couple of years later, and propagated the use of latrines, every household agreed to make one almost overnight. In a report on the impact of the IFAD project on Sadolpara Village, its staff noted that before the IFAD interventions, 'the rural community live[d] in semi-darkness without any contact with the outside world'. Regarding the introduction of latrines, the report states:

> The villagers used to defecate in the open place thereby prevalence of communicable disease and loss of human life were common. . . . But after project intervention ninety nine per cent have constructed latrines, . . . so major changes on the part of hygiene and health can be observed.

Each family built their own latrine, following instructions issued by the IFAD team. The only goods supplied by the latter were a stone slab and about one metre of downpipe. All the other materials required were locally available.

6. The western part of Garo Hills is a 'mild extremely wet agro-climatic zone' with an annual rainfall of 4,851.5 mm, spread out over on average 113 rainy days a year (calculated between 1984 and 2007) (Ray et al. 2013).

7. Anthropology's recent ontological turn has led to a reappropriation of the concept of animism, without its former problematic evolutionist connotations. Early anthropologists such as Tylor (1871) and Frazer (1890) linked animism to what they viewed as the earliest or lowest stage of human evolution. By contrast, what has been coined 'new animism' refers to the 'widespread indigenous and increasingly popular "alternative" understanding that humans share this world with a wide range of persons, only some of whom are human' (Harvey 2005: xi). New animism, in other words, accommodates ontologies that are not based on the nature/culture dichotomy that is foundational to Western modernity.

8. Tiplut Nongbri points out that even though the government officers and the missionaries worked together, they did not necessarily have the same aims: 'The administrators' primary objective was to bring the tribal territories within the political control of the empire and transform tribes into loyal subjects of the sovereign. Whereas the goal of the missionary was to win the native's soul to Christendom that is unbound by political and geographical boundaries' (Nongbri 2014: 91).
9. There are a number of Garo dialects, which (at least historically) were spoken by subgroups or 'sub-tribes'. Many authors continue to quote Playfair on this matter (1909). A more concise list is given by Majumdar, who mentions: Am'beng, A'we, Chisak, Gara-Ganching, Matabeng, Matchi-Dual, Ruga-Chibok, and Atong (Majumdar 1978: 18). The vast majority of the Garo speak either A'we or Am'beng, while the other dialects have far fewer speakers. A'we speakers are predominant in the north of Garo Hills, as well as in adjacent Goalpara, which was where the missionaries initially established themselves (Allen et al. 1993 [1909]: 505). Speakers of Am'beng make up roughly 50 per cent of all Garo and comprise the majority across 'almost the whole western half of the district' (Majumdar 1978: 26). Ongoing debates question whether some of the other dialects should actually be considered dialects of Garo: Atong and Ruga, for example, are not mutually intelligible with other Garo dialects, but are more closely related to the Rabha language (Burling 2003: 176).
10. Folklorist Dewansingh Rongmithu Sangma notes that, according to Garo mythology, Garo 'possessed a literature of their own in their own script on rolls of parchment made from animal skins'. These texts were lost when the ancestors of the Garo migrated from Tibet towards Assam. 'It was while they were wandering from Tibet towards the plains of India that they felt acute shortage of food that they boiled the scrolls of parchment and ate them up. Thus their literature was lost for ever' (Sangma 1960: 1–2). Scott (2009: 24) notes that many of the upland communities across Zomia have myths about scripts that they once possessed and then either accidentally or wilfully lost. He interprets this as an active rejection of the attributes of plains dwellers, as part of a cultural strategy of resisting taxation, conscription, and other forms of control that lowland states tried to impose upon upland communities.
11. Records from the Census of India reveal the gradual increase of the percentage of Christians among Garo: 1901: 0.02%; 1911: 0.03; 1921: 0.04%; 1931: 0.19%; 1941: 37.94%; 1951: 20.58%; 1961: 37.70%; 1971: 54.21% (Bose 1985: xix). In 2001, 95% of Garo self-identified as Christians (Office of the Registrar General and Census Commissioner 2010).
12. The ubiquitous Garo elementary school book *Learning How to Read 1* (*Skichengani Ki'tap 1*) has a section on the 'Human Child' (*Mande Bi'sa*). Its first lines are: 'This child prays to God. God sees you. God sees you and me all

the time.' (*Ia bi'sa Isolo bi'a. Isol uko nika. Isol nang'ko are angko pangnan nika.*) (Skichengani Ki'tap I 1995 [1920]). In Garo, 'Isol' primarily refers to the Christian God. This school book exemplifies the strong association between education and Christianity.

13. For Songsarek Garo, even the preparation of rice beer involves the spirits. Brewing rice beer sees the transformation of rice grains into spirit-like fruit flies, or 'rice bodies' (*chumang*). If these flies do not appear, I was told, the beer will not taste good and will not have its intoxicating effect. Rice beer is not only enjoyed by people, but also by the spirits and the dead. Whenever they consume rice beer, Songsareks begin by pouring a little onto the ground, to provide the first draught to the spirits. Rice beer can also be offered to the dead.

14. The most comprehensive attempt to re-valorize the Garo community religion was made by Dewansing Rongmitu Sangma. In *Jadoreng: The Psycho-Physical Culture of the Garos* (1993), he seeks to reconcile the cosmological premises of the traditional community religion with Western psychology. The book was published twelve years after his death, and even though it did not lead to a revival of the community religion, it does seem to have contributed to its appreciation as an alternative ontology. It is not uncommon for politically aspiring Garo men to 'flirt' with the traditional community religion, drinking rice beer, and proudly stating that they are Songsareks. Yet in practice, with the exception of Dewansing Rongmitu, none of these men have ever really left the Christian church, nor been rejected by it. Perhaps an explanation for the absence of a religious revival movement among the Garo lies in the lenience of the mainstream Christian churches towards those who express interest in the traditional community religion. Whereas Dewansing Rongmitu explicitly extolled Garo philosophy and living in accordance with Songsarek *niam*, other authors have limited themselves to observing and describing traditional knowledge from a 'modernist' perspective. Several Garo scholars have produced comprehensive accounts of the traditional Garo community religion in this way. These include Enothsing Sangma's (unpublished) PhD thesis, 'Traditional Garo Religion in Its Social Matrix' (E.C. Sangma 1984), which includes detailed original accounts that are largely based upon fieldwork, and, more recently, Paulinus R. Marak's *The Garo Tribal Religion: Beliefs and Practices* (2005). The latter seems to be primarily based on published sources, whereas Alva B. Sangma's *Rites of Passage in the Garo Oral Literature* (2012) supplements material sourced from publications in Garo with newly obtained/recorded oral texts as well as observations. Noteworthy is also the pictorial ethnography produced by Timour Claquin Chambugong *The Songsarek Garo of Meghalaya* (Claquin Chambugong 2013).

15. The Census of India 2011, table DDWOOC-01 Appendix MDDS, records a total of at least 19,834 Songsareks residing in Meghalaya (Office of the Registrar General and Census Commissioner n.d.). In addition, a small number of

NOTES 257

Songsareks live in neighbouring parts of Assam (India) and Mymensingh (Bangladesh).

16. The perceived lack of wider political integration corresponds with the regional divergence of dialects mentioned in chapter 2, note 9. D.N. Majumdar writes that in precolonial times, the 'smaller communities which at the present time have combined to form the Garo identity those days had their own dialectical or linguistic peculiarities, varying social customs, and even most probably different clan organisations'.

17. The hills yielded produce such as cotton that was required by people living in the plains. In return, the hill dwellers depended on the plains for supplies of salt, dried fish, tobacco, and betel-nut (Robinson 1841 [1975]: 415). Moreover, the people of the hills did not have the skills to work iron (for knives or axes) or bell metal (for gongs), hence they procured such items from plains dwellers. Some of these objects appear as precious goods on the earliest known drawings and pictures from the area (Eliot 1799: 16; Playfair 1909: 32 (facing)).

18. In addition, Garo were often victims of 'a constant succession of fraud and falsehood' at the markets, where traders took advantage of Garos' need for certain products from the plains to drive hard bargains (Martin 1990 [1838]: 86–90).

19. 'In 1876, a Regulation (No. I of 1876) was passed to prevent entry of unlicensed persons into the hills for trading purposes and to control the acquisition of land in the hill district by persons who were not natives of the district. These provisions were similar to those of the Inner Line Regulations (Regulation No. V of 1873) and were enacted separately in view of the fact that the Inner Line Regulation as such could not be applied to a tract which was entirely surrounded by settled territory.' (Mackenzie 1884, cited in Das (1990: 9). These Inner Line Regulations, and the Inner Line Permits linked to them, remained in place, at least formally, until the mid-1990s. Since they were lifted, much to the dismay of some Garo political bodies, migration into Garo Hills has increased. Some of these political groups therefore continue to call for reinstatement of the Inner Line (*The Shillong Times* 2019).

20. This policy measure, Regulation X of 1822, was the first to define Garo Hills as a politically distinct region (Mackenzie 1995 [1884]: 250; Sinha 2003: 197).

21. The responsibilities and functions of village heads with respect to the administration of justice that were defined in the colonial period were subsequently, with some slight alterations, adopted by the Garo Hills Autonomous District Council, and are specified in the Garo Hills Autonomous District (Administration of Justice) Rules, 1953. The creation of the District Council limited the powers of village heads, at least on paper, by shifting the authority to impose punishment in relation to 'criminal' offences (as defined under the Indian Penal Code) to the courts of the District Council of (what was then) Garo Hills District (Kusum and Bakshi 1982: 28; Gassah 2002: 187).

22. Garo *niam* has also been analysed by Karnesh R. Marak (1964); C.D. Baldwin (1933); Ladia, 1993 #5625; Marak, 1964 #5502}. Disputes and criminal cases are discussed in Marak (1997).
23. Controversies in relation to the concept of 'tribe' reached an early peak in the 1940s, in a debate between the sociologist Ghurye and anthropologist Elwin. Ghurye maintained that from a sociological perspective, there were no grounds for a distinction between 'tribes' and 'castes' (Ghurye 1963 [1943] 6). Elwin (1943: 18) countered this, arguing that 'tribal' societies were unique and uniquely valuable as the custodians of cultural traditions that were distinct but by no means inferior to the Indian 'mainstream'.
24. Since the lists are composed state by state, groups that live divided across state boundaries may have ST status in one state, but not in a neighbouring state. Soon after independence, when Garo Hills became an autonomous district within the state of Assam, Garo living in the autonomous district obtained ST status, but those located elsewhere did not. With the formation of the state of Meghalaya in 1971, all Garo in the new state became ST. But Garo living elsewhere in Assam have, as far as I know, only been designated as ST since 2004, after long and at times violent political campaigns.
25. With their linguistic and cultural similarities, Jaintia (also referred to as Pnar) and Khasi tend to be referred to as a single group. Both belong to the Hynniewtrep people, which also includes War and Bhoi, two much smaller groups. Together, all the Hynniewtrep comprise the majority population in central and eastern Meghalaya (Haokip 2014: 304). Linguistically, Khasi/Pnar and Garo are unrelated, as they belong to different language families (Post and Burling 2016: 14). In contexts of governance, Khasi/Jaintia and Garo typically communicate with one another in English, which is the official language of the state of Meghalaya.
26. Ever since its incorporation into the colonial state, Garo Hills has had an exclusive status, whereby local governance is inspired on Garo *niam*. The legal prohibition of transfers of land to non-Garo first came into effect in 1955 (Act No IV of 1955), to be further tightened with the imposition of the Meghalaya Transfer of Land (Regulation) Act, 1971 (Act I of 1972) (Das 1990: 34). While this has inhibited the transfer of land from Garo to non-Garo, it has not prevented members of smaller 'tribes' (such as Hajong, Koch, Raba) from transferring their land to Garo (Majumdar 1986b: 65).
27. Currently, the distribution is: 40% for Garo, 40% for Khasi/Jaintia, and 5% for the other STs as well as for the Scheduled Castes (Guenauer 2016: 435).
28. Of the sixty seats in the Legislative Assembly of the state of Meghalaya, fifty-five are reserved for members of the Scheduled Tribes (Guenauer 2016: 434).
29. In rural Garo Hills, beef is undoubtedly the most prized meat. At important events, such as political rallies, or all but the least significant funerals, it is almost obligatory to serve beef. In urban settings, beef continues to be eaten, but there is

also a growing appreciation for pork. The Bharatiya Janata Party (BJP), which has gained some political presence in Garo Hills, is known nationally for its condemnation of the slaughter of cattle, but has been careful not to raise the issue among North-East India's hill communities. Nevertheless, Meghalaya's politics have not been left completely untouched by the national controversies—provocative political opponents of the BJP have been known to host 'beef parties' to capitalize on Garos' enjoyment of the meat (Parashar 2017).

30. Violent conflict has marked large parts of North-East India since the earliest days of independence. In addition to the Naga movement for independence, which had already been underway for several decades by the time the Republic of India came into being in 1947, militant groups gained prominence in Manipur, Mizoram, and Assam in the 1960s and 1970s. Their primary objective was to win a certain degree of ethnic self-determination independent of the Indian state, although interethnic conflict has also been a recurrent issue (Kashena 2017). The Indian government attempted to quell these movements by deploying heavily armed security forces, which it empowered to use any measure of violence deemed necessary under the infamous Armed Forces Special Powers Act. These conflicts reached their peak between the 1980s and the early 2000s, and although they have since somewhat died down, with many of the militant groups having entered into peace negotiations with the Indian government, the region continues to be volatile (Baruah 2005a; Bhaumik 2009).

31. Among the militant groups that have been active in Garo Hills until recently are the Garo National Liberation Army (GNLA), Garo Liberation Tigers (GLT), A'chik Tiger Force (ATF), Liberation of A'chik Elite Force (LAEF), A'chik Songna An'pachakgipa Kotok or 'Protector Army of Garo Land' (ASAK), A'chik National Liberation Central Army (ANLCA), A'chik National Co-operative Army (ANCA), A'chik National Liberation Army (ANLA), A'chik National Volunteer Council—Breakaway (ANVC-B), and Mat Memang/Matchadu Matchabet ('Ghost Animal/Half Tiger-Half Human'). New groups have emerged regularly, and expressing the frustration of trying to compile a complete list, some authors have referred to the various groups as an 'alphabet soup' (P. K. 2014). According to India's Institute for Conflict Management's South Asia Terrorism Portal database, at least 399 people were killed between 2001 and 2016 as a result of 'insurgency related incidents' in Garo Hills (Institute for Conflict Management 2019).

32. Most such counter-insurgency operations are not conducted by Meghalaya's own police force (which is primarily made up by Garo), but by the Central Reserve Police Force (CRPF). Central troops are generally Hindi speakers and have difficulty conversing with the local population. The CRPF has several battalions in Garo Hills and most people I have known in rural West Garo Hills have expressed genuine fear of them.

33. Since militancy has died down, some of these extortive practices have been taken over by gangs who are not organized under a political banner. Local newspapers frequently report on abductions of non-Garo traders for ransom. (See, for example, *The Shillong Times* 2018a, accessed 31 January 2020.)

Chapter 3

1. Until fairly recently, Songsareks did not keep track of their children's birth dates. Or if they did, they did not do so according to the Gregorian calendar, which resulted in wild or even 'ridiculously incorrect' guesses (Majumdar 1978: 154). People sometimes stated their age with reference to significant historical events, such as a major accident, an earthquake, or (for older people) the active presence of the Indian Air Force in the skies over the Garo Hills at the time of the Bangladesh liberation war in the early 1970s. Such estimations are not easily converted into the kinds of dates recognized by the Indian state. All adults had official documents such as Voter Identification Cards, but the birth dates stated on these were seldom accurate, especially for older persons.
2. Biomedicine tends to attribute these symptoms to malaria. In addition to performing sacrifices to Risi, followers of the traditional Garo community religion sometimes use antimalarial drugs, such as chloroquine. They do not consider these differing approaches to treatment to be incompatible (section 5.2).
3. Typically, most of the female members of a *ba'saa* live close together in a single village. Upon marriage, men relocate to reside with their wives, which often means moving to a different village than the one in which they were born.
4. Nepali have a long history of residence in Garo Hills, where they have typically herded dairy cattle. Their migration into what is currently India's North-East was part of a diaspora movement out of eastern Nepal that began in the late 19th century (Sinha and Subba 2003).
5. In 2009, the Garo Hills Autonomous District Council passed the 'Garo Customary Law Bill', which restricts membership of the Garo community to children who have been born from two Garo parents. This meant that any children born thereafter to a non-Garo mother or father would not legally belong to the community. As a consequence, Garo customary law, as authorized by the District Council, would no longer apply to them. In effect, this would make it impossible for people of mixed descent to inherit land or other assets, or to qualify for the benefits available to Garo as part of affirmative action policies (Saikia 2017). The bill continues to be controversial, not least because it represents a departure from the existing (customary) practice. After its adoption, the bill was passed on for endorsement to the Governor of Meghalaya, but as of spring 2021 it has not yet been issued.

6. For an extensive discussion on Garo names, including nicknames and name jokes see Burling, Hvenekilde, and Marak (2000).
7. The Sangma and Marak clans function more or less as moieties. Sangma and the third largest clan, Momin, are regarded as equivalent in this sense. The other two clans, Shira and Arengh, are numerically insignificant, and can marry either Sangma or Marak (Burling 1997 [1963]: 23).
8. Writing about European nobility in *The Way of the Masks*, Levi-Strauss defined the House as a 'moral person, holding an estate made up of material and immaterial wealth which perpetuates itself through the transmission of its name down a real or imaginary line, considered legitimate as long as this continuity can express itself in the language of kinship or of affinity, and, most often, of both' (Levi-Strauss 1983: 174).
9. Jewellery may include necklaces made from multiple strings of metal rings (*sillitting*), chains adorned with decades-old twenty-five paisa silver coins (*suki mipal*) or fifty paisa coins (*repa mipal*), necklaces woven from silver wire (*kakam* or *kunal*), or waist belts (*senki ripok*).
10. People distinguish between at least twenty different kinds of gongs. Most gongs are about a foot in diameter; some are slightly smaller. The more valuable ones are decorated with finely etched images. A common gong, such as an *anggar angjong*, is only worth about a hundred rupees. Rare ones like the *assam katta singimari* are valued at thousands of rupees.
11. The agreement reached between the parents of a prospective bride and groom prior to the marriage initiates a 'release period' (*watmiting*), or 'time to capture' (*sekmiting*). It grants the bride's parents an exclusive right to have the groom abducted to their house. People from other Houses are not allowed to abduct him until it has become clear whether the marriage will be accepted or not. The groom should be abducted and the marriage initiated within days, or at the most weeks, after the agreement has been reached.
12. Recorded on video, 2 October 2000.
13. When a marriage by *du'sia* creates a new House, three chicken intestines need to be assessed. The omens of the first two chickens relate to the respective matrilineal groups of the groom and the bride. The third one, the 'chicken of honour', indicates the prosperity and fertility of the House that is coming into being.
14. All three chickens were cooked. Tami's relatives and neighbours ate the meat from the first two. People said that were the bride and the groom to eat it, that would constitute a transgression, because those chickens are associated with them. I was told that if the groom committed such a transgression and then escaped to his own village (as he should attempt to), he would probably be attacked on the way by animals such as tigers, bears, or elephants. No such risk is incurred by eating the meat of the 'chicken of honour'.

15. If a marriage is consummated, it is expected to come into effect. Once, when men were drinking rice beer together, one of them was taunted for having slept with a woman for whom he had been abducted, but had subsequently rejected. His behaviour was considered particularly scandalous because she had become pregnant as a result.
16. As mentioned in the Preface, video footage recorded in the course of Tami and Gushen's marriage was used in the ethnographic documentary *Notes on Man Capture*, which was produced by Nandini Bedi in 2007 (distributed by Magic Lantern Movies, New Delhi. http://magiclanternmovies.in/film/notes-man-capture). The film is also available on YouTube at: https://youtu.be/q9q7QsOd6tw.
17. A married man has two sets of *chra*s: his male matrilineal relatives by birth ('own *chra*', *chratang*), as well as his wife's male matrilineal relatives (who he refers to as *apa-chra*). A married woman acknowledges her own *chra*s, but not the *chra*s of her husband.

Chapter 4

1. Recorded on video, 12 March 2000.
2. *Dikki* is a generic term for a whole range of potent 'jungle onion'-like wild plants, as noted by Dewansingh Rongmuthu (Sangma 1970: 38–42).
3. Several spirits are perceived at once as a single entity and as two constituent ones. Rabokka is also referred to as Dakkara-Rabokka. Rabokka is then the elder brother of Dakkara. There are also some spirits who are thought to be husband and wife, such as Bang-Nawang, the guardian of the afterworld. Bang is Nawang's wife.
4. Audio recording made in the context of ethnographic fieldwork on 19 March 2001.
5. From the age of about 6 or 7, it becomes improper for a boy to sleep in the vicinity of his parents and sisters. Until two or three decades ago, it was common for all the young males in a village to move, at that age, into a bachelors' dormitory, where they lived together until they got married. The dormitories were important sites for the transfer of stories, knowledge, and skills that were central to the community religion, while they also allowed for peer bonding. The dormitories were usually off limits to girls; it was only during village festivals that all villagers, irrespective of age or gender, had access to them. They also served as a place where (male) visitors could rest, and as a 'council hall' where matters of common interest were discussed—in the absence of women (Majumdar 1984: 309–310).
6. In a more general sense, people maintained that their forefathers had originated from Tibet, but they were not any more specific than that. The legend that narrates the Garo migration from Tibet is often cited by Garo folklorists, and quoted by many authors, but no one in Sadolpara was able to recount it to me in

detail (Playfair 1909: 8–12; Sangma 1970: 1–2; Sangma 1981: 4; M.N. Sangma 1984; Sangma 1993).

7. In a chant that is recited during the rituals that are part of the Wangala festival, reference is made to Guira as 'the spirit of the *nokma*'s planted *kusi* boulder, the father's supporting boulder' ('*nokmani kusinibane, do'mani rong'dunibane*'). A similar association is suggested by Playfair, who writes that 'sacrificial stones' are erected in honour of Guira's brother Kalkami (1909: 82). Guira-Kalkami is a double spirit. In Sadolpara, the top of the steps that used to lead to the collective bachelors' house had a wood carving of the head of Guira-Kalkami, providing the spirit with a presence among the youth who lived and gathered there.

8. It is impossible to determine for certain the degree to which boundaries between village territories had been fixed in precolonial times. According to Das (1990: 14), 'after centuries of feuds and fighting, the different clans of Garo Hills came to some tacit understanding as to the boundaries of the clan land of each clan'. The land survey, conducted under the governance of Deputy Commissioner G.D. Walker, resulted in the demarcation of 1,322 distinct village territories. Disputes about land continued to exist, but whereas before 'such disputes (had been) settled by arms and regular fights between the clans concerned', they became primarily a matter of court proceedings (as mentioned in section 2.3). Land that could not, according to the colonial authorities, be clearly identified as part of any single village's territory was taken over by the government. Registering the land rendered those living on it subjects of the colonial, and later Indian state, but it also provided the rural population with valuable ownership titles to the land they lived on and cultivated (Majumdar 1986a: 125).

9. In Sadolpara, most land is held by Houses of the Mangsang Sangma matrilineage, to which the House of the village head and Jiji's House belong. In addition, a further eleven Houses hold title to land. People do not state the area of *a'king* land in absolute terms (such as acres), but by the number of fields that it can accommodate. Most Houses with minor holdings only have small patches of land that cannot accommodate more than five or six fields. The exception to this is one House, which also belongs to the Mangsang Sangma matrilineage, albeit to another matrilineal group. This House claims to have nearly as much land as that of the village head, and at one time it made a serious and ultimately partially successful attempt to have its land registered with the GHADC. The process led to its claim being acknowledged in a written statement, but no map was drawn to indicate where the land was located. The Chambugong Marak and Mrong Marak matrilineal groups also have minor shares of *a'king* land in Sadolpara. According to the genealogies that I recorded, these matrilineages have only been present there for less than five or six generations. Most probably, they bought their land from Mangsang Sangma Houses. The largest share of Chambugong and Mrong

a'king land belongs to the Houses that are the most senior of their groups. Five of the more junior Houses also hold title to land.

10. In everyday conversation, the term *nokma* refers to a 'village head', but is an abbreviated form of the full title: *a'king nokma*. The *a'king nokma* of a village like Sadolpara is registered with the GHADC, but several 'minor' *nokma*s are often also registered. In a broader sense, the term *nokma* can be used to refer to anyone who has significant possessions, anyone who is an 'owner'. Jiji's close kin liked to state that she was a *nokma*, since her House holds significant claims to land, and is the tamer of a *kram* drum. Yet her status as an owner was not acknowledged by the GHADC. According to the current head of the House (Pongjan, the heir of Jiji's husband Baka), as well as Jiji's two sons, the House holds title to *a'king* land with a total size of 300 *bitot*. One *bitot* is large enough for ten fields.
11. Borah and Goswami calculated that in Garo Hills, where the soil and vegetation ideally require a fallow period of at least fifteen years, the maximum population density that can support itself with shifting cultivation to a minimum standard of living is no more than five persons per km^2 (Borah and Goswami 1977). Although I have no exact numbers regarding the current population density in rural West Garo Hills, there is no doubt that it exceeds that figure. Population densities in rural East Garo Hills are much lower, and shifting cultivation does indeed continue to provide people there with relatively abundant harvests. See Bela Malik for an extensive account of the government policies enacted between 1860 and 1970 with respect to shifting cultivation in Garo Hills (Malik 2003).
12. A recent study conducted in West Garo Hills, based on satellite imagery, indicates that the majority of land is currently in use—either for shifting cultivation or for orchards crops. The district now only has small patches of primeval or 'old' forest (Kurien, Lele, and Nagendra 2019: 11).
13. Enothsing Sangma states that 'Garo' regard the *kram* 'as drum of the spirit', and that the spirit is 'believed capable of doing some harm to man and in certain cases it may cause death' (E.C. Sangma 1984: 124).
14. A *kram* drum-owning House is referred to as a 'strong House' (*nok raka*); one that does not own a *kram* drum as a 'lame House' (*nok malam*).
15. One of these is the *mil'am gakasil*, a rare Garo traditional sword. The sword is associated with its own spirit, who demands the sacrifice of a chicken once a year. In Sadolpara at the time of my fieldwork, the only Houses to keep such swords were that of the *a'king nokma* and of the second largest *nokma*. These were also the only Houses to have a *rang ripu*, a precious and particularly powerful gong. I have never seen a *rang ripu*, but was told that its surface is blotted like the skin of someone struck by a contagious disease such as measles. Like any other spirit, the spirit of the gong can bite and thus cause illness. When a sacrifice is performed for the spirit in order to entice it to release a victim it is biting, the gong is beaten once. Otherwise, the *rang ripu* is never played, nor can it be given as *ma'gual*

(section 5.6). Owning such a gong means 'taming' it, comparable to the 'taming' of a *kram* drum. Possession of a *rang ripu* or a *mil'am gakasil* grants a House prestige and raises its status, particularly among Songsareks.

16. *Kram* drums are on display in the extensive ethnographic collections of the District Museum of the Department of Arts and Culture of Meghalaya State in Tura, the Don Bosco Centre for Indigenous Cultures in Shillong, the Madhab Chandra Goswami Anthropological Museum at Guwahati University, the Assam State Museum in Guwahati, and the Indian Museum in Kolkata, to name but a few.
17. Recorded on video, 14 November 2000.
18. Recorded on video, 16 November 2000.
19. I disagree with authors who argue that *marang* has purely negative connotations. According to Sinha, *marang* is 'more a horror than anything else' (Sinha 1966: 99), while Majumdar 'translates' *marang* as 'bad luck" or 'ill-luck' (Majumdar 1978: 137). *Marang* is undoubtedly dangerous, but at times it is unavoidable (childbirth) or even essential for survival (warfare). In the latter sense, Girard's comparison with the notion of violence is insightful: while violence is dangerous and should be avoided, 'justified violence' can be required to defend oneself and one's community against a greater threat (Girard 1977).
20. Every two years, Songsareks conduct an extensive ritual to purge *marang*. This is done in mid-March, before the onset of the rains that indicate the start of the new agricultural year. This ritual, Bilsi Ra'a ('take the year'), relates to the village as a whole. The village is symbolically closed to outsiders for the few days of its duration. Led by the village head, the men hunt together, ideally catching a langur monkey (*ranggol*), but if they are unable to get one, a squirrel may serve as a substitute. A senior man who leads the ritual, and acts as *kamal*, ties the dead animal on a string and drags it through the village. He hits each house with it so that the animal can soak up the *marang* that has collected there in the preceding months. Men accompany him and collect old pestles, brooms, and rice cooking sticks from each of the houses visited. These symbolize the old year. They are discarded outside the village, in the jungle. The dead animal is tied, spreadeagled, to a fork in a tree at the same spot. The next day, no work may be done inside the village, nor should any loud sounds be made. On the evening of the last day of Bilsi Ra'a, the head of each House makes an offering of an egg at his granary, in order to 'wake up' the rice grains that are kept there and prepare them for germination. These grains have been selected from among the rice that was harvested the previous year, and will be sown on the swiddens in the weeks that follow.
21. Saljong is equated to the sun and the moon, as Montgomery Martin already noted in an early 19th century travelogue: 'Saljung in fact is the firmament or visible heavens: the heavenly bodies, sun, moon, and stars, and spirits, who preside

over the hills, woods and rivers, are considered as the agents employed by Saljung to manage the affairs of the world' (1990 [1838]: 97).

22. The *dama* drums used to be kept in the bachelors' dormitory. Each of the young men who lived there carved his own *dama* drum. When he married and left, his drum remained in the bachelors' house, even if he moved to a different village after marriage. Nowadays, these drums are typically kept in another collective place, such as the gazebo-like resting houses (*kachari*) that are often shared by people living in a single ward (Figure 3.5).

23. The celebration of A'galmaka, once initiated, cannot be interrupted. In the course of one of the celebrations of A'galmaka that I attended, a death occurred. Sisi had been a highly respected elderly woman, and many villagers went to her house to participate in the mortuary ritual, yet it was imperative that the celebration of A'galmaka did not stop. A small party continued the visits from house to house. The route of the party could not be changed, so they also had to visit the ward at which the death had occurred. By spending much more time at each house than they would have done otherwise, they slowed down their progress, and by the time they finally reached Sisi's ward, the funeral had been all but concluded.

24. By mid-August, the hill rice ripens. Most of the grains are 'plucked' (*aka*) or 'taken' (*ra'a*) from the stem by hand. A small quantity of the rice is cut with a sickle. This can be rice cut with the stem (*midong*, 'rice on the stalk') or without the stem (*michikkang*, 'rice on the ear'). About a week before the start of the Wangala festival, 'rice on the stalk' is offered to people who have died during the past year. 'Rice on the ear' is kept for the funerals of the year ahead, for the dead to come. The head of each House uses a sickle to harvest the last of the swidden rice on the day that the Jamegapa ('*jam*', granary; '*gapa*', full) festival begins. It is cut as 'rice on the stalk' from stems that have grown at the spot where the altar stood at A'galmaka. After completing the rice harvest in this way, the head of the House offers a pomelo (*jambura*) at the same spot. The fruit is cut into two, and some salt is rubbed onto the inside of each half. While a chant is uttered, the halves are moistened with a little rice beer that has been made from newly harvested rice. The chant includes lines such as: 'The neck of the rice stalk has been hacked, ... The mother of rice has been killed ... Plants, come out, and grow in any direction. Be in harmony with each other, and with the spirits.' ('*Gitok sotahajok. ... Mini ma'ku gitok sotjok. ... Rua ganrikalbune. Ruku'mongrikaljokne.*' Chanting of Jiji M. Sangma, recorded on video on 2 September 2000.) The invocation refers to the cutting of the rice stalks as 'hacking the neck' and thus 'killing' the 'rice mother.' Even in everyday speech, people refer to the harvest of the last rice as 'severing the mother' (Amarata). People explained the symbolism of the offering, telling me that the murder of the 'rice mother' generates *marang*. This *marang* can be neutralized by the sour juice of the pomelo. In precolonial times, men who came back from battle and felt 'drunk with blood' (*anchi peka*) used to

rid themselves of their bloodthirstiness by drinking the juice of sour citrus fruits like lime and pomelo.
25. Wangala celebrations are open to anyone who wants to participate; turning visitors away is not permitted. One way to try to limit the number of visitors is not to communicate the date of the celebrations in advance. This is not a new strategy. Majumdar noted how already in the 1970s, in Matchakolgre, a village close to Tura that at the time had a substantial number of (impoverished) Songsareks, drums were no longer beaten at the time of Wangala. 'Villagers told me that the beating of drums acts as an announcement to the neighbouring villagers, who come in large numbers to participate in the festivities causing considerable expenditure and embarrassment to the local households' (Majumdar 1978: 63).
26. Two of the four crabs that are offered are killed by the village head; the other two are allowed to escape. Biki explained to me, 'These are set free, so that they inform other animals that bite and sting about the two that were killed.' Presumably, this helps to keep other biting and stinging animals at bay. With the killing of the crabs, the *nokma* shows his supremacy over all biting and stinging creatures.
27. Recorded on video, 10 October 2000.

Chapter 5

1. The salesmen waited at the market with dozens if not hundreds of boxes and strips of medications spread out in front of them. In a typical consultation, the salesman would ask his customer, 'What is the problem?' The latter would then, for instance, point at their abdomen and say, with reference to the absent patient: 'She has pain in the stomach.' In response, the salesman would take out some pills. He might advise the client to buy eight pills, to be taken twice daily for four days. If that proved too expensive for the buyer, the number of pills would be halved, adjusting the treatment to the means available. Most people who bought these kinds of medicines were illiterate and relied upon the advice of the salesmen. Medicines that required injection were considered particularly effective by villagers. There was a Community Health Centre in the nearby town of Dadenggri, but that was about one and a half hour away on foot, so it was relatively far for residents of Sadolpara. In addition, more often than not, the—theoretically free—medicines prescribed by the Centre's staff were out of stock, so people would end up having to buy them from a pharmacy anyway.
2. Any food or drink that is touched by a ghost will go bad. To prevent this from happening to rice beer that is brewing, some ashes are always kept on the leaves that seal a vessel. I was told that this fools the ghosts into thinking the ashes are chicken dung, which they detest.

3. The lament narrates the journey that the ghost is about to make to the afterworld, and elderly women like Jiji know it by heart. Jiji recited for me the part that describes the last part of the journey:

> At the place where the ghost has lunch,
> it ties the cow to the boldak tree
> The leaf in which rice has been folded is opened wide,
> the bamboo in which curry has been prepared is split
> *Mi'mang misal cha'ram*
> *Boldak matchu karam*
> *Mipal gangjam engramna*
> *Sangrang ripram pitramna*

Before reaching the afterworld, the ghost is said to pause for lunch. The food and the cow derive from the realm of the living. When the ghost recommences its journey, it has to cross a fork in the path, which is guarded by Bang-Nawang. Bang-Nawang, the guardian of the afterworld, is a double-deity: Bang is a man, and Nawang his wife. Jiji chanted on:

> The male Nawang has a beard
> Female Bang is pregnant
> Her belly round and big like a rice beer vessel
> His mouth wide open, like a carrying basket.
> *Nawang bipa kusumang*
> *Bang bima okgnang*
> *Bikma dikka choketa*
> *Kusik ala kokgita*

The women wail as they chant the dirge, and Jiji told me that it is the duty of women who are only distantly related to the deceased to wail and lament loudly, to help the close relatives of the dead person to 'bring out their grief'. In between spells of lamentation, the women chat about just anything, and sometimes—or rather, often—they crack sexually charged jokes. The jokes lead to sniggering rather than outright laughter on these occasions, indicating a degree of ambivalence about such jokes in this context. Someone once suggested to me that scandalous jokes can serve to break the emotional tension created by the presence of the corpse.

4. Transgressions associated with the manifestation of one's soul in a previous life can trigger a violent death. The sanctions for the transgression have then been 'held back' or 'kept' (*donsua*). A death that results from an attack by a tiger or a bear, or from being caught in the raging fire (*walsari*) that burns the new swiddens, is likely to be due to such a former transgression. If someone suspects that they may be at risk of such sanctions, they can attempt to protect themself by changing their given name. For Songsareks, this requires a sacrifice to the creator spirit Rabokka. When Biki's uncle Gakjang was killed by a tiger, his widow was so afraid that the

same transgression would lead to her own death as well that she changed her given name from 'Miti' to 'Asik Nengjak'. Children are never named after people who have died a violent death, and certainly not after someone who has been killed by a tiger.

5. Decades ago, when Jiji was still a child, a used sling could be washed and given, but nowadays a new one is given instead. When I asked why this has changed, I was told: 'The new cloth is as clean as a washed one, don't you understand'? Nowadays, people in rural West Garo Hills use factory-produced textiles, which are sold relatively cheaply at the market. Five or six decades ago, people would have generally woven their own fabrics, which was very time-consuming. In those days, a piece of cloth such as a sling would have therefore had much greater intrinsic value than its industrially-produced equivalent has today.

6. It would be taboo to slaughter a cow for 'washing the sling' because, as I was told, 'this [ritual] aims to honour mother, and a cow is a mother as well.' More generally, if people need to slaughter cattle for funerals or other ceremonies and they have the option, they will always choose a bull. It is preferable to retain cows for their procreative capacity, and because they can give milk. Milk is not readily available because not many people have cows, while those who are there do not produce much milk. But people who do have access to it boil their tea with milk and sugar in a similar way to how tea is prepared throughout much of South Asia.

7. One such disease is 'T.B.-illness' (*tibi saa*), which causes people to 'dry up slowly, until they have no blood left', as Jiji's eldest daughter described it. People not only use the term 'T.B.' to refer to (presumed) tuberculosis, but also for a disease like leishmaniasis (*kala azar*). Another disease that is considered highly contagious is 'being eaten by worms' (*jo'ong cha'a*). The worms, too small to be seen, consume the flesh of the infected person and mutilate their body. The worms are believed to live in large 'worm balls' (*jong'dik*) in certain streams. Water from these streams infects anyone who drinks it, eats fish caught from it, or uses it for irrigation.

8. Animals such as monster lizards (*aringga*) and electric eels (*na'nil*) are believed to have supernatural qualities. Jiji told me that monster lizards, which can be up to one metre high at the shoulder, kill by piercing their tail through their victim's head, to then drink their blood. Electric eels live in deep pools or in deep places in rivers. It is said that they bite their victim's forehead or navel and then suck their blood. Water spirits (*bugarani*) also cause death by sucking humans' blood. A water spirit is an anthropomorphic being that is said to envy people for their long hair—in the past, Songsareks never used to cut their hair (Burling 1997 [1963]: 321).

9. Biki told me that when his uncle Gakjang was killed in the forest by a tiger, four or five decades ago, the tiger had consumed most of the man. People had been so terrified that they had not even brought what remained of the body to the village, but had cremated it on the spot (see also Sinha 1966: 100).

10. People who are threatened by a tiger can try worshipping it as the spirit Chura. Once or twice a year, such a House is obliged to sacrifice a chicken or a goat. Offering such sacrifices makes the House a 'tamer' of Chura. This results in a status that is somewhat comparable to that which the 'taming' of Risi grants to a *kram* owning-House.
11. Both vessels are associated with spirits. Rice transforms into rice beer with the help of the spirits. A rice storage vessel needs to be associated with a spirit in order to be able to feed the residents of a house. The rice beer and rice storage vessels are made of heavy earthenware. Like all pottery in Garo homes, they are made by Bengalis in the riverine villages in the nearby plains, and bought at the weekly markets. When a new rice storage vessel is acquired, a chicken needs to be sacrificed (*rong'dik dutata*) in order to guide the spirit to the vessel.
12. Hence the second day of a funeral is called *surigala*, a term which refers to the clearing of the house (*suri*: old, worn things; *gala*: to throw).
13. Not long ago, many more gongs were in circulation. Enotsingh Sangma (1984:174) describes how the body of a rich old man was laid out 'over a bed of gongs'. I have never seen such a display at any of the funerals I have attended.
14. The rice is divided into portions that are individually wrapped in leaves. The leaves are folded so that the top of the packet remains open, with the halved egg clearly displayed. 'That way, the ghosts know it is meant for them', explained Jiji's sister Meji. Rice that is meant for human consumption is also always packaged in leaves, but they are folded closed, and thus clearly distinguishable from the food meant for the dead.
15. *Snaka* refers to poison, presumably of vegetable origin, which is made into a paste or liquid and then surreptitiously added to someone's food, tea, or even betel for chewing. A man named Clement told me about a cremation following which 'something hard' had remained among the ashes, which was identified as having been in the stomach of the deceased person. This hard part was left over from the poison that the death was then attributed to. Clement himself had not been present at the funeral, but had heard it said that *snaka* had been the cause of death. Rumours of such happenings spread quickly among people who were not there themselves. If someone dies due to (alleged) *snaka*, unnamed 'others' are held responsible.
16. Cattle are an important gift for the one who died. Slaughtering the gifted cattle enables the animals to follow the ghost to the afterworld, where they constitute a valuable asset. Some of the resulting meat is also prepared for the ghost. Most importantly, the spleen (*kasira*) is cooked in a fresh green bamboo, the split halves of which are placed on either side of the head of the one who died. The spleens of any additional cows slaughtered are boiled and smoked, and given to the ghost in the weeks that follow the mortuary ritual. Historically, an important man (such as a village head), would have been accompanied by

a dog after death. According to Biki, the dog used to be strangled (*ka'sota*), to then be cremated on a pyre next to the pyre of the deceased man. The dog sacrifice apparently used to be occasionally carried out until about fifty or sixty years ago. It came into being to substitute the former practice of human sacrifice. Biki, as well as other people who knew about the subject, had heard that historically, sacrificed men would have been captured from somewhere outside the village, but could theoretically have been just about any male adult. The practice is mentioned by Sinha: 'The post-mortem rituals of the Garos also indicate that the customs demanded killing human being... (who) would serve the spirit of the dead in the Mimang land [Balpakram, the afterworld]' (Sinha 1966: 99). The sacrifice of a man has also been substituted with that of a dog in relation to the 'sacrifice for the village land' (A'songtata, section 4.4), which accompanies the planting of the *a'song* stones, but also in relation to the precautions taken when cultivating 'strong earth' (*a'a raka*, sections 4.3 and 6.5; Chapter 4, note 14).

17. In the early 2000s, a small cow or bull cost about INR 2,000. A chicken could be bought for INR 50–100. Pigs fetched anywhere between INR 800 and 1,200. Prices have gone up since then, and nowadays, in 2020, an average bull can sell for INR 5,000, while large ones may cost up to INR 10,000.

18. The words of Sengseng Mangsang Sangma at Miknang's funeral, as recorded on video, 12 April 2000.

19. The words of Waling Raksam Marak at Nagal's funeral, as recorded on video, 5 August 2000.

20. Certain kinds of jewellery, such as waist belts, are only offered when a woman has died. This means that such jewellery always stays within the same matrilineal group. Heirloom weapons (swords, shields, spears) are only offered at the funerals of men, and these are thus always given to a House that belongs to a matrilineal group distinct from the one of the House in which the death has occurred. Such a House will usually also belong to another clan since marriages do not normally bring together spouses from the same clan. Gongs can be given at the funerals of either men or women, to Houses of the matrilineal group of the House in which the death has occurred, or to other matrilineal groups. The circulation of gongs is thus not restricted to a given matrilineal group or moiety.

21. This was the case at the end of the 19th century as well. Allen wrote: 'These khoras [gongs] are even now made in Goalpara and Mymensingh and are sold according to the weight of metal.... One well known Garo told me without shame ... that he had some few years ago got khoras made in Goalpara on the pattern of an old one he had, that these new ones cost him rupees 6 each, that he buried them in the ground for some months with salt, and then took them out converted in appearance into khoras many generations old, so old as to deceive the best judges,

and so valuable as to have bought him nearly rupees 100 each' (Allen, quoting the 'Report on the general administration of the district in 1886–87' (1980 [1906]: 43)).
22. Majumdar mentions that gongs used to also be hidden outside the house: 'heirlooms as rang [gongs] are buried in a carefully concealed place inside deep jungle as a measure of safety' (Majumdar 1978: 126).
23. Recorded on video, 11 October 2000.
24. Recorded on video, 4 August 2000.
25. Recorded on video, 11 October 2000.
26. Recorded on video, 12 April 2000.
27. Recorded on video, 4 August 2000.
28. Recorded on video, 12 April 2000.
29. Recorded on video, 6 August 2000, for the entire dialogue quoted.
30. Audio recording, 19 August 2000.
31. Audio recording, 19 August 2000.
32. Recorded on video, 5 August 2000, for the entire dialogue quoted.
33. Recorded on video, 11 October 2000.
34. Recorded on video, 12 October 2000.
35. Recorded on video, 11 October 2000.
36. Recorded on video, 27 May 2000.
37. Recorded on video, 6 August 2000.
38. Recorded on video, 5 August 2000.

Chapter 6

1. In Sadolpara, people use the term *nokkrom* for both the female and the male heir. Elsewhere in Garo Hills, the female heir can be referred to as the *nokna*, as mentioned by Burling (1997 [1963]: 76).
2. Audio recording, 19 August 2000.
3. Recorded on video, 26 August 2000.
4. Recorded on video, 11 October 2000.
5. Recorded on video, 12 October 2000, for the entire sequence quoted.
6. Recorded on video, 12 October 2000.
7. Recorded on video, 12 October 2000.
8. The marriage of a man to an additional wife is referred to as *du'si chapa* or *dok'chapa*. Since a replacement marriage implies the continuation of an existing marriage alliance, it only requires the interpretation of the large intestine of a single 'chicken of honour'. Even if replacement results in a man wedding two wives at once (a widow and an additional wife), the interpretation of just one 'chicken of honour' is enough, since both women share the same 'place' in the

marriage. As mentioned in section 3.4, this 'chicken of honour' refers to the prosperity and fertility of the House as a whole.
9. Audio recording, 19 August 2000.
10. Recorded on video, 27 May 2000.
11. Recorded on video, 27 May 2000, for the entire sequence quoted.
12. Recorded on video, 26 August 2000, for the entire sequence quoted.
13. Recorded on video, 26 August 2000, for the two lines quoted.
14. In the last two decades, wages have increased, and villagers can now earn INR 150–250 per day if they work for one another, while the men harvesting bamboo can make up to INR 500 per day).
15. In 2014, a mining ban was imposed across the state of Meghalaya, following a Supreme Court ruling that had been called for by an interest group called the National Green Tribunal. The case was won on the grounds of a national law that states that all subterranean resources belong to the Indian state. This overruled local interpretations of land rights, according to which resources located under the soil belong to the owners of the *a'king* land (Mcduie-Ra and Kikon 2016: 266). In the summer of 2019, the Supreme Court ruled that mining could be resumed (Sitlhou 2019), which may have consequences for mining in Sadolpara in future. Unlike in the eastern part of Garo Hills, where coal mining continued (illicitly) despite the ban, in Sadolpara it was ceased after the ruling.
16. The type of coal mining done in Meghalaya is rather derogatively referred to as 'rat hole' mining in the English press. The key feature of this technique is that no struts are placed. First, parallel tunnels are dug into the coal-bearing layer. These are then gradually widened and connected with each other, until large vaults have been carved out that are only supported by pillars. When the pillars themselves are mined, the ceiling collapses. A man who dug coal told me: 'If we hear the ceiling make a "krr krr" sound, we know that it's time to get out.' This mining technique is dangerous, but in Sadolpara and the surrounding area the tunnels were relatively shallow, which made it less hazardous than elsewhere in the state. In the 2000s, the daily wage for labourers mining coal in and around Sadolpara was INR 100–200 per day.
17. In its first year, a swidden is referred to as *a'ba*; in its second year as *a'breng*.
18. 'Strong earth' can be cultivated, but only if special measures are taken. I was told that in the recent past, when the Songsarek spirits were more widely acknowledged than they are nowadays, the cultivation of strong earth required sacrificing a dog to the particularly malevolent spirits known to reside on such land. The dog had to be either beaten to death or killed by hanging, before being burned in the fire that clears the new fields in preparation for the sowing of the new crops. However, if the spirit concerned 'gave' particularly abundant amounts of rice or millet, a dog might not suffice, and the spirit might 'take' the life of a human being as well. This implies that the growth of rice and millet in particular is dependent

on the willingness of certain resident forest spirits to give, and it indicates that sacrificing a dog can serve as a substitute for the life of a human being—which is also apparent in relation to the sacrificial rituals that were formerly conducted in relation to a *kusi* boulder, or to the sacrifice of a dog at the funeral of a powerful and influential person. Alternatively, the threat posed by the spirits resident on 'strong earth' may be counteracted by planting *dikki*. *Dikki* refers to a category of onion-like herbs that are attributed strong curative capacities. Many people associate *dikki* with a certain spirit, which is believed to be able to control the spirits residing on 'strong earth' (de Maaker 2013a).

19. Such a section within a larger claimed area is called an *a'tot*, and can also be cultivated by unmarried youth of about thirteen years of age and older. Neither unmarried men nor women may attend the meetings at which the locations of the new fields are decided, nor can they themselves claim a field. When unmarried men or women work an *a'tot*, they are allowed to retain the returns of cash crops such as ginger and cotton, but the rest of the yield goes to the household in which they live.

20. The taboo relates to the fear and awe that these animals inspire. Elephants like to feed on rice when the crops are standing in the field, and I was told several stories of people who had been killed when they had attempted to scare away an elephant in the past. To avoid attracting elephants, people do not refer to them directly (the word for elephant is *mongma*), but as 'the big one' (*dal'gipa*). At the beginning of the 20th century, there were reputedly thousands of elephants in Garo Hills, but nowadays sightings have become rare. Tigers are strongly associated with shapeshifting humans, but can also be associated with the spirit Chura (see Chapter 5, note 9), which already constitutes two good reasons for not hunting them. By the early 2000s, tigers were no longer seen in the forest, but people claimed that—as human beings in tiger form–they continued to roam around at night.

21. These frogs are only found for a few weeks a year, from around the end of May to early June. Villagers offer them for sale in the markets of towns like Tura, and many Garo consider them a delicacy.

22. In the dry months, the water level of rivers and streams is low, which makes fishing relatively easy. People fish with casting-nets, a range of fish traps made from bamboo, and fishing rods with hooks. In the 2000s, a vegetable poison (*makkal*) was also used, but with encouragement from the IFAD programme people decided to stop. The poison kills all the fish where it is applied, which significantly reduces the catch in the long run.

23. Expressing a perspective shared by other environmental scientists, P.S. Ramakrishnan has described shifting cultivation as 'a casually managed multispecies complex agro-ecosystem' that, when properly applied, can combine stability with resilience (Ramakrishnan 2007: 98). There can be little doubt that

shifting cultivation has been conducted in a sustainable manner in the hills of South and South East Asia for thousands of years, and that the populations of these uplands have a profound knowledge of the environments they live in. Shifting cultivation becomes unsustainable when loss of land, combined with increasing population pressure, leads to a significant reduction in the duration of fallow periods (Choudhury and Sundriyal 2003: 22). The best way to deal with this, according to a recent report published by Niti Aayog, a prestigious public policy think tank of the Indian government, is not to try to stop farmers from making swiddens, but to encourage innovation in the kinds of crops grown, as well as in exploring ways that the forest can be productive during the years that it is left to recuperate from cultivation (Pant, Tiwari, and Choudhury 2018: 8). This could include, for example, encouraging apiculture, or growing medicinal plants in the forest, as is currently being promoted by the Meghalaya Basin Development Authority (https://mbda.gov.in).
24. Since the 1970s, government agencies have acquired large areas of land in Garo Hills for a variety of purposes. Notable examples include the land obtained for the construction of Baljek airport in Jengal (247 acres of land acquired from the mid-1970s onwards) and for the Tura campus of the North-Eastern Hill University (600 acres land acquired since 1999). The land for these projects became available when the respective village heads agreed to sign NOCs, allowing the land to be converted to *patta*. Village heads agreed quite readily to issuing NOCs when they were offered considerable amounts of money. Often, they only gave a small part of the money received to the other members of the matrilineal group that shared in the right to the land (Fernandes et al. 2016: 45–47). Consequently, many such land deals have given rise to rifts within matrilineal groups, and it is rumoured that the militant groups that were active at the time also often managed to obtain substantial shares of the money transacted.
25. In Bengal, the bigha was standardized under British colonial rule at approximately 1/3 acre. Hence, in metric units a bigha is 1,333 m^2.
26. A group of closely related Houses, usually located in a single ward, is referred to as a *dol*. Among Songsareks, such Houses all relate to the *kram* drum of the most senior House of the *dol*.
27. This initiation of a house as a place where a *kram* drum can be kept involves a day-long celebration, Den'bilsia, which establishes or transforms the relationship of the 'head' of the House with Risi. Den'bilsia calls for the slaughter of a goat, four to five cattle, and five or six chickens. The House of the *kram* drum-tamers bears most of these costs, but its subsidiary Houses are expected to participate and to contribute animals, rice beer, and rice. The roof of the house in which the *kram* drum will be kept is (re-)thatched during Den'bilsia, and the ceremony needs to be performed whenever *kram* drum owners build a new house.

Chapter 7

1. The Indian National Congress has lost significant ground at the national level in recent decades. Compared to other parts of India, the party remains relatively strong in the state of Meghalaya. In the 2018 elections, it won nineteen of the sixty seats of the Meghalaya assembly, making it the second largest party of the state.
2. The Nationalist Congress Party was founded by Garo politician Purno Sangma together with Marathi politicians Sharad Pawar and Tariq Anwar, after the three of them were expelled from the Indian National Congress (INC) for challenging Sonia Gandhi's eligibility to become the INC's leader. Sonia Gandhi, the widow of assassinated INC president and former Prime Minister Rajiv Gandhi, was born in Italy, which Sangma, Pawar, and Anwar believed made her unfit to become prime minister, if elected (UNI 1999).
3. From the age of about 5 or 6, children in villages like Sadolpara are expected to help with certain household chores, such as washing dishes and carrying them back and forth between the house and the water source. It is also very common to let young children take care of babies and toddlers, often their younger siblings, so that their parents can work. Looking after a younger child is referred to as 'carrying' it, and for much of the time the smaller child is indeed carried in a sling by the older one looking after it. If this is done for a child from another household, it may be arranged as a rather formalized relationship involving payment either in cash or in kind (such as a small cow).
4. Purno Sangma engendered a political dynasty: at the age of 29, his daughter Agatha Sangma became the youngest ever minister to serve in the Indian central government (she was Minister for Rural Development from 2009 to 2012), while in 2018, his son Conrad became the Chief Minister of the State of Meghalaya for the National People's Party (NPP). Purno Sangma had been among the three politicians that founded the NPP in 2012, as mentioned in Chapter 7, note 2. Conrad Sangma's younger brother James Sangma currently serves as a minister in the Government of the State of Meghalaya.

Chapter 8

1. I have written about how followers of the traditional Garo community religion 'play' what is perceived as 'real' traditional Garo culture for the camera in 'Critiquing Stereotypes? Documentary as Dialogue with the Garo' (de Maaker 2020). I argue that Songsareks are well aware what kinds of cultural performances documentary filmmakers are likely to expect from them, but that people make clear distinctions between such performances and the interpretation and enactment of *niam* in their daily lives.

References

A'chik National Volunteers Council. 2006. *Memorandum on the demand for the creation of separate Garoland to Dr. Manmohan Singh, the Hon'ble Prime Minister of India.* Cheram: A'chick National Volunteers Council.

Agarwal, Bina. 1994. *A Field of One's Own: Gender and Land Rights in South Asia.* Cambridge: Cambridge University Press.

Allen, Basil C. 1980 [1906]. *Gazetteer of the Khasi and Jaintia Hills, Garo Hills, Lushai Hills* [Photographic Reprint]. Delhi: Mittal Publishers (originally published Allahabad: Pioneer Press).

Allen, Basil C., Edward A. Gait, George H. Allen, and Henry F. Howard. 1993 [1909]. *Gazetter of Bengal and North East India.* New Delhi: Mittal Publications.

Anderson, Benedict. 1983. *Imagined Communities: Reflections on the Origin and Spread of Nationalism.* London: Verso.

Appadurai, Arjun. 1996. *Modernity at Large: Cultural Dimensions of Globalization.* Minneapolis: University of Minnesota Press.

Arbuthnott Report. 1908. *Communicates orders on the proposals made for dealing with the alleged grievances of the Garos in the Goalpara and Garo hills districts.* Edited by Department of Revenue and Agriculture (Land Revenue). Calcutta: Department of Revenue and Agriculture.

Astuti, Rita, and Maurice E.F. Bloch. 2013. 'Are ancestors dead?' In *A Companion to the Anthropology of Religion*, edited by Janice Boddy and Michael Lambek, 103–117. Chichester: Wiley.

Bal, Ellen W., and Willem van Schendel. 2002. 'Beyond the tribal mind set: Studying non-Bengali peoples in West Bengal and Bangladesh'. In *The Concept of Tribal Society*, edited by Georg Pfeffer and Deepak Kumar Behera, 121–139. New Delhi: Concept Publishing Company.

Baldwin, C. D. 1933. *Garo Law.* Mymensingh: Printed at the Lily Press.

Barik, S.K., and Vincent T. Darlong. 2008. *Natural Resource Management Policy Environment in Meghalaya Impacting Livelihood of Forest Poor.* Bogor: Center for International Forestry Research.

Barkataki-Ruscheweyh, Meenaxi. 2018. *Dancing to the State: Ethnic Compulsions of the Tangsa in Assam.* First edition. New Delhi: Oxford University Press.

Barman, Santo. 1994. *Zamindari System in Assam during British Rule (A Case Study of Goalpara District).* Guwahati: Spectrum Publications.

Barooah, Nirode K. 1970. *David Scott in North-East India, 1802–1831: A Study in British Paternalism.* New Delhi: Munshiram Manoharlal.

Barth, Frederik. 1969. *Ethnic Groups and Boundaries: The Social Organization of Culture Difference.* Long Grove, MD: Waveland Press.

Baruah, Sanjib. 2005a. 'The Problem'. Introduction to a themed issue: Gateway to the East, a symposium on Northeast India and the Look East policy. *Seminar*

(550), Available from : https://india-seminar.com/2005/550/550%20problem.htm. Accessed 18 June 2021.

———. 2005b. *Durable Disorder: Understanding the Politics of Northeast India.* New Delhi: Oxford University Press.

———. 2009. 'Introduction'. In *Beyond Counter-insurgency: Breaking the Impasse in Northeast India*, edited by Sanjib Baruah, 1–21. New Delhi: Oxford University Press.

Bates, Crispin. 1995. *Race, Caste and Tribe in Central India: The Early Origins of Indian Anthropometry*: Edinburgh: Centre for South Asian Studies, University of Edinburgh.

Baud, Michiel, and Willem van Schendel. 1997. 'Towards a comparative history of borderlands'. *Journal of World History* no. 8 (2):211–242.

Bayly, Susan. 1999. *Caste Society and Politics in India: From the Eighteenth Century to the Modern Age.* Cambridge: Cambridge University Press.

Bedi, Nandini. 2007a. 'Ambi Jiji's retirement'. Documentary film, 29 minutes. Producer and Commissioning Editor: Rajiv Mehrotra. Produced for *The Open Frame*. New Delhi: PSBT (The Public Service Broadcasting Trust). Available from: https://youtu.be/lZj4AgdK4Xc. Accessed 18 June 2021.

———. 2007b. *Notes on Man Capture.* Documentary film, 43 minutes. Producer: Nandini Bedi. New Delhi: Magic Lantern Movies. Available from: https://youtu.be/q9q7QsOd6tw. Accessed 18 June 2021.

———. 2009. 'The "other" notes on man capture'. *LOVA journal (Tijdschrift voor Feministische Antropologie)* no. 30 (1): 56–65.

Bertrand, Gabrielle. 1958. *Secret Lands Where Women Reign.* London: Robert Hale.

Béteille, André. 1998. 'The idea of indigenous people'. *Current Anthropology* no. 39 (2): 187–192.

Bhat, K.H. 1988. 'Social change in Rengsanggri 1956–1986'. In *Proceedings of the North East India History Association (8th session)*, edited by Jayanta B. Bhattacharjee, 366–372. Shillong: North East India History Association.

Bhattacharjee, Jayanta B. 1973. 'Pattern of British administration in Garoland'. *Journal of Indian History* LI/ Part III (Dec' 73) no. (153):509–520.

———. 1978. *The Garos and the English.* New Delhi: Radiant Publishers.

Bhaumik, Subir. 2009. *Troubled Periphery: Crisis of India's North East.* Sage Studies on India's North East. Los Angeles: Sage.

Bindloss, Joseph. 2009. *Northeast India.* London: Lonely Planet.

Bird-David, Nurit. 1999. '"Animism" revisited: Personhood, environment, and relational epistemology'. *Current Anthropology* no. 40 (Feb 1999):S67–S91.

Björkman, Lisa. 2014. '"You can't buy a vote": Meanings of money in a Mumbai election'. *American Ethnologist* no. 41 (4):617–634. doi: 10.1111/amet.12101.

———. 2015. ' "Vote banking" as politics in Mumbai'. In *Patronage as Politics in South Asia*, edited by Anastasia Piliavsky, 176–195. Cambridge: Cambridge University Press.

Bloch, Maurice, and Jonathan Parry. 1982. *Death and the Regeneration of Life.* Cambridge: Cambridge University Press.

Borah, D., and N.R Goswami. 1977. 'A comparative study of crop production under shifting and terrace cultivation: A case study in Garo Hills, Meghalaya'. *Assam*

REFERENCES 279

Agricultural University Journal (Agroeconomic Research Centre for North East India) 12–40.

Bose, Jyotsna K. 1985. *Culture Change among the Garos*. Calcutta: Institute of Social Research and Applied Anthropology.

Bourdieu, Pierre 1977. *Outline of a Theory of Practice*, trans. Richard Nice. Cambridge: Cambridge University Press.

Brubaker, Rogers. 2012. 'Categories of analysis and categories of practice: A note on the study of Muslims in European countries of immigration'. *Ethnic and Racial Studies* no. 36 (1):1–8. doi: 10.1080/01419870.2012.729674.

Buckser, Andrew, and Stephen D. Glazier. 2003. *The Anthropology of Religious Conversion*. Lanham: Rowman & Littlefield.

Burling, Robbins. 1988. 'Garo beliefs in the afterlife'. In *On the Meaning of Death: Essays on Mortuary Rituals and Eschatological Beliefs*, edited by Sven Cederroth, Claes Corlin and Jan Lindström, 31–38. Uppsala: Acta Universitatis Upsaliensis.

———. 1997 [1963]. *Rengsanggri: Family and Kinship in a Garo Village*. Philadelphia, PA: University of Pennsylvania Press (Reprint, with an additional chapter written in 1997). Tura: Tura Book Room.

———. 2003. 'The Tibeto-Burman languages of Northeastern India'. In *The Sino-Tibetan Languages*, edited by Graham Thurgood and Randy J. LaPolla, 169–191. London: Curzon Press.

Burling, Robbins, Anne Hvenekilde, and Caroline R. Marak. 2000. 'Personal names in a mande (Garo) village'. *Names* no. 48 (2):83–104.

Carey, William. 1919. *A Garo Jungle Book; or, the Mission to the Garos of Assam*. Philadelphia, PA: Judson Press.

Carsten, Janet, and Stephen Hugh-Jones. 1995. *About the House: Lévi-Strauss and beyond*. Cambridge: Cambridge University Press.

Chattopadhyay, S.K., and Milton S. Sangma. 1989. *The Garo Customary Laws*. Shillong: Directorate of Arts and Culture.

Chaube, Shibani K. 1973. *Hill Politics in Northeast India*. Calcutta: Orient Longman.

Choudhury, Dhrupad, and R.C. Sundriyal. 2003. 'Factors contributing to the marginalization of shifting cultivation in North-East India: Micro-scale issues'. *Outlook on Agriculture* no. 32 (1):17–28.

Choudhury, Ratnadip. 2011. 'For Northeast peace, ULFA and NDFB must quit Garo Hills'. *Tehelka* no. 8 (31 (August 20)).

Claquin Chambugong, Timour. 2013. *The Songsarek Garo of Meghalaya*. Genève: Fondation Culturelle Musée Barbier-Mueller.

Clifford, James, and George E. Marcus. 1986. *Writing Culture: The Poetics and Politics of Ethnography*. Berkeley, CA: University of California Press.

Comaroff, John L., and Jean Comaroff. 2018. *The Politics of Custom: Chiefship, Capital, and the State in Contemporary Africa*. Chicago, IL: The University of Chicago Press.

Costa, Giulio. 1954. 'The Garo code of law'. *Anthropos* no. 49 (28):1041–1066.

Das, Debojyoti. 2018. *The Politics of Swidden Farming: Environment and Development in Eastern India*. London: Anthem Press.

Das, Jitendra N. 1990. *A Study of the Land systems of Meghalaya*. Guwahati: Law Research Institute Eastern Region, Guwahati High Court.

de Maaker, Erik. 2000. 'Integrating ethnographic research and filmmaking: Video elicitation for a performance-oriented analysis of the Teyyam ritual'. *Visual Anthropology* no. 13:185–197.

———. 2006a. 'Negotiating Life: Garo Death Rituals and the Transformation of Society', Ph.D. Thesis, Leiden University.

———. 2006b. 'Recording, constructing and reviewing Teyyam, the annual visit of the god Vishnumurti'. In *Reflecting Visual Ethnography: Using the Camera in Anthropological Research*, edited by Metje Postma and Peter Ian Crawford, 103–118. Leiden: CNWS Publications.

———. 2009. 'Narratives of Garo witchcraft'. In *Traditions on the Move: Essays in Honour of Jarich Oosten*, edited by Jan Jansen, Sabine Luning, and Erik de Maaker, 147–156. Amsterdam: Rozenberg Publishers.

———. 2012. 'Negotiations at death: Assessing gifts, mothers, and marriages'. In *Negotiating Rites*, edited by Ute Hüsken and Frank Neubert, 43–57. New York: Oxford University Press.

———. 2013a. 'Have the Mitdes gone silent? Conversion, rhetoric, and the continuing importance of the lower deities in Northeast India'. In *Asia in the Making of Christianity: Conversion, Agency, and Indigeneity, 1600s to the Present*, edited by Richard F. Young and Jonathan A. Seitz, 135–162. Leiden: Brill.

———. 2013b. 'Performing the Garo nation?: Garo Wangala dancing between faith and folklore'. *Asian Ethnology* no. 72 (2):221–239.

———. 2014. 'Researching Garo death rites'. In *Fieldwork in South Asia: Memories, Moments and Experiences*, edited by Sarit K. Chaudhuri and Sucheta Sen Chaudhuri, 167–185. New Delhi: Sage.

———. 2015. 'Ambiguous mortal remains, substitute bodies, and other materializations of the dead among the Garo of Northeast India'. In *Ultimate Ambiguities: Investigating Death and Liminality*, edited by Peter Berger and Justin Kroesen, 15–35. New York: Berghahn.

———. 2018. 'On the nature of indigenous land: Ownership, access and farming in upland Northeast India'. In *Indigeneity on the Move: Varying Manifestations of a Contested Concept*, edited by Eva Gerharz, Nasir Uddin and Pradeep Chakkarath, 29–48. New York: Berghahn.

———. 2019. *Nokdangko Man·rikani: Gamrangko Sualani, Ma·gipa Ong·rikani aro Bia Ka·anirang*, transl. Norinchi G. Momin. (originally published as 'Negotiations at death: Assessing gifts, mothers, and marriages' in Hüsken and Neubert, *Negotiating Rites*, OUP, 2012). Tura: Tura Book Room.

———. 2020. 'Critiquing stereotypes? Documentary as dialogue with the Garo'. In *Media, Indigeneity and Nation In South Asia*, edited by Markus Schleiter and Erik de Maaker, 196–212. Abingdon, Oxon: Routledge.

———. 2021a. 'Who owns the hills? Ownership, inequality and communal sharing in the borderlands of India'. Contribution to a special issue on 'Agrarian Change in Zomia', guest-edited by Erik de Maaker and Deborah E. Tooker. *Asian Ethnology* no. 79 (2):357–375.

———. 2021b. 'Aloof but not abandoned: Relationality and the exploitation of the environment in the Garo Hills of India'. In *Environmental Humanities in the New*

Himalayas: Symbiotic Indigeneity, Commoning, Sustainability, edited by Dan Smyer Yü and Erik de Maaker, 135–151. Abingdon, Oxon: Routledge.

Directorate of Census Operations, Meghalaya. 2014. *District Census Handbook West Garo Hills, Village and Town Directory* Census of India 2011, Meghalaya (Series 18, Part XII-A). Shillong: Ministry of Home Affairs, Government of India.

Directorate of Information and Public Relations. 2002. *The Pristine Culture and Society of The Garos of Meghalaya*. Shillong: Directorate of Information and Public Relations, Govt. of Meghalaya.

Dirks, Nicholas B. 2001. *Castes of Mind: Colonialism and the Making of Modern India*. Princeton, NJ: Princeton University Press.

Downs, Frederick S. 1983. *Christianity in North East India: Historical Perspectives*. Delhi: ISPCK in association with CLC, Gauhati.

Dumont, Louis. 1981. *Homo hierarchicus: The Caste System and Its Implications*, trans. Mark Sainsbury, Louis Dumont and Basia Gulati. Chicago, IL: Chicago University Press.

Duncan, Christopher R. 2003. 'Untangling conversion: Religious change and identity among the forest tobelo of Indonesia'. *Ethnology* no. 42 (4):307–322.

Eliot, John. 1799. 'Observations on the inhabitants of the Garrow hills: Made during a public deputation in the years 1788 and 1789'. *Asiatic Researches or Transactions of the Society Instituted in Bengal for Inquiry into the History and Antiquities, the Arts, Sciences and Literature of Asia*. no. III:17–37.

Elwin, Verrier. 1943. *The Aboriginals*. Bombay: Oxford University Press.

Eriksen, Thomas Hylland. 2001. 'Ethnic identity, national identity and intergroup conflict'. In *Social Identity, Intergroup Conflict and Conflict Reduction*, edited by Richard D. Ashmore, Lee J. Jussim and David Wilder, 42–70. Oxford: Oxford University Press.

Ferguson, James. 1999. *Expectations of Modernity: Myths and Meanings of Urban Life on The Zambian Copperbelt*. Berkeley, CA: University of California Press.

Fernandes, Walter, Veronica Pala, Gita Bharali, and Bitopi Dutta. 2016. *The Development Dilemma: Displacement in Meghalaya 1947–2010*. Guwahati: North-Eastern Social Research Centre.

Foster, Robert J. 1995. *Social Reproduction and History in Melanesia: Mortuary Ritual, Gift Exchange and Custom in the Tanga Islands*. Cambridge: Cambridge University Press.

Frazer, James George. 1890. *The Golden Bough: A Study in Comparative Religion*. London: Macmillan.

Fuller, Chris J. 1988. 'The Hindu pantheon and the legitimation of hierarchy'. *Man* no. 23 (1):19–39. doi: 10.2307/2803031.

Gait, Edward A. 1963. *A History of Assam*. Revised and enlarged by Birinchi K. Barua and H.V. Sreenivasa Murthy (third revised edition). Calcutta: Thacker Spink & Co.

Galanter, Marc. 1984. *Competing Equalities: Law and the Backward Classes in India*: Berkeley: University of California Press.

Garo Hills Autonomous District Council. 2007. *Acts, Rules and Regulations with Amendments* (Second Edition). Tura: The Garo Hills Autonomous District Council.

REFERENCES

Gassah, L.S. 2002. 'Traditional self-governing institutions among the hill population groups of Meghalaya'. In *Traditional Self-Governing Institutions among the Hill Tribes of North-East India*, edited by Atul Goswami, 180–193. New Delhi: Akansha Publishing House.

Geertz, Clifford. 1973. *The Interpretation of Cultures: Selected Essays*. New York: Basic Books.

Gerbrands, Adrian A. 1971. 'Etno-cinematografisch onderzoek bij de kilèngé, west nieuw-britannië'. *Registratie* no. 3:27–33.

Gerbrands, Adrianus Alexander. 1967. *Wow-Ipits: Eight Asmat Woodcarvers of New Guinea*, transl. by Inez Wolf Seeger. The Hague Mouton.

Ghurye, Govind S. 1963 [1943]. *The Scheduled Tribes (The Aborigines So-Called and Their Future)*. Bombay: Bhatkal.

Girard, Rene. 1977. *Violence and the Sacred*. Baltimore, MD: Johns Hopkins University Press.

Godelier, M. 2018. *Claude Lévi-Strauss: A Critical Study of His Thought*, transl. by Nora Scott. London: Verso Books.

Goswami, Madhab C., and Dhirendra N. Majumdar. 1972. *Social Institutions of the Garo of Meghalaya: An Analytical Study*. Calcutta: Nababharat Publishers.

Guenauer, Cornelia. 2016. 'Tribal politics, suits and rock music: Electioneering in Meghalaya'. *South Asia: Journal of South Asian Studies* no. 39 (2):430–443. doi: 10.1080/00856401.2016.1164799.

Gupta, Akhil. 2012. *Red Tape: Bureaucracy, Structural Violence, and Poverty in India*. Durham, NC: Duke University Press.

Gupta, Akhil, and James Ferguson. 1997. *Culture, Power, Place: Explorations in Critical Anthropology*. Durham, NC: Duke University Press.

Gupta, Dhritiman. 2012. 'Centre provides 55% of Rs 65,502 crore North-East states' spend'. The Spending & Policy Research Foundation 2012. 21 January. Available from http://www.indiaspend.com/investigations/centre-provides-55-of-rs-65502-crore-north-east-states-spend.Accessed 18 June 2021.

Hamilton, Francis (formerly Buchanan) 1940 [cf. 1807–1814]. *An Account of Assam with Some Notices Concerning the Neighbouring Territories (also published as: Martin, Robert Montgomery (1990 [1838]), Historical Documents of Eastern India*. Edited by S.K. Bhuyan. Gauhati: Government of Assam in the Department of Historical and Antiquarian Studies, Narayani Handiqui Historical Institute.

Haokip, Thongkholal. 2014. 'Inter-ethnic relations in Meghalaya'. *Asian Ethnicity* no. 15 (3):1–15. doi: 10.1080/14631369.2013.853545.

Harvey, Graham. 2005. *Animism: Respecting the Living World*. London: Hurst & Co.

———. 2019. 'Animism and ecology: Participating in the world community'. *The Ecological Citizen* no. 3:79–84.

Hertz, Robert. 1960 [1907]. *Death and the Right Hand*, transl. Rodney and Claudia Needham. London: Cohen & West.

Hobsbawm, Eric, and Terence Ranger, eds. 1983. *The Invention of Tradition*. Cambridge: Cambridge University Press.

Hindustan Times. 2017. 'BJP leaders who quit last week over cattle trade ban to hold beef fest in Meghalaya'. 10 June.

REFERENCES 283

Huntington, Richard, and Peter Metcalf. 1991. *Celebrations of Death: The Anthropology of Mortuary Ritual*. Cambridge: Cambridge University Press.

Institute for Conflict Management. *Insurgency-related Incidents in Garo Hills Region: 2001–2016*. South Asia Terrorism Portal (SATP) 2019. Url: http://www.satp.org/satporgtp/countries/india/database/Insurgency-related_Incidents_in_Garo_Hills_region_of_Meghalaya.htm Accessed 18 June 2021.

Jeffrey, Craig. 2010. *Timepass: Youth, Class, and the Politics of Waiting In India*. Stanford, CA: Stanford University Press.

Joshi, Vibha. 2012. *A Matter of Belief: Christian Conversion and Healing in North-East India*. New York: Berghahn Books.

Joyce, Rosemary A., and Susan D. Gillespie. 2000. *Beyond Kinship: Social and Material Reproduction in House Societies*. Philadelphia: University of Pennsylvania Press.

Kar, Bodhisattva. 2009. 'When was the postcolonial?' In *Beyond Counter-Insurgency: Breaking the Impasse in Northeast India*, edited by Sanjib Baruah, 49–77. New Delhi: Oxford University Press.

Kar, Parimal C. 1970. *British Annexation of Garo Hills*. Calcutta: Nababharat Publishers.

———. 1982. *Glimpses of the Garos*. Tura: Garo Hills Book Emporium.

Karlsson, Bengt G. 2003. 'Anthropology and the "indigenous slot"—claims to and debates about indigenous peoples' status in India'. *Critique of Anthropology* no. 23 (4):403–423.

———. 2011. *Unruly Hills: A Political Ecology of India's Northeast*. New York: Berghahn Books.

Kashena, Asojiini R. 2017. *Enduring Loss: Stories from the Kuki-Naga Conflict in Manipur*. Guwahati: North Eastern Social Research Centre.

Keane, Webb. 2007. *Christian Moderns: Freedom and Fetish in the Mission Encounter*. Berkeley: University of California Press.

Kikon, Dolly. 2005. 'Operation hornbill festival 2004'. Themed issue: Gateway to the East: a symposium on Northeast India and the Look East Policy. *Seminar* (550), web edition, url: https://www.india-seminar.com/2005/550/550%20dolly%20kikon.htm. Accessed 19 June 2021.

Kumar, Ashish, Bruce G. Marcot, and Rohitkumar Patel. 2017. *Tropical Forests and Fragmentation: A Case of South Garo Hills, Meghalaya, North East India*. Saarbrücken: Lap Lambert Academic Publishing.

Kumar, B. B. 1996. *Re-organization of North-East India: Facts and Documents*. New Delhi: Omsons Publications.

Kurien, Amit J., Sharachchandra Lele, and Harini Nagendra. 2019. 'Farms or forests? Understanding and mapping shifting cultivation using the case study of West Garo Hills, India'. *Land* 8 (9):26.

Kusum, K., and Parvinrai M. Bakshi. 1982. *Customary Law and Justice in the Tribal Areas of Meghalaya*. Bombay: N.M. Tripathi.

Laidlaw, James. 2013. 'Ethics'. In *A Companion to the Anthropology of Religion*, edited by Janice Boddy and Michael Lambek, 171–188. Chichester: Wiley.

Laine, Nicolas. 2012. 'Effects of the 1996 timber ban in Northeast India: The case of the Khamtis of Lohit District, Arunachal Pradesh'. In *Nature, Environment and Society: Conservation, Governance and Transformation in India*, edited by Nicholas Laine and Tanka B. Subba, 73–89. New Delhi: Orient Blackswan.

Lambek, Michael. 2016. 'What is "religion" for anthropology? And what has anthropology brought to "religion"?' In *A Companion to the Anthropology of Religion*, edited by Janice Boddy and Michael Lambek, 1–24. Chichester: Wiley.

Lévi-Strauss, Claude. 1983. *The Way of the Masks*. London: Cape.

———. 1991. 'Maison'. In *Dictionaire de l'ethnologie et de l'anthropologie*, edited by Pierre Bonte and Michael Izard, 434–436. Paris: Presses Universitaires de France.

Li, Victor. 2006. *The Neo-Primitivist Turn: Critical Reflections on Alterity, Culture and Modernity*. Toronto: University of Toronto Press.

Loiwal, Manogya. 2018. 'Meghalaya's most wanted Garo National Liberation Army chief shot dead'. *India Today*. 24 February. Available here: https://www.indiatoday.in/india/story/meghalaya-s-most-wanted-garo-national-libration-army-chief-shot-dead-1176737-2018-02-24.Accessed 19 June 2021.

Longkumer, Arkotong. 2010. *Reform, Identity and Narratives of Belonging: The Heraka Movement of Northeast India*. London: Continuum.

———. 2016. 'Rice-beer, purification and debates over religion and culture in Northeast India'. *South Asia: Journal of South Asian Studies* no. 39 (2): 444–461. doi: 10.1080/00856401.2016.1154645.

M'cosh, John 1975 [1837]. *Topography of Assam*. Calcutta: Bengal Military Orphan Press. Reprint, Delhi: Sanskaran Prakashak.

Mackenzie, Alexander 1995 [1884]. *The North-East Frontier of India* (originally published as: *History of the Relations of the Government with the Hill Tribes of the North-East Frontier of Bengal*). Calcutta: Home Department Press. Reprint, New Delhi: Mittal Publications.

Majumdar, Dhirendra N. 1966. *The Garos: An Account of the Garos of the Present Day*. Gauhati: Lawyers Book Stall.

———. 1976. 'Shifting cultivation, is it a way of life? An analysis of Garo data'. In *Shifting Cultivation in North East India*, edited by Barrister Pakem, Jayanta B. Bhattacharjee, B.B. Dutta, and Basudeb Datta Ray, 14–18. Shillong: North East Indian Council for Social Science Research.

———. 1977. 'Problems of identity in a multi-ethnic setting: A case study in western Meghalaya'. *Bulletin of the Department of Anthropology, Dibrugarh University* no. VI (Cultural and Biological Adaptability of Man with Special Reference to North East India), 38–46.

———. 1978. *A Study of Culture Change in Two Garo Villages*. Calcutta: Anthropological Survey of India.

———. 1980. 'Some aspects of urbanization in Garo Hills'. In *Family, Marriage and Social Change on the Indian Fringe*, edited by Satya M. Dubey, P.K. Bordoloi, and Birendra N. Borthakur, 162–171. New Delhi: Cosmo Publications.

———. 1984. 'A decaying institution—what has happened to the Nokpante? A study among the Garos'. In *The Tribes of North East India*, edited by Sebastian Karotemprell, 307–318. Shillong: Vendrame Missiological Institute.

———. 1985. 'The story about the origin of the Koches and their migration to Garo Hills'. In *Folklore in North-East India*, edited by Soumen Sen, 183–190. New Delhi: Omsons Publications.

―――. 1986a. 'The Garos in the plain areas: A study on the change of the concept of ownership'. In *Land Reforms and Peasant Movement*, edited by Atul Goswami, 124–129. New Delhi: Omsons Publications.

―――. 1986b. 'Problems of land alienation and indebtedness among the Hinduized communities of western Meghalaya'. In *Alienation of Tribal Land and Indebtedness*, edited by B. N. Bordoloi, 58–66. Guwahati: Tribal Research Institute, Assam.

Malik, Bela. 2003. 'The "problem" of shifting cultivation in the Garo Hills of North-East India, 1860–1970'. *Conservation and Society* no. 1 (2 (July-December 2003)):287–315.

Marak, Caroline. 1997. 'Status of women in Garo culture'. In *Women in Meghalaya*, edited by Soumen Sen, 56–72. Delhi: Omsons.

―――. 2005. 'Militancy in Garo Hills: A preliminary note'. *North East India Studies* no. 1 (1):97–104.

Marak, H.A. 1993. *Hundred Drums Wangala Brochure*. Tura: 100 Drums Wangala Organising Committee.

Marak, Julius. 2000. 'Garo Customary Laws and Practices: A Sociological Study'. Originally presented as the author's thesis (Ph.D.), University of Gauhati, 1982. Delhi: Akansha Publishing House.

Marak, Karnesh R. 1964. *The Garos and Their Customary Laws and Usages*. Tura: Brucellis Sangma.

Marak, Krickwin C. 1999. 'Reflection on the missiological approaches to the tribals of North East India'. In *Missiological Approaches in India: Retrospect and Prospect*, edited by Jospeh Mattan and Krickwin C. Marak, 173–199. Mumbai: The Bombay Saint Paul Society.

―――. 1998. 'Christianity among the Garos: An attempt to re-read people's movement from a missiological perspective'. In *Christianity in India: Search for Liberation and Identity*, edited by F. Hrangkhuma, 155–186. Pune: Centre for Mission Studies.

Marak, Kumie R. 1997. *Traditions and Modernity in Matrilineal Tribal Society, Tribal Studies of India Series 178*. New Delhi: Inter-India Publications.

Marak, Paulinus R. 2005. *The Garo Tribal Religion: Beliefs and Practices*. New Delhi: Anshah Publishing House.

Marak, Queenbala. 2012. 'Revisiting Playfair's The Garos: A century later'. *Man In India* no. 91 (3-4):517–529.

―――. 2014. *Food Politics: Studying Food, Identity and Difference among the Garos*. Newcastle upon Tyne: Cambridge Scholars Publishing.

―――. 2018. 'Rice from a·ba: Stories, rituals and practices of the Garos'. *South Asian Anthropologist* no. 18 (2):161–175.

Marshall-Fratani, Ruth. 1998. 'Mediating the global and local in Nigerian Pentecostalism'. *Journal of Religion in Africa* no. 28 (3):278–315.

Martin, Robert Montgomery. 1990 [1838]. *Historical Documents of Eastern India*. Vol. VIII, Assam. Delhi: Caxton Publications.

McDuie-Ra, D.A. 2019. 'Embracing or challenging the "tribe"'. In *Landscape, Culture, and Belonging: Writing the History of Northeast India*, edited by Neeladri Bhattacharya and Joy Pachuau, 66–85. Cambridge: Cambridge University Press.

McDuie-Ra, Duncan, and Dolly Kikon. 2016. 'Tribal communities and coal in Northeast India: The politics of imposing and resisting mining bans'. *Energy Policy* no. 99:261–269. doi: http://dx.doi.org/10.1016/j.enpol.2016.05.021.

Meghalaya Times. 2012. 'Coal mining placing Sadolpara on its last stand'. 6 October 2012, Front page. Accessed 1 December 2017.

Middleton, C. Townsend. 2011. 'Across the interface of state ethnography: Rethinking ethnology and its subjects in multicultural India'. *American Ethnologist* no. 38 (2):249–266. doi: 10.1111/j.1548-1425.2011.01304.x.

Middleton, Townsend. 2013. 'Scheduling tribes: A view from inside India's ethnographic state'. *Focaal, Journal of Global and Historical Anthropology* no. (65):13–22.

Mills, Moffat. 1853 [1984]. *Report on the Province of Assam*. Guwahati: Publication Board of Assam.

Ministry of Tribal Affairs. 2007. *The National Tribal Policy: A Policy for the Scheduled Tribes of India* (draft version). New Delhi: Ministry of Tribal Affairs.

Misra, Sanghamitra. 2011. *Becoming a Borderland: The Politics of Space and Identity in Colonial Northeastern India*. New Delhi: Taylor & Francis.

Morton, Micah F., Jianhua Wang, and Haiying Li. 2016. 'Decolonizing methods: Akha articulations of indigeneity in the Upper Mekong region'. *Asian Ethnicity* no. 17 (4):580–595. doi: 10.1080/14631369.2016.1150775.

Nijland, D.J. 1994. "Film en non-verbale cultuuruitingen bij de tobelo." In *Halmahera and beyond: Social Science Research in the Moluccas*, edited by Leontine E. Visser, 139–163. Leiden: KITLV Press.

Nongbri, Tiplut. 2001. 'Timber ban in North-East India'. *Economic and Political Weekly* no. 36 (21):1893–1900.

———. 2014. *Development, Masculinity and Christianity: Essays and Verses from India's North East*. Shimla: Indian Institute of Advanced Study.

Office of the Registrar General and Census Commissioner. 2010. *C-1 Appendix—2001 Details of Religious Community Shown Under 'Other Religions And Persuasions' In Main Table C-1*. New Delhi: Government of India, Ministry of Home Affairs. Available from: http://censusindia.gov.in/Census_Data_2001/India_at_glance/religion.aspx. Accessed 17 September 2010.

———. 2020. *Census of India 2011*. Government of India, Ministry of Home Affairs. Available from: http://censusindia.gov.in/2011census/population_enumeration.html.Accessed 15 February 2020.

Office of the Sub-Divisional Officer (C). 2010. Proposal for developing Sadolpara—ethnic Garo village as a tourist attraction (project proposal). Dadenggre: Government of Meghalaya, Office of the Sub Divisional Officer (C), Dadenggre Sub-Division, West Garo Hills.

Oppitz, Michael. 2008. 'Preface'. In *Naga Identities: Changing Local Cultures in the Northeast of India*, edited by Michael Oppitz, Thomas Kaiser, Alban von Stockhausen, and Marion Wettstein, 9. Gent: Snoeck Publishers.

Otto, Ton, and Poul Pedersen. 2005. *Tradition and Agency: Tracing Cultural Continuity and Invention*. Aarhus: Aarhus University Press.

Pachuau, Joy L.K. 2014. *Being Mizo: Identity and Belonging in Northeast India*. Delhi: Oxford University Press.

Pant, R.M., B.K. Tiwari, and Dhrupad Choudhury. 2018. Shifting cultivation: Towards a transformational approach. In *Report of Working Group III*. New Delhi: NITI Aayog.

Prakruti, P.K. 2014 'How militant leader's FB addiction brought Meghalaya police to his hideout in the city'. *Bangalore Mirror*, 18 June 2014. Available from: https://bangaloremirror.indiatimes.com/bangalore/cover-story/fb-postings-nimhans-garo-national-liberation-army-smartphones-mnrega-sim-cards-atm-cards-rapiush-sangmamla/articleshow/36724394.cms. Accessed 19 June 2021.

Pels, Peter 2000. 'The rise and fall of the Indian aborigines: Orientalism, eolithic, and the emergence of an ethnology of India, 1833-1869'. In *Colonial Subjects: Essays on the Practical History of Anthropology*, edited by Peter Pels and Oscar Salemink, 82-116. Ann Arbor: The University of Michigan Press.

Pianazzi, A. 1934. *In Garoland*. Calcutta: Catholic Orphan Press.

Playfair, Alan. 1909. *The Garos*. London: David Nutt.

Post, Mark, and Robbins Burling. 2016. 'The Tibeto-Burman languages of Northeast India'. In *The Sino-Tibetan Languages*, edited by Graham Thurgood and Randy J. LaPolla, 213-242. Abingdon: Taylor & Francis.

Raj, Selva J., and Corinne G. Dempsey. 2002. *Popular Christianity in India: Riting between the Lines*. Albany: State University of New York Press.

Ramakrishnan, P.S. 2007. 'Traditional forest knowledge and sustainable forestry: A North-East India perspective'. *Forest Ecology and Management* no. 249 (1-2):91-99. Doi: http://dx.doi.org/10.1016/j.foreco.2007.04.001.

Rambo, Lewis R. 1993. *Understanding Religious Conversion*. New Haven, CT: Yale University Press.

Ramirez, Philippe. 2013. 'Ethnic conversions and transethnic descent groups in the Assam-Meghalaya borderlands'. *Asian Ethnology* no. 72 (2):279-297.

Ray, Lala I.P., P.K. Bora, A.K. Singh, Ram N.J. Singh, and S.M. Feroze. 2013. 'Temporal rainfall distribution characteristics at Tura, Western Meghalaya'. *Indian Journal of Hill Farming* no. 26 (2):35-41.

Robbins, Joel. 2004. *Becoming Sinners: Christianity and Moral Torment in a Papua New Guinea Society*. Berkeley: University of California Press.

Robinson, William. 1841 [1975]. *A Descriptive Account of Assam: With a Sketch of the Local Geography, and a History of the Tea-Plant Of Assam: To Which Is Added a Short Account of the Neighbouring Tribes, Exhibiting History, Manners and Customs*. [photographic reprint]. New Delhi: Mittal Publications.

Roy, Sankar. 1981. 'Aspects of eolithic agriculture and shifting cultivation, Garo Hills, Meghalaya'. *Asian Perspectives* no. 24 (2):193-221.

Rycroft, D.J., and S. Dasgupta. 2011. *The Politics of Belonging in India: Becoming Adivasi*. Abingdon, Oxon: Taylor & Francis.

Saha, Niranjan. 1968. 'A garo village in Assam: Changing pattern of land occupation and income'. *Economic and Political Weekly* no. 3 (44):1693-1696.

———. 1970. 'Carrying capacity of shifting cultivation (a study of Assam hills)'. *Indian Journal of Agricultural Economics* no. XXV (July-Sept, No. 3):220.

Saha, Niranjan, and Murulidhar Barkataky. 1968. *Banshidua: A Socio-Economic Survey of a Garo Village in Assam*. Jorhat: Agro-Economic Research Centre for North East India.

Sahlins, Marshall. 1999. 'Two or three things that I know about culture'. *The Journal of the Royal Anthropological Institute* no. 5 (Sept, 1999):399–421.

Saikia, Arunabh. 2017. 'In Meghalaya's Garo Hills, a bill to codify the tribe's customary laws could hurt women the most'. Published on Scroll.in. Available from: https://scroll.in/article/834180/in-meghalayas-garo-hills-a-bill-to-codify-the-tribes-customary-laws-could-hurt-women-the-most.Accessed 19 June 2021.

Saikia, Arupjyoti. 2011. *Forests and Ecological History of Assam, 1826–2000*. New Delhi: Oxford University Press.

Sangma, Dewansing Rongmuthu. 1936. 'The ancient Garo calendar'. *Journal of the Assam Research Society* no. IV(2):55–56.

———. 1960. *The Folk-Tales of the Garos*. Gauhati: University of Gauhati, Dept. of Publications.

———. 1993. *Jadoreng: The Psycho-Physical Culture of the Garos*, edited by Julius L.R. Marak. Mendipather (East Garo Hills): Salseng C. Marak.

Sangma, Enothsing C. 1984. 'Traditional Garo religion in its social matrix'. Ph.D. Thesis (unpublished), Guwahati University, Guwahati.

Sangma, Jangsan. 1973. *Principles of Garo Law*. Tura: Jangsan Sangma.

Sangma, Mihir N. 1984. 'Traditions of Garo migration'. In *Proceedings of the North East India History Association*, edited by J. N. Bhattacharjee, 71–78. Shillong: North East India History Association.

Sangma, Milton S. 1981. *History and Culture of the Garos*. New Delhi: Books Today.

———. 1983. *History of Garo Literature*. Shillong: North-Eastern Hill University.

———. 1984. 'Garo Traditional Beliefs and Christianity'. In *The Tribes of North East India*, edited by Sebastian Karotemprell, 95–105. Shillong: Vendrame Missiological Institute.

———. 1985. 'Sonaram R. Sangma: A study of his life and works as a Garo nationalist'. *Journal of the North East Indian History Association* no. 6th Agarthala session:323–334.

———. 1986. 'British impact and Garo response'. In *Studies in the History of North-East India*, edited by Jayanta B. Bhattacharjee, 215–233. Shillong: North East India History Association.

———. 1988. 'Inner line regulations for Garo Hills during British rule'. In *Proceedings of the North East India History Association (8th session)*, edited by Jayanta B. Bhattacharjee, 415–427. Shillong: North East India History Association.

———. 1998. 'Working of the Garo Hills Autonomous District Council: An overall view'. In *Power to People in Meghalaya: Sixth Schedule and the 73th Amendment*, edited by Mahendra N. Karna, L.S. Gassah, and C. Joshua Thomas, 131–156. New Delhi: Regency Publications.

Sangma, Semeri Alva B. 2012. *Rites of Passage in the Garo Oral Literature*. New Delhi: Akansha Publishing House.

Sangma, Tharsush. 2002. 'Political movement of Sonaram R. Sangma and its impact upon the Garo society'. PhD. Thesis (unpublished), Guahati University. Available from: https://shodhganga.inflibnet.ac.in/handle/10603/67159. Accessed 19 June 2021.

Sarmah, Kishore Kumar. 1977. 'Christianity and Garo society: A case study of the impact of conversion in three villages of Garo Hills, Meghalaya'. *Bulletin of the Department of Anthropology, Dibrugarh University* no. VI (Cultural and biological adaptability of man with special reference to North East India):47–53.

Scheper-Hughes, Nancy. 1992. *Death without Weeping: The Violence of Everyday Life in Brazil*: Berkeley, CA: University of California Press.

Scott, James C. 2009. *The Art of Not Being Governed: An Anarchist History of Upland Southeast Asia*. New Haven, CT: Yale University Press.

Sheiderman, Sara. 2010. 'Are the central Himalayas in Zomia? Some scholarly and political considerations across time and space'. *Journal of Global History* no. 5:289–312. doi: https://doi-org.ezproxy.leidenuniv.nl:2443/10.1017/S1740022810000094.

Singh, Moirangthem Prakash. 2015. *Basic Statistics of North Eastern Region 2015*. Shillong: North Eastern Council Secretariat, Evaluation and Monitoring Sector, Government of India.

Sinha, Aadhesh C. 2003. 'Sonaram Sangma's struggle for restoration of forest rights and redressal of grievances of the Garos'. In *Readings in History and Culture of the Garos*, edited by Mignonette Momin, 195–211. New Delhi: Regency Publications.

Sinha, Awadhesh C., and Tanka B. Subba. 2003. *The Nepalis in Northeast India: A Community in Search of Indian Identity*. New Delhi: Indus.

Sinha, Tarunchandra C. 1966. *The Psyche of the Garos*. Calcutta: Anthropological Survey of India.

Sitlhou, Makepeace. 2019. 'Return to the rat hole'. *Foreign Policy* (December 24). Available online from: https://foreignpolicy.com/2019/12/24/rat-hole-coal-mine-meghalaya-government-protections-workers-environment/. Accessed 19 June 2021.

Skichengani Ki'tap 1995 [1920]. *Skichengani Ki'tap I*. Tura: Tura Book Room.

Sparkes, Stephen, and Signe Howell. 2003. *The House in Southeast Asia: A Changing Social, Economic and Political Domain*. London: RoutledgeCurzon.

Srinivas, Mysore N. 2003. *Religion and Society among the Coorgs of South India*. Oxford: Oxford University Press.

Srivastava, Vinay K. 2008. 'Concept of "tribe" in the draft national tribal policy'. *Economic and Political Weekly* no. 43 (50): 29–35.

Staples, James. 2019. 'Blurring bovine boundaries: Cow politics and the everyday in South India'. *South Asia: Journal of South Asian Studies* no. 42 (6):1125–1140. doi: 10.1080/00856401.2019.1669951.

Stasch, Rupert. 2009. *Society of Others: Kinship and Mourning in a West Papuan Place*. Berkeley: University of California Press.

Suzuki, Hikaru. 2013. 'Funeral-while-alive as experiential transcendence'. In *Death and Dying in Contemporary Japan*, edited by Hikaru Suzuki, 102–122. London: Routledge.

The Assam Tribune. 18 April 2013. 'Most NE ultra outfits have bases in Bangladesh'. Accessed 26 June 2017.

———. 2 September 2015. "Two more extortionists lynched in Garo Hills." Accessed 21 January 2018..

———. 18 January 2016. 'Dacoit lynched in Garo Hills'. Accessed 25 February 2016..

The Shillong Times. 2 November 2017. 'All souls' day: Remembering one's own'. Available from: http://www.theshillongtimes.com/2017/11/02/all-souls-day-observed-3/. Accessed 27 July 2018.

———. 2018a (13 November 2018). 'Assam ginger merchant abducted in Garo Hills'. Accessed from: http://theshillongtimes.com/2018/11/13/assam-ginger-merchant-abducted-in-garo-hills/.Accessed on 18 November 2018.

———. 2018b (January 18 2018). 'NCP candidate, ex-GNLA rebel among four killed in IED blast'. Available from: http://www.theshillongtimes.com/2018/02/19/ncp-candidate-ex-gnla-rebel-among-four-killed-in-ied-blast/. Accessed on 15 January 2019.

———. 29 January 2019. 'Garo body calls on PM to implement ILP'. Available from: https://theshillongtimes.com/2019/01/29/garo-body-calls-on-pm-to-implement-ilp/. Accessed on 19 June 2021.

The Times of India. 6 April 2014. 'Purno bats for Garoland'. Accessed from: https://timesofindia.indiatimes.com/city/guwahati/Purno-bats-for-Garoland/articleshow/33337834.cms. Accessed on 19 June 2021.

Thomas, John. 2016. *Evangelising the Nation: Religion and the Formation of Naga Political Identity, Transition in Northeastern India.* Abingdon: Routledge.

Tiwari, B.K. 2003. 'Innovations in shifting cultivation, land use and land cover change in higher elevations of Meghalaya, India'. In *Methodological Issues in Mountain Research: A Socio-Ecological Approach,* edited by P. S. Ramakrishnan, K. G. Saxena, Suprava Patnaik and Surendra Singh, 163–175. New Delhi: Oxford and IBH Publishing.

Tooker, Deborah E. 1992. 'Identity systems of highland Burma: "Belief", *akha zan,* and a critique of interiorized notions of ethno-religious identity'. *Man* no. 27 (4):799–819.

———. 2004. 'Modular modern: Shifting forms of collective identity among the *akha* of northern Thailand'. *Anthropological Quarterly* no. 77 (2):243–288. doi: 10.2307/3318315.

Tylor, Edward B. 1871. *Primitive Culture: Researches into the Development of Mythology, Philosophy, Religion, Art, and Custom.* London: J. Murray.

UNI. 18 August 1999. 'Senior Congress leaders quit in Jharkhand'. Rediff on the Net. Available from: https://m.rediff.com/%0D%0Anews/1999/may/24jhar.htm.

van der Veer, Peter. 1996. *Conversion to Modernities: The Globalization of Christianity.* New York: Routledge.

Van Schendel, Willem. 2002. 'Geographies of knowing, geographies of ignorance: Jumping scale in Southeast Asia'. *Environment and Planning D: Society and Space* no. 20:647–668. doi: 10.1068/d16s.

———. 2005. *The Bengal Borderland: Beyond State and Nation in South Asia.* London: Anthem.

Vitebsky, Piers. 2017. *Living without the Dead: Loss and Redemption in a Jungle Cosmos.* Noida: HarperCollins.

Waterson, Roxana. 1990. *The Living House: An Anthropology of Architecture in South-East Asia.* Singapore: Oxford University Press.

———. 1995. 'Houses and hierarchies in island Southeast Asia'. In *About the House: Lévi-Strauss and beyond*, edited by Janet Carsten and Stephen Hugh-Jones, 47–68. Cambridge: Cambridge University Press.

Wouters, Jelle J. P. 2018. *In the Shadows of Naga Insurgency: Tribes, State, and Violence in Northeast India*. New Delhi: Oxford University Press.

Xaxa, V. 2008. *State, Society, and Tribes: Issues in Post-Colonial India*. Noida: Pearson India Education Services.

Index

For the benefit of digital users, indexed terms that span two pages (e.g., 52–53) may, on occasion, appear on only one of those pages.

A Garo Jungle Book, 31–32
a'a raka, 95, 205–6
   ramram, 210–11
A'chik, 2–3, 38
A'chik Dalgipa Baptist Krima (ADBK), 29–30
A'chik National Volunteers Council (ANVC), 53–54
A'galmaka, 115–16, 116f, 118, 123, 125, 266n.23
a'kim, 68, 69, 72–73, 175–76, 181–82, 183, 184, 187–89, 190–92, 193, 238, 248–49
   alliance, 183, 188–89
   bond, 80–81
   claim, 180–81
   debt, 177, 182, 183–84, 185–87, 193, 198–99
   inducing marriage, 68–69
   obligations, 81–82, 188–89, 191–92
   relationships, 181–82
   replacement, 181–82, 187–88, 189, 191–93, 198–99
a'king, 13–14, 102–3, 104–6, 201–3, 228–29, 236–37, 243–44
   land, 106–8, 111–12, 113–14, 116, 174–75, 205–7, 211, 214, 247–48
   nokma, 106–7, 110, 112–13
a'ma, 72–73
a'pal, 213–14
A'songtata, 101–2
A'we, 31–32, 51
   dialect, 31–32
abisi, 145
Acts Rules and Regulations of the Garo Hills Autonomous District Council, 230

affinal kin, 87
affinal relationships, 23
affluent middle class, 235
Agarwal, Bina, 73–74
agricultural ceremonies, 127
   festivals, 125
   rituals, 119
Ajigre, 86
Akha of northern Thailand, 12–13
Akha-ness, 12–13
All Party Hill Leaders Conference (APHLC), 42
Am'beng (or A'beng), 51
ama, 64–65
ama-ma'de, 71
ambi, 13–14, 71, 180
amua, 98–99
Anderson, Benedict, 8–9
Angami Naga, 241–42
angde ba'a, 180–81
animism, 241–42
Apatani, 36
Arbuthnott, 104–6
areca nut, 86, 126, 211, 215–16, 232–33, 234, 242–43
Arunachal Pradesh, 56–57
Asanangre, 51
Assam, 202–3
Assamese, 25–26, 227–28
Astuti, Rita and Maurice Bloch, 12–13
atchu ambini somoi, 12
atchu dal'gipa, 149
atchu, 71–72
audiovisual methodology, 17–18
Autonomous District Councils, 42
Autonomous Districts of Assam, 41–42
autonomous district, 43

ba'saa, 64
Backward Tract, 40
bad earth, 2
bagan, 211
Bakrapul, 52
Bal, Ellen, 46–47
Baljek airport, 236
Balmi *ja'gri*, 119–20
Balpakram, 131–34
Bang-Nawang, 131–32
Bangal chalak, 50
Bangladesh, 56, 199–200, 202–3
Baptist, 81, 93, 129, 177–78, 189–90, 196
  and Catholic constituencies, 29–30
  funeral, 189–90
  law, 129
  missionaries, 34–35
  tenets, 129
Barth, Frederik, 8–9
Baruah, Sanjib, 6
Bates, Crispin, 45
battle of Palashi (Plassey), 37–38
Bedi, Nandini, 90, 152
below poverty line (BPL), 226, 228
Bengali, 25–26, 30–31, 227–28
  Muslims, 25–26, 199–200
  Muslim migrant labourers, 50
  traders, 200–1, 203
Bengaluru, 56–57
Bertrand, Gabrielle, 83
Béteille, André, 46–47
Bharatiya Janata Party (BJP), 46
Bhutan, 4–5, 56
bigil gipok, 13–14, 222–23
Biharis, 25–26
Billy Graham Evangelical Association, 32–33
Bindloss, Jospeh, 2–3
biomedicine, 32, 78–80, 246
Bird-David, Nurit, 30–31
Björkman, Lisa, 224–25
Bloch, Maurice, 12–13, 170–71
Block Development Office (BDO)
Block Office, 59, 226–27, 228
borang, 239–40
Border Security Force (BSF), 49
Bourdieu, Pierre, 69
Brahmaputra river, 41–42, 199–200
  valley, 37–38
British colonial state, 37–38

Brubaker, Rogers, 7–8, 46–47
Burling, Robbins, 17, 32, 36–37, 43–44, 74, 88–89, 104–6, 107, 108–9, 188–89
burungni mitde, 95

Carey, William, 31–32
Carsten, Janet, 69
cartographical surveys, 214
cash crops, 25, 118, 203–4
cast galvanized iron (CGI), 226
category of analysis, 7–8
category of practice, 7–47
Catholic, 81
  priests, 34–35
  schools, 31–32
Census of India 2011, 47
Central Reserve Police Force (CRPF), 54–55
cerebral malaria, 26–28
cha'rimsa, 205–6
chapa, 187–88
chasong, 71
chatchi, 64, 144–45, 194–96
Chattopadhyay, S.K. 43–44
Chaube, Shibani, 31–32
chawari dal'gipa, 71–72
Chenggalgre, 13–14
Chhattisgarh, 52
Chibonggre, 229–30
chika, 97
chra, 84, 237–38
Christianity, 204–6, 218, 219, 243, 245, 247, 248–49
  converts, 33–34
  custom, 189, 190–91
  divinities, 124–25
  eschatology, 133–34
  funerals, 142
  Garo, 124–25, 126, 134–35, 136
  God, 33, 241–42
  Houses, 125–26
  missionaries, 240
  niam, 170, 189
  prayer, 33
chu, 35, 117–18
chu gitchak, 35
chu ringjola, 116, 118
civil servants, 107
Civil Sub-Division, 226–27
coal, 55, 202–3, 209, 232–33, 246, 247–48, 249

INDEX

colonial chroniclers, 38–39
colonial district authorities, 104–6
colonial Southern Africa, 41
Comaroff, John and Jean Comaroff, 41
commodification of land, 216
Community and Rural Development Block, 226
conditional marriage, 76
consanguineal, 87
constitution of the GHADC, 43–44
consumption of beef, 49
  of dog meat, 49
cosmological relationships, 9–10
Costa, Gulio, 43–44
counter-insurgency measures, 54–55
counterterrorism operations, 54–55
  units, 2
cow belt, 56–57
creation of a separate Garo state, 54–55
cultivation cycles, 206–7
cultural agency, 9
  coherence, 3
  fracture, 31–32
  hierarchies, 5, 49
  homogeneity, 3, 21–22
  normativities, 4
custodianship, 106
customary invocation, 89–90

daan, 241–42
Dadenggre, 93–94, 100–1, 160–61, 177–78, 188–89, 226–27, 229–30
Dakkara, 95
Dakkara-Rabokka, 95–97
Dalits, 32–33, 48–49
dama drums, 116–18, 120–21, 122, 123–24, 240
dan, 126
dani, 95–97, 122
danil, 139
Das, Debojyoti, 253n.7
Das, Jitendra, 40, 41–42, 104–6, 107
datanga, 68
debra, 134
  su'gala, 134
delang su'a, 194–96
Delhi, 51
delim, 104–6
demand for a separate Garo state, 52–54

demon—haunted, 36
demonetization, 20–21
Den'bilsia, 110
den'pata, 114
deregata, 65
Dhaka, 51
diagnostic technique, 97
dikka, 138
dikki herb, 95
Dimapur, 124
distinctive administrative status, 40
Dising, 72, 135, 149, 150f, 198–99, 221, 222–23, 224–25, 226, 231
dongnapa atchia, 84
dram, 125–26
du'bik, 76
doka, 76
du'sia, 76, 78, 80–81, 182, 183
du'u rasong, 76–78
Duncan, Christopher, 124–25
Durkheimian notion of morality, 13
Durkheimian perspective, 170–71

earthen vessels, 117–18
earthenware, 74–75
East Garo Hills, 51
economic repertoire, 126
*eleka*s, 40–41
elementary Bengali, 199–200
Eliot, John, 38
elite Garo families, 235
endemic malaria, 39–40
environmental scientists, 212–13
epistemic authority, 35–36
ethnic community, 3
  conversion, 11–12
  Garo culture, 5
  incarceration, 22
  insurgency, 2
  insurgents, 2
  permeability, 11–12
  tourism, 2–3
ethnocommunication, 18
ethnographic analysis, 9–10
  engagement, 3
  fieldwork, 13, 32, 74
  literature, 21–22
  museums, 147, 240
  museum collections, 113

ethnographic analysis, (cont.)
  present, 13
  research, 18
  state, 6
  studies, 3–4
  surveys, 6
ethno-territories, 6

field rotation, 205–6
fieldwork, 4–5, 132
film elicitation, 18
first-person accounts, 19
five Garo Hills districts, 51
forest Tobelo of Halmahera, 124–25
fossilized past, 5
fundamentally egalitarian, 92
funerary gift, 102–3
  niam, 171–72
  rituals, 134–35

Galanter, Marc, 40, 45–46
Gambaregre, 152
gambari, 108–9
Garo animism, 30–31
  belief system, 30–31
  Christianity, 29–30
  college students, 56–57
  conceptualizations of relatedness, 65–66
  conversions, 241–42
  cultural practices, 29–30
  culture, 2–3, 13, 180
  elite, 25–26
  ethnic identity, ethnic activists, 31–32, 120
  ethnicity, 22
  ethnography, 17
  funerals, 10, 16–17
  funerary rituals, 128–29
  graduates, 52
  headmen, 100
  heartland, 51
  interpretations of kinship, 74
  kinship terminology, 63–64, 65–66, 129, 139–40, 170–71
  marriages, 174–75
  medicine, 243
  medium school, 233–34
  middle class, 55–56
  militant groups, 53–55
  nationalist groups, 52
  niam, 11–12, 13, 40, 43–44, 68, 70–71, 74, 84–85
  political community, 51
  political consciousness, 52
  politicians, 52–53
  traditions, 5–6
  'village republics', 40–41
Garo Baptist church, 29–30, 31–32, 34–35
  Baptists, 32–33, 35
Garo Catholics, 133–34
Garo Christians, 125–26, 133–34, 240–42, 246
Garo Customary Law Bill, 260n.5
Garo Hills Autonomous District Council (GHADC), 41–42, 43–44, 63, 104–7, 127, 178–79, 192–93, 213–14, 226, 228–29, 230, 243–44
Garo Hills constituency, 52
  district, 40–41, 235
  Police, 54–55
Garo National Liberation Army (GNLA), 54–55
Garo *niam*, 191, 193, 230, 238–39, 243–44, 248–49
Garo Student Union (GSU), 52
Garoland, 52
Garoness, 12–13, 51, 124, 180
Garrow, 38
genealogical relationships, 112–13
genealogies, 70–71
genealogies of Houses, 72
geographically compact area, 53–54
Gerbrands, Adrian, 18
girijan, 45
gital, 36–37
*gittim*s, 13–14
Goalpara (Assam), 37–38, 51, 238
Government administrators, 216–17
government-funded lower primary school, 234
government of Meghalaya, 5–6
gram snake, 119, 136–37
grapmangtata, 131–32, 140
greng, 147
Grey, Sir William, 38–39
grika, 102
guala, 146
Guira, 95, 101, 102

INDEX   297

gukmittim, 210–11
Guwahati, 51

Hajong, 25–26, 48–49
Hamilton, Francis, 38
Harvest Festival, 180
headhunting, 38–39
heathens, 35–36, 93–94
hegemony of Christianity, 29–30
herbal healer, 93–94
  preparations, 78–80
heritage village, 5
Hertz, Robert, 9–10
hierarchical relationships, 182, 207
hill rice, 212–14
Hindi, 56–57, 227–28
Hindu Garo, 29–30
Hindu nationalism, 47–48
  perspective, 50–51
  temples, 29–30
Hinduism, 30–31
Hinduized, 32–33
Hobsbawn, Eric and Terence Ranger, 8–9
Hornbill Festival, 124
House of Sadol, 101–2
House relationships, 73–74
house tax, 43
Howell, Signe, 69
Hugh-Jones, Stephen, 69
Hyderabad, 56–57

improvised explosive device (IED), 54–55
India's North-East, 34–35
India's union government, 236
Indian armed forces, 49
Indian central government, 52–53
  Constitution, 225
  federal government, 228–29
  independence, 25–26, 104
  interlocutors, 45
  Indian made foreign liquor, 35
  National Congress (INC), 46, 221–22
  railway network, 236
  state's policies, 6
  territory, 199–200
indigenous languages, 56–57
Indira Gandhi National Widow Pension
  Scheme (IGNWPS), 177–78
infant mortality, 10

in-married men, 63–64
Inner Line, 40
institutionalized religion, 30–31
inter-House hierarchies, 71–72
inter-House relationships, 127, 159, 162, 170,
  178–79, 199
interlocutors, 17–18, 19
inventive traditions, 9
inventiveness of tradition, 9
Isol, 241–42
isomorphism, 4

jada, 187
Jaintia, 3–4, 236
Jaintia Hills Autonomous District Council, 42
jak rara, 223
Jamegapa festival, 210
janggi, 130–31
jat, 46–47
Jesuni sam, 243
Jharkhand, 52
jhum, 2–3
jikgite, 173, 184
jikpangma, 184
Jingjal, 52
Job Card, 226
jol onkata, 122
Joshi, Vibha, 241–42

ka'sae den'a, 142
Kabyle of North Africa, 69
kachari, 141
kamal, 30–31, 97
kaman, 203–4
kanga, 114
Kar, Bodhisattva, 2009, 40
Kar, Parimal, 104–6
Karlsson, Bengt, 41, 43–44, 46–47, 52,
  63, 104–6
kattarang, 90–91
kazina, 214
Keane, Webb, 33
Khasi and Mizo, 31–32
Khasi Hills Autonomous District Council, 42
Khasi Hills, 238
Khasi, 3–4, 36, 236
Kikon, Dolly, 51, 124
kima, 165
kimbrong, 167–69, 170

INDEX

kimindam, 98–99
kin group, 76, 81–82, 84
   trial, 81, 86–87, 89–91 92, 110, 175–76, 221
kinship, 71, 139–40
kinship designations, 149–50
kinsperson, 58
Koch, 25–26, 100
kompa, 147–49
Kompru Atop, 97
Korowai (West Irian), 3
kracha'a, 16, 91
kram, 61–63, 68–69, 95, 106–7, 108–13, 116–17, 119, 122–23, 127, 143–44, 149, 150–51, 174–75, 176–79, 180–81, 192, 214, 216–17, 218, 219, 240
kukuri, 114
kusi boulder, 101–4, 106–7, 108, 192, 241–42

Lambek, Michael, 30–31
land management laws, 22
legitimacy of the Indian state, 53–54
Leiden University, 17–18
Leiden Visual Anthropology, 18
Lévi-Strauss, Claude, 69
Lieutenant-Governor of Bengal, 38–39
literature on matrilineality, 83
local hardwoods, 1
Lok Sabha, 236
Lonely Planet Northeast India, 2–3
longpingagipa, 233–34
loskor, 40–41

M'cosh, John, 39–40
ma'chong, 64
ma'dong, 81–82
ma'gual, 146–52, 153–56, 157–58, 162, 179–80, 183–84
   gongs, 183–84
   guala, 183–84
   mahari, 237–38, 248
      bichel, 81, 175–76
      toma, 81
Mahatma Gandhi National Rural Employment Guarantee Act (MGNREGA), 52–53, 226
Majumdar, Dhirendra, 25–26, 31–32, 38–39, 68–69, 88–89, 100, 106, 107, 126, 147, 211

mama, 64–65
mande, 38, 59
   burung, 55
   gital, 84, 183–84
mandeni niam, 189
mandi, 59
Mangdugre, 86
Mangsang matrilineage, 174–75
mangsrea, 98
mania, 12
manjri pillar, 120–21
Marak, Caroline, 80
Marak, Julius, 43–44
Marak, Krickwin, 37
Marak, Metrona, 221–22
Marakapara, 160–61
marang, 114, 115–16, 136, 137, 153–54, 163, 170–71, 180
market economy, 219–20
market-oriented economic activities, 232–33
marriage by abduction, 80
   -related abduction, 80
Marwaris, 25–26
matriarchy, 83
matriculation, 233–34
matrilineage, 64, 69, 70–71, 83, 87, 89–90, 111–12, 114–15, 144–45, 146, 157–58, 181–82, 183–84, 185, 187, 190–91, 197–98, 238
matrilineal affiliation, 180–81
matrilineal, 63, 182
   group(s), 22–23, 63–64, 66, 68–69, 71–72, 73–74, 81–82, 84, 89–91
   kin, 75, 78–80, 81–82, 93–94
   kin, 111–12, 129, 154–55, 157, 173, 175, 176–77, 180–81, 182, 183–84, 185–87, 188–89, 190–91, 199
   kin group, 182, 183, 196
   lines, 171–72
   nephew, 175
   relatedness, 133–34, 155
   relative(s), 82, 84–85, 102–3, 106–8, 109–10, 113–14, 116, 127, 132–33, 134–35, 139–40, 146, 152–53, 155, 168–69, 170, 171, 175–76, 178–79, 180, 181–82, 183, 184, 185–87, 188–89, 190–93, 196, 197–98, 199
   relative(s), 139, 146, 153–54, 168–69, 171, 176–77, 185–87, 188–89
   uncle, 152, 157–58

INDEX 299

matrilineal descent, 65–66, 73–74
matriliny, 139–40
matrilocality, 73–74
McDuie-Ra, Duncan and Dolly Kikon, 253–54n.3, 273n.15
Member of the District Council (MDC), 228–30
Meghalaya, 200–1, 226, 227–28
 Land Transfer Act, 47
 Legislative Assembly, 54–55
 State Police, 54–55
 Tourism Department, 124
Meghalaya's Department of Soil Conservation, 196–97
Meghalaya's Special Force-10 commandos, 54–55
Megonggre, 111–12
melia, 91–92, 185
Members of the Legislative Assembly (MLAs), 221–22, 229–30
Memorandum on the demand for the creation of separate Garoland, 53–54
MGNREGA 'Job Card' scheme, 232–33
mi'mang dakenga, 143–44
mi'mang dila, 188–89
mi'mang, 130–31, 141–42
middle-class Garo, 180, 240
midwife, 58
Miknang, 151–52, 188–89
mil'am, 139
militants, 227
militant activity, 54–55
 groups, 53–54
Mills, Moffat, 39–40
mimi'mang, 141–42
Ministry of Tribal Affairs, 45–46
minor title holders, 106–7
minority community, 100, 124
minority religion, 32–33
mitanga, 189
mitde, 30–31
 manigipa, 30–31
mixed populations, 25–26
Mizo settlement patterns, 10–11
Mizos, 29–30
MLA scheme, 223–24, 226
modern Garo history, 31–32
modern Indian state, 4

modern ontology, 33
modernization theory, 4
mondoli a'pal, 81
Montgomery Martin, Robert, 252n.4
mortuary practices, 9–10
 rituals, 9–11, 147
mosques, 29–30
mouzas, 40–41
Mrong matrilineage, 174–75
Mrongs, 175, 176–77, 180–82
multi-ethnic state, 46–47
Muslim Bengali, 50
Myanmar, 56
Mymensingh, 37–38, 44–45, 51, 238

Naga culture, 124
Naga(s), 29–30, 36
Nagaland, 56–57, 124
Nagamese, 56–57
Nangseng, 129, 162, 189–91
narikki sil, 149, 152–53
natik, 61–62, 109, 111–12
National People's Party (NPP), 52
National Socialist Council of Nagalim (NSCM-IM), 56
National Tribal Policy, 45–46
Nationalist Congress Party (NCP), 54–55, 221–22
New Tribes Mission, 124–25
Ngaju of Kalimantan, 9–10
niam, 11, 13, 21–22, 24, 72, 81, 82, 84–85, 87–89, 90–92, 93, 119, 136–37, 142–43, 147–49, 154–55, 157, 165–66, 170, 171–72, 179–80, 188–89, 191–92
niam chongmot, 12
 of the mande, 12
Nijland, Dirk, 17–18
nok, 68
nok mande, 13–14, 59
nok Nepal, 232–33
nok ruri, 232–33
nokgipa, 95, 176–77
nokkap raka, 110
nokkrom, 175
nokma, 14–15, 33–34, 43, 68–69, 106–7
nokni mitde, 95
nokpante, 99–100
Nokrek mountain, 25

INDEX

non-Garo, 81–82
   minorities, 25–26, 29–30
   missionaries, 37
Nongbri, Tiplut, 31–32, 42, 52–53, 200
normative frameworks, 21–22
North-East India's upland societies, 21–22
North-Eastern hill communities, 32–33
North-Eastern Hill University, 236

Odisha, 10–11
Oldap, 72, 76, 98f, 100, 108–9, 111, 164f, 198–99
on'songa, 68
onna, 173
onsonga, 175
ontological landscape, 21–22
Oppitz, Michael, 36
oral geneology, 72–73
orchard crops, 88–89
Otto, Ton and Poul Pedersen, 9
Outer Line, 40

paddy, 26, 119, 126
paddy cultivation, 126
Pachuau, Joy, 10–11
pagilla, 93–94
pahari, 45
pap, 34–35
Parry, Jonathan, 170–71
Partially Excluded Area, 40
patriarchal bias, 106
patta, 43, 214, 215–16, 228–29, 236–37, 247–48
permanent cultivation, 241
Phulbari, 199–200
pita, 125–26
Playfair, Alan, 43–44
   The Garos, 38
political inequality, 10–11
political movements in India, 52
politicized ethnicities, 51
polytheistic religions, 30–31
pongsi, 97
precolonial times, 10–11, 51, 82
preferential discrimination, 47
   policies, 46
primordialist, 8–9
private property, 216
proposed new Garoland state, 53–54

Protestant Christian churches, 29–30
Protestants, 34–35
Public Distribution System (PDS), 72, 135, 226–27, 232–33
Punjabi, 25–26
purity, 47–48

Rabha, 25–26
Rahman, A.R. 124
Ramakrishnan, P.S., 274–75n.23
Ramirez, Philippe, 11–12
rasong, 91, 92, 135
rehabilitation packages, 54–55
relational epistemology, 30–31
religious denominations, 12
   diversity, 10–11
   landscape, 4
   ontologies, 4
religious practices, 192
Rengsanggri, 74
Republic Day, 225
revivalist religious movements, 36
rice beer, 13–14, 34–35, 58–59, 61–63, 67, 75–76, 78, 80–81, 93–94, 102, 110, 115–18, 120–21, 123, 125, 126–27, 129, 131, 138, 141, 165–66, 173–74, 194–96, 201–2, 245
rice beer vessel, 138
rikgitok, 5–6
Ringre (Tura), 104
Risi, 61–63, 95, 97, 98–99, 108–13, 116–17, 120, 178, 192, 216–17, 241–42
Risi Denchokola ritual, 109–10
Risi Srenggata ritual, 109–10
Roman Catholics, 29–30, 32–33, 125
rong'dik, 138
rong'dikni mitde, 95
Rongram constituency, 221–22
rural gangs, 2
   land management, 22
   tourism, 2
ruri, 12, 190–91, 232–33
rurini niam, 189

Sadol, 100, 101–2
Sadolpara (Sadolbra), 2–3, 4–5, 13–15, 18–19, 26–28, 35–36, 37, 45, 50, 59–61, 67, 73–74, 81–82, 86, 93–94, 99–101, 102–3, 106–7, 108–9, 111–12, 116, 118, 120–21,

123–25, 132, 135, 136–37, 142, 147, 152, 156, 157–58, 159, 160–61, 163–65, 179–81, 188–89, 196–200, 201, 202–3, 204–5, 209, 211, 212–13, 216–17, 227–28, 232, 233–34, 240–41, 243, 246
Saikia, Arupjyoti, 40
Saljong, 115–16, 119–20, 121–22
Saljong *rodila*, 116
salvage ethnography, 240–41
sam A'chik, 37, 130, 243
samsepa, 114
Sangma, Capt. Williamson A., 42
Sangma, Dewansingh Rongmithu, 255n.10, 256n.14
Sangma, Enothsing C., 80
Sangma, E.C., 131–32
Sangma, Jangsan, 43–44
Sangma, Jonathone, 54–55
Sangma, Milton, 38–39, 40, 41–44, 52, 230
Sangma, Purno, 52, 221–22, 236, 276n.4
Sangma, Sonaram, 41, 52, 104–6
sasatsu'a, 121–22
Scheduled District, 40
  Tribes, 45–46, 227–28, 236
Scheper-Huges, Nancy, 10
Scott, James, 92
Secret Lands Where Women Reign, 83
secular medical science, 243
seki donga, 81–82, 184
Seventh Day Adventist(s), 81, 93
shared ethnicity, 51
shifting cultivation, 23–24, 26, 88–89, 107–8, 113–14, 115, 126–27, 203–4, 205–6, 212–13, 247
Shillong, 51
signatory powers, 107
signs of 'development', 1
Sikh gurdwara, 29–30
sin'na-dinga, 61–62, 97, 109–10, 130
Sinha, Aadhesh, 41, 52, 104–6
siphei, 55
Sisi *mikgri*, 119–20
Sixth Schedule Areas, 42
  Schedule of the Indian Constitution, 41–42, 214, 236
skutong, 69, 83–84
sling ritual, 134–35
slums of Brazil, 10
sma channa, 97

snaka, 142
social distance, 26–28
social gap, 228
social hierarchy, 24
  interaction, 1
  networks, 4–5
  socio-religious responsibilities, 112–13
soft agricultural loans, 215–16
sok apsan ringjok, 65
songgitchamgre (old village), 2
Songsarek celebration(s), 34–35, 120–21
  chants and rituals, 96
  custom, 173, 182, 184, 187–88, 189, 192, 198–99
  funeral(s), 128–29, 138, 165, 189–90
  Garo, 134
  House(s), 108–10, 120
  households, 98–99
  marriages, 130–31, 173
  niam, 81–82, 93, 138, 189
  practice(s), 32–33, 80–81, 180, 194–96
  presence, 192
  ritual, 93–94, 97, 99–100
  spirits, 12, 37, 80–81, 93, 99–100
  villagers, 5–6, 34–35
Songsarek(s), 12, 30–31, 32, 36–37, 62–63, 67, 70–71, 73–75, 80, 81, 84, 92, 93–95, 96–97, 99–100, 106–8, 109, 112–14, 118–19, 120, 123, 124, 126–27, 128–29, 130–34, 136, 137–38, 139, 142, 145–46, 147, 155–56, 163–65, 167–68, 170–71, 180–82, 183, 190–91, 193, 196
Songsareks' Wangala celebrations, 95–96
Sonibar-bazar, 86
Sora of Odisha, 10–11, 30–31
sordars, 40–41
South Asia, 3–4
South Asia's patrilineal communities, 83
South Asian communities, 176–77
South East Asia, 92
south-eastern part of Garo Hills, 131–32
South Indian Catholic priests, 31–32
South-East Asian archipelago, 69
Sparkes, Stephen, 69
spatial organization, 73–74
Special Rural Welfare Programme, 223–24
spi, 139
spirit-induced illnesses, 99–100
spring chamber, 223–24

Stasch, Rupert, 3
state administration of Meghalaya, 42
State Bank of India (SBI), 215–16
state bureaucracy, 106
Stoddard, 38–39
Sub-Divisional Officer, 177–78
subsidiary houses, 110
superstition, 2
Suzuki, Hikaru, 134–35
swidden, 58–59, 78, 88–89, 107–8, 111, 113–14, 115–16, 118–19, 126, 131–32, 136–37, 187, 194–96, 204–5, 206, 247
    crops, 22–23, 33–34, 88–89, 95, 108, 110, 115, 119, 124–25, 127, 241
    rice, 119–20

ta'a narot, 210–11
ta'a steng, 210–11
Tangans of Melanesia, 171
tangnapa rongua, 84
TB (Tuberculosis), 225–26
teak forests, 39–40
Telangana, 52
terai, 39–40
the tribal circuit, 2–3
timber ban, 42
toma, 86, 179–80
Tooker, Deborah, 12–13
traditional funeral chants, 58
    Garo community religion, 2–3, 6, 22, 29–31, 35–36, 51, 58, 59, 74, 92, 95, 103–4, 111–13, 119, 123, 129, 232–33, 240–41
    Garo culture, 147
    Garo House, 219, 232–33
    leaders, 41
    normativity, 4
    tribal community, 45
Tura, 16, 20–21, 25, 49, 104, 120, 123, 147, 180, 192–93, 222–23, 227, 228–30
    region, 80, 211
turia, 144–45
tusidil'a, 78

ukam, 155–62, 178
    debt, 158, 160–61
    exchange, 155–57, 158, 159–62, 163
    gong, 156–57
    money, 155–57
    rika, 158
ukama, 156
uncorrupted ethnic Garo culture, 5
Urapmin of Melanesia, 36–37
urban Garo middle class, 82–83
urban standard sanitation, 26–28
urban–rural disparity, 26–28
Uttarakhand, 52

Van Schendel, Willem, 4–5, 44–45, 46–47, 251–52n.1
vegetarianism, 47–48
Village Development Board, 226
village domain, 20–21
    level administrative autonomy, 22
Vitebsky, Piers, 10–11, 30–31
vote bank, 224–25

wa'ge, 98–99
wa'pak, 71
waknol, 64
wanchi, 120
Wangala celebrations, 48–49
Wangala troupe, 180
Wangala, 48–49, 51, 96, 119–26, 173–74, 178, 188–89, 224–25, 239–40
wari, 111–12
washing the sling, 134–36
Waterson, Roxana, 69
West Garo Hills, 2, 13–14, 74, 107–8, 120, 125–26, 128–29, 131–32, 134, 137–38, 142, 146, 155–56, 170, 171–72, 179–80, 192–93, 199, 210, 215–16, 219–20, 226, 246, 248–49
Wild crops, 212–13
Wouters, Jelle, 54–55
writing culture, 4

Xaxa, Virginius, 46

zamindars, 38–39, 40
zan, 12–13